S0-BBV-515

Windows Web Scripting Developer's Guide

indows Web Scripting
Developer's Guide

DAN **HEFLIN**
TODD **NEY**

Osborne/**McGraw-Hill**

Berkeley   New York   St. Louis   San Francisco
Auckland   Bogotá   Hamburg   London   Madrid
Mexico City   Milan   Montreal   New Delhi   Panama City
Paris   São Paulo   Singapore   Sydney
Tokyo   Toronto

Osborne/**McGraw-Hill**
2600 Tenth Street
Berkeley, California 94710
U.S.A.

For information on translations or book distributors outside the U.S.A., or to arrange bulk purchase discounts for sales promotions, premiums, or fund-raisers, please contact Osborne/**McGraw-Hill** at the above address.

Windows Web Scripting Developer's Guide

Copyright © 2000 by The McGraw-Hill Companies. All rights reserved. Printed in the United States of America. Except as permitted under the Copyright Act of 1976, no part of this publication may be reproduced or distributed in any form or by any means, or stored in a database or retrieval system, without the prior written permission of the publisher, with the exception that the program listings may be entered, stored, and executed in a computer system, but they may not be reproduced for publication.

1234567890 DOC DOC 9019876543210

ISBN 0-07-212280-3

Publisher
  Brandon A. Nordin
**Associate Publisher and
Editor-in-Chief**
  Scott Rogers
Acquisitions Editor
  Wendy Rinaldi
Project Editor
  Madhu Prasher
Editorial Assistant
  Monika Faltiss
Technical Editor
  Mark Hammock
Copy Editor
  Barbara Brodnitz

Proofreader
  Carol Burbo
Indexer
  Valerie Robbins
Computer Designers
  Jani Beckwith
  Elizabeth Jang
  E. A. Pauw
  Lauren McCarthy
Illustrators
  Robert Hansen
  Michael Mueller
  Beth Young
Series Design
  Peter F. Hancik

This book was composed with Corel VENTURA™ Publisher.

Information has been obtained by Osborne/**McGraw-Hill** from sources believed to be reliable. However, because of the possibility of human or mechanical error by our sources, Osborne/**McGraw-Hill**, or others, Osborne/**McGraw-Hill** does not guarantee the accuracy, adequacy, or completeness of any information and is not responsible for any errors or omissions or the results obtained from use of such information.

I dedicate this book to the two most influential women in my life, my wife and mom. My wife, Ruth, has supported me in the writing of this book, has taught me a lot about love and life, and has given us two beautiful children, Michelle and David. My mom believed in me and gave me encouragement to accomplish anything in life that I wanted to do.

—Dan Heflin

I would like to dedicate this book to my mom and dad. They have given me encouragement, love, and support throughout my life, and I would like to thank them for everything they have done for me.

—Todd Ney

About the Authors

Dan Heflin has been developing business applications since 1985. He has broad consulting experience in the medical, financial, and manufacturing industries, among others. Besides working with DHTML behaviors, XML and Window Script Components, Dan works with HTML, VBScript, JavaScript, Visual Basic, and C++. Since 1997, he has been a consultant for developing Web applications. He is a regular contributor to Fawcette Technical Publications' *Visual Basic Programmer's Journal*. Dan is also a founding partner of Premier Business Software, Inc. (www.premierbusinesssoft.com). Premier Business Software, Inc., creates Web sites and Internet/intranet applications for Fortune 500 companies.

Dan lives in the suburbs of Chicago with his wife, Ruth, and two kids, Michelle and David. For fun, he likes to watch hockey and quote lines from comedy movies ("Throw me a frickin' bone, people"). He can be reached at dheflin@premierbusinesssoft.com.

Todd Ney is the cofounder of Premier Business Software, Inc. (www.premierbusinesssoft.com), an Internet/intranet development company. He has worked with numerous Fortune 500 companies in the manufacturing, medical, and insurance industries. He looks forward to building the company into a technologist's dream, continually working with the latest technology. His roots are in software development, specializing in DHTML, Visual Basic, scripting, XML, database development, and other cutting-edge development environments. He is also a frequent contributor to *Visual Basic Programmer's Journal*. Todd lives in Milwaukee, where he enjoys watching the Milwaukee Bucks, trying to hit a golf ball straight, and attending various cultural events. He can be reached at tney@premierbusinesssoft.com.

AT A GLANCE

CONTENTS

Part IV

Advanced Internet Explorer Functionality

Part VI

Sample Application

Part VII

Appendixes

ACKNOWLEDGMENTS

First and foremost, we would like to thank our friends and families for all of their love and support, not only on this project, but in every day of our lives.

We would like to thank the Academy....

Mark Hammock deserves thanks for his technical editing and suggestions for this book and the quick recovery from his illness.

We would like to thank Komatsu America and its employees for allowing us the opportunity to leave for a few months to work on the book and return to our old jobs.

Finally, we would like to thank Wendy Rinaldi for giving us the opportunity to write this book and Monika Faltiss and the entire production staff at Osborne for working with us to bring this book to publication.

PREFACE

Web scripting technology began with Microsoft Internet Explorer 3 and Netscape Navigator 3, which introduced dynamic client-side content and changed the look of a Web page in the client's browser. These extraordinary new concepts just hinted at the coming ability to build browser-based applications.

These concepts really took off with the release of version 4 of the browser products. Microsoft especially stepped up the available functionality by allowing us to replace entire sections of HTML code with code that was generated on the client machine, as well as allowing us to dynamically change styles or the look of elements. In that same release, Microsoft introduced the concept of XML and the features and functionality that a cross-platform structured data transfer store can provide.

The 5.0 releases of the browser have solidified (or will solidify, in the case of Netscape) these new and immature technologies into a true development platform. Also, in addition to just using scripting in the browser, new technologies have recently been introduced that allow us to leverage our scripting knowledge to build server-side components for our Web servers.

All of these great developments have led to some growing pains in two different areas: cross-browser compatibility, and separation of the script code and data from the HTML itself. Thankfully, we have recently seen some strides being made on both accounts. Cross-browser compatibility will hopefully be aided by the W3 Consortium (the Web standards body) and will allow us to develop dynamic content applications using a common set of code. As far as separation of data and scripting from content is concerned, many of the features that are being built and endorsed as standards, such as HTML components, XML, and the XML document object model, are covered right here in these pages.

We hope that this book will help you learn some of the exciting development techniques found in the newest versions of the browser and scripting, such as HTML components, XML technologies, Windows Script Components, and remote scripting. In addition to introducing you to these technologies, we will give you ideas of how to apply these concepts in your Internet development strategies. Finally, we have included a fairly extensive appendix section; this resource serves as a quick look-up section for the syntax and functionality of the covered technologies.

PART I

An Overview of Web Scripting Technologies

CHAPTER 1

Introduction

Using scripting languages in Web site development is becoming more common every day. Almost every Web page you visit these days uses at least some form of scripting. And as we begin to create more advanced Web solutions, we find ourselves wanting to reuse code and needing a platform-neutral method for transporting data. With Microsoft's Internet Explorer 5.0, we are finally able to create reusable scripting solutions, and as we move forward to future versions of the Microsoft and Netscape browsers, we will see even more importance being placed on these technologies. Reusable HTML components (DHTML behaviors and element behaviors) and XML, for instance, are not just buzzwords that are here today and gone tomorrow, but rather they are the future of both client-side and server-side Web development.

SCRIPTING TECHNOLOGIES AT A GLANCE

In general this book is about how to use scripting to build Internet applications using the latest technologies of DHTML behaviors, XML, Windows Script Components, advanced features found in Internet Explorer 5.0, and remote scripting.

▼ DHTML behaviors allow you to create reusable components that contain DHTML and logic that can easily be applied to an HTML element to extend the element's built-in functionality. These lightweight components encapsulate your script and provide an easy mechanism to separate the code from the Web page content. This allows you to share code across multiple pages and improves the manageability of your Web-based application. It is important to note that in this book we cover both the HTML component (HTC) and Windows Script Component (WSC) methods of building behaviors.

■ Extensible Markup Language, or XML, is an exciting new markup language that provides a mechanism for describing structured data. The specification for XML is defined by the World Wide Web Consortium (W3C) and provides a uniform method of exchanging data between applications. In this book, we concentrate on using: the XML document object model (DOM), Extensible Style Language (XSL), and XML schemas. The XML DOM provides a common method to access data from an XML document. XSL allows us to transform XML data into an HTML document or into another XML document. XML schemas allow us to define the structure, data types, and constraints of XML documents.

■ Windows Script Components allow you to develop components that can be used as DHTML behaviors, Component Object Model (COM) components, or Active Server Page components. The nice thing about WSCs is that you can create these components using the same scripting languages you are already familiar with. This allows you to easily create components that contain reusable code without needing to learn a completely new language and set of syntaxes.

■ Advanced DHTML features found in IE 5.0 enable you to create the more fully featured applications that users have come to expect. These features include the ability to enable drag-and-drop and mouse capturing. In addition, IE 5.0 introduces a new concept called HTML applications for creating HTML pages that are installed on a user's system. These pages do not have the security restrictions normally applied to Web pages, but they allow you to easily update the application and provide all the features the browser supports.

▲ Remote scripting allows you to communicate and retrieve data from the server without the need for refreshing the page. This functionality, combined with DHTML, allows you to create a client/server-type architecture from inside an HTML page.

We have designed this book to be used by individuals who have some basic Web experience and are familiar with JavaScript and basic DHTML concepts: webmasters, HTML authors and designers, and Windows developers who want to learn to build Web applications, for example.

This book is designed to show you how to exploit these new technologies and begin building Web applications using the latest in Web technologies.

RESOURCES AND DEVELOPMENT AIDS

To implement most of the technologies in this book, all that is required to build components and XML on the client-side is Internet Explorer 5.0 or later and your favorite text editor. We would, however, recommend using Microsoft Visual InterDev 6.0 or later if you are new to DHTML. Visual InterDev can be helpful with learning the DHTML syntax. To debug the code it is also helpful to have the Microsoft Script Debugger (freely available from Microsoft's Web site at http://msdn.microsoft.com/scripting) or Microsoft Visual InterDev 6.0 or later. It is important to note that Visual InterDev 6.0 requires service pack three to allow debugging of DHTML behaviors.

In all of our examples of technologies that interact with the server, we used Microsoft Internet Information Server 4.0 or later running on Microsoft Windows NT 4.0 or later. You should also have the 5.0 or later version of the JavaScript engine installed on your server. This JavaScript engine can be downloaded as a separate component (freely available from Microsoft's Web site at http://msdn.microsoft.com/scripting) and is installed automatically with IE 5.0. If you wish to run XML on the server, you will need to install the XML components, which can be installed as a separate component (http://msdn.microsoft.com/xml) or as part of IE 5.0.

We used the Active Server Page programming environment to build our server-based solutions. It is important to note that with the exception of Remote Scripting and Active Server Page Windows Script Components (because these technologies are directly tied to Active Server Pages), all of the functionality we show could easily be ported to a different environment, such as CGI or Java Servlets.

In some of our server-based examples, we needed to utilize a database to show you how an application would interact in a real world scenario. For these examples, we utilized Microsoft Access 97 and Microsoft ActiveX Data Object (ADO) to retrieve the data. In order to run these applications, you will need to have both of these tools installed (the latest version of ADO is available as a free download from Microsoft at http://www.microsoft.com/data). We used Access because of its wide usage, but we would recommend a more scalable database, such as Microsoft SQL Server or Oracle, in a production environment.

The final component that is required to run our applications is the remote scripting runtime files (only required for the remote scripting functionality). These runtime components can be downloaded from the scripting area of the MSDN Web site at http://msdn.microsoft.com/scripting.

OVERVIEW OF THIS BOOK'S CONTENTS

We are now going to introduce you to the layout, content, and conventions of this book so you know where we are heading in our scripting journey.

Layout of the Book

After this introductory chapter, we have divided the rest of the book into four major parts covering scripting technologies, followed by a part that consists of the final chapter, which shows you how to integrate all of the technologies into one application.

HTML Components

After a quick overview of DHTML and cascading style sheets (CSS), we introduce you to how to use behaviors from inside a Web page and how to interact with this new technology. Next we introduce you to the behaviors that are built into Internet Explorer 5.0 and provide such functionality as persisting data, downloading files, and determining client capabilities. Once you know the basic functionality of behaviors, we next lead you through developing your own scripting component. With a basic understanding of the functionality available in IE 5.0 under your belt, we introduce you to some of the new functionality in the preview edition of IE 5.5. This functionality further extends the concept of HTML components and shows the direction Microsoft is taking and the commitment Microsoft is making to the technology. With a complete understanding of the functionality of HTML components, we show you how to debug components and script using the Script Debugger and Visual InterDev. Finally, we lead you through creating a grid component that could be used in a real-world situation.

XML Technologies

First we introduce you to the basic syntax of XML, and then we lead you through retrieving and modifying the XML using the XML document object model (XML DOM). Next we introduce you to the XML data source object (XMLDSO), which allows us to easily build XML data entry and modification applications. The next XML topic we cover is Extensible Style Languages (XSL); XSL allows us to query and transform XML data to HTML or other XML documents. The final XML topic we introduce you to is the new specification of XML schemas, which allow you to specify the structure and rules about XML documents using XML itself. Putting it all together, we build a sample shopping cart application that uses XML on the server and client to show you how to tie all of the XML technologies together into a sample application.

Advanced Internet Explorer Functionality

We begin our coverage of the advanced IE functionality with an introduction to HTML applications, which are applications that are built using HTML pages. These pages allow access to the user's system, as well as more control of the user interface, and they do not have the same security restrictions that a normal Web page has. We also introduce you to data transfer functionality, such as cut/copy/paste and drag-and-drop, now available in IE 5.0. Finally, we introduce you to mouse capturing, which allows one central location to trap all mouse activity on a page.

Windows Script Components and Remote Scripting

We first introduce you to the basic concepts of WSC, which are Component Object Model (COM) components and can be used both on the client side as DHTML behaviors and also on the server as reusable components. Next we introduce you to WSCs that have full accessibility to the Active Server Page objects and allow us to reuse ASP code. Finally we introduce you to remote scripting. This functionality allows you to make trips to the server to retrieve data without requiring a complete page refresh.

A Real-World Sample Application

In the final chapter, we lead you though a sample application that uses most of the technologies covered in this book, resulting in a complete Web application. The application is comprised of a client application (an HTML application) that allows a user to fill in a timesheet while being away from the network, as well as an online viewer portion that allows you to view completed timesheets from a browser.

Appendixes

In addition to leading you through examples of all of these great technologies, we have included some quick-reference appendixes so the book can serve as a handy reference guide. In the appendixes we cover the important tags, properties, methods, and syntax you will need once you become comfortable with the general concepts.

Downloading the Samples

We have included all of the complete, nonsnippet samples available as a single compressed file (zip format) on the Osborne Web site (http://www.osborne.com) for you to download and play with. The layout of the zip file is fairly straightforward, with each of the samples located in a directory related to the chapter number. It is important to note that to run the ASP files, you will need to move these files to an ASP-aware server, such as Microsoft Internet Information Server or Personal Web Server.

NOTE: All development was done in JavaScript, both on the client side and on the server side.

The Future of Scripting Technology

It is, of course, difficult to say exactly where this technology is headed, but we will give some predictions based on items that are currently under development. The W3 Consortium currently is considering a proposal from Netscape and Microsoft to develop a standard way to build DHTML behaviors. Based on the early developments from the consortium, it looks like the final standard will look similar to the syntax currently in HTML components. Additionally, Microsoft will continue to extend the functionality and fully support the use of DHTML behaviors, as is evident from our chapter on the preliminary version of IE 5.5.

If XML isn't everywhere right now, in the future it probably will be. Look for XML support to be added to all the major database products. This will allow us to store, search, and index XML documents. In addition, Microsoft currently is proposing a set of standards to handle routing of XML documents (BizTalk) and to replace proprietary remote object standards (DCOM, CORBA, RMI) with an XML-based standard called Simple Object Access Protocol (SOAP). Look for industry-specific XML schemas that will define common ways for entire industries to share data between applications. Finally look for more XML-based standards from the W3C to extend and standardize XSL syntax.

PART II

HTML Components

CHAPTER 2

Introduction to DHTML Behaviors

Almost every major Web site that is being developed today uses some form of Dynamic HTML and cascading style sheets to provide a more interactive and engaging browsing experience. Everywhere you look, Dynamic HTML is being used to individualize the look or content of a particular page, and many users have now come to expect this level of interactivity.

Dynamic HTML, or DHTML as it is commonly called, provides the ability to change the content or look of an existing Web page from the client's browser. By modifying the page on the client, we can eliminate the all-too-often long delay caused by refreshing the page from the server. These pages are modified through a scripting language, such as JavaScript or Visual Basic Script (both provide a simple and easy-to-learn syntax). In addition, cascading style sheets, or CSS, let you centrally define the look of a particular HTML element, an HTML page, or a complete Web site. You can also change the look of the client using client-side scripts and CSS.

The purpose of this book is not to cover basic DHTML or CSS, so we are not going to cover the complete list of objects or try to teach you everything there is to know about DHTML or CSS. But rather we would like to touch on some of the highlights of both technologies as they apply to this book.

OVERVIEW OF CSS

Cascading style sheets (CSS) are a simple mechanism for adding styles such as fonts, colors, and spacing to a single or group of HTML documents or elements. HTML style sheets give HTML developers the control over formatting that traditional desktop publishing designers have enjoyed for years. With style sheets, you can finally specify point sizes, page margins, spacing between lines, and exact positioning of HTML elements. You can also create any number of formatting variations for a single HTML tag. In addition to these features, CSS allow you to separate the formatting information from the actual HTML, simplifying code reuse.

Applying Style Sheets

Cascading style sheets can be applied to an HTML document by one of four methods: importing, linking, embedding, or in-line. Imported style sheets bring the contents of a style sheet into an existing style element. Because the imported method is rarely used, and the same functionality is better supported using linked sheets, we will not cover imported style sheets. Linked CSS provide the ability to store all of the formatting information in a separate file, which can then be linked to several HTML pages or even a complete Web site. When you change the one style sheet file, you change the look of all of the linked pages without having to modify each of the pages individually. The following script demonstrates the use of a linked CSS to set the background color and fonts for the body and paragraphs in a page.

SimpleStyle.htm

```
<HTML>
<HEAD>
<TITLE>Sample Linked CSS</TITLE>
<LINK REL="STYLESHEET" TYPE="text/css"HREF=" SimpleStyle.css">
</HEAD>
<BODY>
<P>Bigger Text</P>
Simple Small Text
</BODY>
</HTML>
```

The SimpleStyle.css style sheet is as follows:

```
body
{font-family:"Verdana,Sans-Serif"; font-size:10pt; background:gray;}
P
{font-family:"Verdana,Sans-Serif"; font-size: 16pt; color:white;}
```

Embedded style sheets are similar in syntax to that of linked style sheets; however, they are included in the same file as the HTML to which they are being applied. Embedded style sheets allow you to define in one place all the style elements of the complete page and make changing the page's look much easier. Let's return to our previous example to show the syntax for an embedded style sheet:

Embedded.htm

```
<HTML>
<HEAD>
<TITLE>Sample Embedded CSS</TITLE>
</HEAD>
<STYLE>
body {font-family:"Verdana,Sans-Serif"; font-size:10pt; background:gray; }
P {font-family:"Verdana,Sans-Serif"; font-size: 16pt; color:white; }
</STYLE>
<BODY>
<P>Bigger Text</P>
Simple Small Text
</BODY>
</HTML>
```

The final way to apply a style sheet is to put the style inside the applicable HTML element. This method is similar to setting the attributes of a given HTML element; the only difference is the syntax that is used. These in-line style sheets are useful if you wish to apply a style to a single tag or only a few sections of a document. Once again, let's return to our prior example to show how to apply an in-line style sheet:

Inline.htm

```
<HTML>
<HEAD>
<TITLE>Sample In-Line CSS</TITLE>
</HEAD>
<BODY style="font-family:Verdana,Sans-Serif; font-size:10pt;
background:gray;">
<P style="font-family:Verdana,Sans-Serif; font-size:16pt;
color:white;">Bigger Text</P>
Simple Small Text
</BODY>
</HTML>
```

One important thing to note is the way conflicts are handled if multiple styles are applied to the same element: the "closest" style is always the one that is applied. What this means is that if a tag has an in-line style (the closest because it is part of the tag), the in-line style is applied, regardless of any previously declared, conflicting style declarations. Once the current tag goes out of scope (ends), the in-line style precedence also ends, and the previous style (if any) goes back into effect. The next in order of precedence are embedded styles (because they are part of the document), then linked styles (because they are external to the page), and lastly the imported style sheet.

Style Sheet Selectors

In the previous examples, we have been using the HTML element type to define the selector (the elements that the style sheet should be applied to). However, another very useful technique that can be used with embedded and linked CSS is using the CLASS attribute of an HTML element to define the selector. This method allows us to define a subset of elements of the same or different type that the style should be applied to. For example, let's say we want to have an HTML page that applies the same font to both a paragraph and a table cell. This result could be achieved using the CLASS attribute. To designate that we are applying a style to a CLASS of elements we use a (.) in the style tag prior to the class name. We expand on the previous example to show you how to accomplish this:

Class.htm

```
<HTML>
<HEAD>
<TITLE>Sample CSS Using CLASS</TITLE>
</HEAD>
<STYLE>
body {font-family:"Verdana,Sans-Serif"; font-size:10pt; background:gray; }
.sameFont {font-family:"Verdana,Sans-Serif"; font-size: 16pt; color:white;
} </STYLE>
<BODY>
<P CLASS="sameFont">Bigger Text</P>
Simple Small Text
```

```
<TABLE>
    <TR>
        <TD CLASS="sameFont">Matching</TD>
        <TD>Not the same</TD>
    </TR>
</TABLE>
</BODY>
</HTML>
```

You can also define the selector by using the ID of the element you wish to have the style applied to. The effect is the same as applying an in-line style, except for the fact that all of the style information can be put in one central location, instead of on each tag. To designate that we are applying a style to a particular ID of an element, we use a # in the style tag prior to the ID value. The following example takes our in-line example and uses the ID selector method:

Id.htm

```
<HTML>
<HEAD>
<TITLE>Sample CSS Using ID</TITLE>
</HEAD>
<STYLE>
#Bod {font-family:"Verdana,Sans-Serif"; font-size:10pt; background:gray;}
#Para {font-family:"Verdana,Sans-Serif"; font-size: 16pt; color:white;}
</STYLE>
<BODY id="Bod">
<P id="Para">Bigger Text</P>
Simple Small Text
</BODY>
</HTML>
```

OVERVIEW OF DHTML

Dynamic HTML, as its name suggests, provides a mechanism to create interactive pages based on the standard HTML that we have all become familiar with. DHTML allows the page's author to change the look and feel of any element on a particular page without requiring additional interaction with the server. With DHTML you can use dynamic styles to make simple changes to the look of a particular element or use the document object model to change whole portions of the page. In addition to facilitating changes in documents, DHTML also allows the author to trap events for any element on the page and take action when an event occurs.

The key to DHTML is the *document object model*, also known as the DOM. The DOM is a standard, advanced by the W3 Consortium (the independent Internet standards committee) as a common way to build dynamic pages that work across disparate programming languages, browsers, and operating systems. The DOM is the foundation of turning HTML elements into event-generating programmable objects, both individually or as a group of elements. DHTML's DOM is a simple hierarchical system that makes all of the objects (HTML elements, the page itself, and so on) in a page accessible to a scripting language, such as JavaScript. In the DOM there is a document object that represents the page itself, and all of the other objects branch off from this object. Not all of the objects branch directly off of the document object; some are inside of another HTML element, such as an input element being a child of a form element, and are referred to as child elements. If there is more than one child element inside of the parent HTML element, the child elements refer to each other as sibling elements.

There are two major features that DHTML contains: dynamic styles and dynamic content. Dynamic styles allow us to create programmable style sheets, and dynamic content allows us to add, delete, or replace HTML elements using scripting.

Dynamic Styles

In our overview of CSS, we showed you how to apply styles to a particular element. The next thing that we want to do is to dynamically change the style based on the user's action. Thankfully this is easily done through dynamic styles, which are nothing more than styles that are modified through a scripting language. For instance, let's take our simple example again. Let's say that now when the user puts their mouse over the paragraph, we want to make the text in the paragraph tag "Bigger text" even larger. In addition, once the user moves the mouse off of the area we want to return the text back to its original size. Changing the text size is as simple as setting the paragraph's style.fontSize value as shown in the following example:

FontSize.htm

```
<HTML>
<HEAD>
<TITLE>Sample In-Line CSS</TITLE>
</HEAD>
<BODY style="font-family:Verdana,Sans-Serif; font-size:10pt;
background:gray;">
<P onmouseover="style.fontSize='20pt'" onmouseout="style.fontSize='16pt'"
style="font-family:Verdana,Sans-Serif; font-size:16pt;
color:white;">Bigger Text</P>
Simple Small Text
</BODY>
</HTML>
```

In this example we are using in-line JavaScript and the event handlers onmouseover and onmouseout to set the font size. The style subobject allows us to dynamically change the font or any other style when an event occurs within the viewer's browser. What you will notice changing when you reference a style through script versus in tags are the names of the properties. These changes are simply made to provide a syntax that is compatible with the DOM and matches the standard of the JavaScript scripting language. Dynamic style sheets provide us with a great deal of functionality without our having to learn a completely new set of tags or objects.

Dynamic Content

Dynamic content allows developers to change the HTML elements in a page, and you can effectively change the complete page on the client side. The DOM provides four properties that are supported by all block style elements (for example, DIV, SPAN, TABLE, TR, P, and so on) that allow us to change the content of a given block. The four properties are innerHTML, outerHMTL, innerText, and outerText.

The innerHTML and innerText properties allow you to change the content inside a particular element but not the containing element tag itself. The outerHTML and outerText properties allow you to change not only the content inside of the element but the element tag itself. With innerHTML and outerHTML, if the string contains HTML tags it is parsed, and the elements are inserted into the document. With innerText and outerText, if the string contains HTML the HTML tags are displayed directly in the page. In addition, the innerText value can be used to retrieve only the text from an element. This can be helpful if you want to retrieve the data from an element, without having to deal with the formatting tags.

The following example shows you how to use the innerHTML and innerText properties to add user-defined data to a page. In addition, the example shows how you can use the innerText to view the HTML source on the page.

Inner.htm

```
<HTML>
<SCRIPT Language="JavaScript">
var status="HTML";
function setText(){
    if (status == "Text")
        alert("You must change the viewing mode to display HTML.");
    else
        userData.innerHTML = theText.value;
}
function showSourceHTML(){
    if (status == "HTML"){
        container.innerText = container.innerHTML;
        status = "Text";
    }
    else{
        container.innerHTML = container.innerText;
        status = "HTML";
    }
}
</SCRIPT>
<HEAD>
<TITLE>Dynamic Content</TITLE>
```

```
</HEAD>
<BODY>
<DIV ID="container"><P><Strong>This is a sample to show you how to work
with setting HTML and Text</Strong></P>
<DIV ID="userData"></DIV>
</DIV>
<P>Type In HTML to display above:<INPUT ID="theText" TYPE="TEXT" />
<INPUT TYPE="BUTTON" VALUE="Set HTML" onClick="setText()" /></P>
<INPUT ID="showSourceHTML" TYPE="BUTTON" VALUE="Show Source / HTML"
onClick="showSourceHTML()" />
</BODY>
</HTML>
```

Modifying Individual Elements

With Internet Explorer 5.0, Microsoft introduced another way to deal with adding, deleting, and modifying individual elements: allowing elements to be cloned from other elements or created from a simple text string. In addition, elements can be deleted or replaced using a simple method call.

The cloneNode method has been added to HTML elements object model to allow another element to be created from the original element. When using the cloneNode method, the object, attributes, and, if specified, the child nodes are also cloned. In addition to cloning nodes, you can create HTML elements using the createElement method. The createElement method takes one parameter, which is a valid HTML string for an element. Attributes can also be passed in as part of the string, as long as the string is valid HTML. Both the cloneNode and createElement methods return an element object that can be further modified (for example, setting attributes, using innerHTML, and so on) in code before associating it with the document. However, you cannot reference the object by its ID until it has been inserted into the current document.

Now that you have created a new element object, you need to insert it into the document. This is done using the insertBefore or the appendChild methods. The insertBefore method is invoked on the object you wish to insert the new element into. In addition, the method allows you to specify the child in the hierarchy of the calling element to insert the new object before. The appendChild method inserts the element at the end of the children collection of the calling object.

The following example shows how to use the cloneNode, createElement, insertBefore, and appendChild methods:

Child.htm

```
<HTML>
<HEAD>
<TITLE>Dynamic Content</TITLE>
</HEAD>
<SCRIPT LANGUAGE="JavaScript">
function clone(cloneObj){
    var newNode;
    newNode = cloneObj.cloneNode(false);
    newNode.innerHTML = "Cloned " + cloneObj.innerText;
    cloneObj.insertBefore(newNode);
    window.event.cancelBubble = true;
}
function create(createObj){
    var newNode;
    newNode = document.createElement("<P>");
    newNode.innerText = "New Paragraph";
    createObj.appendChild(newNode);
}
</SCRIPT>
<BODY>
<DIV onClick="clone(this)" style="color:red">
Click here to add a cloned node inside this DIV
</DIV>
<BR>
<DIV onClick="create(this)">Click here to add a new paragraph to this
DIV</DIV>
</BODY>
</HTML>
```

The DOM also contains methods to remove or replace a particular child or node. Table 2-1 lists the different methods and parameters for each call, including the creation and insertion methods we have already covered.

Method	Parameters	Return Value	Example
appendChild	Element to append	Appended element	NewEl = object. appendChild(NewEl)
cloneNode	Clone children (true/*false)	Cloned element	Cloned = original. cloneNode(false)
createElement	Element to create (HTML string)	New element	NewEl = object. createElement ("<DIV>")
insertbefore	New element to insert; optionally: object that new element is to be inserted before	New element	NewEl =object. insertBefore (NewEl, Child)
replaceChild	New element, or element to be replaced	Replaced element	OldEl = object. replaceChild (NewEl, OldEl)
replaceNode	New element (to replace existing object)	Replaced element	OldEl = OldEl. replaceNode(NewEl)
removeChild	Element to remove	Removed element	RemEl = object. removeChild(RemEl)
removeNode	Remove child elements (true/*false)	Removed element	RemEl = RemEl. removeNode(true);

(* = default value)

Table 2-1.   DHTML DOM Calls to Interact with a Particular Child or Node

Collections and Events

There are two very useful collections in the DOM that contain the elements in the document and the children of a particular element. The *all* collection is available both on the document level and also for each HTML element. At the document level, this collection contains all of the elements in a document. At the element level, it contains all its own elements. The *children* collection is available at the element level and contains only the direct descendants of the element and not the descendants of its children.

Up to this point we have shown code using simple event capturing. For example, we have used the onClick event handler to capture mouse clicks on an individual element, as follows:

```
<DIV onClick="create(this)">Click here to add a new paragraph to this
DIV<//DIV>
```

However, there is another way to capture events at a higher level, using event bubbling. *Event bubbling* is a powerful way of handling events in an HTML document. Event bubbling works in the following way: first, the event handler for the affected element is called; next, the event is raised to the element's parent, regardless of whether the event was handled at the element level. The event keeps being raised up, or bubbled, until the event is bubbled up to the window object or another event handler that cancels the bubbling. You may have noticed in our example of dynamic content we had the line

```
window.event.cancelBubble = true;
```

What we are doing here is stopping the event from being bubbled up to the event handler for the parent of the element. The parent element, after you have added a child to the original DIV, would be the original DIV, so when you click on the child you end up with double the number of children that you might expect. To see this in action, take that example and comment out the cancel bubble line. This is pretty cool and can be a useful functionality as long as you remember to turn it off in the situations where you don't want the bubbling to occur.

DHTML REUSE AND ENCAPSULATION

Every important development tool needs to be able to encapsulate functionality. Encapsulation provides users with a well-defined interface to a set of functionality in a way that hides the internal workings of the code. If you are familiar with any of the major development environments (such as Visual Basic, C++, and Java), you know that they all provide a mechanism to *componitize* (encapsulate) and reuse code. By providing encapsulation, the HTML and script can be reused by other applications and developers, without the need for them to reinvent the wheel.

Before the advent of Dynamic HTML, there was little need to reuse code simply because there wasn't much scripting code being used. However, since we have entered the era of dynamic Web sites,

HTML pages must quickly provide feedback and interact with the user. Dynamic HTML and scripting give us the ability to respond to users and change the look of the application based on the requests the user has made. As described in the overview, DHTML and scripting allow us to look at every HTML element as a scriptable object. In other words, you can change the properties and look of every piece of HTML in a document.

Once we achieved this new functionality, however, we found ourselves writing hundreds of lines of code for each page to provide this new level of interactivity. Because each HTML page is often thought of as its own entity, one kept writing the same code over and over again and not reusing the code already written and tested.

Another bar to encapsulation and reuse was lack of a good mechanism. Prior to Microsoft Internet Explorer 5.0, one way to provide encapsulation for script was to use include files to import an existing script library. These included script files were simply external files that were imported into the existing pages at runtime by the server, providing minimal levels of code reuse and functionality. (Part of the problem with include files is that they don't have a mechanism to raise events and interact with the HTML on the page.)

The only other mechanism to encapsulate DHTML functionality was the scriptlet. *Scriptlets* were Microsoft's first attempt at developing reusable HTML components. The concept was good, but because of the way it was implemented it caused problems when interacting with other HTML elements on a page. In brief, a scriptlet interacts with a Web page similar to the way an ActiveX control does. The scriptlet was created using the object tag in HTML and ran in its own window inside of the existing page. Scriptlets were somewhat of a sore thumb in that they didn't fit well within the HTML of the page—they didn't feel or look like native HTML. Scriptlets had their own rectangular opaque area that covered the hosting page, and because of this they did not fit smoothly into a textured background or other HTML elements.

Enter DHTML Behaviors

Developers were looking for a seamless way to separate the code and functionality from the display content without having to learn a new language or environment. In addition, a method programmers could use to develop components that contain effects—and a method that could be easily used by an interface designer—would make development of large projects easier to manage.

With the release of Internet Explorer 5.0, Microsoft introduced a new piece of functionality called DHTML behaviors, which make the encapsulation and reusability much easier. DHTML behaviors are simple, lightweight script- or binary-based components that encapsulate specific functionality or behaviors on a page. Behaviors are most often developed using script, but they can also be developed using C++ to create binary components. Binary behaviors can be useful if you have very sensitive business rules that you wish to implement. When applied to a standard HTML element on a page, a behavior can enhance that element's default functionality and includes any new methods, properties, or events of the behavior.

Behaviors provide easy separation of script from content, which not only makes it easy to reuse code across multiple pages but also contributes to the improved manageability of the page. In addition to this, developers can create a "super component" that combines several HTML elements to create a new component that can have a new programming interface. We will discuss how to create behaviors and cover more technical details of behaviors in Chapter 4, but right now we will show you how easy it is to use behaviors in your Web pages.

Applying Behaviors

In order to support the functionality available in DHTML behaviors, the DOM and CSS needed to have several new pieces of functionality added. What Microsoft did in IE 5.0 was to add functionality to the browser (rather than changing existing technology) so that older browsers could just ignore the new piece of functionality, a graceful way to degrade the content to older browsers.

Behaviors are applied to an element using a CSS or a method call to the DOM. Using CSS, behaviors can be applied as easily as changing the font on an HTML element. Through CSS, behaviors can be applied using the new behavior attribute. The behavior attribute can be specified on an element just like any CSS attribute. The following shows the different ways of specifying a behavior from a CSS:

An in-line style:

```
<DIV STYLE="behavior:url(foo.htc)"> An in-line style applied
behavior</DIV>
```

By defining an embedded style, using the HTML element as a selector:

```
<STYLE>
    DIV {behavior:url(foo.htc)}
</STYLE>
<BODY>
<DIV> An embedded style applied behavior</DIV>
</BODY>
```

By defining an embedded style, using a class name as a selector:

```
<STYLE>
    .foo   {behavior:url(foo.htc)}
</STYLE>
<BODY>
<DIV CLASS="foo"> An embedded style using a class applied behavior</DIV>
</BODY>
```

By using the style object of the element in script:

```
<SCRIPT LANGUAGE="JavaScript">
function init(){
    foo.style.behavior = "url(foo.htc)";
}
</SCRIPT>
<BODY onLoad="init()">
<DIV id="foo"> A style object applied behavior</DIV>
</BODY>
```

The primary focus of this book is on creating behaviors in script; however, one item you need to be aware of is that if a behavior was developed using C++ (not very common) versus script, the syntax of applying the behavior is slightly different. Because C++ behaviors are binary content, the way to include them into a page is to use the object tag. Once you have created the reference in the object tag, you set the URL in the behavior style to the value of the ID for the object element prefixed with a #. The following is an example:

```
<STYLE> .foo {behavior:url(#binaryObject)}
</STYLE>
<OBJECT ID="binaryObject" ... ></OBJECT>
<DIV id="foo"></DIV>
```

In addition to using a style sheet, a behavior may be added using the addBehavior method on the item you wish to apply the behavior to. The addBehavior method is the dynamic way of applying a behavior to an element through script. Another feature of the addBehavior method is that if an element is removed from the document hierarchy, the behavior stays attached to the element. If you are using the CSS methods, other than through in-line implementation, the behavior is automatically detached from the element when it is removed from the hierarchy. The addBehavior method returns an integer value, which is an identifier that can later be used to remove the behavior. The following shows the use of the addBehavior method:

```
<SCRIPT LANGUAGE="JavaScript">
function init(){
    identifier = foo.addBehaviorl("foo.htc");
}
</SCRIPT>
<BODY onLoad="init()">
<DIV id="foo"> An addBehavior applied behavior</DIV>
</BODY>
```

User-Defined Tags

So far we have shown applying behaviors to a standard HTML element. In some cases the new functionality may not be intended to enhance the existing functionality of an HTML element but rather to provide nonvisual functionality. For example, you may have a behavior that returns the capabilities of the user's browser, such as whether it supports Java or cookies. These nonvisual behaviors don't extend an existing HTML element, but rather they provide you with additional information. In such cases, you will want to apply the behavior to your own user-defined tag.

You can create a user-defined XML element to apply the behavior to. The way this is done is to create a name space for your document and then prefix your new element with that name space. A name space provides you the ability to define your elements so that they do not conflict with an existing HTML element. In addition to this, name spaces turn your user-defined elements into DHTML objects that support events and the basic DHTML functionality, such as innerHTML and innerText. Setting up a name space is done by adding XMLNS:MyNamespace (where MyNamespace is a user-defined name) to the <html> tag at the beginning of the document. In addition to specifying the name space, you can define a uniform resource name (URN) that uniquely identifies the name space; this is something similar to a uniform resource locator (URL) in that it should globally identify a name space. The following is an example of using the URN: XMLNS:MyNamespace="MyGloballyUniqueName". Now when you create your user-defined element, you prefix the element with MyNamespace:newElement (where newElement is the your new user-defined element).

Here's an example of creating your own name space and element and applying a behavior to it. In addition, the tag we are creating is named INPUT, which shows that we can create an element that has the same name as a standard HTML element, but because we are using a name space there isn't a conflict.

```
<HTML XMLNS:TEST>
<SCRIPT>
function getSetting(){
    alert(foo.getSetting("CookiesEnabled"));
}
</SCRIPT>
<BODY onLoad="getSetting()">
<TEST:INPUT ID="foo" STYLE="behavior:url(foo.htc)"></TEST:INPUT>
</BODY>
</HTML>
```

Calling Methods and Setting Properties

In the previous code, you may have noticed that we are calling a method of our user-defined element. The code:

foo.getSetting ("CookiesEnabled") is a call to the new functionality provided by the behavior and becomes transparent to the developer that a behavior is being used. We also see this with properties. If you wish to set a property that is part of a behavior, you can set the value in the tag of the element that the behavior is associated to. For example, if a behavior, foo, has a property bar it could be set as simple as this:

```
<STYLE>
    DIV {behavior:url(foo.htc)}
</STYLE>
<BODY>
<DIV bar="PropertyValue"> An embedded style applied behavior</DIV>
</BODY>
```

As a component, a DHTML behavior has its own object model that may expose properties, methods, and events. Once a behavior is applied to an element, the element's properties, methods, and events are extended to include those exposed through the behavior.

Multiple Behaviors

In all the examples up to this point we have shown you how to add a single behavior to an element. However, you can add multiple behaviors to the same element if you would like. The addBehavior method automatically appends the behavior to a list of behaviors being applied to the element and does not overwrite other behaviors that have been previously attached. In addition to the addBehavior method, you can apply multiple behaviors using the behavior CSS attribute for an element using a space-delimited string. For example:

```
<DIV STYLE="behavior:url(foo.htc) url(bar.htc)">Multiple behaviors</DIV>
```

If conflicts exist between the two behaviors because of common methods, properties, or events, the behavior that was last applied or the last behavior in the list is the behavior that is called.

Other DOM Additions

In addition to addBehavior and the behavior attribute of CSS, Table 2-2 lists the methods that have also been added to the DHTML DOM to

New DHTML Extension	Parameters	Return Value	Description
attachEvent - Method	Event to capture; function to call when event fires	If function was successful (true/false)	Binds the specified function to an event that is fired by the object. The function is automatically called when the event fires on the object.
behaviorUrns - Collection	None	See description	Returns a collection of URN strings identifying the behaviors attached to the element.
detachEvent - Method	Event to detach; function that was called when event was fired	None	Unbinds a specific function from an event, which stops the function from automatically being called when the event fires on the object.
removeBehavior - Method	Identifier returned from the addBehavior method	If function was successful (true/false)	Used to detach a behavior from an element.
scopeName - Property	None	See description	Returns the name space for the element. If the element is a standard HTML element it returns the value "HTML."
srcUrn - Property	None	See description	Retrieves the URN for the behavior that fired the event.
tagUrn - Property	None	See description	A read-only value that returns the URN for user-defined tags and returns null for standard HTML tags.
urns - Method	String that specifies the behavior's URN	See description	Retrieves a collection of elements a particular behavior is attached to, based on the behavior's URN.

Table 2-2.   Methods That Have Been Added to DHTML DOM to Support DHTML Behaviors

support behaviors. Note: Uniform resource names (URNs) specify the identity of a resource. For example inside a behavior's code, you can specify its URN so that the behavior can be uniquely identified.

DHTML Behaviors and Security

DHTML behavior files are downloaded from a Web site or retrieved from the browser's cache when they are referenced in a Web page. Since behaviors are downloadable files, there are security issues that need to be understood in order to use them properly. There are two types of security concerns: the browser security level and the domain where the behavior is being downloaded.

The browser security level has to do with the types of objects that are being downloaded from a site. The same security rules apply to behaviors as they do to the page that uses the behavior. The browser maintains these settings, and behaviors are considered the same as an HTML page.

For the domain security, the behavior must be downloaded from the same domain as the page that requests the behavior. For example, if the page's site is from http://myserver, and it requests a behavior from http://yourserver, the page will display an "Access Denied" error. Also the page and the behavior must use the same protocol, otherwise when the page is downloaded it will display the "Access Denied" error, as well.

Summary

In this chapter we have gone over the functionality in CSS and DHTML that we will use through the remainder of the book. In addition we have covered how to apply behaviors to an HTML element or your own user-defined element. We also have shown that a DHTML behavior's functionality is transparent once the behavior has been applied to that element. In the next chapter we will show you how to use the built-in behaviors in Internet Explorer 5.0.

CHAPTER 3

IE 5 DHTML Default Behaviors

At the end of the last chapter we discussed DHTML behaviors and their importance in Web development. To recap, some of the benefits of DHTML behaviors are encapsulation, code reuse, and developing HTML components. Internet Explorer 5 comes with some prebuilt DHTML behaviors. They are referred to as *default behaviors*. Table 3-1 lists the default behaviors that are included with IE 5.

Behavior	Purpose
anchor	Allows the browser to display files and folders on a Web server in a Web folder view. This behavior works with the httpFolder behavior.
anim	Uses DirectAnimation® to display DirectAnimation objects and sounds in the browser. This behavior uses the Microsoft's Liquid Motions technology (lmlib.dll).
animation	Displays a timed animation element on a Web page.
audio	Plays a timed audio element on a Web page.
clientCaps	Retrieves information about the capabilities of the client browser and the environment in which it is executing.
download	Downloads a file from the same domain where the calling page is located, notifying a specified callback function when complete.
homePage	Contains home page information for the user.
httpFolder	Displays a Web site as a set of files and folders in a folder view.

Table 3-1.   IE 5's Default Behaviors

Behavior	Purpose
img	Displays a timed image element on a Web page.
media	Displays a media element on a Web page.
par	Defines an independent timeline container for a set of elements on a Web page.
saveFavorite	Saves a Web page's state in the Favorite's user data when the user adds the page to their Favorites. The page persists across user sessions.
saveHistory	Persists a Web page's state in the History user data area. The page persists for only the session (until the browser is closed).
saveSnapShot	Persists a Web page's data when it is saved locally as HTML only.
seq	Defines a sequential timeline container for a set of elements on a Web page.
time	Defines an active timeline for elements on the Web page.
userData	Persists data in the user data area.
video	Plays a timed video element on a Web page.

Table 3-1.   IE 5's Default Behaviors *(continued)*

In this chapter we will demonstrate the benefits of DHTML behaviors by showing how to apply some of the default behaviors. Throughout this chapter, we will show

▼ What each of the default behaviors does.

■ How to declare behaviors using XML name spaces and CSS.

- How the page's DOM refers to a behavior.
- The calling properties and methods of the default behaviors.
▲ How a behavior is a reusable component.

CLIENTCAPS DEFAULT BEHAVIOR

The clientCaps behavior does what its name implies: it gives information about the client's computer that is running IE 5. The capabilities include both hardware and software attributes. This behavior also shows which IE 5 components are installed, and it also has methods for downloading and installing them, if needed. One of the more useful features of clientCaps is its information on the screen height and width. The behavior has two sets of height and width properties: height/width and availHeight/availWidth. The difference between the two is that the availHeight and availWidth properties take into account the Windows taskbar, while the height and width properties give you the screen resolution. With this information, you can program your Web page to resize based on the user's screen size.

Figure 3-1 shows the clientCaps behavior in action. It was run on the machine that we use to write this book, so if you run it on your machine your results may be different. We have broken the clientCap's attributes into five sections: screen dimensions, screen color, browser capabilities, miscellaneous client capabilities, and components installed. The first four sections are self-explanatory. For each section a description is given for the clientCaps property, with the actual clientCaps property shown in parenthesis.

The Components Installed section shows the available components that are included with IE 5, whether they are installed on the client's computer, and their version number. If a component is not installed on the client computer, an install button is displayed in the Installed column. If the user presses the button, it will download that component from the Internet and install it on the client's computer. This feature is handy when your page needs an IE 5 component: it can check to see if it is installed and then download it if it needs to be installed.

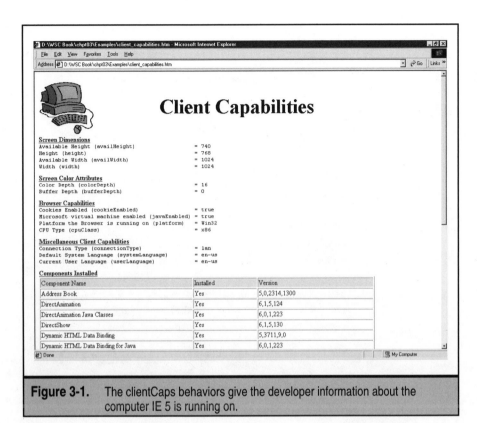

Figure 3-1. The clientCaps behaviors give the developer information about the computer IE 5 is running on.

The code listing below, from the file client_capabilities.htm, shows how the page in Figure 3-1 was implemented:

client_capabilities.htm

```
<html XMLNS:CC>
<head>
<STYLE>
    @media all { CC\:clientCaps {behavior:url(#default#clientCaps)}}
    .Title { color:darkblue;font-weight:bold;text-decoration:underline }
    .Values { position:relative;top:-20 }
</Style>
<title>Client Capabilities</title>
</head>
<body onload="getClientCaps()" bgcolor="#00FFCC">
    <CC:clientCaps id=clientCaps />
    <table border="0" width="100%">
      <tr>
```

```
        <td width="30%"><img border="0" src="computer.gif" width="135"
height="132"></td>
        <td width="70%">
          <p align="left"><b><font size="7">Client
Capabilities</font></b></p>
        </td>
      </tr>
    </table>
    <div>
      <span class=title>Screen Dimensions</span>
      <pre id=displayScreenDim class=values></pre>
    </div>
    <div style="position:relative;top:-45">
      <span class=title>Screen Color Attributes</span>
      <pre id=displayColorAttr class=values></pre>
    </div>
    <div style="position:relative;top:-90">
      <span class=title>Browser Capabilities</span>
      <pre id=displayBrowserCaps class=values></pre>
    </div>
    <div style="position: relative; top: -135; width: 700; height: 6">
      <span class=title>Miscellaneous Client </span>
      <span class=title>Capabilities</span>
      <pre id=displayMiscCaps class=values></pre>
    </div>
    <div style="position:relative;top:-180">
      <span class=title>Components Installed</span>
        <table id=tblComponent border="1" width="84%">
        <tr>
        <td width="36%" bgcolor="#C0C0C0">Component Name</td>
        <td width="15%" bgcolor="#C0C0C0">Installed</td>
        <td width="28%" bgcolor="#C0C0C0">Version</td>
        </tr>
        </table>
    </div>
</body>
<script language=javascript>
function getClientCaps(){
var sTemp = '';
var sHTML;
var newRow;
    sTemp = sTemp + 'Available Height (availHeight) =
' +clientCaps.availHeight  + '\n';
```

```
    sTemp = sTemp + 'Height (height) = ' + clientCaps.height + '\n';
    sTemp = sTemp + 'Available Width (availWidth) =
' + clientCaps.availWidth + '\n';
    sTemp = sTemp + 'Width (width) = ' + clientCaps.width + '\n\n';
    displayScreenDim.innerText = sTemp;
    sTemp = 'Color Depth (colorDepth) = ' + clientCaps.colorDepth + '\n';
    sTemp = sTemp + 'Buffer Depth (bufferDepth) =
' + clientCaps.bufferDepth + '\n\n';
    displayColorAttr.innerText = sTemp;
    sTemp = 'Cookies Enabled (cookieEnabled) = '
+ clientCaps.cookieEnabled + '\n';
    sTemp = sTemp + 'Microsoft virtual machine enabled (javaEnabled) =
'+ clientCaps.javaEnabled + '\n';
    sTemp = sTemp + 'Platform the Browser is running on (platform)   =
' + clientCaps.platform + '\n';
    sTemp = sTemp + 'CPU Type (cpuClass) = ' + clientCaps.cpuClass + '\n\n';
    displayBrowserCaps.innerText = sTemp;
    sTemp = 'Connection Type (connectionType) =
' + clientCaps.connectionType + '\n';
sTemp = sTemp + 'Default System Language (systemLanguage)      =
' + clientCaps.systemLanguage + '\n';
    sTemp = sTemp + 'Current User Language (userLanguage)        =
' + clientCaps.userLanguage + '\n\n';
    displayMiscCaps.innerText = sTemp;
    showComponentStatus();
}
function showComponentStatus(){
    displayComponent('Address Book',
'{7790769C-0471-11D2-AF11-00C04FA35D02}');
    displayComponent('DirectAnimation',
        '{283807B5-2C60-11D0-A31D-00AA00B92C03}');
    displayComponent('DirectAnimation Java Classes',
        '{4F216970-C90C-11D1-B5C7-0000F8051515}');
    displayComponent('DirectShow',
 '{44BBA848-CC51-11CF-AAFA-00AA00B6015C}');
    displayComponent('Dynamic HTML Data Binding',
        '{9381D8F2-0288-11D0-9501-00AA00B911A5}');
    displayComponent('Dynamic HTML Data Binding for Java',
        '{4F216970-C90C-11D1-B5C7-0000F8051515}');
    displayComponent('Internet Connection Wizard',
        '{5A8D6EE0-3E18-11D0-821E-444553540000}');
    displayComponent('Internet Explorer 5 Web Browser',
        '{89820200-ECBD-11CF-8B85-00AA005B4383}');
```

```
        displayComponent('Internet Explorer Classes for Java',
            '{08B0E5C0-4FCB-11CF-AAA5-00401C608555}');
        displayComponent('Internet Explorer Help',
            '{45EA75A0-A269-11D1-B5BF-0000F8051515}');
        displayComponent('Internet Explorer Help Engine',
            '{DE5AED00-A4BF-11D1-9948-00C04F98BBC9}');
        displayComponent('Windows Media Player',
            '{22D6F312-B0F6-11D0-94AB-0080C74C7E95}');
        displayComponent('NetMeeting NT',
    '{44BBA842-CC51-11CF-AAFA-00AA00B6015B}');
        displayComponent('Offline Browsing Pack',
            '{3AF36230-A269-11D1-B5BF-0000F8051515}');
        displayComponent('Outlook Express',
            '{44BBA840-CC51-11CF-AAFA-00AA00B6015C}');
        displayComponent('Task Scheduler',
            '{CC2A9BA0-3BDD-11D0-821E-444553540000}');
        displayComponent('Microsoft virtual machine',
            '{08B0E5C0-4FCB-11CF-AAA5-00401C608500}');
        displayComponent('VRML 2.0 Viewer',
            '{90A7533D-88FE-11D0-9DBE-0000C0411FC3}');
        displayComponent('Wallet', '{1CDEE860-E95B-11CF-B1B0-00AA00BBAD66}');
}
function displayComponent(compDesc, compID){
var newCell;
var sFunc;
    newRow = document.all.tblComponent.insertRow();
    newCell = newRow .insertCell();
    newCell.width = '36%';
    newCell.innerText = compDesc;
    newCell = newRow .insertCell();
    newCell.width = '15%';
    if (clientCaps.isComponentInstalled(compID, "componentID")){
        newCell.innerText = 'Yes';
        newCell = newRow .insertCell();
        newCell.width = '28%';
        newCell.innerText = clientCaps.getComponentVersion
(compID, "ComponentID");
    }
    else{
        sFunc = "addComponent('" + compID + "');";
        newCell.innerHTML = '<input type="button" value="Install"
name="installComp" onclick="' + sFunc + '">'
        newCell = newRow .insertCell();
        newCell.width = '28%';
```

```
            newCell.innerText = ' ';
        }
    }
function addComponent(compID){
var bAvailable;
var i;
var row;
        clientCaps.addComponentRequest(compID, 'componentid');
        bAvailable = clientCaps.doComponentRequest();
        if (bAvailable == true){
            //remove the rows from table and redisplay them
            for (i=document.all.tblComponent.rows.length - 1; i > 0 ; i--){
                    row = document.all.tblComponent.rows[i];
                    row.removeNode(true);
            }
            showComponentStatus();
        }
    }
}
</script>
</html>
```

To use clientCaps, the first thing you need to do on the HTML page is to instantiate the behavior so the page has a reference to the behavior. Our example page uses an XML name space to create a unique XML element inside the <html> tag:

```
<html XMLNS:CC>
```

The name space was given a name of CC. The name space is then used to create an XML element. This element is then used on the page to create an instantiation of the clientCaps behavior. The example page uses a cascading style sheet to assign the clientCaps behavior to an element on the page:

```
@media all { CC\:clientCaps {behavior:url(#default#clientCaps)}}
```

The @media all is a CSS rule that states this style sheet covers all media (screen, print, and so on) in which this page is displayed. The CC\:clientCaps is the name space with the name of the XML element that it used on the page. The \ before the : is used to tell the browser that the : is not used as an attribute:value combination, as is used in a CSS. Whenever that XML element is used on the page, it has the following style sheet assigned to it:

```
behavior:url(#default#clientCaps)
```

This is actually assigning the clientCaps behavior to the XML element CC:clientCaps.

NOTE: We will see how to attach a behavior directly to the XML name space and not use a CSS in another example.

The clientCaps behavior is attached to the page after the <body> tag by adding the following XML element to the page:

```
<CC:clientCaps id=clientCaps />
```

The page can now reference the behavior by the clientCaps ID attribute.

When the onload event fires for the <body> tag, it calls the getClientCaps() function. This function creates the first four sections of the page. Each section calls properties of the clientCaps behavior, which are displayed on the page. For example, to get the available width of the screen, the following property is called:

```
clientCaps.availHeight
```

clientCaps is the ID of the clientCaps behavior, and the availHeight is a property of the behavior.

To see how a method is called, let's look at the displayComponent function to see how it checks if a component is installed already. The displayComponent() function is called for each possible component that can be installed with IE 5 from the showComponentStatus() function. The displayComponent() function checks to see if the component is already installed:

```
if (clientCaps.isComponentInstalled(compID, "componentID"))
```

The isComponetInstalled uses the GUID (globally unique ID) of the component to see if the component is installed on the client's computer. If it is installed, then clientCaps gets the version number of the installed component by calling

```
clientCaps.getComponentVersion(compID, "ComponentID")
```

If the component is not installed, the addComponent() function is called. This function allows the user to download the component and install the component on the client's computer. The first thing the addComponent() function does is add the component to a collection:

```
clientCaps.addComponentRequest(compID, 'componentid')
```

The addComponentRequest method loads many components into a collection, so the download can be called once to download all the components at one time. This example downloads only one component at a time. To download the component(s), the following method is called:

```
bAvailable = clientCaps.doComponentRequest()
```

The bAvailable variable is used to check if the download succeeded.

THE DOWNLOAD DEFAULT BEHAVIOR

The IE 5 download behavior is used to download files from within the browser. This means that the page does not have to be reloaded from the server. There is, however, a restriction on the type of files that can be downloaded: the download behavior will only download text files. If another file type is downloaded, only the file's format type is downloaded and not the actual file contents. Another restriction is that the download behavior will only download files that are within the same domain as the page that is executing the download behavior. The download behavior supports only one member, the startDownload method. This method is used to start the download and calls a script function when the download has completed. The script function receives the file's contents as a parameter.

This behavior can be very useful for passing text data from a Web server to the page without refreshing the entire page. For example, if there is a drop-down menu on the page, and it is filled with data based on radio buttons selected on the page, then some script could call the download behavior's startDownload method to load the drop-down menu. Let's look at an example of this.

Download Behavior Example

Figure 3-2 shows a page with a set of radio buttons and a drop-down menu (<select> tag) on it. Choosing the Cities radio button and pressing the View Values button loads the drop-down menu with data from the file cities.txt. Choosing the States radio button and pressing the View Values button loads the drop-down menu with data from the states.txt file. The entire page is not downloaded from the Web site, only the data that needs to be changed. The code is shown below:

citiesstates.htm

```
<html XMLNS:IE>
<head>
<title>Pick Either Cities or States</title>
</head>
<script language="JavaScript">
function getValues(){
var sFileName;
    //clear the select
    document.all.objSelect.length = 0;

    //select the appropiate file
    if (document.all.optSelectChoice(0).checked == true)
        sFileName = 'cities.txt';
    else
        sFileName = 'states.txt';

    //download the file
    objDownload.startDownload(sFileName, onDownloadDone);
}
function onDownloadDone(data) {
var arrTemp;
var i;
var sTemp = new String;

    //split the data into array elements
    arrTemp = data.split("|");

    //load the data into the select
    for (i = 0; i < arrTemp.length; i++){
        document.all.objSelect.length++;
        document.all.objSelect.options[i].text = arrTemp[i];
    }
}
</script>
<body bgcolor="#0099FF">
<IE:Download ID="objDownload" STYLE="behavior:url(#default#download)" />
<p align="center"><font size="5">Pick Either Cities or States</font></p>
<form >
```

```
    <table border="0" width="364">
      <tr>
        <td width="106">Select Choice: </td>
        <td width="116"><input type="radio" value="V1" checked
name="optSelectChoice">Cities
          <input type="radio" name="optSelectChoice" value="V2">States</td>
        <td width="122"><input type="button" value="View Values"
onclick="getValues()" name="btnSelectValues"></td>
      </tr>
      <tr>
        <td width="106">Select Values:</td>
        <td width="116"><select size="1" name="objSelect">
          </select></td>
        <td width="122"></td>
      </tr>
    </table>
</form>
</body>
</html>
```

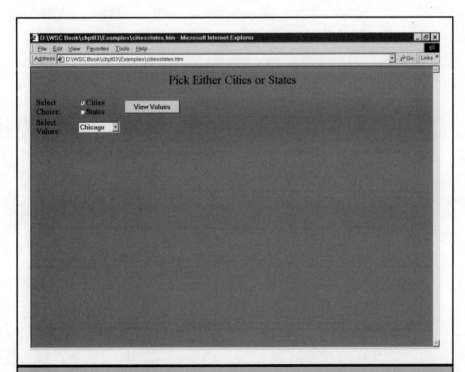

Figure 3-2.   The DHTML default download behavior downloads files from the server without the server having to reload the entire Web page.

The statement that follows the <body> tag in the code listing creates a reference to the download behavior in the page:

```
<IE:Download ID="objDownload" STYLE="behavior:url(#default#download)" />
```

The IE element is created as an XML name space in the first line in the listing:

```
<html XMLNS:IE>
```

The download behavior is referenced in the page using the ID objDownload. The btnSelectValues button's onclick event calls the getValues() function. This function decides which file to download (either the cities or states), then the function calls the download behavior's startDownload method:

```
objDownload.startDownload(sFileName, onDownloadDone)
```

The sFileName parameter is the file we wish to download, and the onDownloadDone parameter specifies the function to be called when the download is complete. When the onDownloadDone function is executed, it loads the <select> tag with data from the file. The file in this example uses a | (pipe) to delimit the data, but the file could be any layout, even an XML file, as long as the receiving page knows how to parse the file's contents.

ANCHOR AND HTTPFOLDER DEFAULT BEHAVIORS

Web Folders are a new way to display and manage a Web site's files and folders in IE 5. The Web Folders feature displays a Web site's directory structure in the same manner as Windows Explorer does when it uses a Listview (Explorer's right pane) to display files and folders. Figure 3-3 contrasts the traditional Internet way of displaying files and folders (top) and the Web Folders way of doing the same thing (bottom).

IE 5 contains two DHTML default behaviors that incorporate the use of Web Folders: the anchor and the httpFolder behaviors. These behaviors have the same functionality but give the developer different implementations of working with Web Folders. The anchor behavior is used with the <A> tag to display a Web Folder. The httpFolder behavior is used when you want to display a Web Folder

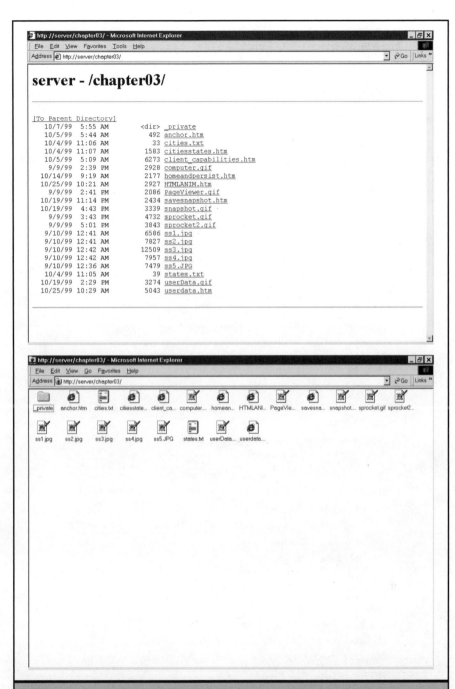

Figure 3-3.   Web Folders (bottom) give the user a more Windows-like interface to display and manage a Web site's files and folders, as opposed to the traditional Internet display (top).

using script code. The following listing shows how the two behaviors are used:

anchor.htm

```
<html XMLNS:IE>
<head>
<title>Open in Web Folder View</title>
<STYLE>
    A {behavior: url(#default#AnchorClick);}
</STYLE>
</head>
<script language="JavaScript">
function gotoFolder(){
    if (document.all.selWindowType.value == "self")
        document.all.objHttpFolder.navigate("http://localhost/chapter03/");
    else

document.all.objHttpFolder.navigateFrame("http://localhost/chapter03/",
"top");
}
</script>
<body bgcolor="#FFCC66">
<IE:httpFolder id="objHttpFolder" style="behavior:url(#default#httpFolder)"
/>
<table border="0" width="100%">
  <tr>
    <td width="16%"><font color="#FF0000"><img border="0"
src="anchor.jpg" align="left" width="70" height="70"></font> </td>
    <td width="84%">
      <p align="center"><font size="6"><font color="#FF0000">
Anchor</font> DHTML
Default Behavior</font></td>
  </tr>
</table>
<p><br>
Click <A HREF = http://localhost/chapter03/
FOLDER = http://localhost/chapter03/
TARGET = "self">Here</A> to view the Chapter 3 examples directory</p>
<table border="0" width="100%">
  <tr>
    <td width="16%"><img border="0" src="folder.jpg" width="64"
```

```
height="64"></td>
    <td width="84%">
       <p align="center"><font size="6"><font
color="#FF0000">httpFolders</font>
    DHTML Default Behavior</font></td>
  </tr
</table>
<p>Select a window and press the 'View Folder' button to display
the Chapter 3
example directory</p>
<form>
  <table border="0" width="100%">
    <tr>
       <td width="36%">Window: <select size="1" name="selWindowType"
id="selWindowType">
          <option value="self">Self</option>
          <option value="top">New Window</option>
       </select></td>
       <td width="64%"><input onclick="gotoFolder()" type="button"
value="View Folder" name="btnViewFolder"></td>
    </tr>
  </table>
</form>
</body>
</html>
```

The Anchor Behavior Example

Let's first cover how Web Folders are implemented using the anchor
behavior, then we will cover how to use Web Folders through script.
Please note that in order to run this example on your computer, you
may need to see the section "Web Folder Requirements and Security"
following this section. The anchor behavior is attached to the <A
HREF> using the style declaration

```
A {behavior: url(#default#AnchorClick);}
```

NOTE: This style sheet causes all <A> tags on the page to have the anchor
behavior attached to them. If we had other <A> tags on the page, they would
not have to use the anchor behavior.

Looking at the <A HREF> tag on the page, we see that it contains some new attributes that are used by the anchor behavior:

```
<A HREF = "http://localhost/chapter03/" FOLDER =
"http://localhost/chapter03/" TARGET = "self"
```

When the user clicks on the anchor within the page, it opens the Web site's directory using the folder attribute (in this case http://localhost/chapter03/). The target attribute is used by the behavior to decide the window in which it will display the Web Folder. The acceptable values for the target attribute are "self," "top," or the name of an existing frame or window. The "self" value displays the Web Folder in the page's window that received the onclick event from the <A HREF> tag. The "top" value creates a new window to display the Web Folder. Any other name value opens the Web Folder in the specified frame or window. A new window is created if the name is invalid (does not exist).

The httpFolder Behavior Example

To use the httpFolder behavior, an XML name space was created in the <HTML> tag and a reference was added to the page using the XML element:

```
<IE:httpFolder id="objHttpFolder" style=
"behavior:url(#default#httpFolder)" />
```

The onclick event of the page's input button calls the gotoFolder() function when it is clicked:

```
<input onclick="gotoFolder()" type="button" value="View Folder"
name="btnViewFolder">
```

The gotoFolder() function decides which window the Web Folder is to be displayed in by the option selected in the selWindowType drop-down menu. If the Web Folder will be displayed in the same window, the function executes the httpFolder's navigate method and passes the Web Folder to display

```
document.all.objHttpFolder.navigate("http://localhost/chapter03/");
```

The httpFolder behavior's navigate method uses the current window to display the Web Folder.

If the Web Folder is to be displayed in a new window, then the httpFolder's navigateFrame is executed, passing it the Web Folder to display and target frame as a parameter. The "top" parameter used in our example tells it to display the specified Web Folder in a new browser window:

```
document.all.objHttpFolder.navigateFrame("http://localhost/chapter03/",
"top");
```

> **NOTE:**   The navigateFrame's second parameter could also have been another frame already on the page or a new page.

Web Folder Requirements and Security

To use Web Folders, the Web server must support Front Page Extensions (version 97, 98, or 2000), or it must be a WebDav (Web Distributed Authoring and Versioning) server. A WebDav is a set of HTTP 1.1 extensions that allows a user to read and write documents over the Web. The other requirement is that the Author and Browse permissions must enabled. If you want Web Folders enabled for a Web site using IIS (Microsoft's Internet Information Server), you need to install the FrontPage server extensions on IIS and give Execute permissions to the Web site. These two steps need to be done for each Web site that is to be Web Folder enabled.

Web sites that have the Web Folder feature should set up more stringent security. The reason for this security concern is because a user can browse and modify contents of the Web site when Web Folders are enabled on the site.

DATA-PERSISTENT DEFAULT BEHAVIORS

IE 5 comes with four default behaviors that keep Web page data on the client's computer (or *persists* the data): saveHistory, saveFavorite, saveSnapshot, and userData. When and how long the data persists is determined by the behavior used, as indicated in Table 3-2.

Behavior	When Data Persists	When Persisted Data Is Available	Length of Data Persistence
saveHistory	When navigating away from the page	On return to the page using the Back or Forward button	Current session only
saveFavorite	When the page is saved as a favorite	When selecting the page from the Favorite menu or through a shortcut	Across sessions (until the Favorite is removed)
saveSnapshot	When the page is saved locally as a Web page (HTML only)	When displaying the locally saved HTML page	As long as the page is saved
userData	When the save methods are called through script	When the load method is called from script code	Developer decides

Table 3-2.   The IE 5 DHTML Default Behaviors for Persistent Web Page Data

The saveHistory, saveFavorite, and saveSnapshot behaviors need no script code to persist the data, although they do have properties and methods that can be called through script to persist it. The userData behavior relies on script code to make the data persistent.

homePage, saveHistory, and saveFavorite Behaviors Example

There is another default behavior that persists a specific type of data: the homePage behavior. The homePage behavior contains information about the user's home page setting. This behavior has methods to set the user's home page, navigate to the user's home page, and check if the current page is the user's home page. The homePage behavior needs script code to be used.

Figure 3-4 shows a Web page using the homePage, saveHistory, and saveFavorite behaviors. The Web page is divided into three sections: the top section shows the capabilities of the homePage behavior; the middle section will use the saveHistory behavior to persist data in a text box when the page is navigated away from; and the last section will use the saveFavorite behavior to persist data in a text box when the page is saved as a favorite.

The homePage section tests to see if a URL is the user's home page, then it navigates to the user's home page and sets a new home page for the user. The saveHistory section allows the user to enter data in the text box, saving that data if the user navigates away from the page.

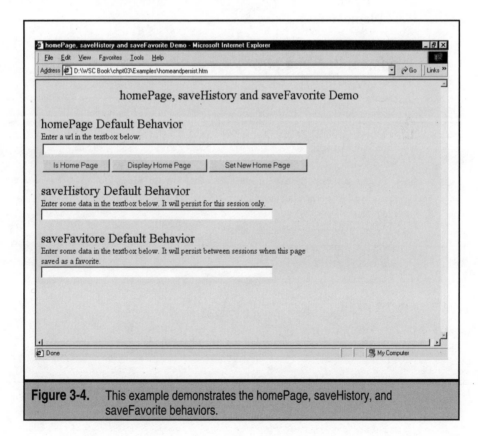

Figure 3-4.   This example demonstrates the homePage, saveHistory, and saveFavorite behaviors.

The next time the page is displayed using the Back or Forward buttons, the persisted data is redisplayed in the text box. At first, one might wonder how this behavior differs from standard browser caching. After all, you can browse away from a page containing a form. Using your Back button you can then return to that page with your form-field data still intact. To demonstrate the difference when using the saveHistory behavior, you simply need to refresh the page. Doing so, you'll see that the data has not merely been cached: it has truly been persisted and remains part of the page, even after reloading the page from the server.

The saveFavorite section will persist the data entered in the text box when the page is saved as a favorite. When the page is redisplayed by selecting it from the Favorite menu, the persisted data will be displayed with the page.

The following code listing shows how these behaviors were implemented:

homeandpersist.htm

```
<html XMLNS:HP>
<head>
<META NAME="save" CONTENT="history">
<META NAME="save" CONTENT="favorite">
<title>homePage, saveHistory and saveFavorite Demo</title>
<STYLE>
    .saveHistory {behavior:url(#default#savehistory);}
    .saveFavorite {behavior:url(#default#savefavorite);}
</STYLE>
<script language="JavaScript">
function isHomePage(){
var bolHomePage;
    bolHomePage = objHomePage.isHomePage(document.all.sURL.value);
    if (bolHomePage)
        alert(document.all.sURL.value + " is your home page.");
    else
        alert(document.all.sURL.value + " is not your home page.");
}
function displayHomePage(){
    objHomePage.navigateHomePage();
}
function setHomePage(){
```

```
        objHomePage.setHomePage(document.all.sURL.value);
}
</script>
</head>
<body bgcolor="#FFFFCC">
<HP:homePage id="objHomePage" style="behavior:url(#default#homepage)" />
<p align="center"><font size="5">homePage, saveHistory and
saveFavorite Demo<br>
<br>
</font></p>
<form >
 <font size="5">homePage Default Behavior</font>
 <br>
 Enter a url in the textbox below:
  <table border="0" width="101%">
    <tr>
      <td width="49%"><input type="text" id="sURL" size="71"></td>
    </tr>
  </table>
 <table border="0" width="98">
  <tr>
    <td width="26%" align="center">
       <input onclick="isHomePage()" type="button" value="Is Home Page"
name="btnIsHomePage">
    </td>
    <td width="38%" align="center">
       <input onclick="displayHomePage()" type="button"
value="Display Home Page" name="btnDisplayHomePage">
    </td>
    <td width="36%" align="center">
       <input onclick="setHomePage()" type="button"
value="Set New Home Page" name="btnSetHomePage">
    </td>
  </tr>
 </table>
  <br>
 <font size="5">saveHistory Default Behavior</font>
 <br> Enter some data in the textbox below. It will persist for
this session only.
 <br><input type="text" class="saveHistory" name="txtHistory" size="62">
 <p><font size="5">saveFavitore Default Behavior</font>
 <br> Enter some data in the textbox below. It will persist between sessions
when this page
```

```
 <br> saved as a favorite.
 <br><input type="text" class="saveFavorite" name="txtFavorite" size="62">
</form>
</body>
</html>
```

The first behavior we cover is the homePage behavior. It is declared on the page using an XML name space called HP because it needs an ID to be referenced in the script code to access its methods. The <HTML> tag declares the name space:

```
<html XMLNS:HP>
```

After the page's <body> tag, the HP name space is used and attaches the homePage behavior in its style attribute:

```
<HP:homePage id="objHomePage" style="behavior:url(#default#homepage)" />
```

The homePage will be referenced in the script code using the ID objHomePage.

On the page there are three buttons that are used to call functions, which call methods of the homePage behavior through their respective onclick events. The button labeled Is Home Page calls the isHomePage() function. This function uses the isHomePage method to check if the text typed into the text box is the user's current home page. There is a restriction on this method for it to work properly: the user needs to be in the domain of the current setting of the home page in order for this method to return that the URL is the current home page. For example, if the current home page is www.yahoo.com, and the user was at www.microsoft.com, and the user typed in the textbox www.yahoo.com, the method isHomePage would return false. It would only return true if the user was someplace on the Yahoo! Web site.

The button labeled Display Home Page calls the displayHomePage() function when it is clicked. The displayHomePage() functions calls the homePage behavior's displayHomePage method to navigate the browser to the current home page setting. The last button labeled Set New Home Page calls the setHomePage() function when it is clicked. This function sets the user's home page to what was entered into the text box by calling the homePage behaviors' setHomePage method.

The saveHistory and the saveFavorite behaviors are declared in the same fashion using style sheets:

```
.saveHistory {behavior:url(#default#savehistory);}
.saveFavorite {behavior:url(#default#savefavorite);}
```

The styles are attached to <input> tags using the class attribute:

```
<input type="text" class="saveHistory" name="txtHistory" size="62">
<input type="text" class="saveFavorite" name="txtFavorite" size="62">
```

The <meta> tags at the top of the HTML page are the items that tell the IE 5 browser how to persist the data. For the saveHistory behavior the following <meta> tag is used to persist the data as history data:

```
<META NAME="save" CONTENT="history">
```

This tag tells the IE 5 browser that if the saveHistory behavior is used for any tags on this page to save the save as history data. The <meta> tag for saveFavorite behavior is very similar:

```
<META NAME="save" CONTENT="favorite">
```

This tag tells IE 5 to save any saveFavorite behavior data as favorite data.

saveSnapshot Default DHTML Behavior Example

The saveSnapshot behavior can be used to persist data when a Web page is saved locally as an HTML-only page. The types of data items that can be saved are values, styles, dynamically updated content, and scripting variables. Using this behavior, body and individual table elements cannot be persisted. The scripting data types that can be persisted are string, Boolean, and integer variants. The following code listing shows an implementation of the saveSnapshot behavior:

savesnapshot.htm

```
<html>
<head>
<meta name="save" CONTENT="snapshot">
<title>saveSnapshot Default DHTML Behavior</title>
<style>
```

```
        .saveSnapshot { behavior:url(#default#savesnapshot) }
</style>
</head>
<body bgcolor="#FF00FF">
<table border="0" width="100%" height="82">
  <tr>
     <td width="15%" height="78"><img border="0" src="snapshot.gif"
width="64" height="64"></td>
     <td width="85%" valign="middle" align="center" height="78">
       <p align="center"><font size="5"><b>saveSnapshot DHTML
Default Behavior      Demo</b></font></p>
       <p> </td>
  </tr>
</table>
<font size="3">This page will use the saveSnapshot DHTML behavior
to save the data on the page when it is saved as an HTML
Web Page, HTML Only.<br>
<br>
</font>
<form>
  <table border="0" width="99%">
   <tr>
     <td width="38%">Textbox:</td>
     <td width="67%"><input class="saveSnapshot" type="text" id="txtItem1" size="20"></td>
   </tr>
   <tr>
     <td width="38%">Scrolling Textbox:</td>
     <td width="67%"><textarea class="saveSnapshot" rows="3"
id="txtScrolling" cols="32"></textarea></td>
   </tr>
   <tr>
     <td width="38%">Checkbox:</td>
     <td width="67%"><input  class="saveSnapshot" type="checkbox" id="chkItem" value="ON"></td>
   </tr>
   <tr>
     <td width="38%">Radio Buttons</td>
     <td width="67%"><input class="saveSnapshot" type="radio"
checked name="optButton" id="optButton">One   
       <input class="saveSnapshot" type="radio" name="optButton"
id="optButton" >Two</td>
   </tr>
   <tr>
```

```
      <td width="38%">Single Item Drop Down:</td>
      <td width="67%">
        <select class="saveSnapshot" size="1" id="ddSingle">
          <option selected value="1">Item 1</option>
          <option value="2">Item 2</option>
          <option value="3">Item 3</option>
          <option value="4">Item 4</option>
          <option value="5">Item 5</option>
        </select></td>
    </tr>
    <tr>
      <td width="38%">Multiple Item Drop Down:</td>
      <td width="67%"><select class="saveSnapshot" size="3" id="ddMultiple"
multiple name="ddMultiple">
          <option value="1">Item 1</option>
          <option value="2">Item 2</option>
          <option value="3">Item 3</option>
          <option value="4">Item 4</option>
          <option value="5">Item 5</option>
        </select></td>
    </tr>
  </table>
</form>
</body>
</html>
```

The saveSnapshot is implemented very similar to the way the saveHistory and saveFavorite behaviors are implemented. It uses a <meta> tag:

```
<meta name="save" CONTENT="snapshot">
```

This tag lets the browser know that it should persist the data for any tag that has the saveSnapshot behavior attached to it. In the code listing, this is done with a style sheet and a class attribute in the <input> tag of the item to be persisted. To actually persist the data, the user needs to save the page locally as an HTML-only page using the Save As option from the File menu. Once the page is saved, the file can be redisplayed in the browser by using the Open command from the File menu. When the file is opened, the data that was on the page when it was saved will appear, and any data variables will be set. While this behavior acts in a similar manner to the saveHistory and saveFavorite behaviors, it differs greatly in its persistence implementation, as the saved page is actually altered to contain the information being persisted as hard-coded values within the source code.

userData DHTML Default Behavior

The saveHistory, saveFavorite, and the saveSnapshot behaviors all have inherent problems from a development viewpoint. The saveHistory behavior does not persist data across sessions—that is, once the browser is closed, the saved data is gone. For the saveFavorite behavior to persist data, the Web page needs to be saved as a favorite. The saveSnapShot behavior saves the Web page to a file, so if the page is refreshed, the persisted data does not show up. The userData behavior overcomes these limitations by giving the developer more power and control of what data is persisted, when it is persisted, and for how long it is persisted.

The userData behavior is used to persist data using script code. The data is persisted to the UserData store, which is on the client's machine. This UserData store can be thought of as a cookie on steroids. The UserData store is not saved in the Internet temporary files directory, and using the userData behavior it is easier to save and reload data than when using cookies.

The UserData store can also contain up to 64K of data per page and 640K per domain. The location of the UserData store differs depending on what OS the client is running, as Table 3-3 notes.

OS	Location
NT	Winnt\Profiles\Administrator\Application Data\Internet Explorer\UserData Where Winnt is the NT directory, Administrator is the current user
Windows 95 and 98	Windows\Application Data\Microsoft\Internet Explorer\UserData Where Windows is the Windows directory

Table 3-3. Locations of the UserData Store

In the UserData directory there is an index file called index.dat that keeps track of the UserData store. Each file in the UserData directory, except for the index file, is an XML file. If you double-click on a file in a UserData store, it will open an IE 5 window, which will display an XML structure. We will look at an example of this later. The data persisted in the UserData store is persisted across sessions.

userData DHTML Default Behavior Example

The userData behavior example shows how data is persisted in the UserData store by using script code instead attaching the behavior to individual tags that need to be persisted. Figure 3-5 shows a Web page that uses the userData behavior. The two buttons at the bottom allow the user to save the data on the page to the UserData store and to load the data from the UserData store back onto the page.

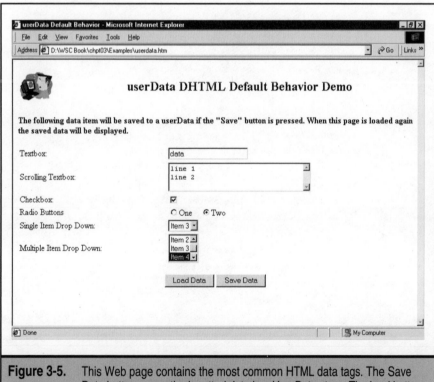

Figure 3-5.   This Web page contains the most common HTML data tags. The Save Data button saves the inputted data in a UserData store. The load button reloads the data from the UserData store and displays it on the page.

The following code listing shows how this is implemented:

userdata.htm

```
<html XMLNS:IE>
<head>
<title>userData Default Behavior</title>
</head>
<script language="JavaScript">
function LoadData(){
var objUD;
var objDDSingle;
var objDDMultiple;
var data;
var value = new Array();
var i;
var j;

    objUD = document.all.objUserData;
    objUD.load("userDataDemo");
    document.all.txtItem1.value = objUD.getAttribute(document.all.txtItem1.id);
    document.all.txtScrolling.innerText = objUD.getAttribute(document.all.txtScrolling.id);
    if (objUD.getAttribute(document.all.chkItem.id) == "true")
        document.all.chkItem.checked = true;
    else
        document.all.chkItem.checked = false;
    document.all.optButton(0).checked =
objUD.getAttribute(document.all.optButton(0).id + "0");
    document.all.optButton(1).checked = objUD.getAttribute(document.all.optButton(1).id + "1");
    value.length = 1;
    value[0] = objUD.getAttribute(document.all.ddSingle.id);
    objDDSingle = document.all.ddSingle;
    if (value[0] != null){
        for (i =0; i < objDDSingle.length; ++i){
            if (objDDSingle.options(i).value ==
 value[0]){objDDSingle.options(i).selected = true;
                    break;
            }
        }
    }
```

```
objDDMultiple = document.all.ddMultiple;
data = objUD.getAttribute(objDDMultiple.id);
for (j=0; j < objDDMultiple.options.length; j++){
     objDDMultiple.options[j].selected = false;
}
value = data.split(",");
for (i=0; i < value.length; i++){
     for (j=0; j < objDDMultiple.options.length; j++){
          if (objDDMultiple.options[j].value == value[i]){
               objDDMultiple.options[j].selected = true;
               break;
          }
     }
}
}
function SaveData(){
var objUD;
var objDDSingle;
var objDDMultiple;
var value  = new Array()
var i;
     objUD = document.all.objUserData;
     objUD.setAttribute(document.all.txtItem1.id,
document.all.txtItem1.value);
     objUD.setAttribute(document.all.txtScrolling.id,
document.all.txtScrolling.innerText);
     objUD.setAttribute(document.all.chkItem.id,
document.all.chkItem.checked)
     objUD.setAttribute(document.all.optButton(0).id + "0",
document.all.optButton(0).checked)
     objUD.setAttribute(document.all.optButton(1).id + "1",
document.all.optButton(1).checked)
     value.length++;
     objDDSingle = document.all.ddSingle;
     if (objDDSingle.selectedIndex != null)
          value[0] = objDDSingle.options(objDDSingle.selectedIndex).value;
     else
          value[0] = null;
     objUD.setAttribute(document.all.ddSingle.id, value);
     value.length = 0;
     objDDMultiple = document.all.ddMultiple;
```

```
            for (i = 0; i < objDDMultiple.length; ++i){
                if (objDDMultiple.options(i).selected == true){
                    value.length++;
                    value[value.length - 1] = objDDMultiple.options(i).value;
                }
            }
        objUD.setAttribute(document.all.ddMultiple.id, value.toString());
        objUD.save("userDataDemo");
}
</script>
<body bgcolor="red">
<IE:userData id="objUserData" style="behavior:url(#default#userData)" />
<table border="0" width="100%">
  <tr>
    <td width="12%"><img border="0" src="userData.gif" width="64"
height="64"></td>
    <td width="88%">
        <p align="center"><font size="5"><b>userData DHTML Default Behavior
Demo</b></font></td>
  </tr>
</table>
<font size="3"><br>
<b>The following data item will be saved to a userData if the
&quot;Save&quot; button is pressed. When this page is loaded again the saved
data will be displayed.</b><br>
</font>
<form>
  <table border="0" width="99%">
    <tr>
      <td width="38%">Textbox:</td>
      <td width="67%"><input type="text" id="txtItem1" size="20"></td>
    </tr>
    <tr>
      <td width="38%">Scrolling Textbox:</td>
      <td width="67%"><textarea rows="3" id="txtScrolling"
cols="32"></textarea></td>
    </tr>
    <tr>
      <td width="38%">Checkbox:</td>
      <td width="67%"><input type="checkbox" id="chkItem" value="ON"></td>
    </tr>
```

```
  <tr>
    <td width="38%">Radio Buttons</td>
    <td width="67%"><input type="radio" checked name="optButton"
id="optButton">One   
      <input type="radio" name="optButton" id="optButton" >Two</td>
  </tr>
  <tr>
    <td width="38%">Single Item Drop Down:</td>
    <td width="67%"><select size="1" id="ddSingle">
      <option selected value="1">Item 1</option>
      <option value="2">Item 2</option>
      <option value="3">Item 3</option>
      <option value="4">Item 4</option>
      <option value="5">Item 5</option>
    </select></td>
  </tr>
  <tr>
    <td width="38%">Multiple Item Drop Down:</td>
    <td width="67%"><select size="3" id="ddMultiple" multiple
name="ddMultiple">
      <option value="1">Item 1</option>
      <option value="2">Item 2</option>
      <option value="3">Item 3</option>
      <option value="4">Item 4</option>
      <option value="5">Item 5</option>
    </select></td>
  </tr>
</table>
<p align="center">
  <input type="button" value="Load Data" id="btnLoad"
onclick="LoadData()">
  <input type="submit" value="Save Data" name="btnSave"
onclick="SaveData()">
</p>
</form>
</body>
</html>
```

The userData behavior is declared using an XML name space with objUserData as its ID:

```
<IE:userData id="objUserData" style="behavior:url(#default#userData)" />
```

The <input> and <select> tags on the page do not have the userData behavior attached to them, although they could. The data on the page is persisted when the Save Data button is pressed. The Save Data button's onclick event calls a function called SaveData(). This function uses properties and methods from the userData behavior to persist the data. The first thing this function does is set a variable to the userData object.

```
objUD = document.all.objUserData;
```

It uses objUD as a reference to the userData object to save the fully qualified name out each time. It then calls the userData setAttributes method:

```
objUD.setAttribute(document.all.txtItem1.id, document.all.txtItem1.value);
```

This method places a name and its corresponding value in the UserData store. In this example, a text box's data is saved in the UserData store with the name of the ID of the <input> tag, with the data being the value (text) in the text box. One additional method needs to be called to actually write out the data we're saving to the UserData store:

```
objUD.save("userDataDemo")
```

The save method takes as a parameter the name of the UserData store that the data will be persisted to. This name is created in the UserData store directory. The userData behavior's save method must be called after the data is placed in the UserData store with the setAttribute method for the data to be written out to the UserData store. Other types of <input> tags can also be saved, and even <select> tag data, or any desired data, can be saved using this implementation.

To load the data back onto the page, the page needs to access the saved UserData store. In the example, the saved UserData store is called userdataDemo, and it is retrieved through a call to the UserData's load method:

```
objUD.load("userDataDemo");
```

where objUD is the reference to the userData behavior's ID. Then the getAttribute method is called to retrieve the data. An example of this is our repopulating of the saved text box from the above example:

```
document.all.txtItem1.value = objUD.getAttribute(document.all.txtItem1.id);
```

The userData behavior's getAttribute method is called to retrieve the data. The text box's ID is used by this method to indicate which data item to retrieve from the UserData store. The resulting data is then displayed in the text box.

If we look at the UserData store directory, we will find an XML file called userDataDemo.xml that contains the persisted data. The XML file should look something like Figure 3-6. For the above example text boxes, the persisted value is represented by the value

```
txtItem1="Demo"
```

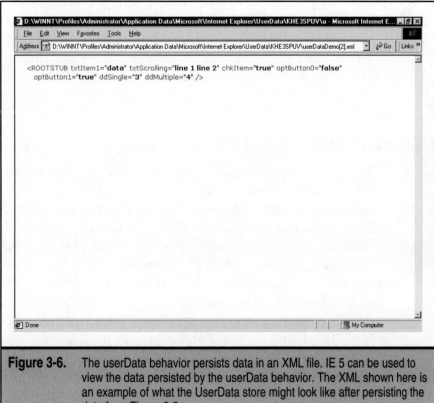

Figure 3-6. The userData behavior persists data in an XML file. IE 5 can be used to view the data persisted by the userData behavior. The XML shown here is an example of what the UserData store might look like after persisting the data from Figure 3-5.

THE MULTIMEDIA DHTML DEFAULT BEHAVIORS

IE 5 contains six default behaviors that work with multimedia (refer to Table 3-1). The benefits of using these behaviors are they allow more interactivity in Web pages with less server interaction; multimedia plug-ins are not required; and multimedia-rich presentations can be displayed without the need for volumes of script. One of the main shared features of these multimedia behaviors is that they all have access to the new feature of IE 5: HTML+TIME capabilities.

IE 5 HTML+TIME Feature

HTML+TIME gives the browser the ability to create a time line for synchronizing HTML tags. The time line, which itself is built using HTML tags, designates when HTML elements are to be displayed on the page. The HTML+TIME feature is based on the SMIL 1.0 Recommendation. Microsoft has submitted its implementation to the World Wide Web Consortium (W3C) for approval. There are three behaviors that are used to create an HTML+TIME time line: the time, par, and seq behaviors.

Multimedia and HTML+TIME Example

This example uses the anim behavior along with the HTML+TIME time behavior. Figure 3-7 actually contains two examples. On the left side, a pair of sprockets continue to turn while the page is displayed. The sprockets are actually two GIF files that are rotated using the anim behavior. On the right side of the page is a slide presentation, containing five slides. This slide presentation was created without any script code, using only the time behavior to show the slides. Each slide is shown for 4 seconds along with its caption. Both the pictures and captions are run in sequence using the seq setting as their time line. This setting is a value of the timeline attribute of the time behavior and *not* the seq default behavior. Since Figure 3-7 is just a screen capture, it does not show the animation that is occurring, so we suggest you run this page yourself to see it at work.

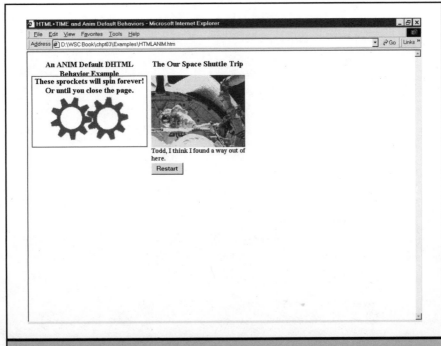

Figure 3-7.   The sprocket images on the left are rotated using the anim behavior, and the slide presentation on the right uses the time behavior.

The following code listing shows how the page is implemented:

HTMLANIM.htm

```
<html>
<head>
<XML:NAMESPACE PREFIX="anim"/>
<title>HTML+TIME and Anim Default Behaviors</title>
<STYLE>
  anim\:DA    { behavior: url(#default#anim); }
</STYLE>
</head>
<script language="Jscript">
function startPage(){
```

```
        startData();
    }
    function startData(){
    var m;
        m = divTest.statics;
        img1 = m.ImportImage("sprocket.gif");
        rotImg = img1.Transform(m.Rotate2RateDegrees(60));
        document.all.divTest.Image = rotImg;
        m = divTest2.statics;
        img1 = m.ImportImage("sprocket2.gif");
        rotImg = img1.Transform(m.Rotate2RateDegrees(-60));
        document.all.divTest2.Image = rotImg;
    }
    function restartShow(){
        document.all.showPics.beginElement();
        document.all.showText.beginElement();
    }
</script>
<body onload="startPage()">
<div style="width:300; height:180;position:absolute;top:20">
    <h4 align="center">An ANIM Default DHTML Behavior Example</h4>
    <div style="border:2 solid red;width:300;
height:180;position:absolute;top:40">
        <h4 align="center">These sprockets will spin forever! Or until
you close the page.</h4>
        <anim:DA ID="divTest" STYLE="position:absolute; top:5; width:200;
height:200; z-index: 1;" />
        <anim:DA ID="divTest2" STYLE="position:absolute; top:5; left:95;
width:200; height:200; z-index: 1;" />
    </div>
</div>
<div style="width:240; height:175;position:absolute;top:20;left:320" >
    <h4 align="center">Our Space Shuttle Trip</h4>
    <span style="behavior:url(#default#time)" t:TIMELINE="seq" id="showPics">
    <img style="behavior:url(#default#time);position:absolute;top:40;"
t:DUR="4" src="ss1.jpg" >
    <img style="behavior:url(#default#time);position:absolute;top:40;"
t:DUR="4" src="ss2.jpg" >
    <img style="behavior:url(#default#time);position:absolute;top:40;"
t:DUR="4" src="ss3.jpg" >
    <img style="behavior:url(#default#time);position:absolute;top:40;"
```

```
t:DUR="4" src="ss4.jpg" >
    <img style="behavior:url(#default#time);position:absolute;top:40;"
src="ss5.jpg" >
</span>
<span style="behavior:url(#default#time)" t:TIMELINE="seq" id="showText">
    <h5 style="behavior:url(#default#time);position:absolute;top:220"
t:DUR="4">Hey Todd, what's this button for?</h5>
    <h5 style="behavior:url(#default#time);position:absolute;top:220"
t:DUR="4">Oooooooooooh nooooooo, I think I know what it is and it's not
good.</h5>
    <h5 style="behavior:url(#default#time);position:absolute;top:220"
t:DUR="4">Todd, I think I found a way out of here.</h5>
    <h5 style="behavior:url(#default#time);position:absolute;top:220"
t:DUR="4">We finally made it back home.</h5>
    <h5 style="behavior:url(#default#time);position:absolute;top:220" >Hey!
Now, where are we going? Let us out of here. Momma!</h5>
</span>
<input type="button" name="Restart" value="Restart"
style="position:absolute;top:260" onclick="restartShow()">
</div>
</body>
</html>
```

Beginning with the sproket example, the two anim behaviors are created on the page using an XML name space and referenced in the page using the following three lines:

```
<XML:NAMESPACE PREFIX="anim"/>
<anim:DA ID="divTest" STYLE="position:absolute; top:5; width:200;
height:200; z-index: 1;" />
<anim:DA ID="divTest2" STYLE="position:absolute; top:5; left:95; width:200;
height:200; z-index: 1;" />
```

We need 2 anim behaviors on the page because each GIF sprocket file needs to be animated. One sprocket turns clockwise, and the other turns counter-clockwise.

In the <body> tag there is an onload event that calls the startPage() function. The startPage function takes each GIF and transforms it into a DirectAnimation object, rotating each one in the opposite direction. For more information on how DirectAnimation works, see Microsoft's Web site.

The slide presentation consists of two <span> tags that are used to contain the images and their captions. Each <span> tag has a time behavior attached to it.

```
<span style="behavior:url(#default#time)" t:TIMELINE="seq" id="showPics">
<span style="behavior:url(#default#time)" t:TIMELINE="seq" id="showText">
```

The HTML tags within the beginning <span> tag and the corresponding </span> tag are the tags that will be used in the time line. Each of the <span> tags contains a t:timeline="seq" attribute. This attribute tells the time line how to display the tags within that time line. The *t* is an IE 5 built-in reference to the time behavior. In this case, each tag is displayed in sequence. Within the <span> tag, each HTML tag element has a t:DUR attribute: t:DUR="4".

```
<img style="behavior:url(#default#time);position:absolute;top:40;" t:DUR="4"
src="ss2.jpg" >
```

This attribute is used by the time behavior to set the duration of how long each image element will be displayed. In this example, the image is shown for 4 seconds before sequentially displaying the next image. The last <image> tag in the time line does not have a DUR attribute and continues to be displayed as long as the page is open or until the slide presentation is restarted. When the Restart button at the bottom of the slide presentation is pressed, the function restartShow() is called by its onclick event. This function calls the beginElement method for each of the time behaviors to restart the time line at the beginning.

SUMMARY

In this chapter we showed how to use the IE 5 DHTML default behaviors. We covered different techniques on how to declare behaviors on a page. We showed that behaviors can be reused, and we touched on the use of most of the IE 5 default behaviors.

CHAPTER 4

Architecture of an HTML Component

In the past, if your pages needed to share common user interface functionality, you needed to use a custom component, perhaps an ActiveX control, a Java applet, or a set of HTML tags and script code cut and pasted into Web pages that needed the functionality. There were many disadvantages to using these types of components. A component developed in-house required someone on staff to know, or learn, the component's language. A purchased component might not do exactly what was needed. Compiled components had to be downloaded to the client's computer, and users might not want to wait for what could sometimes be a lengthy process. Additionally, there were security issues involved when using some components.

But now, using DHTML, HTML tags, script code, and a little XML, you can create your own components, known as HTML components (or HTC). HTML components are just like objects, in that they have properties, methods, and events. Because they reside on a Web page, they can also access the page's DHTML object model (DOM) and receive notifications from it.

The HTML component shown in Figure 4-1 is a frame that encloses the set of HTML elements. If you are familiar with Windows applications, you know that frames are used to give a context to a set of controls. While HTML does not have a frame tag, a frame component can be developed as an HTML component and reused on other pages. The frame in Figure 4-1 is an HTML component written using DHTML and HTML tags.

Not all HTML components must offer a user interface. An example of this type of nonvisual behavior could be a behavior that validates the data entered into forms across multiple Web pages.

In this chapter we will explore the architecture of an HTML component, along with

▼ What DHTML behaviors and HTML components are, as well as the benefits of using them.

■ The HTML component file (.htc) and specific XML elements that define the component.

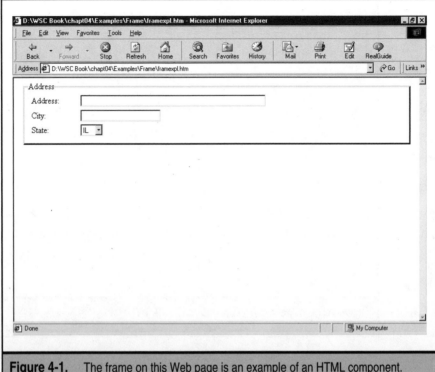

Figure 4-1.   The frame on this Web page is an example of an HTML component.

■ Using the HTML Component Wizard to create an HTML
   component skeleton file.

▲ Creating your first HTML component and using it on a
   Web page

DHTML BEHAVIORS AND HTML COMPONENTS

DHTML behaviors are Web components that contain specific
functionality. That specific functionality is attached to an HTML tag.
DHTML behaviors can be created in a number of ways, as Table 4-1
indicates. In this chapter we will cover creating DHTML behaviors as
an HTML component (also known as an HTC). HTCs use DHTML,
scripting code, and specific XML elements to create a behavior.

DHTML Behavior Implementation	Description
HTML component (HTC)	Uses DHTML, HTML, scripting, and XML to define the component.
Windows scripting component (WSC)	Uses Microsoft's scripting technology to create DHTML behaviors. This technology is also used to create COM objects with script. (Covered in Chapter 16.)
C++ and Active Template Library (ATL)	Uses COM interfaces to build binary DHTML behaviors. These behaviors are not covered in this book.

Table 4-1. Different Ways to Implement DHTML Behaviors

The HTC implementation has many benefits over the other implementations. HTCs are easier to build than components created with WSC and C++. With HTC, a Web developer needs to know only HTML, the DHTML DOM, and a small set of XML elements. With WSCs, a Web developer needs to know the workings of XML; because it uses more complex XML elements to define a behavior than that used in HTCs. Also, the Web developer needs to know how WSCs work, whereas with an HTC, they should already know the core technology (HTML and DHTML DOM) of an HTC. Developing behaviors using C++ incurs the cost of a big learning curve, and there is more code to write than with an HTC.

How an HTC Works Under the Covers

The Internet Explorer 5 engine, MSHTML.DLL, does not talk directly to an HTC. Instead, a proxy DLL called SCROBJ.DLL serves as an interface between the HTC and IE engine. The proxy DLL uses interface handlers to talk to the HTC. These interface handlers are used to simplify the COM interfaces exposed to the Web page. An HTC is just a wrapper that makes calls to the interface handler.The illustration shows how this works.

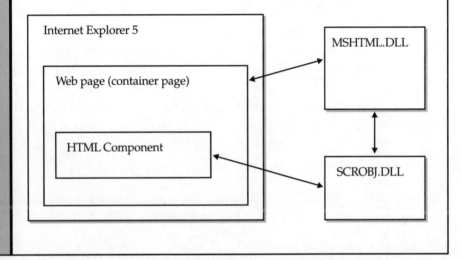

HTML COMPONENT FILE ARCHITECTURE

An HTC file is a text file that contains HTML elements, script code, and HTC-specific elements. The file has an extension of .htc. The HTC file exposes properties, methods, and events that define the behavior's functionality. The HTC-specific elements are XML elements that are used by IE 5 to create the behavior's public interface to its containing page. In the next couple of sections, we will cover the HTC-specific XML elements, that is, elements, methods, and events. An HTC also has an object that it has access to—the element object. This object refers to the element (HTML tag) that the HTC is attached to.

HTC Elements

Table 4-2 shows the HTC-specific XML elements that are used to define the behavior's interface.

We will cover the HTC elements in the order they are usually found in the HTC file. Each of the elements has a Name and ID attribute, with the exception of the Attach element, which does not have a Name attribute. The Name attribute is used by the containing document to refer to the element. The ID attribute is used to refer to the element in the HTML component itself.

Element	Purpose
Attach	Binds an event from the component's container to the component
Component	Used in the HTC file to define it as a component
Event	Used by the HTC to create an event that is exposed to its container
Method	A public procedure of the component that is exposed to the component's container
Property	A public attribute of the component

Table 4-2.   XML Elements Used by HTC to Expose Its Interface to Its Container

The Component element is a required element because it is used to identify the contents of the file as an HTML component. Its syntax is

```
<PUBLIC:COMPONENT
    NAME = sName *
URN = sURN
    ID = sID *



....</PUBLIC:COMPONENT>
```

(* denotes that the attribute is explained at the start of "HTC Elements.")

The Component element has three attributes. The Name attribute is useful when the containing page's element has more than one behavior attached to it. For example, if the tag <DIV ID="aDiv"> has multiple behaviors attached to it, you refer to the behavior with the name myHTC with the syntax aDiv.myHTC.xxx, where xxx is a method or property of the myHTC behavior. The URN (uniform resource name) element uniquely identifies the component. This allows events that are fired up to a containing page with the same event name to be identified by the containing page. The containing page can identify the component by using the event object's scrURN property to check which component fired the event. (The event object is covered in the HTC event section later in the chapter.) All the other HTC elements are placed inside the beginning and ending Component element tags.

The Property element defines attributes of the component. Its syntax is

```
<PUBLIC:PROPERTY
    Name = sName *
    ID = sID *
    InternalName = sInternameName
    Get = sGetFunctionName
    Put = sPutFunctionName
    Persist = bPersist
    Value = vDefaultValue
/>
```

(* denotes that the attribute is explained at the start of "HTC Elements.")

The only required attribute of the Property component is the Name attribute. If the InternalName attribute is set, it is used inside the HTC component to refer to the property; otherwise the Name attribute is used for that purpose. The Get and Put attributes are used by the component to execute functions that retrieve and set values of the Property, respectively. If these attributes are not set to function names, then the value of the Property is stored internally in the HTC. If the function names are set, then there must be corresponding functions within <script> tags in the HTC file that define them. To create read-only properties, define only the Get attribute function. For write-only properties, define only the Put attribute function. The Boolean Persist attribute value is set to either true or false. If the value is true, then the Property's value is persisted with the component's containing page. The Value attribute sets the Property's default value. This could be used to initialize the value of the Property.

The Method element is used by the component to expose procedures to the container. The syntax of the Method element is

```
<PUBLIC:METHOD
    Name = sName *
    InternalName = sInternalName
    ID = sID *
/>
```

(* denotes that the attribute is explained at the start of "HTC Elements.")

The Name attribute is the only required attribute of the Method element. The Name attribute is the name given to the function in the script that will be executed. When specified, the InternalName attribute is used by the component to refer to the Method within the component.

The Event element is used to create an event object that the component fires up to the component's container. Its syntax is

```
<PUBLIC:EVENT
    NAME = sName *
    ID = sEventID *
/>
```

(* denotes that the attribute is explained at the start of "HTC Elements.")

The Name attribute is required, and it is the name of the event that will be received by the component's container. We will see how events are fired in the "HTC Methods" section, later in this chapter.

The Attach element is used by the component to bind an event from the container to a procedure in the component. The syntax of the Attach element is

```
<PUBLIC:ATTACH
    Event = sEvent
    For = document | element | window
    OnEvent = sEventHandler
    ID = sID *
/>
```

(* denotes that the attribute is explained at the start of "HTC Elements.")

The Event and OnEvent attributes are required. The Event attribute is the name of the container event the component will trap. The For attribute is used to identify what DHTML object the event will trap. The default value of the For attribute is the element object. The element object is the container element that has the component attached to it. The OnEvent attribute is the name of a procedure within the <script> tags in the component that will be called when the event is fired.

HTC Methods

There are two intrinsic methods of HTCs, and they are both used in firing events up to the component's container. The methods are createEventObject and fire. The createEventObject method creates an event object that is used to pass event information to the receiver of the event. The event object has properties and methods and can be used by the component to pass data to the container that receives the event. The fire method is used to raise an event object up to the component's container. An example of the use of these two methods is as follows:

```
objEvt = createEventObject();
objEvt.result = "some data here";
evtClick.fire(objEvt);
```

The first statement creates an event object. The event's result property is then set to "some data here". This event object, objEvt, is passed with the event when it is fired up to the container. The container can then use the event object's result property data in the event. This is how the container page is set up to be notified of the event:

```
<div style="behavior:url(frame.htc)"
onSomeEvent="doProcessEvent"></div>
```

Assuming the event was named onSomeEvent in the HTC, the element that has the behavior attached to it declares the event and sets a procedure to execute when the event fires. This is no different than trapping any other event for an HTML tag.

HTC Events

HTCs also have intrinsic events that are fired from the DHTML DOM specifically for HTCs. The events are oncontentready, ondetach, and ondocumentready. The HTC Attach element is used to trap these events in the HTC. Table 4-3 outlines the purpose of the events.

Timing and Scope Rules

Timing needs to be taken into account when the elements of the HTC and the DHTML DOM are available after an HTC is instantiated by the containing page. Until the HTC is available, its properties may not be available by the containing page's script code. Therefore, it is best to wait for the HTC's ondocumentready event to fire before attempting to make any DHTML DOM changes within the HTC. It is best not to reference the HTC on the containing page until the window's onload event fires. If the HTC needs to be referenced before the container's onload event fires, then the element's readyState property must be set to "complete" before the HTC can be

Event	Purpose
oncontentready	Fires when the element that the behavior is attached to has been parsed by the browser.
ondetach	Fires before the behavior is removed from the element it is attached to.
ondocumentready	Fires when the containing page has been parsed. This event fires after all scripts, images, Microsoft ActiveX controls, and other elements on the page have completed downloading. This event is fired after the window.onload event fires.

Table 4-3.   Events That Can Be Trapped by an HTC

referenced. Trapping the onreadystatechange event for the element checks the readyState value. It is safe to set properties of the HTC in the containing page's element tag as long as the property does not reference any elements in the HTC. For example, if an HTC has a property called acctNo, it is safe to do the following:

```
<div id="myDiv" style="behavior:url(someHTC.htc)"
acctNO="1234"></div>
```

Scope rules have been set up to resolve naming conflicts. There are three name spaces used to resolve these conflicts: the behavior's, the element's, and those of the containing page. The following is the order of precedence, from highest to lowest:

▼ the behavior

■ the elements the behavior is attached to

▲ the containing page's window object

HTML COMPONENT WIZARD

To help in the creation of HTCs, we have created an HTML Component Wizard (HTC Wizard) application. The HTC Wizard will create an HTC skeleton file. We will use the Wizard to create the frame component that was shown in Figure 4-1.

There are limitations to the HTC wizard:

▼ The HTC Wizard is used to create an HTC file, but it does not have a great deal of validation. For example, it does not check for duplicate property names.

■ It does check for the existence of required element attributes. For example, it will check that the Name attribute has been entered for a property.

■ It limits the number of entries that may be entered for properties, methods, events, and attached event elements.

▲ It creates script code only in JScript.

The HTC Wizard was created as an HTML application. HTML applications are new in IE 5, and they run inside the browser, without any server interaction. We cover HTML applications in Chapter 13 and therefore will not cover the architecture of the HTC Wizard. Instead we will concentrate on how to create an HTC using the HTC Wizard.

To use the HTC Wizard, refer to Chapter 1 for information about downloading it. To start the HTC Wizard, either open the file, HTCWiz.hta, in the browser, or double-click on the file. Both methods display the first page of the HTC Wizard, the Create Component Element page, which is shown in Figure 4-2.

The Create Component Element page will create the component element in the HTC file. The two required items are the file location and file/component name. The file location is the path of the location where the HTC will be created. The file/component name is used to name the HTC file and will be the name of the component. The URN is the

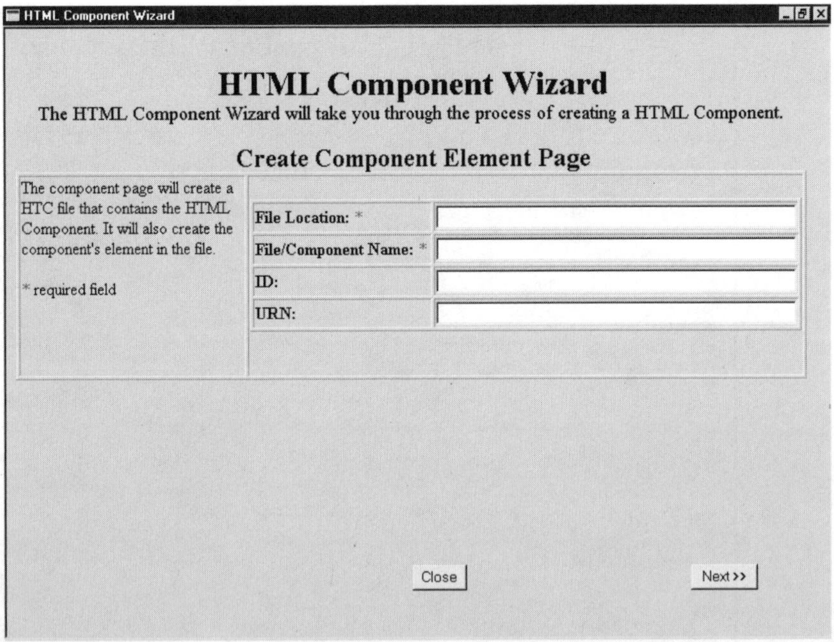

Figure 4-2. The HTML Component Wizard creates a skeleton HTC file.

uniform resource name and is used to uniquely distinguish this component from other components. Enter a file location and enter "frame" for the file/component name. Press the Next button to go to the Create Property Elements page.

The Create Property Elements page allows up to 15 properties to be entered for the HTC. While it requires only the name of the property, it also has data entry fields for the property's ID, internal name, read, write, persist value, and default value (see Figure 4-3).

You can use the properties in Table 4-4 on the Create Property Elements page to create the properties for the frame component.

After entering the properties, press the Next button to go to the Method Elements page. On the Method Elements page, add the following two methods: **appendElement** and **removeElement**. These

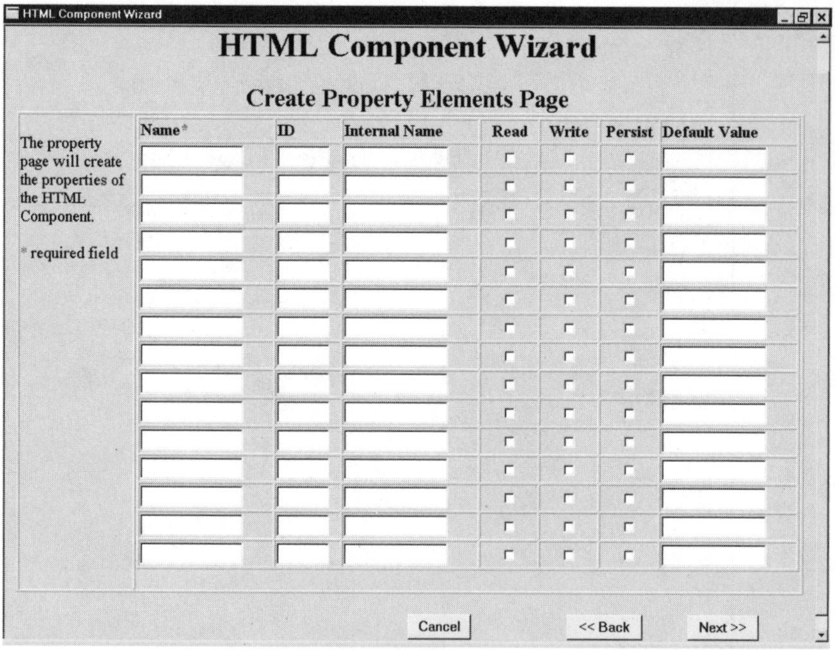

Figure 4-3. The Create Property Elements page of the HTC Wizard is where you can enter up to 15 properties for the HTC.

methods allow the frame component to append and/or delete HTML elements from the frame.

Press the Next button to go to the Event Elements page. Add two events with their IDs: **onappendElement** (ID: **evtOnAppendElement**) and **onremoveElement** (ID: **evtOnRemoveElement**). The onappendElement event is fired when an HTML element is appended to a frame. The onremoveElement is fired when an HTML element is removed from a frame.

Press the Next button to go to the Create Attach Elements page. The frame component does attach one event: the **ondocumentready** event. The Create Attach Elements page allows the HTC component to trap events from the containing page (see Figure 4-4). The required

Name	ID	Internal Name	Read	Write	Persist	Default Value
Caption			Yes	Yes		
borderwidth			Yes	Yes		
borderstyle			Yes	Yes		
bordercolor			Yes	Yes		
Height			Yes	Yes		
Width			Yes	Yes		
Top			Yes	Yes		
Left			Yes	Yes		
Margin			Yes	Yes		
Color			Yes	Yes		
Font			Yes	Yes		
backgroundimage			Yes	Yes		
backgroundcolor			Yes	Yes		

Table 4-4.   The Properties for the Frame Component

items for an attached element are the event procedure name and the container's event that will be trapped. The event procedure is the name of the procedure in the script code that will be called when the event is raised in the HTC. Enter **ShowDocument** in the event procedure name's field and **ondocumentready** in the container event's field. Also set the Source of Event field to **element**.

After the Create Attach Elements values have been entered, press the Finish button to create the HTC component. When the HTC Wizard is done, it should display a message stating that the component was successfully created and then close itself.

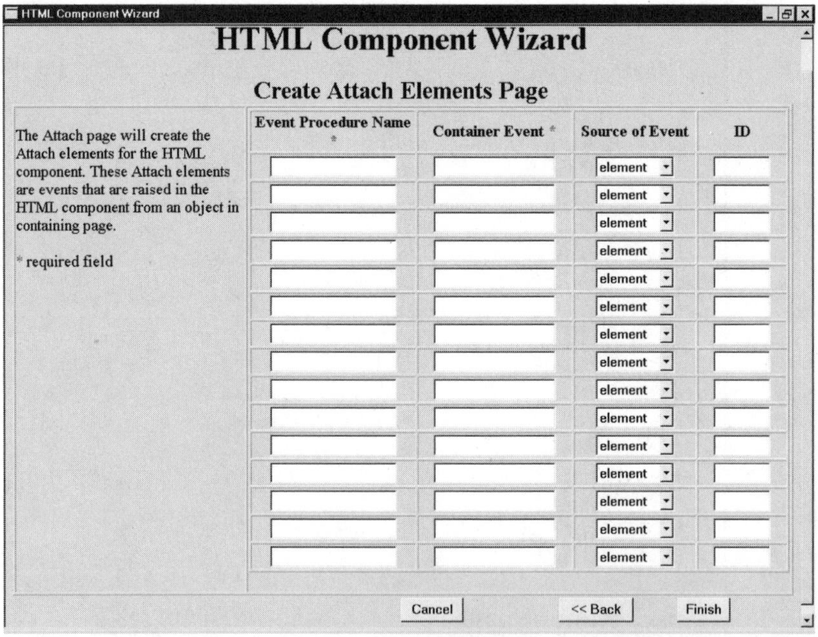

Figure 4-4. The Create Attach Elements page allows the HTC to trap the events of its container.

HTC FRAME COMPONENT FILE LAYOUT

If you take a look at the frame.htc that was created by the HTC Wizard, it will have the properties and will have attached the ondocumentready event. The properties' get and put function stubs are created along with variables to retain the properties. At this point we have a frame component that does absolutely nothing. We need to add code to the functions to get it to look like Figure 4-1. The listing below shows the completed frame component's code:

frame.htc

```
<PUBLIC:COMPONENT
    NAME="frame"
    URN="frame"

>
```

```
<PUBLIC:PROPERTY NAME="caption" GET="getcaption" PUT="putcaption"/>
<PUBLIC:PROPERTY NAME="borderwidth" GET="getborderwidth"
PUT="putborderwidth"/>
<PUBLIC:PROPERTY NAME="borderstyle" GET="getborderstyle"
PUT="putborderstyle"/>
<PUBLIC:PROPERTY NAME="bordercolor" GET="getbordercolor"
PUT="putbordercolor"/>
<PUBLIC:PROPERTY NAME="height" GET="getheight"/>
<PUBLIC:PROPERTY NAME="width" GET="getwidth" />
<PUBLIC:PROPERTY NAME="top" GET="gettop" PUT="puttop"/>
<PUBLIC:PROPERTY NAME="left" GET="getleft" PUT="putleft"/>
<PUBLIC:PROPERTY NAME="margin" GET="getmargin" PUT="putmargin"/>
<PUBLIC:PROPERTY NAME="color" GET="getcolor" PUT="putcolor"/>
<PUBLIC:PROPERTY NAME="font" GET="getfont" PUT="putfont"/>
<PUBLIC:PROPERTY NAME="backgroundimage" GET="getbgimg" PUT="putbgimg"/>
<PUBLIC:PROPERTY NAME="backgroundcolor" GET="getbgcolor" PUT="putbgcolor"/>
<PUBLIC:METHOD Name="appendElement" />
<PUBLIC:METHOD Name="removeElement" />
<PUBLIC:EVENT Name=onappendElement id=evtOnAppendElement />
<PUBLIC:EVENT Name=onremoveElement id=evtOnRemoveElement />
<PUBLIC:ATTACH EVENT="ondocumentready" ONEVENT="ShowDocument()" />

<script language="JavaScript">
var vcaption = null;
var vborderwidth = null;
var vborderstyle = null;
var vbordercolor = null;
var vheight = null;
var vwidth = null;
var vtop = null;
var vleft = null;
var vmargin = null;
var vcolor = null;
var vfont = null;
var vbackgroundimage = null;
var vbackgroundcolor = null;

function putcaption(text){
var s, s1;
var re;

    s = text;
    re = / /g;
    s1 = s.replace(re, " ");
```

```
        if (vcaption != null)
            eval(element.id + "pbsLabel").innerHTML = s1;
        vcaption = s1;
}
function getcaption(){
    return vcaption;
}
function putborderwidth(width){
    if (isNaN(parseInt(width, 10)))
        alert('The border width value is not numeric - ' + width);
    else{
        if (vborderwidth != null)
            eval(element.id + "pbsFrame").style.borderWidth = width;
        vborderwidth = width;
    }
}
function getborderwidth(){
    return eval(element.id + "pbsFrame").style.borderWidth;
}
function putborderstyle(style){
    if (style != 'inset' && style != 'outset' && style != 'none'
        && style != 'dotted' && style != 'dashed' && style != 'solid'
        && style != 'double' && style != 'groove' && style != 'ridge')
        alert('The border style value is not valid - ' + style);
    else{
        if (vborderstyle != null)
            eval(element.id + "pbsFrame").style.borderStyle = style;
        vborderstyle = style;
    }
}
function getborderstyle(){
    return eval(element.id + "pbsFrame").style.borderStyle;
}
function putbordercolor(color){
    if (color == '' || color == 'null' || color == null)
        alert('A border color was not assigned.');
    else{
        if (vbordercolor != null)
            eval(element.id + "pbsFrame").style.borderColor = color;
        vbordercolor = color;
    }
}
function getbordercolor(){
    return eval(element.id + "pbsFrame").style.borderColor;
```

```
}
function getheight(){
    return (eval(element.id + "pbsLabel").getBoundingClientRect().bottom -
eval(element.id + "pbsLabel").getBoundingClientRect().top);
}
function getwidth(){
    return (eval(element.id + "pbsLabel").getBoundingClientRect().right -
eval(element.id + "pbsLabel").getBoundingClientRect().left);
}
function puttop(top){
    if (isNaN(parseInt(top, 10)))
        alert('The frame top value is numeric - ' + top);
    else{
        if (vtop != null)
            eval(element.id + "pbsFrame").style.top = top;
        vtop = top;
    }
}
function gettop(){
    return eval(element.id + "pbsFrame").style.top;
}
function putleft(left){
    if (isNaN(parseInt(left, 10)))
        alert('The frame left value is numeric - ' + left);
    else{
        if (vleft != null)
            eval(element.id + "pbsFrame").style.left = left;
        vleft = left;
    }
}function getleft(){
    return eval(element.id + "pbsFrame").style.left;
}
function putmargin(margin){
    if (isNaN(parseInt(margin, 10)))
        alert('The frame margin value is numeric - ' + margin);
    else{
        if (vmargin != null)
            eval(element.id + "pbsFrame").style.padding = margin;
        vmargin = margin;
    }
}
function getmargin(){
    return eval(element.id + "pbsFrame").style.padding;
}
```

```
function putcolor(color){
    if (vcolor != null)
        eval(element.id + "pbsLabel").style.color = color;
    vcolor = color;
}
function getcolor(){
    return eval(element.id + "pbsLabel").style.color;
}
function putbgcolor(bgcolor){
    if (vbackgroundcolor != null){
        eval(element.id + "pbsFrame").style.backgroundColor = bgcolor;
        eval(element.id + "pbsLabel").style.backgroundColor = bgcolor;
    }
    vbackgroundcolor = bgcolor;
}
function getbgcolor(){
    return eval(element.id + "pbsLabel").style.backgroundColor;
}
function putbgimg(img){
    if (vbackgroundimage != null){
        eval(element.id + "pbsFrame").style.backgroundImage = 'url('
+ img +')';
        eval(element.id + "pbsLabel").style.backgroundImage = 'url('
+ img +
')';
    }
    vbackgroundimage = img;
}
function getbgimg(){
    return eval(element.id + "pbsLabel").style.backgroundImage;
}
function putfont(font){
    if (vfont != null)
        eval(element.id + "pbsLabel").style.fontFamily = font;
    vfont = font;
}
function getfont(){
    return eval(element.id + "pbsLabel").style.fontFamily;
}
function ShowDocument(){
var eFrame;
var eLabel;

    if (vcaption == null)
        vcaption = '';
```

```
eFrame = document.createElement("<div id='" + element.id + "pbsFrame'></div>");
eFrame.style.position = 'relative';
eFrame.style.borderWidth = 3;
eFrame.style.borderStyle = 'outset';
eFrame.style.margin = 8;
eFrame.style.width = '100%';
eFrame.style.backgroundColor = 'white';
if (vmargin != null)
    eFrame.style.padding = vmargin;
else
    vmargin = '';
if (vborderwidth != null)
    eFrame.style.borderWidth = vborderwidth;
else
    vborderwidth = '';
if (vborderstyle != null)
    eFrame.style.borderStyle = vborderstyle;
else
    vborderstyle = '';
if (vbordercolor != null)
    eFrame.style.borderColor = vbordercolor;
else
    vborderwidth = '';
if (vtop != null)
    eFrame.style.top = vtop;
else
    vtop = '';
if (vleft != null)
    eFrame.style.left = vleft;
else
    vleft = '';
if (vbackgroundimage != null)
    eFrame.style.backgroundImage = 'url(' + vbackgroundimage + ')';
if (vbackgroundcolor != null)
    eFrame.style.backgroundColor = vbackgroundcolor;
eFrame.innerHTML = element.innerHTML;
element.innerHTML = '';
element.insertBefore(eFrame, null);

eLabel = document.createElement("<div id='" + element.id + "pbsLabel
style='border-style:solid;border-width:1'></div>");
eLabel.style.position = 'absolute';
eLabel.style.top = -12;
eLabel.style.height = 20;
```

```
        eLabel.style.left = 7;
        eLabel.style.zIndex = 1;
        if (vcolor != null)
            eLabel.style.color = vcolor;
        else
            vcolor = '';
        if (vfont != null)
            eLabel.style.fontFamily = vfont;
        else
            vfont = '';
        if (vbackgroundimage != null)
            eLabel.style.backgroundImage = 'url(' + vbackgroundimage + ')';
        else
            vbackgroundimage = '';
        if (vbackgroundcolor != null)
            eLabel.style.backgroundColor = vbackgroundcolor;
            else
             vbackgroundcolor = '';
        eLabel.innerHTML = '<span id="txtLabel">' + vcaption + '</span>'
        eLabel.style.backgroundColor = eFrame.style.backgroundColor;
        eFrame.insertBefore(eLabel, null);
}
function appendElement(objEle){
var objEvent;
        eval(element.id + "pbsFrame").appendChild(objEle);
        objEvent = createEventObject();
        objEvent.result = true;
        objEvent.element = objEle;
        evtOnAppendElement.fire(objEvent);
}
function removeElement(strEleID){
var objEvent;
var objNode;
        objEvent = createEventObject();
        objEvent.result = true;
        objEvent.element = eval(element.id + "pbsFrame").children(strEleID);
        evtOnRemoveElement.fire(objEvent);
        if (objEvent.result){
            objNode = eval(element.id + "pbsFrame").children(strEleID);
            if (objNode != null){
                    try{
                            eval(element.id +
pbsFrame").removeChild(objNode);
                    }
```

```
                    catch(error){
                        alert("Element with ID " + strEleID + " could
not be deleted because there is more than 1 element with that ID.");
                    }
                }
            }
        }
        </script>
        </PUBLIC:COMPONENT>
```

Frame Component Details

We will examine the HTC file from two perspectives: the implementation of the frame and the HTC elements that make up the HTC file. As we mentioned before, the frame component is used strictly as a user interface component to group (that is, give a unique context to) a set of HTML elements.

The frame component UI is built dynamically in the ShowDocument function, which was bound to the ondocumentready event by the use of the Attach element:

```
<PUBLIC:ATTACH EVENT="ondocumentready" ONEVENT="ShowDocument()" />
```

The ShowDocument used the DHTML DOM to create a new <div> element. This element is used by the component to create its border. The <div>'s ID attribute is dynamically created using the attached element's ID and the constant "pbsFrame". The ID is dynamically built to uniquely identify this element on the page, avoiding possible conflicts when there are multiple frame components on one Web page. Since the element has a unique ID, the component can reference it and be assured that it has the correct one. This is how the <div> is assigned a unique ID within the Web page:

```
eFrame = document.createElement("<div id='" + element.id + "pbsFrame'
></div>");
```

For each property variable that is used by the element, the ShowDocument function checks to see that it is not null. If it is not null, the function sets the new element's style to the property's variable value. If the property variable is null, ShowDocument sets the property variable to nonblank. The reason for this logic is to allow the container page to set a property when the attached element is on the page as an attribute of the tag. The following code shows how the page attaches a behavior and sets a property:

```
<div style="behavior:url(frame.htc) id="frmHomeDirChild" caption="File
Information" margin="20">
```

The <div> tag is used on the containing page to instantiate the frame component using the style attribute. At the same time, the frame's caption and margin are set through the caption and margin attributes. What is happening with these two properties is that their put functions are being called before the ondocumentready event is fired. The properties' variables are initialized to null when the behavior is instantiated. When the put functions are executed, they first test to see if the property variable value is null, and then they save the value into the property variable. If the variable value is null, that indicates that the ShowDocument has not been called. The component has not yet created its HTML elements, so the elements' styles have not been changed. Then in the ShowDocument function, the property variables are tested for not null, so the component can be built with any property values that have already been set. This same concept is used for most of the frame component's properties.

Back to the ShowDocument function: the new <div> element is inserted into the element that the HTC is attached to. It does this by using the element object:

```
element.insertBefore(eFrame, null);
```

The eFrame object is the <div> element. The insertBefore method inserts the eFrame object into the attached element object. So the elements from the component are now children of the HTC's attached element. Another <div> element object is created called eLabel. This <div> element will contain the caption at the top of the frame. It is positioned with some hard-coded values and some styles of the newly created element are set. It is then inserted into the first <div> element, causing the new element to be a child of the pbsFrame element. This is done using the following statement:

```
eFrame.insertBefore(eLabel, null);
```

The rest of the HTC file contains properties to change the look and location of the frame. Table 4-5 contains the purpose of each property. Most of the properties have get and put functions.

Property	Purpose	Used By (Element ID)
caption	Sets or retrieves the caption of the frame.	PbsLabel
borderwidth, borderstyle, bordercolor	Sets or retrieves the frame's border characteristics: width, style, and color.	PbsFrame
height and width	Height and width of the frame. These are read-only properties that return the label's height and width.	PbsLabel
top and left	The coordinates for the placement of the frame on the page.	PbsFrame
margin	The amount of space between the frame border and the HTML elements contained within the frame.	PbsFrame
color	The color of the caption text.	PbsLabel
font	The font of the caption text. The format of the font property is the same as the CSS font property.	PbsLabel
backgroundimage	The frame and caption's background image.	pbsFrame, pbsLabel
backgroundcolor	The frame and caption's background color.	pbsFrame, pbsLabel

Table 4-5. Properties of frame.htc

One thing that you might notice about this component is that it is missing a resize function. It is not needed by this component because it uses <div> elements that resize themselves based on what other elements are contained within them.

The property functions in the HTC file use the underlying CSS properties of the two dynamic elements (pbsFrame and pbsLabel) to change the look of the frame. For example, to change the value of the borderStyle property, the statement is

```
eval(element.id + "pbsFrame").style.borderStyle = style;
```

Assuming the style value is a valid style, the style's borderStyle property is set for the <div> tag that was created. All the other properties do the same kind of thing. To find the valid value for a property, you need to look at what CSS property is being changed and set it with one of the valid values for that CSS property. For example, the CSS borderStyle property has the following valid values on the Windows platform: none, solid, double, groove, ridge, inset, and outset. The frame's borderstyle property's put function validates that the value passed in is one of those acceptable values.

The frame component has two methods. The appendElement method is used to add HTML elements to the end of the frame. The caller must pass a string HTML tag to the appendElement method. The appendElement method takes the element object and calls the appendChild method of the frame's pbsFrame object, like this:

```
eval(element.id + "pbsFrame").appendChild(objEle);
```

The appendElement method then creates an event object and sets its element property to the element object passed into the method. The event is then fired up to the component's container. The code to do this is shown here:

```
objEvent = createEventObject();
objEvent.result = true;
objEvent.element = objEle;
evtOnAppendElement.fire(objEvent);
```

The event was declared in the beginning of the component with this statement:

```
<PUBLIC:EVENT Name=onappendElement id=evtOnAppendElement />
```

This allows the container to now manipulate the newly added element. For example, if a text input element was created, the container could then set the value property of it.

The other method is the removeElement, which is used to remove an element that was added to the frame with the appendElement method. To remove an element, the element's ID is passed to the removeElement method. Before the element is removed from the frame, the removeElement method creates an event object. The event's result property is set to 'true', and its element property is set to the element object that is about to be deleted. The event is then fired up to the container. After the event is processed by the container, execute will return to the frame after the event's fire statement. The container can set the event object's result property to 'false', which will cause the removeElement method not to remove the element. If the result value is 'true', then the element object is retrieved from the frame using the frame's children collection with this statement:

```
objNode = eval(element.id + "pbsFrame").children(strEleID);
```

The children collection uses the element's ID to get the element object. The objNode is then tested for null to see if an element was found with that ID. If it is not null, then the following code is executed:

```
try{
    eval(element.id + "pbsFrame").removeChild(objNode);
}
catch(error){
    alert("Element with ID " + strEleID + " could not be deleted because there
is more than 1 element with that ID.");
}
```

The try and catch statements are used for trapping errors. The code in the try section is executed, and if there are any errors the catch section of code is executed. The reason for this error handling is because if there are two or more elements that have the ID that is being removed an error will occur. The removeChild method of the pbsFrame element is used to remove the element object.

USING THE FRAME COMPONENT

Let's take a look at how the frame component is used on a page. Figure 4-5 shows four frame components on a Web page. The top frame is used to group address information data entry fields. The second frame is used to append or remove an HTML element to the address frame. The third and fourth frames are used for Home Directory information. The Home Directory frames demonstrate how a frame can contain another frame.

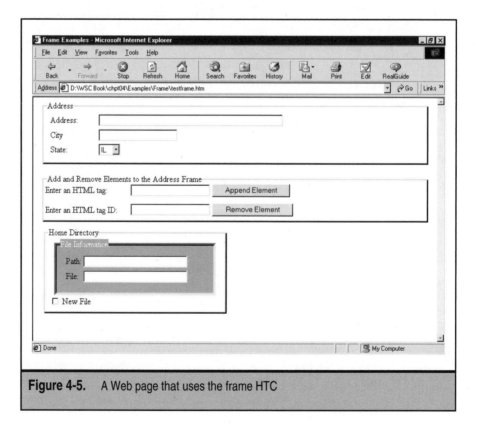

Figure 4-5.   A Web page that uses the frame HTC

The following listing shows how the frames were implemented in the Web page:

testframe.htm

```
<html>
<head>
<title>Frame Examples</title>
<style>
 .frame { behavior:url(frame.htc) ; }
</style>
</head>
<script language="JavaScript">
function initPage(){
    if (document.readyState == 'complete'){
        frmAddress.margin = "10";
        frmHomeDir.margin = "10";
        frmHomeDirChild.borderstyle ="inset";
        frmHomeDirChild.borderwidth = 5;
        frmHomeDirChild.color = "white";
        frmHomeDirChild.backgroundcolor = "gray";
    }
}
function appendElement(strTag){
var objEle;
    objEle = document.createElement("<" + strTag + ">");
    frmAddress.appendElement(objEle);
}
function removeElement(strID){
    frmAddress.removeElement(strID);
}
function eleAdded(){
var objSel;
    if (window.event.element.id == 'ccc'){
        objSel = window.event.element;
        for(i = 0; i < 10; i++){
            objSel.length++;
            objSel.options[objSel.length -1].text = i;
        }
    }
}
```

```
function eleRemoved(){
    if (window.event.element.id == 'ccc')
        window.event.result = false;
}
</script>
<body bgcolor="#FFFFFF" onload="initPage()">
<div class="frame" id="frmAddress" Caption="Address">
  <table border="0" width="100%">
    <tr>
      <td width="13%">Address:</td>
      <td width="87%"><input type="text" name="T1" size="49"></td>
    </tr>
    <tr>
      <td width="13%">City</td>
      <td width="87%"><input type="text" name="T1" size="20"></td>
    </tr>
    <tr>
      <td width="13%">State:</td>
      <td width="87%">
        <select size="1" name="D1">
            <option>IL</option>
            <option>MA</option>
            <option>ND</option>
            <option>RI</option>
            <option>WI</option>
        </select>
      </td>
    </tr>
  </table>
</div>
<br>
<div class="frame" id="frmElementManagement" Caption="Add and Remove
elements to the Address Frame"><table border="0" height=75>
    <tr>
        <td width="164">Enter an HTML tag:</td>
        <td width="150"><input type="text" id="appElementStr" ></td>
        <td width="146"><input type="button" id="btnAppendElement"
onclick="appendElement(document.all.appElementStr.value)"
value="Append
Element"></td>
    </tr>
```

```
    <tr>
        <td width="164">Enter an HTML tag ID:</td>
        <td width="150"><input type="text" id="remElementStr" ></td>
        <td width="146"><input type="button" id="btnRemoveElement"
onclick="removeElement(document.all.remElementStr.value)" value="Remove
Element"></td>
    </tr>
</table>
</div>
<table border="0" width="51%" height="92">
  <tr>
    <td>
        <div  class="frame" id="frmHomeDir" Caption="Home Directory">
        <div  class="frame" id="frmHomeDirChild" Caption="File Information"
margin="20">
            <table border="0" width="100%">
              <tr>
                <td width="13%">Path:</td>
                <td width="87%"><input type="text" name="T1" size="27"></td>
              </tr>
              <tr>
                <td width="13%">File:</td>
                <td width="87%"><input type="text" name="T1" size="27"></td>
              </tr>
            </table>
        </div>
        <input type="checkbox" name="chkBox">New File
      </div>
    </td>
  </tr>
</table>
</body>
```

The Web page has three frame components: frmAddress,
frmHomeDir, and frmHomeDirChild. Each frame is instantiated
using a <div> tag. Each <div> tag uses the Class attribute to
attach the frame HTC to it. The class is created using the following
style declaration:

```
<style>
 .frame { behavior:url(frame.htc); }
</style>
```

The frmAddress frame contains a table that holds the address data entry fields. The table is used merely to align the labels and data entry fields contained within. The Home Directory frames are a little bit more complex. The frmHomeDir frame is contained within a table and contains the frmHomeDirChild frame. The frmHomeDirChild also contains a table for the data fields that it contains. The frmAddress and frmHomeDir frames set the caption when they are instantiated. The frmHomeDirChild sets two properties when it is instantiated, the caption and the margin. The margin property is set there just to show how properties can be set when the behavior is instantiated on the page.

The initPage() function is called when the body of the Web page is loaded. In this function the frmAddress and frmHomeDir margin's are set and the frmHomeDirChild's border is changed, and its text color is set along with its background color.

The appendElement function is called when the Append Element button's onclick event is raised. The button also passes the value of the appElementStr <input> tag to the function. The value of the appElementStr input element needs to be a valid HTML tag. For example, enter **select id='ccc'** in the text box and press the Append Element button. The appendElement function will create an element using the document object's createElement method, using the string that it was passed. Then it calls the address frame's appendElement method. As we saw earlier, the frame component's appendElement method will fire the onappendelement event to the container. The onappendelement event is attached to the address frame when it was declared on the page, like this:

```
<div  class="frame" id="frmAddress" Caption="Address"
onappendelement="eleAdded()" onremoveElement="eleRemoved()">
```

When the onappendelement event is fired on the page, it calls the eleAdded function. The eleAdderd checks to see if the element added has an ID of "ccc". If the element has that ID, then the numbers 0–9 are added as items to the <select> tag. It is assumed that the element is a <select> tag.

The same kind of process is used for removing elements, except the removeElement function removes elements by the element's ID.

The eleRemove function is called when the onremoveElement event is raised before the element is to be removed. The eleRemove event can set the event object's result property to false to cancel the removal of the element. This is demonstrated in the eleRemove function when an element with the ID of "ccc" is to be removed.

Elements are deleted from the address frame by using the Remove Element button and remElementStr text box. To see how this process works, enter **input type=check id=chkTest** into the text box next to the Append Element button and press the Append Element button. A checkbox should now show up in the address frame. Enter **chkTest** into the text box next to the Remove Element button and press the Remove Element button. The checkbox should now be gone from the address frame.

SUMMARY

In this chapter we covered the major characteristics of HTML components. We compared them against other DHTML behavior implementations. We covered how HTCs communicate with a Web page and the DLLs that are used in the process. The syntax for an HTC file was shown and the XML elements that are used to define it. We used the HTC Wizard to create a skeleton HTC file for a frame component. Finally we saw how the frame HTC is used on a Web page.

CHAPTER 5

Advanced HTML Component Features in Internet Explorer 5.5

HTML component technology has taken Web developers to the next step in Web site development. Now a Web developer can organize a Web site into sets of components or objects that can be reused throughout the Web site. One advantage of using components is that they make the Web site easier to create and maintain because a component's logic is encapsulated. That is to say, a component contains all the logic that it needs to do its job. For example, when a multicolumn list box component is created for a Web site, all of its functionality is contained inside the component, and it only exposes the properties, methods, and events (its public interface) to the outside world, allowing the outside world to tell it what to do. The world outside the component cannot, and should not be able to, tell the list box how to perform its function.

The first version of the HTML component technology (DHTML behaviors) was a vast improvement over what was previously available. There were some problems with the components, though. While the technology did give a Web developer the ability to encapsulate logic within a component, it had an encapsulation leak. This leak existed because the HTML component's container had access to the component's underlying HTML. Another problem was that the HTML components were downloaded asynchronously while the rest of a Web page was downloaded synchronously, one element at a time. This forced the Web developer to check to see when the HTML component was ready to be processed. Another problem with HTML components was that they were attached to an HTML tag on the Web page, so they were not true HTML elements. They just added or gave functionality to an existing HTML tag.

In the latest release of Internet Explorer (version 5.5), these issues are addressed. In this chapter, we will show the following features that IE 5.5 adds to HTML components, making them even better:

▼ New and updated HTML component XML elements, objects, and events.

■ How to make an HTML component into a true HTML element and not have it attached to another HTML tag.

- Using the new ViewLink feature to encapsulate the component's HTML from its container.

- How to have a component download synchronously like the rest of the Web page's HTML elements.

- The Web page's use of cascading style sheets on components and components' use of CSS.

▲ How events are raised to the Web page.

NOTE: At the time of this writing, we were working with a beta copy of Internet Explorer 5.5. Therefore, some features of the final release of IE 5.5 may not work exactly as stated in this chapter.

IMPROVEMENTS TO HTML COMPONENT ARCHITECTURE

As we stated earlier, the first version of HTML components exposed the component's HTML to its container. This problem has been addressed by the ViewLink feature in the latest version of Internet Explorer. A component is linked to the container and does not get embedded into it. The container's document tree does not have any knowledge of the component's document tree. This new type of component is called an Element behavior. It is basically implemented in the same manner as a DHTML behavior, but also contains markup (HTML).

A DHTML behavior is attached to an HTML tag either by an XML name space or a CSS style. A DHTML behavior extends the functionality of the HTML tag. On the other hand, an Element behavior is not attached to an HTML tag, but is itself a custom tag in the container. A DHTML behavior is downloaded to the client asynchronously. The new Element behavior uses a different mechanism to download, the <?IMPORT> processing instruction. This instruction causes the component to be downloaded synchronously like the rest of the Web page's elements.

Element behaviors should be viewed as a new version of HTML components. The older version, DHTML behaviors, is backward compatible with IE 5.5, but Element behaviors are recommended when IE 5.5 or later is being used as the browser of choice. The Element behavior implementation improves upon DHTML behaviors and makes it easier for the developer to use HTML components.

Overview of the Element Behavior Architecture

To understand how an Element behavior functions, along with what items are used with an Element behavior, see Figure 5-1. It obviously starts with IE 5.5 and the main Web page. The Web page is considered the primary document. The primary document has a custom element in it called the master element. The master element is the element that declares the Element behavior on the primary document (Web page).

An Element behavior is divided into two main sections: the <head> tag and the <body> tag. These sections are wrapped within an <html> tag. The <head> section contains the component's HTC-specific XML elements and script. This section is the same as a DHTML behavior with some minor differences. The <body> section

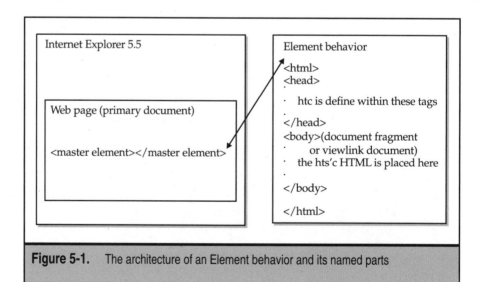

Figure 5-1.   The architecture of an Element behavior and its named parts

is where the component defines its HTML tags. The <body> section is referred to as either the document fragment or the viewlink document. The <body> section is what is linked to the primary document. It is considered linked because the primary document does not know about the Element behavior's HTML document.

As you can see, there are differences between a DHTML behavior and an Element behavior. Table 5-1 compares the two types of behaviors.

Feature	DHTML Behavior	Element Behavior
Contains it own HTML	No	Yes
Its parent has knowledge of its HTML	Yes	No
Download method	Asynchronous	Synchronous
Has its own custom HTML element	No	Yes
Uses another HTML tag to attach to it	Yes	No
Uses the HTML component XML elements	Yes	Yes

Table 5-1.   DHTML Behaviors versus Element Behaviors

Changes to the HTML Component Implementation

Before we take a look at how Element behaviors are implemented, we need to cover the changes to the HTML component's architecture. The following HTC-specific XML elements have been either modified or added: the <component> and <defaults> elements and the defaults and document objects.

Changes to the <component> Element

Additional attributes have been added to the <component> element. These new attributes are used only for Element behaviors. The syntax of the <component> element is

```
<PUBLIC:COMPONENT
    NAME = sName
    URN = sURN
    ID = sID
    tagName = sTagName
    lightWeight = true | false
    literalContent = true | false
    supportsEditMode = true | false
/>
```

NOTE: Default values are in bold.

The four new attributes (tagName, lightWeight, literalContent, and supportsEditMode) are all optional. The lightWeight, literalContent, and supportsEditMode attributes are used only if the tagName attribute is used.

The tagName attribute is used to specify the tag name on the master element that is used to declare the HTML component. This attribute also allows the HTML component to have markup (HTML elements) in the .htc file. The lightWeight attribute specifies if the markup should be parsed each time the tagName is used on the Web page (primary document). The literalContent attribute specifies if the content in the tag that defines the tagName (master element) is treated as a data island and is not parsed or rendered. If the value of this attribute is set to false, then the content is treated as content and is parsed and rendered. The supportsEditMode attribute specifies whether the markup in the HTML component is editable. The attribute, if true, gives the container page (primary document) access to the component's underlying HTML.

The <defaults> Element and defaults Object

The <defaults> element and defaults object are both new to this version of HTML components. The <defaults> element is used to define the value when the component is parsed, and the defaults object is used to set its properties in script. We will only cover the <defaults> element and not the defaults object because they both serve the same purpose and have the same properties. The only difference between them is how they are executed. The syntax for the <defaults> element is

```
<PUBLIC:DEFAULTS
    tabStop = true | false
    style = sStyle
    contentEditable = inherit | true | false
    canHaveHTML = true | false
    viewInheritStyle = true | false
    viewMasterTab = true | false
    viewLinkContent = true | false
/>
```

NOTE: Default values are in bold.

All the attributes are optional. The tabStop attribute states whether the tags in the HTC can be tabbed to. The style attribute is used to set the CCS for a component's container's tag (master element). If a style attribute already exits on the container's tag, then that style is given precedence. An element in the component's document is given precedence over the master element.

The contentEditable attribute states whether the contents of the component are editable. The inherit value states that the component will be editable based on its parent's contentEditable value. The canHaveHTML attribute states whether the container's tag that defines the component (master element) can contain HTML markup. The InheritStyle attribute controls whether the component inherits styles from the container page (primary document). The viewMasterTab attribute states whether the container's tag (master element) is included in the tab sequence of the container (primary document). The viewLinkContent attribute is used to state whether the markup in the component is to be used as a ViewLink instead of as a DHTML behavior.

Implementing an Element Behavior

Implementing an Element behavior is very similar to the way a DHTML behavior is implemented; however, there are a couple of differences. The following code listing shows an Element behavior that is used as a link component.

link.htc

```
<html>
<head>
<PUBLIC:COMPONENT tagName=LINK >
<PUBLIC:DEFAULTS viewLinkContent />
<PUBLIC:METHOD NAME="setLink" />
<PUBLIC:PROPERTY NAME="text" GET="gettext" PUT="puttext" />
<PUBLIC:PROPERTY NAME="URL" GET="geturl" PUT="puturl" />
<PUBLIC:ATTACH for="elememt" event="oncontentready"
onevent="setLink('Fired by the oncontentready event','')" />
<SCRIPT LANGUAGE="JScript">
var vtext = "Microsoft's MSDN Workshop";
var vurl = "http://msdn.microsoft.com/workshop";
function gettext(){
    return vtext;
}
function puttext(vValue){
    vtext = vValue;
}
function geturl(){
    return vurl;
}
function puturl(vValue){
    vurl = vValue;
}
```

```
function setLink(text,URL){
    alert("in setLink");
    document.all.linkitem.innerText = text;
    document.all.linkitem.href = URL;
    vtext = text;
    vurl = URL;
}
function clickLink(){
    alert("Clicked the Link component's link.");
}
</SCRIPT>
</PUBLIC:COMPONENT>
</head>
<body onload='setLink(vtext,vurl)'>
Below is the Link component's link:<br>
<a id="linkitem" onclick="clickLink()"></a>
</body>
</html>
```

This simple component creates a hyperlink that can be modified. The component is broken up into two sections, <head> and <body>, wrapped inside an <html> tag. While this structure is not required, it provides a good separation between the component's logic and its user interface. The <head> tag contains the HTML component architecture elements, and the <body> tag contains the component's HTML markup that is displayed in the primary document.

Looking at the component's code, we can see that it creates a custom tag called LINK on the <PUBLIC:COMPONENT> element. This tag name will be used by the primary document to declare the component on the document. The <PUBLIC:DEFAULTS> element states that this component should be included in the primary document as a ViewLink component, as opposed to a DHTML behavior. The other <PUBLIC> elements are the standard HTML component elements that make up the component's public interface.

The setLink function is called in two places: on the <body> tag's onload event and the component's oncontentready event for the element (master element). The setLink function is used to set the anchor (<a>) tag's href and innerText (the visual name of the hyperlink). When the component is instantiated on the Web page, the oncontentready event will fire first, and then the onload event will fire. You will see this demonstrated because the setLink function has an alert statement to pause the processing of the component. When the processing is paused, you will be able to see the <a> tag's text on the Web page.

The Web page (primary document) that uses the link component follows.

linktest.htm

```
<html XMLNS:IE>
<head>
    <?IMPORT NAMESPACE="IE" IMPLEMENTATION="link.htc">
</head>
<script language="JavaScript">
function switchLinks(text, url){
    objLink.setLink(document.all.linkitem.innerText,
document.all.linkitem.href);
    document.all.linkitem.innerText = text;
    document.all.linkitem.href = url;
}
function clickedLinkObject(){
    alert("Click Event for the component in the primary document");
}
</script>
<body>
<p>
Below is the primary document's link:<br>
<a id="linkitem" href="http://www.microsoft.com">Microsoft's Web Site</a>
</p>
<IE:LINK id="objLink" onclick="clickedLinkObject()"></IE:LINK><br>
<input type=button value="Switch Links" onclick="switchLinks(objLink.text,

objLink.URL)">
</body>
</html>
```

The following items need to be done to the page to use the component as a ViewLinked component on the Web page:

▼ An XML name space must be declared in the <html> tag.

- The <?IMPORT> processing instruction must be added within the <head> tags.

▲ The <namespace:component tagname> tag must be used to ViewLink the component onto the page.

The <?IMPORT> (it is not case sensitive) processing instruction associates the XML name space and the ViewLink component. The NameSpace parameter is the name of the XML name space to use. The example uses IE, which is defined in the <html> tag. The Implementation parameter gives the file name of the component, in this case link.htc. The <?IMPORT> instruction also causes the component to be downloaded synchronously.

Now that the XML name space is associated with the component file, a custom tag can be created in the Web page. The custom tag is created with the name of the name space and the tagname attribute that is located on the <PUBLIC:COMPONENT> element of the .htc file. In the example page, the custom tag is

```
<IE:LINK id="objLink" onclick="clickedLinkObject()"></IE:LINK>
```

Figure 5-2 shows how this Web page looks after it is first loaded. The page allows the two hyperlinks to be switched. While this particular functionality is not very interesting, the page demonstrates that the component is not part of the page's document tree. The Web page has an anchor (<a>) tag containing the ID of linkitem. Looking at the component's code, it also has a anchor tag with the same ID. When the Switch button on the Web page is clicked, the switchLinks function is called and is passed the component's text and URL values. This function calls the component's setLink method, which sets the URL and text of the component's hyperlink. The setLink method is passed the text and URL of the linkitem on the Web page. Looking back at the setLink method of the component, it takes those values and sets the document.all.linkitem's innerText and href properties. This reference to the document.all.linkitem object is the component's linkitem <a> tag. When the setLink method returns to the switchLinks function, it also sets the document.all.linkitem object's innerText and href properties. This time, the document.all.linkitem object refers to the <a> tag on the Web page.

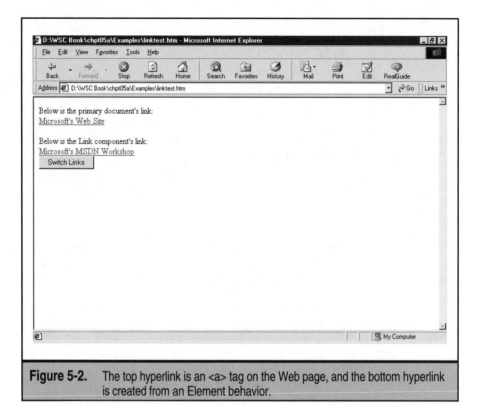

Figure 5-2. The top hyperlink is an <a> tag on the Web page, and the bottom hyperlink is created from an Element behavior.

This works because the component's document tree (DOM) is encapsulated, and the Web page has no information about it. If the same type of functionality were attempted using a DHTML behavior, it would not work because the DHTML behavior's document tree is known by the Web page. The document tree would have two linkitem objects, and a reference to a property using document.all.linkitem would cause an error. The linkitem objects would have been placed in a collection and would have to be referenced using the syntax: document.all.linkitem(0) and document.all.linkitem(1).

NESTING ELEMENT BEHAVIORS

Element behaviors can be placed inside (nested within) each other. The code listing that follows is an inputbox component that contains a text box:

Inputbox.htc

```
<html>
<head>
<PUBLIC:COMPONENT tagName="inputbox" >
<PUBLIC:DEFAULTS viewLinkContent="true" viewMasterTab="true"
viewInheritStyle=false style="font-size:48"/>
<PUBLIC:PROPERTY NAME="value" get="getvalue" put="putvalue"/>
<PUBLIC:Method NAME="setTabSeq" />
<SCRIPT LANGUAGE="JavaScript">
function getvalue(){
    return input.value;
}
function putvalue(data){
   input.value = data;
}
function setTabSeq(data){
   defaults.tabStop = data;
}
</SCRIPT>
</PUBLIC:COMPONENT>
</head>
<body >
<input id="input" style="color:red" type="text">
</body>
</html>
```

This component is placed in another component, which follows.

Csstabeb.htc

```
<html XMLNS:IE>
<head>
<?IMPORT NAMESPACE="IE" IMPLEMENTATION="inputbox.htc">
<PUBLIC:COMPONENT tagName="csstabeb" >
<PUBLIC:DEFAULTS viewLinkContent="true" viewMasterTab="true"
```

```
viewInheritStyle=false style="font-size:48"/>
<PUBLIC:METHOD NAME="setTabSeq" />
<PUBLIC:PROPERTY NAME="tbValue" get="gettbValue" put="puttbValue"/>
<SCRIPT LANGUAGE="JavaScript">
function setTabSeq(bolvalue){
     defaults.tabStop = bolvalue;
     textbox.setTabSeq(bolvalue);
}
function gettbValue(){
     return textbox.value;
}
function puttbValue(data){
     textbox.value = data;
}
function clicked(){
     alert("Component was clicked.");
}
</SCRIPT>
</PUBLIC:COMPONENT>
</head>
<body onclick="clicked()">
<div style="border:1 solid;">This is a area component<br>
<div style="font-size:12">All the area inside the box
outline</div><br>
is the area the component takes<br>
<br>
<IE:inputbox id="textbox"></IE:inputbox>
<br>
Every thing outside this box the is the primary document area<br>
</div>
</body>
</html>
```

The inputbox is contained within the csstabeb component. The csstabeb component uses the <?IMPORT> attribute to point to the inputbox htc file. The csstabeb component creates a custom tag in its <body> tag to contain the inputbox component.

The inputbox component is used as a text box component. This component may not seem very exciting, but it demonstrates that Element behaviors can be composed of other Element behaviors.

The inputbox component has one property, the value property. This property is used to get data in and out of the text box. The csstabeb component uses the inputbox's value property to get and set the inputbox's value. This is done by the csstabeb's tbValue property. A Web page (primary document) now has access to the inputbox's value through the csstabeb component.

The inputbox component also has a setTabSeq method. This method is used to set the defaults object's tabStop property. This property allows/disallows the inputbox's text box to participate in the tab sequence of the Web page.

The csstabeb component displays text and the inputbox component markup in its <body> tag. The csstabeb component is used as a transport to get to the inputbox's value and sets the inputbox's tab state.

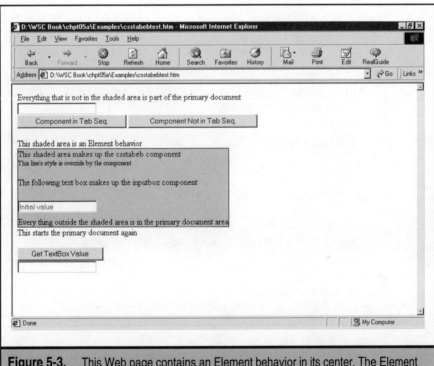

Figure 5-3.   This Web page contains an Element behavior in its center. The Element behavior's text box's participation in the tab sequence of the Web page can be changed using the two top buttons.

TABBING, EVENT BUBBLING, AND INHERITED CSS IN ELEMENT BEHAVIORS

Since an Element behavior is not part of the primary document's tree, it has the ability to tab to and from the primary document and raise events to the primary document. An Element behavior can receive style sheets from the primary document to change its functionality, but it also has the capability to override those same style sheets. Figure 5-3 shows a Web page that has an Element behavior in the middle of it. Actually, there are two Element behaviors on the page: csstabeb and inputbox. Since the inputbox is contained within the csstabeb component, it is displayed on the page. This page will be used to demonstrate tabbing, event bubbling, and inheriting CSS.

The following code listing is for the Web page that uses these Element behaviors.

Csstabebtest.htm

```
<html XMLNS:IE>
<head>
    <?IMPORT NAMESPACE="IE" IMPLEMENTATION="csstabeb.htc">
</head>
<script language="JavaScript">
function setTabSeq(value){
   objArea.setTabSeq(value);
}
function init(){
   objArea.tbValue = "Initial value";
}
function clicked(){
   alert("Primary document was clicked.");
}
</script>
<body onload="init()>
<p>
This are in the primary document<br>
<input type="text"><br>
<input type="button" value="Component in Tab Seq."
onclick="setTabSeq(true)">
<input type="button" value="Component Not in Tab Seq."
onclick="setTabSeq(false)">
</p>
```

```
<IE:csstabeb id="objArea" style="font-size:24;background-color:lightgrey"
"onclick="clicked()"></IE:csstabeb><br>
<p>
<input type="button" value="Get TextBox Value" onclick="{alert('Textbox
value = ' + objArea.tbValue);}">
<br>And so is this<br>
<input type="text">
Any area outside the above box is considered the primary documents
</p>
</body>
</html>
```

Tabbing between the Primary Document and Element Behavior

By default, controls in the Element behavior are not tabbed to from the primary document. There are two attributes that are used by Element behaviors to set up tabbing between the primary document and the Element behavior. The tabStop attribute lets the Element behavior participate in the tab order of the primary document. If the tabStop attribute is true, then the Element behavior participates; otherwise, it does not. When the viewMasterTab attribute is set to true, the master element (the element on the primary document that declares the behavior) participates in the tab order of the primary document.

Our example Element behavior uses two buttons on the Web page to set the behavior of the tab sequence of the primary document. If the Component In Tab Seq. button is pressed, the text box in the behavior can be tabbed to. If the other button is pressed, the behavior's text box will be removed from the tab sequence. Both buttons' onclick events call the csstabeb's setTabSeq function, which in turn calls the behavior's setTabSeq method, setting the csstabeb's tabStop property and calling the inputbox's setTabSeq method to set its tabStop property. The csstabeb's tabStop is set because if it is turned off and the inputbox's tabStop is turned on, the inputbox's tab will not be in the tab sequence. It is like a hierarchy, so if the csstabeb's tab stop is turned off, any other components inside of it cannot be tabbed to. The Component In Tab Seq. button's onclick event passes true to turn the tab sequence on; the other button sends false to remove the text box from the tab sequence.

The behavior also sets the viewMasterTab attribute to false in the <defaults> element. If this attribute was set to true, then the first time the Element behavior was tabbed to, the master element would receive the tab. In the example, this would cause the caveat to disappear and to reappear in the text box the next time the tab key was pressed. The caveat disappears because the master element does not have any controls to tab to.

Event Bubbling and Element Behaviors

If a DHTML behavior trapped a click event, that event would never be raised to its master element. This is because the DHTML behavior is part of the document tree. Since Element behaviors have their own document tree, IE 5.5 automatically raises events to the primary document. This is called *event bubbling*.

To demonstrate event bubbling, click the component on the Web page. Two message boxes are displayed. The first states that the component was clicked, and the second states that the primary document was clicked. This is because the component (csstabeb.htc) traps the onclick event in its <body> tag and the master element also traps the onclick event. When the component is clicked, it processes its onclick event, and the event is then bubbled up to the master element.

Most events from Element behaviors are bubbled up to the master element and the primary document. If an event does not get raised automatically, the element's fireEvent method can be used to raise the event up the tree.

CSS and Element Behaviors

If you look at the Element behavior in Figure 5-3, you will see that it contains two different font sizes. This is because the larger font is inherited from the master element on the Web page, and the smaller font overrides that setting.

Looking at the master element on the Web page, you will see that it contains a font size style of 24 (the larger font). In the behavior, the font size of 12 is given to the specific line in the behavior, thus overriding the master element. By default, the behavior inherits the CSS of the master element. This can be changed by setting the viewInheritStyle attribute of the behavior's <defaults> element to "false".

SUMMARY

In this chapter, we covered the improved HTML component architecture available using Element behaviors. Element behaviors were developed to help components hide their markup from the component's container. Element behaviors are linked into documents and are download synchronously. We discussed the new and modified HTC-specific XML elements used to create Element behaviors. We showed a couple of examples on how to use Element behaviors and how to nest them inside of other Element behaviors.

CHAPTER 6

Debugging Script Code and HTML Components

If you have ever worked in other development environments, such as Visual Basic and Visual C++, you probably have noticed that those products are equipped with very robust debugging environments. These debuggers can stop the execution of code by placing a *breakpoint* in the source code; they can view and change values of variables; and some can even go back to code that was already executed and execute it again. These are just some of the features of a code debugger. A development environment is not really needed to develop Web pages built with only HTML because a basic HTML Web page is just a text file with formatting codes that is read and interpreted by the browser. Of course, we do recommend using a development environment, such as Microsoft's FrontPage or Microsoft's InterDev, to develop Web pages because it makes developing Web pages and sites a lot easier.

This chapter will cover two debugging tools that can help in troubleshooting HTML components and script code. The first tool that we'll cover is Microsoft's Script Debugger. It is a free tool that can be downloaded from Microsoft's site. Next, we'll cover the debugging facilities within Microsoft's Visual InterDev product. Visual InterDev is not free, but it contains a richer feature set and can be used to create Web pages, HTML components, and Web applications. Each debugger has its advantages and disadvantages, so our main reasons for covering these two debuggers in particular are

▼ A developer does not have to purchase a separate product for debugging, as the script debugger can be downloaded and used for free.

▲ They are the only debuggers that support HTML components.

Using these two debugging environments, we will cover the following areas:

▼ Debugging HTML components, using the Frame component created in Chapter 4 as an example.

■ The features of the Scripting Debugger and Visual InterDev's debugger.

■ How to start a debugging session.

- Setting breakpoints, viewing and changing variable values, and executing code with each debugger.

▲ The advantages and disadvantages of each debugging tool.

THE MICROSOFT SCRIPT DEBUGGER

The Microsoft Script Debugger can extend any ActiveX Scripting host application. One of these host applications is Internet Explorer, which allows developers to debug client-side script code that is in the browser. The Script Debugger can also be used in conjunction with Microsoft's Internet Information Server (IIS) to debug server-side script code such as ASP and the external interactions of Java applets. While we will not cover these types of debugging in this book, it is important to note that the concepts are the same.

The Script Debugger can be freely downloaded from http://msdn.microsoft.com/scripting (at the time of this writing) and used without cost. The current version of the Script Debugger is version 1.0 for Windows 95 and 98 and version 1.0a for NT 4.0 and Windows 2000. While the Script Debugger will work with either IE 4 or IE 5, we will be debugging HTML components, so you should have IE 5 installed. After downloading and installing the Script Debugger, Internet Explorer needs to be closed and restarted in order for the Script Debugger to be integrated into the IE View menu (see Figure 6-1).

There are some guidelines that should be used when working with the Script Debugger. When Internet Explorer 5 is installed, it turns the script-debugging feature off. You'll therefore need to turn it on. To enable script debugging after installing IE 5, do the following:

1. From the Tools menu, select Internet Options.

2. Click on the Advanced tab.

3. In the Browsing section of the Settings window, make sure that the Disable Script Debugging checkbox in not checked.

Running multiple instances of the Script Debugger is not recommended, as it can cause unexpected results. If the script code is being debugged in IE 5, it is recommended that IE 5 be run in standalone mode and not in ActiveX Desktop mode. We will not

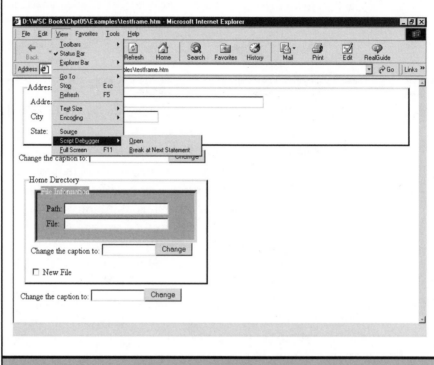

Figure 6-1. Once it is installed, the Script Debugger is integrated into IE's View menu.

be covering every feature of the Script Debugger, so use the help documentation to aid in the debugging of your script. This documentation is very comprehensive and is a great help.

Script Debugger Environment

The Script Debugger uses four main windows (see figure 6-2 later in the chapter) to help with the debugging process: the Source Code window (the left window), the Running Documents window, the Call Stack window, and the Command window. It also contains a menu and toolbar used to manage these windows and its environment.

The Source Code window contains the HTML page that is currently being debugged. This window can be used to manage breakpoints and to follow code execution. The following list tells you how to use some of the more common functions of the debugger. (Note: The code currently being debugged cannot be edited in the source code window. The same file can be opened and can be changed within the debugger, but the debugger will not know about those changes until the page is refreshed in the browser and reloaded into the debugger.)

▼ To set a breakpoint (a place to stop the execution of the code and display the debugger), move the cursor to the line where the execution is to be stopped and then either press F9, select Toggle Breakpoint from the Debug menu, or press the Toggle Breakpoint button on the debug toolbar.

■ To remove a breakpoint, follow the same procedure as setting a breakpoint.

■ To clear all breakpoints, either press CTRL+SHIFT+F9, select Clear All Breakpoints from the Debug menu, or press the Clear All Breakpoints button on the debug toolbar.

■ To follow the code into a procedure (step in), either press F8, select Step In from the Debug menu, or press the Step Into button on the debug toolbar.

■ To bypass a procedure by executing its code and breaking on the next line of code within the current procedure (step over), either press SHIFT+F8, select Step Over from the Debug menu, or press the Step Over button on the debug toolbar.

■ To exit a procedure by finishing its execution and breaking on the next line of code in its calling procedure, if any, (step out), either press CTRL+SHIFT+F8, select Step Out from the Debug menu, or press the Step Out button on the debug toolbar.

■ To continue code execution after a breakpoint (run), either press F5, select Run from the Debug menu, press the Run button on the debug toolbar.

- To stop the debugger, either press SHIFT+F5, select Stop Debugging from the Debug menu, or press the Stop Debugging button on the debug toolbar.

▲ To set a breakpoint on the next line of script code (break at next statement), either select Break at Next Statement from the Debug menu, press the Break at Next Statement button on the debug toolbar, or, within Internet Explorer, select Break at Next Statement from the View I Script Debugger menu.

The Running Documents window displays a list of all applications that are hosting active scripting on the computer. Under each application node is a list of documents currently being debugged for that application. To view a document's source code, double-click on it. The debugger will open a new Source Code window for the document. If you right-click on the Web document, a Next Statement breakpoint can be set.

The Call Stack window displays a list of the active procedures and running threads. The debugger keeps track of active procedures, adding them to the Call Stack window when they are called and removing them when their execution is complete. The combo box at the top of the Call Stack window is used to select the running thread. This feature is usually available only when debugging Java applets.

The Command window is used to execute commands while debugging the script code. It can be used to display values of variables and object properties and can be used to change their values. Procedures and object methods can also be executed within this window. To execute code in the Command window, use the same script language that the currently executing script code is written in. For example, if the code executing is JavaScript, then you can't type in a VBScript Trim command. Items in the Source Code window can even be copied and pasted into a Command window to be executed.

Script Debugger Example

There are several ways to start the Script Debugger, the first of which is to start it from IE 5. Load the Web page to be debugged and from IE's View menu, select Script Debugger/Open, and the Script Debugger will be initiated. The second way to start the Script Debugger is from inside the running script code. This is done by placing a "stop" statement (for VBScript) or "debugger" statement (for JavaScript) in the script code. When the script-specific statement is executed, the debugger pops up and points to that statement. The last way to load the debugger is when a runtime error occurs and the browser asks if the error should be debugged. If the answer is yes, the debugger is loaded and shows the line that contains the error.

Let's walk through some debugging sessions using the Script Debugger applied against the Frame HTML component from the last chapter. We will see how the debugger is started, how to view and change variables, and how to set breakpoints. This debugging session will show how a caption is set on the frame by walking through the code to where testframe.htm sets a caption. We start by doing the following:

1. Load the testframe.htm document from Chapter 4 into Internet Explorer 5.x.

2. Open the Script Debugger by selecting View I Script Debugger I Open. The Script Debugger should now be open, with testframe.htm in the Source Code window. The screen should look something like Figure 6-2.

NOTE: If Visual Studio is installed on your system, the Microsoft Development Environment will open instead of the Microsoft Script Debugger. If this is the case, you can simply continue this exercise using the MDE instead of the Script Debugger. Refer to the Visual InterDev debugging section to see its functions before following the debugging sessions.

3. Expand the Running Document's tree. One of the nodes is for the testframe.htm document and should have three frame.htc documents under it. These are the three frame components used in the page.

4. In the Source Code window, set a breakpoint on the line

```
objFrame.caption = txtNewCaption;
```

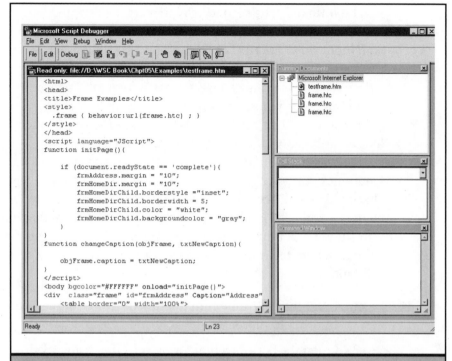

Figure 6-2. The Script Debugger environment with the testframe.htm loaded

within the changeCaption function by placing the cursor at that line and pressing F9. The line should be now be highlighted.

5. Switch back to Internet Explorer and enter a new caption in the first change caption text box and press its Change button. The Script Debugger should pop up, halting execution at the line where you set the breakpoint.

6. Press F8 to go into the frame's code. A new Source Code window should open with the execution pointer in the putcaption function.

7. In the Command window, type the word **text** and press ENTER. The value that is returned should be the new value that was entered on the testframe page for the caption. "text" is a parameter that is passed into the putcaption function.

8. Look at the Call Stack window. There should be three procedures listed. The top item should be the putcaption function that was called by the second item in the list, changeCaption function. The changeCaption was in turn called from the JavaScript – anonymous function.

9. Double-click the JavaScript – anonymous function item in the Call Stack window to discover what started this hold process. The testframe.htm Source Code window should display the HTML line that contains the button that was pressed to change the caption. The button's onclick event called the changeCaption function.

10. Press F8 to go back to the frame.htc Source Code window. The next line of code is executed.

11. Press CTRL+SHIFT+F8 to step out of the frame's putcaption function and back into the testframe's changeCaption function.

12. To demonstrate that the page's DOM is available and can be changed, we are going to change the first button's caption from "Change" to "Set New Caption." Type **document.all.btnFirstFrame.value** in the Command window and press the ENTER key. The button's value, Change, should be displayed. Now on the next line of the Command window, type **document.all.btnFirstFrame.value="Set New Caption"** and again press the ENTER key. This sets the new caption on the button. Figure 6-3 shows how the Script Debugger should look like at this point.

13. Click on the Source code window and press F5 to run the rest of the source code and to return to the testframe Web page. The top most button on the page should have the newly set caption.

Using the Script Debugger to Walk through Code

The best way to understand how an application or a piece of logic works is to walk through the code step by step. In this debugging session, you will see how to stop execution of the code from within the script code itself. We will use the testframe.htm document again, except this time we will watch the script code when the page is

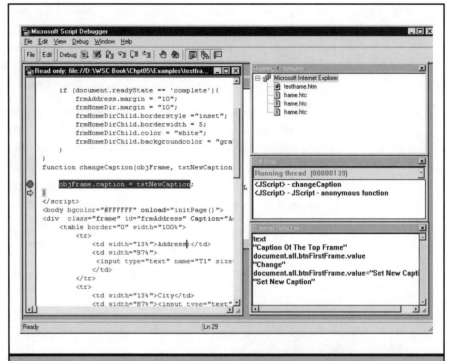

Figure 6-3. What the Script Debugger environment looks like after step 12

loaded. In the first debugging session, we loaded testframe.htm into the browser before the debugger was started. By the time the debugger was displayed, the testframe's onload event had already executed. In this session, we will watch the testframe's onload event while it executes. In order to do this, we need to change testframe.htm as follows:

1. Edit testframe.htm with your favorite editor. Make the following line the first statement in the initPage function:

   ```
   debugger;
   ```

   The initPage should now look like this:

   ```
   function initPage(){
   debugger;
           if (document.readyState == 'complete'){
   ```

2. Now load testframe.htm into Internet Explorer 5.x, and the Script Debugger will pop up as execution is halted at the debugger statement. The debugger statement is used in JScript to pop up the debugger. The equivalent within VBScript is the stop statement.

3. Now try switching back to Internet Explorer: you cannot go back to Internet Explorer because the debugger has control.

4. Notice in the Call Stack window that there is an entry for an anonymous JavaScript function. If you double-click on it, it will show that the <body> tag's onload event called the initPage function.

5. Press F8 to watch the code in the initPage or press F5 to continue to run the script code. When normal execution is resumed, the page is again displayed in Internet Explorer.

Debugger Runtime Errors

In this debugging session, we will create a deliberate error in the script to see how the Script Debugger reacts. There will be two errors generated: one in the testframe.htm document and one in the frame component. Let's place the errors in the script code:

1. Edit the testframe.htm file and change the IF statement in the initPage function to read

    ```
    if (documentx.readyState == 'complete'){
    ```

    We added an "x" to the end of the document object's name. Save the changes in testframe.htm.

2. Edit the frame.htc file and remove the vcaption declaration directly after the statement

    ```
    <script language="JavaScript">
    ```

    Save the changes in frame.htc.

Now that the errors have been placed in the script code, open testframe.htm in Internet Explorer.

1. Load the testframe.htm document in the browser, and you'll see the error displayed in Figure 6-4. The error indicates that vcaption is undefined. This error is going to be shown six times. The reason for the six times is because there are three frame components on the page, and the vcaption variable is referenced twice when each component is loaded into the page.

2. Answer Yes to the question, "Do you wish to Debug?" The Script Debugger will open with the execution stopped at the first reference to the vcaption variable. The Script Debugger does not allow editing of the current file, but you can open another instance of the file and add the vcaption declaration. The change won't take effect until the page is refreshed.

3. Answer No to the other five vcaption "Do you wish to Debug?" errors.

4. The last error to be displayed is the "documentx is undefined" error. Answer Yes to debug this error. The Script Debugger will pop up and show the statement that contains the error.

5. Press F5 to continue to load the page.

Quirks of the Script Debugger

There are some problems with the Script Debugger when debugging HTML components. Sometimes the debugger does not load the page.

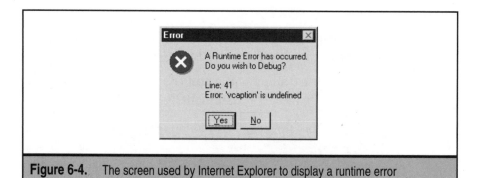

Figure 6-4.   The screen used by Internet Explorer to display a runtime error

The Script Debugger pops up, but there is no source code to debug. When this happens, stop the debugger but do not close it. Go back to Internet Explorer and refresh the page. The next time the debugger is displayed, the source code should be loaded. If the source code is still not loaded, you may need to uninstall Script Debugger and reinstall it. One of its most user-unfriendly quirks is the Source Code window interaction with other windows. If one of the other windows has focus, you have to return focus to the Source Code window in order to execute any of its commands. For example, if the Command window has focus, and you want to finish running the script code by pressing F5, you first have to set focus back to the Source Code window, or the F5 run command is ignored.

THE MICROSOFT VISUAL INTERDEV DEBUGGER

Microsoft Visual InterDev is a much more robust debugger than the Script Debugger. But, of course, you get what you pay for. The Script Debugger is free, whereas Visual InterDev is a product that you need to pay for. Again in this section on Visual InterDev debugging, we will only look at how to use Visual InterDev to debug script code and HTML components. There are many other resources that specifically cover all the features of Visual InterDev in great detail.

Before we get started, there are some prerequisites for debugging HTML components with Visual InterDev. You must install Visual InterDev version 6 and Visual Studio Service Pack 3. If the Script Debugger is installed on the same computer as Visual InterDev, Visual InterDev will become the default script debugger. (As previously noted, you can still use the Script Debugger by loading the Web page first and manually starting the Script Debugger application, MSSCRDBG.EXE. The page's source code needs to be loaded by selecting it from the Running Document's window tree. The default location for it is the Microsoft Script Debugger directory under the Program Files directory.)

Debugging with Visual InterDev

The easiest way to start debugging with Visual InterDev is to load
the page to be debugged into Internet Explorer and open the
debugger by selecting View | Script Debugger | Open. Let's starts
a debugging session using the frame component:

1. Start Internet Explorer and load testframe.htm (see Figure 6-5).

2. Open Visual InterDev for debugging by selecting View | Script
   Debugger | Open. Visual InterDev should start up.

3. Visual InterDev will ask if you want to open a project for
   debugging. Answer No to this question. The testframe.htm
   Source Code window will be shown.

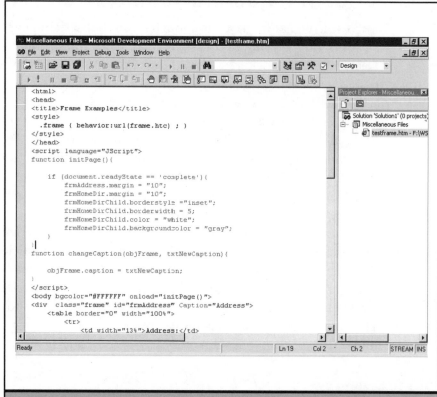

Figure 6-5. The testframe.htm document is loaded in Visual InterDev and is ready for debugging.

NOTE: Visual InterDev projects are used to debug server-side script. This book does not cover server-side script debugging, therefore we will not be covering Visual InterDev projects.

4. In the source code window, place a breakpoint (see the following bulleted list for common Visual InterDev debugging commands) on the following line of code in the changeCaption function:

```
objFrame.caption = txtNewCaption;
```

5. If the Project Explorer window is not visible, open it (CTRL+ALT+J). Observe that there is only one file in the project—testframe.htm.

6. Switch back to Internet Explorer. The Run command will not work because Visual InterDev is not running the page. The page started Visual InterDev for debugging.

7. Enter a caption in the first Change Caption text box and press its Change button. Visual InterDev should be shown at the breakpoint we set previously.

8. If the Immediate window is not visible, then open it (CTRL+ALT+I). Type **txtNewCaption** into the Immediate window and press ENTER. The Immediate window should display the value that was entered into the text box because the text box value is passed into this function.

9. On the breakpoint line, highlight objFrame.caption and place the mouse over it. A ToolTip should be displayed that shows the current frame's caption value.

10. Now highlight just objFrame in the breakpoint line and place the mouse over it. The following tooltip is displayed:

```
objFrame = {...}
```

This indicates that this variable is an object with properties, and it does not know which of its properties to display.

11. To display the properties of the objFrame object, place the cursor on it and right-click to display a context menu. From

the context menu, select Add Watch. A Watch window opens up with the objFrame displayed, with a + sign next to it.

12. To see the properties of the objFrame variable, expand it by clicking on the + sign. Figure 6-6 shows the properties of the objFrame object. The properties are DOM properties for the HTML tag, in this case a <div> tag. You can click twice (*not* double-click) on a property to change the value of the property.

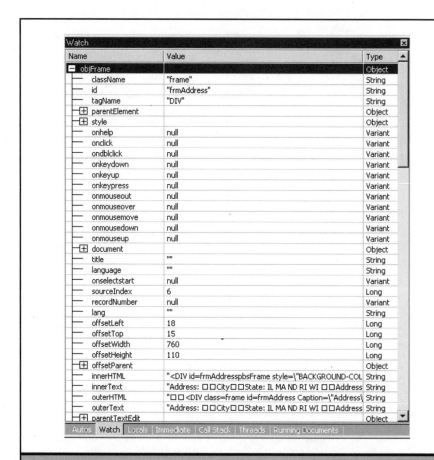

Figure 6-6. The Watch window in Visual InterDev gives a view of all the properties of an object.

13. Go back to the Source Code window at the breakpoint. Press F11 to go into the frame component's source code. Two things happen: a new Source Code window opens for the frame.htc file, and the frame.htc file is added to the Project Explorer window. In the Source Code window, the execution pointer should be at the first line in the putcaption function.

14. Move the cursor to the second line in the putcaption function:

    ```
    vcaption = s1;
    ```

15. Press CTRL+F10, and the code will execute until it gets to the line with the cursor. This feature acts like a temporary breakpoint.

16. Press F5 to continue to execute the rest of the code and return to Internet Explorer. The frame should now have a new caption on it.

From this Visual InterDev debugging session, you can see that the Visual InterDev debugger functions the same way as the Script Debugger. This will be the only debugging session that we will cover using Visual InterDev. You can take the other Script Debugger sessions, previously covered in the chapter, and use Visual InterDev on them to get more of a feel for using this product.

The following list contains the most commonly used Visual InterDev debugger commands:

 ▼ To set a breakpoint (a place to stop the execution of the code so the debugger is displayed), move the cursor to the line where the execution is to be stopped and then either press F9, place the cursor on a line and select Insert Breakpoint from the context menu, press the Insert Breakpoint button on the debug toolbar, or click on the gray area to the left of the desired line of code.

 ■ To remove a breakpoint, move the cursor to the line where the execution will be stopped and then either press F9, place the cursor on a line and select Remove Breakpoint from the context menu, press the Insert Breakpoint button on the debug toolbar, or click on the gray area to the left of the desired line of code.

- To clear all breakpoints, either press CTRL+SHIFT+F9, select the Clear All Breakpoints item from the Debug menu, or press the Clear All Breakpoints button on the debug toolbar.

- To follow the code into a procedure (step in), either press F11, select Step In from the Debug menu, or press the Step Into button on the debug toolbar.

- To bypass a procedure (step over), either press F10, select Step Over from the Debug menu, or press the Step Over button on the debug toolbar.

- To exit a procedure (step out), either press SHIFT+F11, select Step Out from the Debug menu, or press the Step Out button on the debug toolbar.

- To continue to run after a breakpoint (run), either press F5, select Start from the Debug menu, or press the Start button on the debug toolbar.

- To stop the debugger, either press SHIFT+F5, select Start Without Debugging from the Debug menu, or press the End button on the debug toolbar.

- To set the next line to execute (which allows you to reexecute or bypass lines of code), either press CTRL+SHIFT+F10 or move the cursor to the line and select Set Next Statement from the Source Code window's context menu.

▲ To add a variable to the Watch window, either press SHIFT+F9, click twice on a blank line in the Watch window, and enter the variable to be watched in the name column; or highlight the variable in the source code window and select Add Watch from the context menu; or highlight the variable in the Source Code window and select Add Watch from the Debug menu.

Visual InterDev has many more debugging features that can be used to debug script code. The Watch window can be combined with six other features into one window. Look at the bottom of Figure 6-6 and notice the tabs at the bottom. The Autos tab displays the variables in the scope of the current line of execution within the procedure. The Locals tab displays the variables that are within the current stack frame. The Immediate tab is used to enter expressions to be evaluated. The Call Stack tab keeps track of what procedure was called by what procedure. The Threads tab displays information about threads that are running.

The Running Documents tab displays all of the documents that are loaded along with the Web page. It also contains a very powerful feature to keep track of processes, allowing processes that are running to be debugged. Another feature is that a breakpoint can be conditional. These conditions are not like the properties of an object, but instead they control how the breakpoint behaves. A condition on a breakpoint tells the breakpoint to halt execution only when certain criteria are met. For example, if a breakpoint is on the line x++; a condition can be set so that when x = 5 the breakpoint will halt execution. Another condition of a breakpoint is for the number of times a line is executed. For example, after a line is executed four times, the code will stop and the debugger will be displayed. As you can see, Visual InterDev debugging is very flexible and powerful.

COMPARING THE SCRIPT DEBUGGER AND VISUAL INTERDEV

Table 6-1 compares the debugging features of the Script Debugger and Visual InterDev.

While Script Debugger's features aren't as robust as those of Visual InterDev, it does get the job done—and at a lesser price. Visual InterDev, on the other hand, contains a much richer feature set for debugging script code and is therefore more productive. Of course, it also costs more than the freeware Script Debugger. Another advantage of Visual InterDev is that it is not only a debugger but also

Feature	Script Debugger	InterDev
Breakpoints	Yes	Yes
Breakpoint properties	No	Yes
Step into, out of, and over code	Yes	Yes
Run to cursor	No	Yes
Change line execution	No	Yes
Break at next statement	Yes	No
Command window	Yes	Yes
Watch variables	No	Yes
Call stack	Yes	Yes
Process information	Yes, limited (Running Documents window)	Yes

Table 6-1.   Features of the Script Debugger and InterDev

a complete development environment. It can be used to develop Web pages, HTML components, and Web applications.

SUMMARY

In this chapter we covered script debugging. We examined two tools that can be used to help debug script code and HTML components: the Microsoft Script Debugger and Microsoft Visual InterDev products. We demonstrated the features of both debuggers with many hands-on debugging sessions. We gave techniques on how to debug script code. Though we did not cover all the features of either of the debuggers, we gave a good sampling of their capabilities.

CHAPTER 7

Creating a Real-World HTML Component

In Chapter 4 we covered the architecture of an HTML component and showed how to create an HTML component, the Frame component. The Frame component is very useful, but it is also very simple. It does not contain any user interaction—it is really just used to help organize other Web page components. In this chapter we will create a Grid HTML component to demonstrate more HTML component features and at the same time create a component that is very useful on Web pages.

If you have ever used other development tools, such as Visual Basic, that use grid controls, you already know how versatile and important grids are in many applications. Grids allow the most data to be presented to the user in a compact format, as Figure 7-1 demonstrates. HTML's closest representation of a grid is the <table> tag. A <table> tag is not as dynamic as a grid control. User data cannot be entered directly into a cell of an HTML table the same way data can sometimes be entered directly into a traditional grid's cells. Grids also often have the ability to validate user-inputted data immediately after being entered. 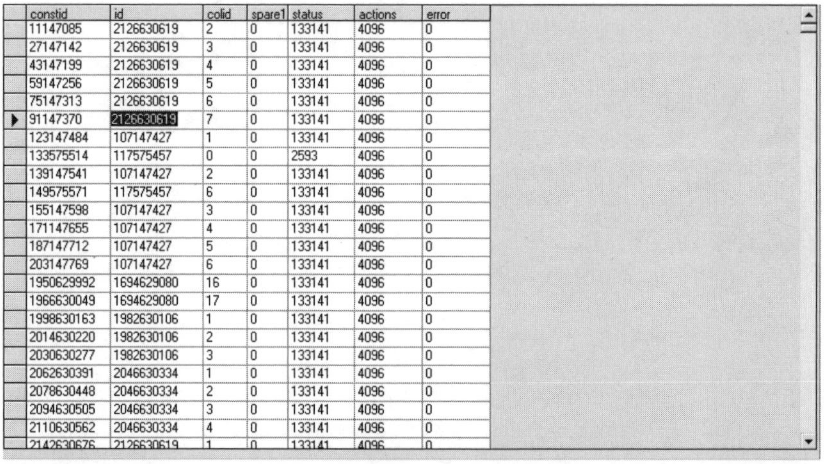

constid	id	colid	spare1	status	actions	error
11147085	2126630619	2	0	133141	4096	0
27147142	2126630619	3	0	133141	4096	0
43147199	2126630619	4	0	133141	4096	0
59147256	2126630619	5	0	133141	4096	0
75147313	2126630619	6	0	133141	4096	0
91147370	2126630619	7	0	133141	4096	0
123147484	107147427	1	0	133141	4096	0
133575514	117575457	0	0	2593	4096	0
139147541	107147427	2	0	133141	4096	0
149575571	117575457	6	0	133141	4096	0
155147598	107147427	3	0	133141	4096	0
171147655	107147427	4	0	133141	4096	0
187147712	107147427	5	0	133141	4096	0
203147769	107147427	6	0	133141	4096	0
1950629992	1694629080	16	0	133141	4096	0
1966630049	1694629080	17	0	133141	4096	0
1998630163	1982630106	1	0	133141	4096	0
2014630220	1982630106	2	0	133141	4096	0
2030630277	1982630106	3	0	133141	4096	0
2062630391	2046630334	1	0	133141	4096	0
2078630448	2046630334	2	0	133141	4096	0
2094630505	2046630334	3	0	133141	4096	0
2110630562	2046630334	4	0	133141	4096	0
2142630676	2126630619	1	0	133141	4096	0

Figure 7-1. A grid control allows a user to view a lot of data and provides the ability to enter data all in one place.

In this chapter we will cover the following topics while developing our HTML Grid component:

▼ The development process of creating an HTML component.

■ The Grid component's architecture.

■ Detailed use of DHTML and cascading style sheets.

■ How to use of the Grid component's features.

▲ Potential feature extensions for the Grid component.

HTML COMPONENT DEVELOPMENT PROCESS

The first task in creating an HTML component is just like any other piece of software: you need to put a project plan together for the component. The project plan does not have to be on paper, though it is the preferred way. Here are the basic tasks that need to be done to create a successful component:

▼ Determine first of all if a component is needed.

■ Define the feature set the component will provide the user.

■ Define the public interface (properties, methods, and events) of the component.

■ Define the component's user interface, if there will be one.

■ Determine how the component may be implemented.

▲ Create a test page to debug and test the component.

Determining if a Component Is Needed

There are many factors in determining if a component should be created. Following are some of the questions to ask (listed from most important to least important):

▼ Do you have the resources (time and money) to create the component?

■ Is the environment you work in familiar with component technology and experienced working with it?

■ Is there duplicate functionality in the application, or will specific functionality be used in more than one place—either in this application or in another application? (The functionality can either be UI or business logic.)

■ Are there other components in the application, and will creating a component make the maintenance of the application easier or harder?

▲ What is the likelihood of the component being reused in this and other applications?

There are advantages and disadvantages to creating a component:

▼ Creating the component could take more time from the project time line.

■ The application is easier to maintain.

■ The component could be reused in another application.

■ If the component is reused, time is saved in the project that is reusing the component.

■ If the component is reused, any changes to the component need to be tested in all applications that use the component.

■ Reusing components between applications makes your applications more tightly coupled to each other.

▲ If a component is not reused, but the logic is copied from it then there are two or more places with the same logic that will need to be maintained.

Defining Component Features

The first thing to do when defining the component's features is to identify the component users. In most cases there are two component users: the developer, who uses the component on a page, and the Web page user, if the component has a user interface. Each of these users has a different perceptive of the component. The developer would like the component to be easily integrated with the page and easy to program with. The Web page user, on the other hand, does not care how easy the component is to program with: they want the component to be easy to use on the page.

Once the users have been identified, you will need to query those users to find out what they want the component to do. For example, the developer might want to give the component a save feature that would save all the data in the component to a file. The Web page user might want the component to have a save button on the component so they can save the data wherever they like.

Features of the component can also be taken from existing logic. For example, if you had a procedure that calculated a value based on some business logic, you could take the code and incorporate it into a component. In this case you would probably not need any user to identify the features of the component.

Determining the Component's Public Interface

Once the user's features have been identified, those features are taken to create the component's public interface. The component's public interface is made up of properties, methods, and events. For example, the component could contain a caption property that can be changed, a save method that saves the component's data to a file, and background color that is changed whenever the mouse pointer goes over it by trapping the onmouseover event of its container.

Determining the Component's User Interface

In creating a component's user interface, the question that needs to be asked is does the component need a user interaction. For example, with a grid control the answer is yes. But with a validation component, the answer probably is no, because it raises errors up to its container. Assuming the component needs a user interface, the next step is to determine how it should look and act. To help in developing the user interface, it is best to create a prototype for the user. This will allow the user to see the component and how it works. In creating the user interface, you can use existing HTML tags (input, select, tables, and so on) or use a combination of HTML tags. For example, the frame component in Chapter 4 uses a couple of <div> tags to create it.

After determining that the component needs a user interface, it is now a good time to prototype the component. The prototype is not a full-function component, although it may have some features that work. A feature is implemented so that some of the concepts can be thought out. The prototype should be written in a language or tool that you are familiar with. Prototyping gives you a chance to explore any questions that you might have about the component before actually implementing it.

Component Implementation and Testing Page

Now that you have the features, public interface, and user interface defined, you can start coding the HTML component. You need to decide what script language the component will be written with. HTML components can be created with either VBScript or JavaScript. We like to use both languages. We mainly use JavaScript and supplement it with VBScript where needed—VBScript is much better at handling dates, for instance. Now it's just a matter of writing the functionality of the component using the DHTML DOM and script code.

As you are writing the component, you might want to test it in a Web page. Create a simple Web page that contains just the component and any other items the component needs. On this page you simulate the component's public interface and test its functionality during the writing process by calling its properties, methods, and events.

THE GRID COMPONENT ARCHITECTURE

In this section we are going to cover the creation of our Grid HTML component. We will use the development process from the previous section to show how they affect the way you create a component.

The Grid's Features

The reason we created the Grid component was because HTML does not have a tag with that functionality. We needed an HTML tag with the similar functionality of a spreadsheet to making the maintenance of data easier on the user. Figure 7-2 shows the grid on a Web page. We created the Grid component with the following features:

▼ The Grid component can either be editable or static.

■ It allows you to insert or delete rows dynamically.

■ It allows for multiple columns and sets and retrieves the column headings.

■ The size of the Grid (height and width) can be set so that it contains only a portion of the page.

■ It adds vertical scroll bars if the rows extended past the bottom of the Grid's height.

■ It has the ability to display or remove the column headers.

■ The container can retrieve the data at either the cell level or for the entire Grid.

■ The Grid can notify the container before and after editing a cell, and it also has the ability to cancel the edits.

■ It has the ability to return the number of columns and rows.

▲ Information can load into the Grid from an array of data or one cell at a time.

Name	Address	City	State	Zip
Bill Jones	123 Main Str	Addison	MA	60123
Mary Smith	614 Avers	Madison	WI	12563-0098
Michelle K. Heflin	60 Wilton Lane	Elmhurt	FL	09908-9883
David J. Heflin	123 Lake Str.	Vernon	CA	53245
Sue Cook	4 N 45 E. Clark	Fileds	IA	45637-8888

Figure 7-2. This editable Grid component was created using the HTML component architecture.

The Grid's Public Interface

Based on the features that we have determined for the Grid component, we can now create its public interface (see Table 7-1).

Grid Feature	Public Interface	
	Name	Type
Make Grid editable or static	Editable	Property (read/write)
Insert and delete rows dynamically	insertRow, deleteRow	Methods
Get/set the number of columns	Cols	Property (read/write)
Size the Grid	width, height	Properties (read/write)
Add vertical scroll bars if the rows extend past the bottom of the Grid's height	N/A	N/A
Display column headers or remove them from the Grid	ShowColHeaders	Property
Notify the container before and after editing a cell and also provide the ability to cancel the edits	onStartEdit, onEndEdit	Events
Return the number of columns and rows	cols, rows	Properties
Load and retrieve data from the Grid	LoadGridData, getGridData	Methods
Load and retrieve data at the cell level	Column	Property

Table 7-1.   The Grid Component's Features

Now we have to decide what type to make each of the public interfaces. The criteria for deciding if a public interface should be a property, is if the public interface is an attribute of the component and if you want the developer to assign the value to the component. For example, the width of the Grid is a property because it is an attribute of the Grid component. A method is used when the component needs to perform some function, such as loading or retrieving data. An event is used when the component needs to notify its container of some action.

The Grid User Interface

Looking at Figure 7-2 you can see that the Grid component has a basic grid user interface. It has column headings, rows, and columns, and the rows can be scrolled up and down. The column headings can be turned on and off. What you can't tell from the figure is that the Grid is editable when you click on a cell, it places the cursor there. Also, as rows are added or deleted, the Grid will expand or contract in size if the Grid component's height is not set. If the height is set, then vertical scroll bars will appear and disappear as needed.

The Grid's Implementation

Since HTML does not have a grid element, we need to implement the Grid component using the tags that it does have. The main HTML tags that we used to create the Grid component are shown below. The Grid's outermost HTML tag is the Web page's tag that has the Grid component attached to it. This tag could be a number of different tags, such as a <div> or <span>, or it could be an XML name space. Inside the container's tag is where the Grid component is actually created by adding HTML elements to it. Each of the elements added has the container element's ID prefixed with another name to create the element's ID. This will guarantee that each of the Grid's elements are unique on the page, assuming that the container element's ID is unique. Note in the screen below that there are spaces between all the

Grid's elements; these are shown so that you can see which elements are used, as they do not show up when the Grid is displayed.

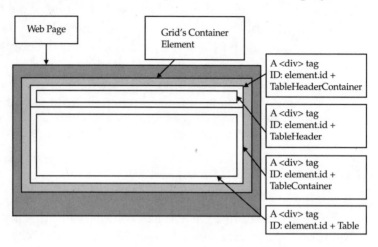

There are four main HTML elements that make up the Grid component: two sets of <div> and <table> tags. The top set is used to create the Grid's column header, and the bottom set is used to create the data display portion of the Grid. The reason for the two sets of tags is to allow the table data portion of the Grid to be scrolled while the column header is stationary. An HTML table is used because it uses row and cells similarly to the way a grid uses rows and columns. The DHTML DOM table object has many useful properties and methods to manipulate tables by rows and cells (column). The HTML <div> tags are used because they provide the capability to scroll elements that are within them. This is how the data portion of the Grid will be scrolled. We will see how this works later in the chapter. Right now, let's take a look at the code used to create these elements in the Grid component.

```
function ShowDocument(){
var eTable;
var eTableHeader;
var eTableContainer;
var eTableHeaderContainer;
var newRow;
var headerRow;
    eTableHeaderContainer = document.createElement("<div id='" + element.id
+ "TableHeaderContainer' ></div>");
    eTableHeaderContainer.style.overflowY = 'auto';
```

```
    eTableHeaderContainer.style.width = vwidth + "%";
    element.insertBefore(eTableHeaderContainer, null);
    eTableHeader = document.createElement("<table id='" + element.id +
"TableHeader' ></table>");
    eTableHeader.width = "100%";
    eTableHeader.style.borderWidth = 2;
    eTableHeader.style.borderBottomWidth = 0;
    eTableHeader.style.borderStyle = 'solid';
    eTableHeader.style.borderColor = 'black';
    eTableHeader.style.backgroundColor = 'silver';
    eTableHeader.style.borderCollapse = 'collapse';
    eTableHeader.style.tableLayout = 'fixed';
    buildRow(eTableHeader, 0);
    headerRow = eTableHeader.rows(0);
    if (vcolHeaders != 0){
        for (i = 0; i < vcolHeaders.length; i++){
            headerRow.children(i).style.borderStyle = 'inset';
            headerRow.children(i).style.borderWidth = '2';
            headerRow.children(i).innerText = vcolHeaders[i];
        }
    }
    if (!bolShowHeaders)
        eTableHeader.style.display = 'none';
        eTableHeaderContainer.insertBefore(eTableHeader, null);
        eTableContainer = document.createElement("<div id='" + element.id +
"TableContainer' ></div>");
    eTableContainer.style.overflowY = 'auto';
    if (vheight != null)
        eTableContainer.style.height = vheight;
    eTableContainer.style.width = vwidth + "%";
    element.insertBefore(eTableContainer, null);
    eTable = document.createElement("<table id='" + element.id + "Table'
></table>");
    eTable.noWrap = true;
    eTable.style.wordBreak = 'keep-all'
    eTable.style.borderWidth = 2;
    eTable.style.borderStyle = 'solid';
    eTable.style.borderColor = 'black';
    eTable.style.borderCollapse = 'collapse';
    eTable.style.tableLayout = 'fixed';
    eTable.style.width = "100%";
    eTableContainer.insertBefore(eTable, null);
}
```

NOTE: The entire code listing for the Grid component will not be shown in this chapter because it is too long. Refer to Chapter 1 for the location of the grid.htc file.

The ShowDocument function is called when the Grid component receives the ondocumentready event. The Grid declares this event using the DHTML behavior's Attach element. The ShowDocument function creates the four elements using the DHTML DOM document object's createElement method. For example, to create the column header container it does the following:

```
eTableHeaderContainer = document.createElement("<div id='" + element.id +
"TableHeaderContainer' ></div>");
```

The createElement method returns the element object that it created. In the example above, the eTableHeaderContainer is the newly created div object. The element object's properties can be set and retrieved, and its methods can be called. The table header container's style's width is set using the vwidth variable that is set via the Grid component's width property. The table header container is then inserted into the Web page's element using the following code:

```
element.insertBefore(eTableHeaderContainer, null);
```

The element object is the element in the Web page to which the component is attached. Its insertBefore method causes the eTableHeaderContainer object (the table header container) to be placed inside the element. The second parameter (null) is used to make the inserted element a child of an existing child in the element. In this case, the null value indicates that the table header container is not to be inserted as a child of another child of the element. After this line of code executes, the element's HTML would look like this, assuming it is a <span> tag:

```
<span id="someID"><div id="someIDTableHeaderContainer"></div></span>
```

A table element is created next. This table is used for the column headings. Some of the table element's properties are set to give it the look and feel of a grid column header. Its background is set to silver to give a shaded look, and it is given a black border. Its border is collapsed to join the row and cell borders to make it look more like a grid instead of an HTML table. The buildRow function (not exposed outside the component) is called to add a row to the table header element object. The row is then placed into a variable using the rows method of the table object, like this:

```
headerRow = eTableHeader.rows(0);
```

eTableHeader is the table object created earlier. It represents the table header. Since it is a table object, the rows collection is used to return a row object. The rows collection has one parameter, which is the row number to retrieve. Next the vcolheaders array, which contains the column headers, is checked to see if it has any entries. If it does have entries, then each entry is placed in the column header's columns using the syntax:

```
headerRow.children(i).innerHTML = vcolHeaders(i);
```

The children property of the headRow returns a cell of the row. Each cell's border width and style are set to give it a 3-D look. The last thing that is done to the column header object is to check if it should be displayed. The bolShowHeaders variable is used to specify whether the column headers should be displayed. It is set by the showColHeaders property of the component. By default it is set to true. If the column headers are not to be displayed, then the table object's display style property is set to "none." The table object is then inserted into the column header container object using the following code:

```
eTableHeaderContainer.insertBefore(eTableHeader, null);
```

The rest of the ShowDocument function creates a div element object and the table container, which contains the data portion of the Grid. Its overflowY style property is set to auto to allow it to display a vertical scroll bar when necessary. The table container is inserted into the attached element of the Web page. A table element object is created to hold the data for the Grid and is inserted into the table container.

Notice that the widths of both table elements are set to 100%. This causes the tables to always be the same size as their containers, div elements. The Grid's width is changed by setting the width of the two div elements. When the Grid's width is changed, the tables resize automatically inside the div elements.

The Grid's Functionality

In this section we will cover how the Grid component functions. If you place it on a Web page, by default it will not show up. The Grid's properties need to be set, and its methods need to executed in order for the grid to show on the page. This section covers how the Grid component

▼ adds and deletes rows

■ assigns and retrieves data at the cell and grid levels

▲ allows editing cells in the grid, as well as which events are fired to the Grid's container during editing

Adding Rows

Rows can be added and removed from the Grid by using the insertRow and deleteRow methods. An example of inserting a row is shown below:

```
objGrid.insertRow(insertBeforeRow);
```

NOTE: In the rest of the examples, objGrid will refer to the Web page's element that has the Grid component attached to it.

The insertRow method takes a row number as its solitary parameter. The row number is the row before which the new row will be inserted. For example, if the row passed into the insertRow method is 2, the new row will be place before row 2 in the grid. This will cause the current row 2 to become row 3. If 0 is passed to the insertRow method, it will insert a new row at the end of the grid. The Grid component's rows are 1 based. To insert a row, the Grid's insertRow method calls the buildRow function to create a row and insert it:

```
function insertRow(rowIndex){
    buildRow(eval(element.id + "Table"), rowIndex);
}
function buildRow(eleTableID, rowIndex){
var newRow;
var newCell;
    if (rowIndex == null)
        rowIndex = 0;
    if (eleTableID.rows.length < rowIndex - 1)
        rowIndex = 0;
    if (rowIndex < 0){
        alert("Invalid insert row: " + rowIndex);
        return;
    }
    newRow = eleTableID.insertRow(rowIndex - 1);
    if (vcols > 0){
        for (i = 0; i < vcols; i++){
            newCell = newRow.insertCell();
            newCell.width = ((1 / vcols) * 100)  + "%";
            newCell.height = vcellheight;
            newCell.innerText = " ";
            newCell.style.borderWidth = 2;
            newCell.style.borderColor = 'black';
            newCell.style.borderStyle = 'solid';
        }
    }
}
```

The buildRow function passes both the Table element and where
the new row should be inserted. It then validates the row number
passed to it. If the row number is null, then it set the value to 0 to
insert the row at the end of the grid. If a row number is passed in that
is larger than the number of rows in the table, then the row number
is set to 0 to insert the row at the end. If the row number passed in is
less then 0, then an error occurs. After these checks, a row element is
inserted into the table element using the table element's insertBefore

method. Then the cell elements are inserted into the row element and their style attributes are set.

Removing Rows

To delete a row, the Grid's deleteRow method is called, passing the row number to delete. The deleteRow method looks like this:

```
function deleteRow(rowIndex){
var regExp;
    if (rowIndex == null)
        return;
    regExp = / /g;
    if (rowIndex.replace(regExp, "") == "")
        return;
    if (eval(element.id + "Table").rows.length <= rowIndex - 1)
        return;
    objRow = eval(element.id + "Table").rows(rowIndex - 1);
    objRow.removeNode(true);
}
```

The deleteRow method makes sure a row number is passed in. It uses a regular expression to remove blank characters from the row number if there were any. It also checks that the row number exists within the table. It then gets the row from the rows collection of the table element and deletes the row by calling the row element's removeNode method. The true parameter causes all the children of the node being deleted to also be deleted.

Assigning and Retrieving Data at the Column Level

Data can be assigned and retrieved in two ways: for an individual column or for the entire grid. To assign/retrieve data by individual column, use the column property. The code below shows how to do this using the first row and first column of the grid:

```
Data = objGrid.column(1,1);
objGrid.column(1,1) = "Hello there";
```

To retrieve the data, the column get property is called. Its code is listed below:

```
function getColumnData(rowIdx, colIdx){
var headerRow;
var rowCnt;
    rowCnt = eval(element.id + "Table").rows.length;
    if ((rowIdx - 1 >= 0) && (rowIdx <= rowCnt)){
        headerRow = eval(element.id + "Table").rows.item(rowIdx - 1);
        if ((colIdx - 1 >= 0) && (colIdx <= cols)){
            if (headerRow.children(colIdx - 1).children.length > 0)
                return vlastEditedItem.children(0).value;
            else
                return headerRow.children(colIdx - 1).innerText;
        }
    }
}
```

The getColumnData function gets the row element by using the row number. It verifies that the row exists and then verifies that the column number is in the range of existing columns. The row element's children collection refers to the elements that are in the row element. For example, a row element would contain column elements (<td> HTML tag) for the table's cells. The cell elements are the children of the row element and are therefore in the row element's children collection. The cells can also have children. The following If statement checks if there are children for a cell:

```
if (headerRow.children(colIdx - 1).children.length > 0)
```

headerRow.children(colIdx - 1) represents the row and column, and the children.length checks if the column has children. If it does have children, then the vlastEditedItem.children(0).value is returned. This object is a text input element that is inside the cell of the table because the column is currently being edited. We will go over how editing a column works in the next section. If the column is not being edited, then the cell's innerHTML is returned.

The column's put function (putColumnData) uses the same logic to put data into to the column data. The column's data is passed to it, and it places the data into the column.

Assigning and Retrieving Data at the Grid Level

To load the data into the entire Grid, use the loadGridData method. The loadGridData method takes an array of data. Since JavaScript arrays are one-dimensional, the loadGridData method will divide the array into rows based on the number of columns the Grid component has. The loadGridData method's code is listed below:

```
function loadGridData(arrData){
var i;
var j;
var idx = 0;
var cntTblRow;
var row;
    if (vlastEditedItem != null)
        editCell(vlastEditedItem, true);
    cntTblRow = eval(element.id + "Table").rows.length;
    for (i = 0; i < arrData.length / vcols; i++){
        if (cntTblRow < i + 1)
            buildRow(eval(element.id + "Table"), 0);
        row = eval(element.id + "Table").rows(i);
        for (j = 0; j < vcols; j++){
            row.cells(j).innerText = arrData[idx];
            idx++;
        }
    }
}
```

The first thing the loadGridData method does is check if the Grid is being edited, and if it is, it saves the data being edited into the column that is being edited. It gets the number of rows the table element has. Then it loops through the array and divides it by the number of columns the Grid component has; thus it is looping by row. For each row of data in the array, the loop checks to see if the row exists. If the row does not exist, a new row is created with a call to the buildRow function. The current row element is then retrieved from the table element, and each row's cell data is set using the cell's innerText property. The idx variable is used as in index into the array.

To retrieve data from the entire Grid, use the getGridData method. This method functions in the same manner as the loadGrid method except it returns an array of data.

Editing Capabilities of the Grid

The Grid component has an editable property that can be turned on to edit a column of the Grid, or it can be used to turn off editing. By default the editable property is turned on. The Grid has two ways of editing columns: by the user clicking on the column or by using the editColumnData method. They both use the same logic, except in how they identify which column to edit.

We will examine how editing is done using the onclick event. The Grid component declares a public onclick event that is attached to the element in this manner:

```
<PUBLIC:ATTACH EVENT="onclick" for="element" ONEVENT="onClick()" />
```

The above declaration causes the Web page's element that has the Grid component attached to it to pass the event to the Grid component. The Grid then calls the onClick function:

```
function onClick(){
  if (!bolEditable)
        return;
  if (window.event.srcElement.tagName == 'TD')
        if (window.event.srcElement.parentElement.parentElement.parentElement.id ==
eval(element.id + "Table").id){
            if (vlastEditedItem != null)
                if (!editCell(vlastEditedItem, true)){
                    return;
                }
            if (editCell(window.event.srcElement, false))
                vlastEditedItem = window.event.srcElement;
        }

}
```

The first thing the onClick function does is check to make sure the Grid is editable. If it is not, it stops and returns. If it is editable, it uses the window object's event source element to make sure that the onClick event was raised for table's cell (<td> tag) element. If it was, it checks to make sure that the cell belongs to the data portion table of the Grid. Assuming that it is the cell of the data portion table, it checks the vlastEditedItem variable for null. The vlastEditedItem variable is used to hold the table cell that is currently being edited.

Next the editCell function is called to set up the editing mechanism. The editCell function serves two functions: to save data that is being edited back into the cell that is currently being edited and to place a text input element in the cell. The code for the editCell function follows:

```
function editCell(ele, save){
var eInputTextBox;
var data;
var regExp = / /g;
var objEvent;
    if (save){
        data = vlastEditedItem.children(0).value;
        objEvent = createEventObject();
        objEvent.data = data;
        objEvent.result = true;
        eeID.fire(objEvent);
        if (objEvent.result){
            ele.removeChild(ele.children(0));
            vlastEditedItem = null;
            ele.innerText = data;
            ele.title = data;
        }
        else{
            eval(element.id + "CellInputTextBox").focus();
            return false;
        }
    }
    else{
        objEvent = createEventObject();
        objEvent.data = ele.innerText;
        objEvent.result = true;
        seID.fire(objEvent);
        if (!objEvent.result)
            return false;
        eInputTextBox = document.createElement("<input style='border:0
none' type='text' id='" + element.id + "CellInputTextBox' ></input>");
        eInputTextBox.value = ele.innerText;
        eInputTextBox.style.width = "100%";
```

```
        eInputTextBox.style.height = "100%";
        ele.innerText = "";
        ele.insertBefore(eInputTextBox, null);
        eInputTextBox.focus();
    }
    return true;
}
```

Assuming that the table is currently being edited, the onClick function calls the editCell function to save the data in the cell by passing true to editCell as its second parameter. In the editCell function, it checks if the data should be saved. If yes, then it stores the input element's data in a temp variable. An event object is created to inform the Web page element that the editing for this cell is about to end. The event passes the edited data value up to the Web page element. In order for the Web page's element to respond to the event, it must declare the onEndEdit event like this:

```
<div class="grid" id="objGrid" onEndEdit="endEdit()"></div>
```

The editCell function then waits for a reply from the Web page element. The Web page element can send a result back like this:

```
function endEdit(){
    window.event.result = false;
}
```

When endEdit executes, it sets the result property of the window's event object. When this function ends, control is returned to the statement after the event was raised in the editCell function. If the Web page element does not trap the onClick event, the event returns immediately to the editCell function. The editCell function looks at the window event object's result property. If it is true, the text input element is removed from the cell, the data from the input element is placed into the cell's innerText property, and the cell's title is set to be the data. The title property is like a tool tip: it is used in case all the data does not show in the cell; then a tool tip will pop up when the mouse is over the cell. If the event object's result is false, the input element is given the focus, and editCell returns false and stops.

Back in the onClick function, if the first call to editCell returns false, then the onClick function ends, and the editing of the new cell is not done. If it returns true, the second call to editCell is made to allow the clicked cell to be edited. This time, when editCell is called it passes both the element that was clicked and false as parameters, telling editCell to edit the cell. In the editCell function, an event is created to notify the Web page element that an edit is about to start. This is the same idea as the onEndEdit event, except this one tells the container that an edit is about to start.

If the Web page element traps the event, it can send back the event with a true or false to editCell. If it sends true, then a text input element is created and assigned the cell's innerText. The cell's innerText is then cleared, and the input element is inserted into the cell. The input element is then given focus. If the Web page element sends back a false, then the edit is canceled.

Miscellaneous Functions

The Grid component provides a couple of miscellaneous functions. The read-only rows property returns the number of rows in the Grid. The cols property returns the number of columns the Grid has. It will set the number of columns if it has not already been set. Once the number of columns has been set, that number cannot be changed. When working with a grid, it is best to pass the number of columns that the grid will have when the grid is instantiated on the Web page. The colsHeader property is used to assign and retrieve individual column headers, and the colHeaders property is used to assign the entire column header. The colHeaders property uses a string with each column heading separated by a comma to assign the column headings. The colHeaders property will return a string in the same manner when it retrieves the column headings. The width and height of the Grid component can be set with the width and height properties. The width is the percentage of the page's width. The height property can be set in either pixels or percent of the page's height.

AN EXAMPLE OF A TEST PAGE

As the component is being developed, it is a good idea to test it. Since a component cannot be executed directly, it will need a test page. The test page is only used by the person developing the component so it does not need to be real fancy. Still, it should execute all the component's functions. The test page should be saved with the component in a source code management tool so that as the component is changed the test page can be used to retest it. Figure 7-3 shows the test page we used for the Grid component.

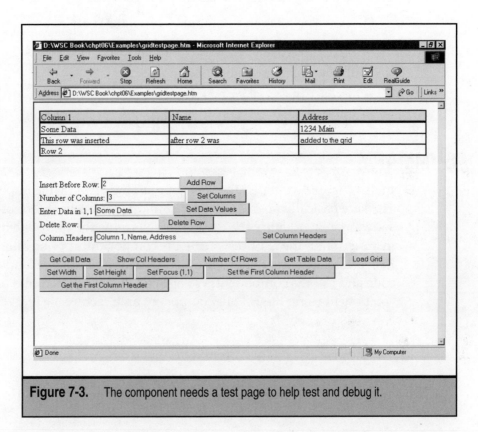

Figure 7-3. The component needs a test page to help test and debug it.

THE GRID COMPONENT EXTENSION

One of the nice features of the Grid component is that its file size is only 11K. The Grid component is tiny when compared to some ActiveX grid controls, which are 200K to 800K in size. The Grid component does not have all the features of ActiveX grid controls, but it could be extended to include them. Here are just a few features that could be added:

▼ Navigating the Grid with the arrow keys.

■ Using the Tab key at the end of a row to insert a new row.

■ An event that tells when a row is about to be deleted.

■ A <select> tag in a column to simulate a combo box control.

■ Sorting the Grid by a column.

■ Built-in column validation.

■ Giving the Grid a 3-D look.

▲ Tying the Grid's data to an XML data source.

SUMMARY

In this chapter we stated the steps of building an HTML component. They are basically no different than building any other piece of software: first, identify the users and determine the component's features. From the features, create the component's public interface, then create the component's user interface, if it needs one, and then code and test the component. We applied these steps to build a Grid component using the HTML component architecture.

PART III

XML Technologies

CHAPTER 8

XML and the XML Document Object Model

A common statement we have been hearing to describe people's excitement for XML (Extensible Markup Language) is "XML will do for data what HTML has done for the user interface." You also may have heard it and wondered what it really means, or you may have been skeptical about this new XML technology. We are going to show you how to use XML, and we'll discuss the advantages of using this exciting new technology. In the next five chapters, we will take you through XML and the technology involved with the data sharing standard.

In this chapter we introduce you to XML and show you how to create an XML document. Then we show you how to use the XML document object model (DOM) to

▼ Load and save an XML document.

■ Gather information about and navigate the XML tree.

■ Get and set data and attributes.

■ Modify the XML tree.

▲ Send data back to the server.

OVERVIEW OF XML

Through the use of HTML, OSS, JavaScript, GIFs, and JPEGs, we have a common way to describe to users the visual display of a particular page. This is a very necessary set of standards; however, these interface elements are both inappropriate and insufficient to describe and manage data. You might be thinking, "But I have data in my Web pages," but in reality this data is a display mechanism (HTML) describing how the page should look.

What is needed is a common way to exchange data, a way so that every piece of software can easily recognize the data and its format. What we are about to show you is how to separate data from your Web pages, a separation similar to what we showed you with DHTML behaviors. DHTML behaviors provide a separation of display logic from the script logic and functionality. XML provides a mechanism to separate the data from the display logic, and it provides a common mechanism to access this new data. This common data format could be used as a vehicle for businesses to exchange transactions or to share databases. Simply put, XML provides a standard method for moving structured data around on the Internet, just as we move HTML pages around today.

XML is a markup language that is used to describe documents that contain structured information. The XML syntax is currently only a 1.0 specification, but considering its young age, it is remarkably useful and complete. The data in an XML document is stored within a hierarchical tree-type structure, which allows for relationships to be defined between the data. The syntax of XML is similar to HTML in that it is a simple, text tag–based language. But where XML differs is in the fact it is extensible, a type of metalanguage. What this means is that with XML you can define your own tags and structural relationships, without being limited to the set of predefined tags that are made available to you by the browser.

With XML, the interpretation of the data or the semantics is implemented by the viewing application that processes the data. Because the viewing application determines the semantics, or how to display the data, multiple views of the same data can be presented to the user. This is particularly useful in Web pages where the data can be manipulated and viewed in multiple formats without returning to the server to download the data simply because the user wishes to see the data in a different format.

You can have more meaningful searches under XML. The reason for this is that, with XML, data can be more uniquely tagged, allowing for more meaningful searches. With this unique tagging system, it is now possible to have searching applications look for detailed information about a particular item without knowing the schema of a particular database.

Because of the XML's extensibility and flexibility, data from different sources can be exchanged without the need to know the underlying data format or where the data came from. In connection with this, industry standard formats can be developed to allow business-to-business sharing of information. This type of sharing will be similar to today's EDI (electronic data interchange) but without the costs and difficulties of implementing such a system. Currently there are efforts already underway from Microsoft and other companies (such as the BizTalk Organization, http://www.biztalk.org) to develop a set of industry standard XML schemas, and we expect to see a lot of development in these areas in the next couple of years.

ANATOMY OF AN XML DOCUMENT

An XML document is composed of XML elements, similar to the way an HTML page is composed of HTML elements. To help eliminate confusion, we need to note that an XML element is sometimes referred to as a node, because the layout of an XML document is tree based. An XML element is made up of a start tag, an end tag, and the data in between. The start and end tags serve to describe the data that is between the two tags. The data inside the start and end tags is the value for that element. For example, the following XML element is Artist and the data or the value is Citizen King:

```
<Artist>Citizen King</Artist>
```

The element's tag name, Artist, describes the value that is inside of the tag. By using this tag's name, we can differentiate between different data that might be in the same document but that has a different meaning. For example, we could have another element in the same document that describes works for that Artist:

```
<Title>Mobile Estates</Title>
```

One important thing to note about XML is that it is case-sensitive, so

```
<Title><title>
```

would be considered two different elements.

In addition to the data that is inside of the start and end tags of an element, you can also have attributes that further describe the element or contain additional information about the element. Attributes are not required items and you can also have multiple attributes on one element if so desired; however, a particular attribute name can be used only once for an element. Attributes simply contain the name of the attribute and the value of the attribute in quotes, separated by an = sign. For example the following Title element contains the Year the Title was released:

```
<Title Year="1999">Mobile Estates</Title>
```

If you have multiple attributes for a particular element, the order in which they appear does not matter. The following shows the use of multiple attributes:

```
<Title Year="1999" Label="Warner Brothers">Mobile Estates</Title>
```

In addition, attributes are useful because you can set the default value, which cannot be done with an element.

The next thing to do with your XML elements is to create an XML document out of the individual elements. An XML document always starts out with a unique first element that acts as the root node for the document. Elements can have nested elements inside of them, but this is not a requirement. By nesting elements inside of another element, we are creating a relationship between the elements and defining the structure of the data. The following shows a simple XML document with the unique root element of CDList:

CdList1.xml

```
<CDList>
  <Artist>
    <Name>Citizen King</Name>
    <Titles>
       <Title Year="1999" Label="Warner Brothers">Mobile Estates</Title>
       <Title Year="1996" Label="Don't Records">Brown Paper Bag</Title>
    </Titles>
  </Artist>
  <Artist>
    <Name>Live</Name>
    <Titles>
       <Title Year="1997" Label="Radioactive Records">Secret Samadhi</Title>
       <Title Year="1994" Label="Radioactive Records">Throwing Copper</Title>
    </Titles>
  </Artist>
</CDList>
```

Writing Well-Formed Documents

XML is a highly structured language, and it is important that all XML be well-formed. By well-formed, what we are saying is that the document must follow a certain set of rules so that any parser can recognize the data and the format. Some of the rules of well-formatted documents (known as well-formed XML) we have covered already, but here's the complete list:

▼ Start tags must have end tags to match.

■ XML tags are case-sensitive.

■ Each XML document must have a unique root element for the complete document.

■ Elements cannot overlap. Overlapping is when you have an end tag of an element after the end tag of a prior element. For example the following is not well-formed:

```
<Artist>Compilation
  <Title>Hits of the 90s<SubTitle>
  </Title>A Decade of Alternative Music</SubTitle>
</Artist>
```

To fix the problem of the tags overlapping you rewrite as follows:

```
<Artist>Compilation
  <Title>Hits of the 90s</Title>
  <SubTitle>A Decade of Alternative Music</SubTitle>
</Artist>
```

■ Denote empty elements with either

```
<title/>
```

or

```
<title></title>
```

▲ Reserved characters: several characters are used directly as part of the XML syntax and so need to be replaced with a special sequence of case-sensitive characters, called *entities* in XML:

Reserved Character	Replacement
<	&lt;
&	&amp;
>	&gt;
"	&quot;
'	&apos;

For example, the text *Hits & Works from the 90's* would need to be encoded as *Hits & Works from the 90's*.

Making XML Self-Documenting

In addition to the rules enforced by the well-formatting standard, you can also attach a set of rules that describe the document and the relationship between elements, making the document self-describing. These rules can help an application understand the layout of the data if it does not have a built-in description of the format. There are currently two methods for creating the rules that accompany the document: document type definitions (DTD) and schemas. Schemas are a new technology, which will eventually replace DTD; they are based on XML itself and thus are extensible and allow the author to move beyond the functionality found in DTDs. We cover schemas later on in this book in Chapter 11; however, we want to make you aware that there is a way to create your own user-defined rules for the document layout.

Serving Up XML Documents

You might be asking yourself, "Now that I know the format of an XML document, what do I do with it?" Simply put, the same things you do with HTML. Because XML is transferred the same as any other text document, you can save your XML to a file with the extension of .xml and make the file available statically. If you wish, you can generate your XML document dynamically using the same tools, such as Active Server Pages or CGI, that you use to your generate HTML on the server. In addition to these standard tools, Microsoft (using

ADO 2.5 or later and SQL Server add-on tools) and other vendors are creating tools that will allow you to automatically pull data from a database in XML document format. These tools will provide some excellent functionality, but they are beyond the scope of this book.

> **NOTE:** If you are using Active Server Pages to dynamically create your XML documents, you must set the content type to text/xml before any XML is sent to the browser. The following shows you how to set the content type: *<% Response.ContentType = "text/xml" %>* .

Using Internet Explorer's XML Parser to Display XML

By default, Internet Explorer 5.0 has the ability to display an XML document in a tree format. This display can be a useful tool to validate that your XML file is well-formed, and it can also be used to get a quick view of your XML document. IE 5 has a built-in XML parser, which is responsible for taking the text stream and validating its format. Figure 8-1 shows an example of our well-formed list of

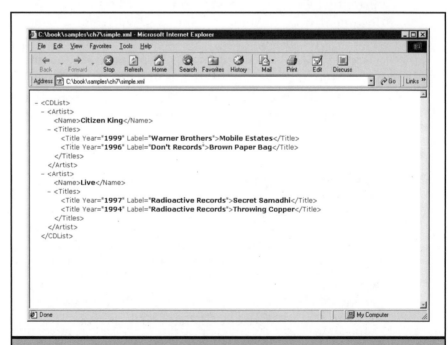

Figure 8-1. Internet Explorer's built-in tree view of a document

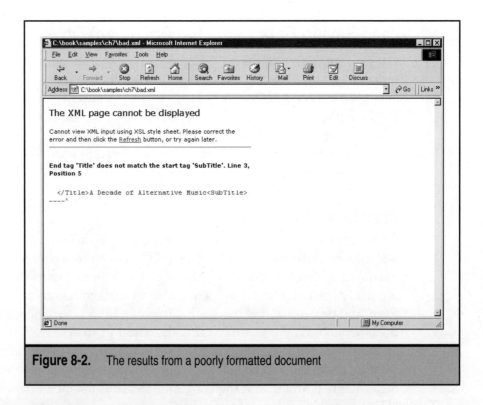

Figure 8-2.   The results from a poorly formatted document

CDs in IE 5. In contrast, Figure 8-2 shows our example of a poorly
formed XML document and what the output is from IE 5.

USING THE XML DOM

The XML document object model (DOM) is a set of objects that can be
used to programmatically navigate and access the data in an XML
document. The DOM is based on a tree model, and each XML element
is known as a *node*. After the XML document has been loaded, the
XML parser automatically creates all of the different objects that make
up the object model. One important thing to note is that the discussion
of the document object model is based on the object model available in
IE 5, which is the only browser that currently natively supports XML.
Microsoft has added extensions to the W3C Consortium's version of
the DOM to support the following functionality: name spaces, data
types, XML schemas, XSL operations, asynchronous loading, and
document saving. Almost all of this functionality is currently under
consideration by the W3C for addition to the standard DOM.

Loading and Saving Data Using the Document Object

The first step in using the DOM is to load an XML document (official name: XMLDOMDocument) so that the parser can create all of the objects based on the document loaded. The document object is the object that represents the top of the tree, and it is used to load the data and act as the gateway to the remainder of the child objects. The document object is the only object that is created in code—all of the other objects are accessed or are created from the document object.

Creating the Document Object

The document object can be created using several different methods, depending on the environment (from HTML or from script) in which the object is being created. It is important to remember that XML DOM is equally useful on both the client platform and on the server platform, and because of this there are different methods to create the document object. If you are creating the object in an HTML page, there is a new tag named (fittingly) XML that provides the functionality of creating the document object. This type of functionality is becoming increasingly popular, and there are more reasons to embed data into HTML pages. This type of functionality is referred to as *XML data islands*, because we are embedding a piece of data inside a larger HTML document. The document object can be created very simply using data islands. All that you need to do is to add an XML tag to your HTML document. This new XML tag should have the ID attribute set, because it will be the way you can reference the document object. The following shows an example of creating the document object from an XML data island:

```
<HTML>
...
<XML ID="MyXMLDocumentObject" />
...
</HTML>
```

To create an XML object or any other type of ActiveX object using JavaScript, you can employ the following method to create the new object: new ActiveXObject. When you are creating the object from script, there are two types of threading models that can be used: free-threaded or rental threaded. By threading models we are referring to the way that the object reacts to concurrent access by different processes, or threads. In most cases you will want to create the object using the rental-threaded model, because of its increased performance and because in most cases you will not have multiple threads accessing your XML document object. There are cases where multiple threads may be accessing the document object, such as in a server scenario, where you will want to make sure that the threads do not interfere with one another, and in these cases you would want to create a free-threaded object. An example of this is if you were to load an XML document to be used by multiple people and potentially multiple threads (such as an application-level variable in Active Server Pages).

Here is an example of how to create a rental-threaded model:

```
var Rental = new ActiveXObject("Microsoft.XMLDOM");
```

This example shows how to create a free-threaded model:

```
var Free = new ActiveXObject("Microsoft.FreeThreadedXMLDOM");
```

Security Issues and Compatibility

One thing you need to be aware of is that if you are creating your document objects using script within a Web page, there are potential compatibility and security issues. The new ActiveXObject will probably be supported only by Internet Explorer and not other browsers such as Netscape's. This really isn't much of an issue now because Netscape doesn't currently support XML, but they likely will in the near future (sometime in 2000). Another thing to be aware of is that if the user has their security settings set to High in Internet Explorer, the browser will not allow the creation of an ActiveXObject even though the object is included with the browser. You can, of course, trap for this error and display a message to the user, but we recommend using the XML tag if you are using XML from inside of the browser. On the server side, the new ActiveXObject is the only way to create the document object and by default becomes the preferred technique.

Loading Data

In addition to simply creating the document object, the XML tag allows you to load the document object with data from inside the tag. There are two nonscript methods to load data into data islands: include the actual XML inside the HTML page or reference an external document.

An in-line XML data island can embed the XML directly inside of the XML tag, as follows:

```
<HTML>
...
<XML ID="Inline">
  <MusicalArtist>
    <Artist>Match Box 20</Artist>
    <Artist>Smashing Pumpkins</Artist>
  </MusicalArtist>
</XML>
...
</HTML>
```

The more commonly used and more functional version of data islands is to load the document from another external source, as shown here:

```
<HTML>
...
<XML ID="ExternalFile" SRC="http://myserver.com/artists.xml" />
...
</HTML>
```

There are two methods that are built into the document object that allow you to load XML from script. These methods can be executed against document objects that were created using either the HTML tag method or the script method. The two methods are loadXML and load. The loadXML method takes one parameter, which is a string containing the XML to load into the document object and returns the status of whether the data was successfully loaded. The following example shows how to use the loadXML method:

loadXML.htm

```
<html>
<script Language="JavaScript">
function loadXML(){
  var result = myDoc.loadXML("<MusicalArtist><Artist>Match Box
20</Artist><Artist>Smashing Pumpkins</Artist></MusicalArtist>");
}
</script>
<body onLoad="loadXML()">
<xml id="myDoc"></xml>
</body>
</html>
```

The load method is similar to the loadXML method, except the one parameter that this method takes is a URL for the location of the XML document. Like the loadXML method, the load method returns the status of whether the document was successfully loaded. The following is an example of calling the load method:

```
var result = myDoc.load("http://myserver.com/sample.xml");
```

Prior to loading the data into an XML document object, there are flags that can be set to affect the way the XML document is parsed. One of the most important flags is the async flag. This flag tells the parser if asynchronous download of the XML document is permitted. The default value for this flag is true, which means the parser will return immediately from the load or loadXML call, and the next line of your code will be executed, possibly before the parser has parsed the complete document. In some cases this may cause a problem if you want to access the object right after the call. To handle these cases, you can set the async property to false, and the parser will not return from the call until the complete document has been loaded and parsed.

Loading Data Asynchronously

In some cases, however, you may wish to implement a background or asynchronous loading of the data. By leaving the async property set to its default true, the parser will return from the call and asynchronously begin

Status (Ready State Value)	Description
loading	The load is in progress, but the data has not started parsing yet.
loaded	The object is reading and parsing data, but the object model is not yet available.
interactive	A portion of the data has been read and parsed, and the object model is available on a partial basis, but it is read only.
complete	The document has been completely loaded, and if successful, the entire complete object model is available. Note: a completed, yet unsuccessful load will also return complete.

Table 8-1. Possible Values of the readyState Property

downloading and parsing the document. This is great functionality, but it would be nice to be notified when the parser has completed. To do this, you can set the onreadystatechange property of the document object to the name of the event handler (function) that should be called, or you can trap the onreadystatechange event for the object. Inside of the function where you trap the ready state change, you will need to check the value of the readyState property to see if the document has completed loading. The reason for this is because the ready state has different values depending on what state the document is in. The onreadystatechange event is fired any time the ready state changes values. Table 8-1 lists the different states of the readyState property and the meaning of each. (Note: currently the documentation on the Microsoft Developers Network Site states that an integer value is returned, but this is not the case because the string values shown in the table are the values actually returned.)

The following shows an example of how to asynchronously download an XML document and how to know when the parser has made the object model available for full use:

Async.htm

```
<html>
<script Language="JavaScript">
function loadXML(){
  AsyncDoc.onreadystatechange = checkState;
  AsyncDoc.load("big.xml");
}
function checkState(){
  var currentState = AsyncDoc.readyState;
  if (currentState == "complete")
    alert("Document is ready for use.");
}
</script>
<xml ID="AsyncDoc"></xml>
<input type="button" value="Load File Async." onclick="loadXML()">
</html>
```

One thing to note about the prior example is that if you are capturing the onreadystatechange where the XML file is resident on your local machine or is available on a fast network link, the parser loads and parses the file very quickly. All of the events are raised for the different ready states, but the order in which the events are processed may not be what you expect. The reason for this is because the events are occurring too rapidly for the script to handle the events, and this causes the unpredictable event processing sequence.

Once you have started an asynchronous download, you can call the abort method on the document object to stop the object from continuing to be downloaded. An important thing to note is that any data that has been downloaded and parsed up to this point is discarded. If you call the abort after the readyState has changed to complete, no action is taken and the document remains intact.

Using the Parse Error Object

If there is any incorrectly formed XML you can retrieve detailed error information about it from the parse error object (official name: XMLDOMParseError), which is part of the DOM. The parse error object can be retrieved via the parseError property that is part of the document object. The object contains detailed information about the last error that occurred while parsing the document. The object includes properties to retrieve the error number, line number, character position, and text description for the error. The following shows an example of using the parse error object to retrieve the description of the error. For a full list of all of the properties in the parse error object, see Table 8-2.

Bad.htm

```
<html>
<script Language="JavaScript">
function load(){
    myTag.load("bad.xml");
    alert("The reason why the file is bad is: " + myTag.parseError.reason);
}
</script>
<body onLoad="load()">
<xml id="myTag"></xml>
</body>
</html>
```

Property	Description
errorCode	Contains the error number for the last error.
filepos	Returns the exact character number in the file where the error occurred.
line	Returns the line number where the error occurred.
linepos	Returns the position in the line of the error.
reason	Returns a text description of the error.
srcText	Returns the text of the line where the error occurred.
url	Returns the URL of the document containing the error.

Table 8-2. Properties of the Parse Error Object

Saving Data

The document object contains a save method that you can simply pass in the location to which the XML file should be saved. There are, of course, browser restrictions on saving the document to a client's machine, and any attempt to do so will result in a permission denied error; however, in a server environment, it is only limited to the operating system's file security. In addition to simply passing in the path of where to save the file, other objects can be passed into the save method, which gives the save method different functionality. One of the objects that can be passed into the save method is the response object from an Active Server Page. If you pass in the response object, the document is sent back to the client that called the script. In addition to the response object, you can pass in another document object, which has the same effect as saving the document and then reloading it into the object that was passed in, checking the persistability of the XML document.

Gathering Information and Navigating the XML Tree

After having successfully loaded the XML document, you will want to navigate in the tree and eventually remove the data from the XML nodes. One thing we need to discuss at this point is the different objects you will be encountering while navigating the document. To fully understand the implementation of the object model, you need to understand how the object model is constructed. There is a set of base objects from which other objects can be built or, in many cases, be used directly to implement the object model. These base objects include the following: XMLDOMDocument, XMLDOMNode, XMLDOMNodeList, XMLDOMNamedNodeMap, XMLDOMParseError, XMLHttpRequest, and XTLRuntime. We have already become familiar with the XMLDOMDocument and the XMLDOMParseError base objects in our discussion about loading and saving data, and we will be discussing most of the other objects later in this chapter.

The XMLDOMNode is an object that is used as the base element for some of the most important objects in the object model, the XMLDOMElement object and the XMLDOMAttribute object. These objects use the base functionality available in the XMLDOMNode object to hold onto data and navigational functionality and extend this functionality to add the support needed for elements and attributes.

In order to illustrate the details of navigating the different nodes in a document, we need to make you aware of some simple properties that are available to both types of objects (document objects and node objects). The nodeName property simply returns the name of the XML element. For example, if the XML for an element was *<sample>Data</sample>*, the nodeName properties value would be *sample*. Another simple but useful property is the xml property. The xml property returns a string that contains all of the XML, including attributes, for that node and all of the XML for the descendant nodes.

When talking about navigation, once again the document object is where all of the functionality begins. The document object contains the documentElement property; this property returns an object (XMLDOMElement) that represents the root node of the XML document. It is important to note that with the document element, we are actually now dealing with the data from the XML document and not the document object we used to load and manage the data.

Finding Elements by Name

As we have stated earlier, the documentElement property of the document object represents the root of the XML document; it is from here we begin navigating to the different nodes in the document. Both XML elements and the document object support a method called getElementsByTagName. This method is used to find all of the descendant elements that match the string parameter passed in, which is the element name to find. If you wish, you can pass in "*" to return all of the descendent elements of the element or all the elements in the document (if executed against the document object). The method returns an object, which is a collection of XML elements that have matching names. This type of object is called an XML node list (XMLDOMNodeList).

The node list supports both a sequential navigation through the collection and also random navigation through the index property. The following is an example of using the XML node list object and also the getElementsByTagName method. In addition to this, Table 8-3 lists all of the methods and properties of the XML node

list object. The example allows the user to enter in the name of the
XML nodes to search for and then navigate through the list of
elements returned, and it displays the XML for the current element.
The sample allows the user to sequentially navigate through the
document, or if they choose the user can enter the specific node
number they wish to see the XML for.

Navigate1.htm

```
<html>
<script Language="JavaScript">
var matchingNodes=null;
var position;
function getMatching(){
  var searchName = xmlName.value;
  matchingNodes = xmlDoc.documentElement.getElementsByTagName(searchName);
  if (matchingNodes.length == 0){
    alert("No matching nodes.");
    status.innerHTML = "";
  }
  else{
    position = 0;
    setStatus();
    rawXML.innerText = matchingNodes.item(0).xml;
  }
}
function setStatus(){
  navStatus.innerHTML = "Matching nodes: " + matchingNodes.length +
" Current position: " + position;
}
function move(){
  var newNode = matchingNodes.nextNode();
  if (newNode == null){
    alert("At end of list. I will reset the list to the beginning");
    matchingNodes.reset();
    newNode = matchingNodes.nextNode();
  }
  rawXML.innerText = newNode.xml;
  position++;
```

```
      setStatus();
   }
   function getRandom(){
     var randomNode = nodeNumber.value;
     var newNode = matchingNodes.item(randomNode);
     if (newNode == null)
       alert("Node does not exist.");
     else
       alert(newNode.xml);
   }
   </script>
   <body>
   <p align="center"><b>Get Named Node Example</b></p>
   <xml ID="xmlDoc" src="big.xml"></xml>
   Search For:<input type="Text" ID="xmlName">
   <input type="button" value="Find Matching" onClick="getMatching()"><BR>
   <div ID="navStatus"> </div>
   <p><input type="button" value="Move Next" onClick="move()"></p>
   <p>Nodes XML:</p>
   <div ID="rawXML"> </div>
   <p>Look Up Node Number:<input type="Text" ID="nodeNumber" length="4">
   <input type="button" value="Get Node's XML" onClick="getRandom()"></p>
   </body>
   </html>
```

Property/Method()	Description
item(index)	Provides random access to the collection and is used to return a specific member of the collection.
length	The number of items in the collection.
nextNode()	Used for sequential access to the collection. Returns the next node in the collection, or returns null if we are at the end of the collection.
reset()	Resets the collection pointer to the beginning of the collection.

Table 8-3.   Properties and Methods for the XML Node List Object

Navigating through the Document

In addition to finding a collection of nodes, you can navigate through the document's elements individually. From any element in the tree you can access the parent, children, or siblings of that element. To access the element's parent, you can simply call the parentNode property of the element, and you will be returned a reference to the parent or a null if the element has no parent. If you wish to navigate from a particular element to its sibling, you can call either the previousSibling or nextSibling to get a reference to the element's sibling (or a null if the requested sibling does not exist).

In addition to dealing with the sibling and parent of an element, you can work with the children of the element. By calling the hasChildNodes method, you can determine if the element has any children. After you know that the element has children you can get the first or last child nodes by getting the values of the firstChild or lastChild properties. In addition to these methods to view the children of an element, you can get an XML node list containing all of the children of the element by calling the childNodes property. The following code shows examples of all of the methods and properties to navigate up and down an XML document.

Navigate2.htm

```
<html>
<script Language="JavaScript">
var activeElement;
var showXML=false;
function loadXML(){
  xmlDocObject.async = false;
  xmlDocObject.load("big.xml");
  activeElement = xmlDocObject.documentElement.firstChild;
  setMessages();
}
function changeActive(direction){
  var tempElement;
  switch (direction) {
    case "Next":
      tempElement = activeElement.nextSibling;
      break;
```

```
       case "Previous":
         tempElement = activeElement.previousSibling;
         break;
       case "ParentElement":
         tempElement = activeElement.parentNode;
         break;
       case "First":
         tempElement = activeElement.firstChild;
         break;
       case "Last":
         tempElement = activeElement.lastChild;
     }
   if (tempElement == null)
     alert("Action causes an invalid active element.");
   else{
     activeElement = tempElement;
     setMessages();
   }
 }
function setMessages(){
   if (showXML == true)
     xmlSource.innerText =  "Current Elements XML:" + activeElement.xml;
   else
     xmlSource.innerText = "";
   if (activeElement.hasChildNodes() == false)
     info.innerText = "The current element does not have children.
The node type is: " + activeElement.nodeName;
   else
     info.innerText = "The current element has " +
activeElement.childNodes.length + " direct children. The node type is: " +
activeElement.nodeName;
   }
function showHide(){
   if (showXML == false){
     xmlSource.innerText =  activeElement.xml;
     showXML = true;
   }
```

```
  else{
    xmlSource.innerText = "";
    showXML = false;
  }
}
</script>
<body onLoad="loadXML()">
<xml ID="xmlDocObject"></xml>
<p align="center"><b>Simply Navigating An XML Document</b></p>
<div ID="xmlSource"> </div><p><div ID="info"> </div>
<input type="button" value="Next Sibling" onClick="changeActive('Next')">
<input type="button" value="Previous Sibling"
onClick="changeActive('Previous')">
<input type="button" value="Set Parent Active"
onClick="changeActive('ParentElement')">
<input type="button" value="First Child" onClick="changeActive('First')">
<input type="button" value="Last Child" onClick="changeActive('Last')">
<input type="button" value="Show / Hide Source" onClick="showHide()">
</body></html>
```

Using XSL to Navigate

In addition to the methods that we have already discussed for
navigating the XML document, there are additional methods that
use the Extensible Stylesheet Language (XSL) to navigate XML data
structures. The navigational methods of selectSingleNode and
selectNodes use XSL pattern matching to return the first node or
all the nodes that match the XSL query. We cover these methods,
the XSL pattern matching syntax, and XSL overall in Chapter 10, but
we wanted to mention these methods here because they are very
powerful tools that are available to navigate the XML tree.

Getting and Setting Data and Attributes in a Node

Getting there is only half of the fun. Now that we have finally arrived
at the node we wish to interrogate, it is time to get and set the value
for the node and also retrieve the values of, and create attributes for,
the node.

Getting and Setting Data

To retrieve and set an element's value (the text in between the tags), you can use the text property of the node. There is, however, an issue to be aware of when using the text property that involves getting the value from a parent element. To illustrate the issue, let's say you have an XML document that looks like the following:

```
<sample>
  <node1>Data For Node 1
    <node2>Some Data</node2>
  </node1>
</sample>
```

Now you make your way down to the node1 element, and you wish to retrieve the data for that node using the text method. What you would expect to be returned is the string *Data For Node 1*, but what you really get is *Data For Node 1 Some Data*. The reason for this is that the text method is returning all of the text that is inside of the tag, whether it is inside of another tag or not.

The answer to how to fix the problem of getting the text from the parent node can be found in our example that dealt with navigating the nodes of an XML document. If you played around with that example, you may have noticed something a little curious when you navigated down to what you thought was the lowest-level node. What is interesting is that the node actually has a child. If you navigate down to that child node, you will notice that the element type is #text. What we have found here is the text node that is created by the parser to hold onto the data for that particular node.

If an element has data between the tags, an XML text object is created to hold onto that data, and this object becomes the first child of that element. In cases where there is both data and other XML elements between the tags, the text object is created and becomes the first child of the element and becomes a sibling to the other XML elements. So to solve the problem we had above, we can access the text object and remove the data from that object itself by using the object's text property or the nodeValue property.

The nodeValue property returns a null value for an XML element. Because the node does not contain the value, the value is actually in the text node, as we have discovered. In essence what the text property for an XML element is doing is mapping the value to the text node's value. To get the text object, you can simply use the first child to get the text node, or you can loop through the nodes looking for the element where the nodeType equals 3 (NODE_TEXT), which is the #text node. One thing to note about using the first child method is that it is not documented that the text object will always be the first child; this is just the way that the parser is currently implemented. The following is a code snippet, which is a function that fixes the problem and returns the text value for the passed in element.

```
function getTextValue(element){
  var col = element.childNodes;
  var node = col.nextNode();
  while (node != null){
    if (node.nodeType == 3)
      return node.text;
    node = col.nextNode();
}}
```

It is our recommendation that you do not use the parent node to store data in the fashion we have shown. However we are aware in some cases you may not be in charge of formulating the XML document layout, and this is why we showed you the work around. A preferable solution would be to create a node under the parent to store the data or to store the data in an attribute of the parent element. Not only will this lead to cleaner code, but it will also make humanly reading the XML easier.

Working with Attributes

Retrieving, adding, and deleting data from attributes involves working with a type of object we have yet to cover, called a named node collection (official name: XMLDOMNamedNodeMap collection object). A named node collection object is similar to the XML node collection object, except, as the name suggests, the elements can be referenced by name in addition to being referenced by index or sequential access. For a list of the properties and methods of a named node collection object, see Table 8-4.

Property/Method()	Description
getNamedItem(name)	Retrieves the item with the specified name.
getQualifiedItem(baseName, nameSpaceURI)	Returns the attribute with the specified name space and attribute name.
item(index)	Provides random access to the collection and is used to return a specific member of the collection.
length	The number of items in the collection.
nextNode()	Used for sequential access to the collection. Returns the next node in the collection, or returns null if we are at the end of the collection.
removeNamedItem(name)	Removes an item with the specified name.
removeQualifiedItem(baseName, nameSpaceURI)	Removes the attribute with the specified name space and attribute name.
reset()	Resets the collection pointer to the beginning of the collection.
setNamedItem(itemObject)	Adds or replaces (if the item already exists) the supplied item in the collection.

Table 8-4. Properties and Methods for a Named Node Map Collection

As you may have already noticed, attribute objects (official name: XMLDOMAttribute) are associated with elements and are not considered part of the document tree. Because of this, attributes are not available as part of the child collections. So to support attributes, the XML element must expose properties and methods to allow us to work with attributes. You can obtain the named collection of attributes for an element by retrieving the attributes property for the XML element. In addition to this, the element object contains a few additional methods, which basically map to the named node map collection, to make working with attributes even easier. Table 8-5 lists the XML element's methods to deal with attributes; if you look at them, you will notice a pretty straightforward correlation to the methods and properties in the named node map collection.

The setAttribute method does more work under the covers than any other method. We probably should have showed you first how to create an attribute manually so you would appreciate the functionality in the method. Not that creating an attribute manually is that difficult—it is just that sometimes we are amazed at the completeness of a 1.0 version of a specification. We will quickly show you how to create an attribute manually because there are some occasions, when you are implementing advanced techniques, when you will need to create them in this fashion.

Method	Description
getAttribute(name)	Returns the value of the named attribute.
getAttributeNode(name)	Returns the attribute object of the named attribute.
removeAttribute(name)	Removes the named attribute from the collection.
removeAttributeNode(attribute Object)	Removes the specified attribute object from the collection.
setAttribute(name, value)	Adds or replaces (if the item already exists) the attribute in the collection and sets its value.
setAttributeNode(attribute Object)	Adds or replaces (if the item already exists) the specified attribute object in the collection.

Table 8-5.   Methods in an XML Element Object That Work with Attributes

To create an attribute manually we go back to our old friend, the XML document object. This object contains the createAttribute method, which takes a parameter that is the name of the attribute to create. After you have created the attribute, you can set the value of it using the value property of the newly created attribute object. Finally you can associate the attribute to the element using either the element's setAttributeNode method or by using the attribute's named node collection and calling the setNamedItem method. The following is a code snippet to create a *year* attribute manually.

```
var newAttribute = xmlDocObject.createAttribute("Year");
newAttribute.value = "1999";
activeElement.attributes.setNamedItem(newAttribute);
```

The following is an example of retrieving, setting, and deleting attributes from an element. The sample allows the user to modify the attributes of an element and displays the values for each of the attributes. One thing we need to mention is that in this example we are using the name property of the attribute object, so we can show you both the attribute name and its value.

Attribute.htm

```
<html>
<script Language="JavaScript">
var theElement;
function load(){
  xmlDocObject.async = false;
  xmlDocObject.loadXML("<sample><singleNode>The
Value</singleNode></sample>");
  theElement = xmlDocObject.documentElement.firstChild;
  displayAttributes();
}
function displayAttributes(){
  var attributeObj = null;
  var attributesColl;
  var innerString = "";
  attributesColl = theElement.attributes;
  attributeObj = attributesColl.nextNode();
```

```
  while (attributeObj != null){
    innerString = innerString + attributeObj.name + " = " +
attributeObj.value + "<BR>";
    attributeObj = attributesColl.nextNode();
  }
  AttributeValues.innerHTML = innerString;
}
function setAttr(){
  var attName = NewName.value;
  var attValue = NewValue.value;
  theElement.setAttribute(attName, attValue);
  displayAttributes();
}
function deleteAttr(){
  var attName = NewName.value;
  theElement.removeAttribute(attName);
  displayAttributes();
}
</script>
<body onLoad="load()">
<p align="center"><b>Manipulate Attributes</b></p>
<xml ID="xmlDocObject"></xml>
Attribute Values:<BR>
<div ID="AttributeValues"></div>
<p>Attribute Name:<input type="text" ID="NewName">
Value:<input type="text" ID="NewValue"></p>
<input type="button" value="Set Attribute" onClick="setAttr()">
<input type="button" value="Remove Attribute" onClick="deleteAttr()">
</body></html>
```

Modifying the XML Tree

In the prior sections we concentrated on how to load data and then get the data out of XML elements, but what if you want to modify the document tree in code? Modifying the XML tree like most data interaction is broken down into three simple actions adding, replacing, and deleting.

Adding XML Elements

There are two steps involved in adding elements to the XML
document: creating the element and associating the element to a
location in the XML tree. To create a new element, you can either
create an element from a string or clone an existing element. The
createElement method is a member of the XML document object
and takes a single parameter, which is the name of the element to
create. The createElement method returns a new XML element object
that you can then set the value and attributes for. The following
snippet creates a new *Artist* node and then sets the value to Garbage:

```
newNode = xmlDocObject.createElement("Artist");
newNode.text = "Garbage";
```

The cloneNode method is a member of an XML element object and
can be used to clone an element and all of its children. The cloneNode
method also has one parameter, which is a true/false value that
indicates whether the child of the node should be cloned or just the
node itself. When using the cloneNode method, the element and all
of its attributes are copied to the new element. However, the copying
of the text or data for the element is dependent on whether you are
cloning the children for the element. The reason for this is as we have
discussed before: the text or data for an element is actually a child node
of that element. So by cloning the children of the node we are copying
the text for the node also.

Now that we have created a new XML element, we need to make
it part of the document tree. There are two methods to add an element
to the document, both of which add the new element to the child
collection of another element. One method makes the new element
the last child in the collection, and the other method allows you to
specify the location of the new element in the collection of children.
The appendChild method takes one parameter, which is the new
element object, and adds the new node to the end of the collection
of children. The insertBefore method takes two parameters, the new
element and a reference element. The reference element is the element
that the new element should be inserted before. It is important to note
that the reference element must be a child of the element you wish to
insert the new element into or a null value. By passing in a null value,

the item is inserted at the end of the collection of children, which is the same functionality as the appendChild method. Both the appendChild and insertBefore methods return the new element if the calls were successful; otherwise an error will be raised. We will now show you examples of each method to help clarify how the methods work. Each method adds a new child element to the root of the document.

The appendChild method:

```
var root = xmlDocObject.documentElement;
var result = root.appendChild(newElement);
```

The insertBefore method:

```
var root = xmlDocObject.documentElement;
var result = root.insertBefore(newElement, root.firstChild);
```

Replacing and Deleting XML Elements

The methods used for updating and deleting XML elements are similar in nature to the appendChild and insertChild methods. The replaceChild method, which is a member of an element object, allows you to update or remove a child from a particular element. The replaceChild method takes two parameters: the new node and the child node to replace. If you pass in null for the new node parameter, the existing node will be removed. The value that is returned from this method is the node that was replaced. The following code snippet shows how to use the replace method to replace the first nonroot element in a document:

```
var root = xmlDocObject.documentElement;
var replaced = root.replaceChild(newElement, root.firstChild);
```

The removeChild method is also a member of the element object. The method takes one parameter, which is the object to remove, and returns the node that was removed if the method was successful. The following is an example of using the removeChild method:

```
var removed  = someNode.removeChild(objToRemove);
```

The following is a simple example of adding, updating, and deleting elements from an XML document. The sample consists of a single element inside of the root element to start with. All of the methods are executed against the single element and modify the children of this element.

ModifyElements.htm

```
<html>
<script Language="JavaScript">
var workElement;
var lastElement = null;
function load(){
  xmlDocObject.async = false;
  xmlDocObject.loadXML("<root><workArea>The Value</workArea></root>");
  workElement = xmlDocObject.documentElement.firstChild;
  displayXML();
}
function displayXML(){
  RawXML.innerText = xmlDocObject.xml;
}
function addNode(){
  var elementName = NewName.value;
  lastElement = xmlDocObject.createElement(elementName);
  lastElement.text = NewValue.value;
  workElement.appendChild(lastElement);
  displayXML();
}
function addClone(){
  lastElement = workElement.cloneNode(true);
  workElement.insertBefore(lastElement, workElement.firstChild);
  displayXML();
}
function undo(){
  if (lastElement != null){
    workElement.removeChild(lastElement);
    displayXML();
  }
}
function reset(){
```

```
    var newNode = xmlDocObject.createElement("workArea");

    newNode.text = "The Value";

    oldElement = xmlDocObject.documentElement.firstChild;

    xmlDocObject.documentElement.replaceChild(newNode, oldElement);

    lastElement = null;

    displayXML();

}</script>
<body onLoad="load()">
<p align="center"><b>Manipulate Elements - All changes are from
the first child</b></p>
<xml ID="xmlDocObject"></xml>
Document XML:<BR>
<div ID="RawXML"></div>
<p>Element Name:<input type="text" ID="NewName">
Value:<input type="text" ID="NewValue">
<input type="button" value="Create Element" onClick="addNode()"></p>
<input type="button" value="Clone Node" onClick="addClone()">
<input type="button" value="Undo" onClick="undo()">
<input type="button" value="Reset" onClick="reset()">
</body></html>
```

Sending Data Back to the Server

In a typical browser scenario, after having made modifications to the data and the elements in the XML document, the next thing to do is to save the changes back to the server. It would be nice if the XML tag were included inside a form element so you could automatically send the data back to the server as part of the form. However, this functionality is not supported, and sending data back is a little more of a manual process. There are three methods to send data back to the server, two of which involve using standard HTML and a third that involves using an object available through the XML DOM.

Sending by Standard HTML Techniques

The basic premise behind sending the document using standard HTML techniques is to place the XML string into a hidden HTML form element and then submit the form to the server. To get a string that contains the complete XML for the document, you use the xml property of the XML document object. Next you send this string to the server using one of two techniques.

HIDDEN TEXT ELEMENT One of the methods to send an XML document back to the server is through the use of a nonvisible text field. The way this method works is you retrieve the XML string, prior to submitting the HTML form to the server, and put the string into the contents of the hidden field. Then when the form is sent to the server, the XML string is also sent. On the server side, you can then take the string and load a document object on the server from the string and retrieve the data from the document tree.

The following is an example of using a hidden text field to send the XML data to the server:

HiddenText.htm

```
<html>
<script Language="JavaScript">
function setXMLString(){
  document.all.xmlTransport.value = xmlDocObject.xml;
}
</script>
<body>
<p>Example of Submitting an XML Document to the Server</p>
<xml ID="xmlDocObject" src="simple.xml"></xml>
<form method="GET" action="test.asp" onsubmit="setXMLString()">
<input type="text" name="xmlTransport" style="visibility:hidden">
<input type="submit">
</form></body></html>
```

HIDDEN FRAME A similar but slightly more complicated way of submitting the XML document is using a hidden frame. Using this technique you would set the XML string to the value of a text box in a hidden frame that could either be an in-line frame or a normal HTML frame. The advantage of this technique is that the complete page that is modifying the XML document does not need to be submitted—only the XML document string itself. Using the hidden frame method allows you to make multiple calls to the server and get or send data without leaving the current page.

The following example uses a frame to submit data to the server; there are three pages involved: the frames page, the main page (the page where modification of the XML document would occur), and finally the hidden page used to upload the data. If you were to use this method in a production environment, we recommend that you check to make sure that the current hidden page is actually the page that sends the data before making calls to the hidden page. In addition, to support multiple calls to the server, the ASP, or whatever mechanism you use to capture the XML documents, data would need to return the HTML for the hidden page.

Frame.htm

```
<html>
<frameset rows="0,*" border="0">
  <frame name="hidden" src="hiddenPage.htm">
  <frame name="main" src="mainPage.htm">
</frameset></html>
```

mainPage.htm

```
<html>
<script Language="JavaScript">
function sendXML(){
//Need to add check to make sure the hidden frame
// contains the correct page.
  try{
    alert(parent.hidden.submitXML(xmlDocObject.xml));
  }
  catch(e){
    alert("An error occurred.");
  }
}
</script>
<body>
<p>Example of Submitting an XML Document to the Server</p>
```

```
<xml ID="xmlDocObject" src="simple.xml"></xml>
<input type="button" onClick="sendXML()" value="Send XML">
</body></html>
```

hiddenPage.htm

```
<html>
<script Language="JavaScript">
function submitXML(xmlString){
  try{
    document.all.xmlTransport.value = xmlString;
    xmlForm.submit();
    return "Successfully submitted data."
  }
  catch(e){
    return "An error occurred."
  }
}</script>
<body>
<form ID="xmlForm" method="GET" action=" test.asp">
<input type="text" name="xmlTransport">
</form>
</body>
</html>
```

Sending with the XMLHttpRequest Object

The very useful XMLHttpRequest can be used to both receive and send XML and HTML documents. The object is relatively simple in design, having only 14 different members (methods, properties). However, the object provides functionality not exposed inside the average browser's interface. The object allows you access to the lower-level functionality of sending and receiving data from the browser. For instance you can view and set the HTTP headers and asynchronously or synchronously send and receive data from a server without leaving the current page. We will focus on the functionality that the object provides to send and receive XML, but if you ever need lower-level control of sending and receiving data from an HTML page, this object might be a good place to start.

With so few methods and properties, the object is pretty easy to use after you have seen it work once. The first task in using the XMLHttpRequest object is to create or instantiate the object. This is done in JavaScript using the new ActiveXObject. The following is an example of creating the request object:

```
var xmlRequestObject = new ActiveXObject("Microsoft.XMLHTTP");
```

Now that we have created the object, it is time to get the processing started by calling the open method to initialize an HTTP request. The open method takes five parameters, which are listed in Table 8-6.

Parameter	Description
HTTP method	The HTTP method parameter refers to the method used to open the connection to the server, for example GET, POST, or PUT.
Requested URL	The requested URL is a file or application to call on the server and must be an absolute path, for example http://myserver/somepath/file, not a relative path such as somepath/file.
Asynchronous indicator	If the call is asynchronous(true, the default) or synchronous (false)
User name	Used to authenticate the user, if there is security on the requested URL.
Password	Used to authenticate the user, if there is security on the requested URL.

Table 8-6. Parameters to the XMLHTTPRequest Object's Open Method

One thing to note about the user name and password, if you are making a request to a nonsecure item you can pass in an empty string (that is, ""). If you pass in an empty string and logon is required, the browser's logon dialog will automatically be shown to gather the user information for the request. The following are examples of calls to the open method to synchronously send and receive an XML document from a nonsecured site.

Sending a XML document to the server:

```
xmlRequestObject.open("PUT",
"http://myserver/getClientXML.asp",
false, "", "");
```

Getting an XML document from a server:

```
xmlRequestObject.open("GET",
"http://myserver/sendClientXML.asp",
false, "", "");
```

From this point, sending and receiving data take two slightly different paths. We will show you how to receive an XML file first and then how to send a file.

So far we have basically told the object where to go and how to get there. Now to receive data we need to tell the object to actually make the trip to the server, which is done by calling the send method. The send method takes one parameter (we will discuss this parameter in more detail when we cover sending a file) that we simply pass in an empty string for. If we are executing the request asynchronously, we will need to set up our monitor of the readyState for the request prior to calling the send method. The method for monitoring the readyState is the same method we discussed earlier in this chapter, and we refer you to the previous "Loading Data Asynchronously" section for details on how this is done.

At this point our request is on its way to the server and we are awaiting the response. After the request has returned from the server, we can access the XML through the responseXML property, which returns us our old friend, the XML document object. The request object checks for errors in formatting of the XML and functions the same way as the load method of an XML document.

NOTE: If you are not getting an object returned from the responseXML property, you should look at the responseText property to see if any data is being returned. If the data is being returned in the responseText property, the object is not recognizing the data as XML and you probably are not setting the content type to text/xml (To do this in ASPs, set the Response.ConentType = "text/xml").

Now that you have gotten a little bit comfortable with the XMLHTTPRequest object and have learned yet another way to receive XML documents, we will show how to send a document to the server. It is actually a relatively simple process, because the objects themselves handle most of the complexities. All that you need to do is to call the open method, which we covered earlier, and then call the send method, passing in the value of the XMLDocument property from your XML document object. The XMLDocument property returns a reference to the XML document object model exposed by the document object. The HTTP request object then encodes the XML and sends the string to the server. On the server side the process is quite simple also, because the XML document object's load method also supports another way of loading data we have yet to cover. The load method allows you to pass in an Active Server Page request object, which has been sent an encoded XML string, and the object automatically loads the data into the XML document object on the server.

The following is an example of using the XMLHTTPRequest object to send data and get data from a server. The example is designed just to show the movement of the XML and does not modify the data on the client. We are also showing how you can use the responseText property to send status messages back to the page. In addition to the client code, we have included the Active Server Page code to show you an example of how to handle sending data on the server.

ClientCode.htm

```
<html>
<script Language="JavaScript">
function sendXML(){
```

```
    var xmlRequestObject = new ActiveXObject("Microsoft.XMLHTTP");
  xmlRequestObject.open("POST", "http://localhost/receiveXML.asp",
false, "", "");
    xmlRequestObject.send(xmlDocObject.XMLDocument);
    alert(xmlRequestObject.responseText);
}
function getXML(){
    var xmlRequestObject = new ActiveXObject("Microsoft.XMLHTTP");
    xmlRequestObject.open("GET", "http://localhost/simple.xml", false,
"", "");
    xmlRequestObject.send("");
    xmlDocObject.XMLDocument = xmlRequestObject.responseXML;
}
</script>
<body onLoad="getXML()">
<p><b>Example Loading and Sending Data using XMLHTTPRequest Object</b></p>
<xml ID="xmlDocObject"></xml>
<INPUT TYPE="button" onClick="sendXML()" value="Send Data">
</body></html>
```

receiveXML.asp

```
<%@ LANGUAGE=JavaScript %>
<%
    var xmlDocObject = Server.CreateObject("Microsoft.XMLDOM");
  xmlDocObject.async=false;
  xmlDocObject.load(Request);
  //Just write out the xml data back to the client
  Response.Write(xmlDocObject.xml);
%>
```

SUMMARY

In this chapter we covered a lot of information about XML. We started out showing you what XML is and how to build your own XML documents. From there we jumped into the XML document object model, which is rather large and can be overwhelming, and showed you how to interact with your XML documents from script. We have not covered all of the DOM yet; we will be getting to more a little later in the book, but we feel we have covered 40 percent of the object model that you will be using probably 90 percent of the time.

9

The XML Data Source Object and Data Binding

In Chapter 8 we introduced you to XML, showed you how to build an XML document, and showed you how to use the XML document object model (DOM) to navigate and modify data in the XML tree. In addition to using the DOM, Microsoft has introduced another object and concept in Internet Explorer that allows us to easily display XML data using standard HTML elements. This new technology is called the XML data source object, and it allows us to bind an HTML element to a piece of XML data.

In this chapter we will be covering the following:

▼   An overview of data binding and its architecture.

▲   Using the XML data source object, including how to bind elements and how to use the object to manipulate data.

OVERVIEW OF DATA BINDING

Beginning with Internet Explorer 4.0, Microsoft introduced the concept of *data binding*, which allows developers to easily create data-centric HTML pages. Data binding is a set of extensions that are built into standard HTML elements that allow an HTML element to be attached to a piece of data in a data source object (DSO). A data source object is a new object built into IE that provides data to a page. This data can come from a number of sources, including XML, a comma-separated value (CSV) list, or an ActiveX Data Object (ADO) recordset. Because the functionality of data binding is built on standard HTML elements, minimal scripting is required to create a page that is based on the data from a DSO.

Data binding has the following advantages:

▼   Data is made available through the DSO and is not embedded directly into an HTML element.

■   Once an HTML element is bound to a piece of data, the element's value automatically changes as the underlying data changes.

■   Data binding provides a great mechanism to view a one-of-many type presentation (for example, the editing or viewing of one customer in a list of customers).

▲ Data binding provides a mechanism to easily build a table of an unknown quantity of multiple items (for example, creating a table that consist of a list of customers).

The Architecture of Data Binding

The data binding architecture is based on four major components: data source objects, data consumers, the binding agent, and the table repeater agent. Figure 9-1 is an illustration of how these objects fit together.

The *data source object* (DSO) is responsible for transmitting the data from the server to the client machine and maintaining the data on the client. The data source provides data to MSHTML (the DLL that is the viewer of HTML in IE) in the form of OLE-DB or an OLE-DB Simple Provider. MSHTML then extends the object model of

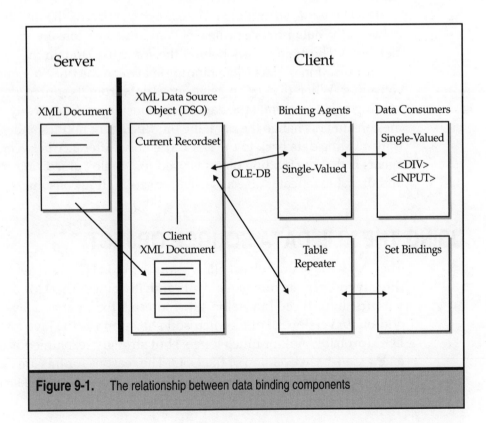

Figure 9-1.   The relationship between data binding components

the DSO and adds a common set of properties, methods, and events. This final object model can then be accessed from script. The exposed data is made available in a recordset format. A *recordset format* is similar to a database table: it is composed of one or more rows, also known as records, that contain one or more columns.

Data consumers are standard HTML elements that have been extended to support receiving data from the DSO. These elements are used to display the DSO data to which they are attached. The following is a list of some of the HTML elements, which have been extended to support being a data consumer: input, span, div, object, applet, and table. There are two types of data consumers: single-valued and set-binding consumers. Most consumers are single-valued consumers, meaning the element is bound to only one column in the current record of the recordset. Set-binding consumers, such as tables, are bound to the complete set of data or the complete recordset (all the rows in the recordset are consumed by the rows of a table).

The *binding agent* and the *table repeater agent* act as the middlemen between the data provider (the DSO) and the data consumers (HTML elements). The agents work behind the scene to maintain the synchronization of data (data binding) between the provider and consumer. When the DSO receives new data from its source, the binding agent transmits the data to the consumers. Conversely, when the consumers change the data, the binding agent notifies and transmits the data back to the DSO. The only difference between the agents is that the binding object is used for single-valued consumers and the table repeater object is used for set-binding consumers.

USING THE XML DATA SOURCE OBJECT

The XML data source object allows you to bind HTML elements directly to XML document elements and attributes. The XML DSO was first introduced in version 4.0 of Internet Explorer as a Java add-on. In version 5.0 of IE, Microsoft still supports the Java XML DSO (probably not for much longer) but strongly recommends using a new C++-based version of the DSO. The reasons for this are due to the increased performance of the C++-based version and the fact that

C++ DSO now supports binding directly to XML data islands, without the need to explicitly create a DSO using the object tag. Because of this we will restrict our focus to the C++ XML DSO.

As we talked about in our discussion of XML in the previous chapter, an XML data island is nothing more than XML documents that are referenced by or included in an HTML page. Most of the examples in this chapter have the XML included directly in the HTML page. This is done to simplify the viewing of both the data and the data binding techniques. As you'll see in this chapter, binding HTML elements to an XML data island is pretty easy to do, thanks to the new version of the XML DSO and enhancements to standard HTML elements.

Attributes Supporting Binding of Single-Valued Consumers

In order to support binding, standard HTML elements have been extended to support the role of a data consumer. It is important to note that these changes are not unique to XML DSO use but apply to binding in general. The most important steps in single-valued data binding are telling the binding agent what data source to connect to and which field or column to bind to. To support binding through declaration, two new attributes, DATASRC and DATAFLD, were added to HTML elements. These attributes are the keys to supporting binding in standard HTML tags. The DATASRC attribute tells the binding agent what DSO the element should be bound to. (One important note about the DATASRC attribute is that the value of the data source name is always prefixed by a # sign.) The DATAFLD attribute is then used to tell the binding agent what column (attribute or element) within the current record of the DSO-supplied recordset the element should be bound to. Please note that the value of the DATAFLD attribute is not case-sensitive like most other XML access techniques.

The following example shows how to notify the binding agent to use the DSO with the name of xmlDSO and to bind the *div* to the *Name* element in the XML document:

```
<div ID="sample" DATASRC="#xmlDSO" DATAFLD="Name"></div>
```

Another attribute was also added to selected elements to tell the browser how to display the bound data, either as HTML or as text. These elements, such as the div, span, label, and body, support the DATAFORMATAS attribute, which has the two possible values of "html" or "text."

Table 9-1 lists all of the HTML elements that are single-valued consumers, whether that value is updatable, and the attributes of the element that are bound to the data source.

Defining an XML DSO

Naturally, the next question is, "How do I define an XML DSO?" The answer is, "You already have." This is true, of course, if you have created an XML data island, because behind the scenes, the XML document object created using the XML tag is actually an XML DSO. This is, as we stated before, how IE 5 has become aware of data islands: it automatically makes them into XML DSOs. This is pretty cool stuff, because with only learning a couple of new attributes we can go ahead and build an example that puts data binding to work. The following is a very simple example that pulls the value of the *band* element from an in-line XML document and displays the value in a div.

simpleBinding.htm

```
<html>
<body>
<xml ID="bandList">
<Bands>
  <Band>
    <Name>Citizen King</Name>
  </Band>
</Bands>
</xml>
<div DATASRC="#bandList" DATAFLD="Name"></div>
</body></html>
```

Element	Supports Updating	Bound Property
A	False	href
APPLET	True	Property value via PARAM
BUTTON	False	innerText, innerHTML
DIV	False	innerText, innerHTML
FRAME	False	src
IFRAME	False	src
IMG	False	src
INPUT TYPE=CHECKBOX	True	checked
INPUT TYPE=HIDDEN	True	value
INPUT TYPE=LABEL	True	value
INPUT TYPE=PASSWORD	True	value
INPUT TYPE=RADIO	True	checked
INPUT TYPE=TEXT	True	value
LABEL	False	innerText, innerHTML
MARQUEE	False	innerText, innerHTML
SELECT	True	obj.options(obj.selected Index).text
SPAN	False	innerText, innerHTML
TEXTAREA	True	value

Table 9-1.   Single-valued HTML Elements That Support Binding

In addition to using the XML tag to create a XML DSO object, you can also use the object tag. We don't recommend using this technique, but we show it in the following example as a way to see what the XML tag is doing for us and also as a possible alternative to using the XML tag.

object.htm

```
<html>
<script Language="JavaScript">
function loadDSO(){
   bandList.XMLDocument.loadXML("<Bands><Band><Name>Citizen
King</Name></Band></Bands>");
}</script>
<body onLoad="loadDSO()">
<object width="0" height="0" ID="bandList"
classid="clsid:550dda30-0541-11d2-9ca9-0060b0ec3d39"
></object>
<div DATASRC="#bandList" DATAFLD="Name"></div>
</body></html>
```

Attributes Supporting Set-Binding Consumers

Table elements are the only common set-binding consumers. In order to support data binding, tables have been enhanced to support the DATASRC attribute. In addition to this, another attribute has been added to the table object to support how the data is displayed in the table. However, before we can discuss this new attribute, we need to discuss and show you the way a table displays data as a set-binding consumer.

The default behavior of a bound table is to create a row in the table for each sibling of the root element. However, the binding does not automatically create any of the column elements for that row. To create columns inside of the row, you must create the column elements manually using the TD tag. Unfortunately, you cannot bind the data directly to the TD element. Instead, you need to create a container within the element to display the data. The container element is actually any one of the single-valued consumers, which is bound to a particular column. The defining of the TD tag and the container elements forms the template for the columns. One thing to note is that if you are using a single-valued consumer inside of a bound table, you do not need to specify the DATASRC property.

The following example shows how to create a bound table. In addition to showing the code, we show you the output in Figure 9-2 so you can see what is actually generated.

boundTable.htm

```
<html>
<body>
<xml ID="bandList">
<Bands>
  <Band>
    <Name>Beatles</Name>
    <NumberOfMembers>4</NumberOfMembers>
    <HomeTown>Liverpool England</HomeTown>
  </Band>
  <Band>
    <Name>Citizen King</Name>
    <NumberOfMembers>5</NumberOfMembers>
    <HomeTown>Milwaukee, WI</HomeTown>
  </Band>
  <Band>
    <Name>Live</Name>
    <NumberOfMembers>4</NumberOfMembers>
    <HomeTown>Hershey, PA</HomeTown>
  </Band>
</Bands>
</XML>
<p align="center"><img src="cd.gif"></p>
<p align="center"><b>A List Of Bands That I Have Listened To
Recently</b></p>
<table DATASRC="#bandList" border="1" align="center">
  <thead><th>Band</th><th># of Members</th><th>Home City</th></thead>
  <tr>
    <td><div DATAFLD="Name"></td>
    <td align="center"><div DATAFLD="NumberOfMembers"></td>
    <td><div DATAFLD="HomeTown"></td>
  </tr>
</table></body></html>
```

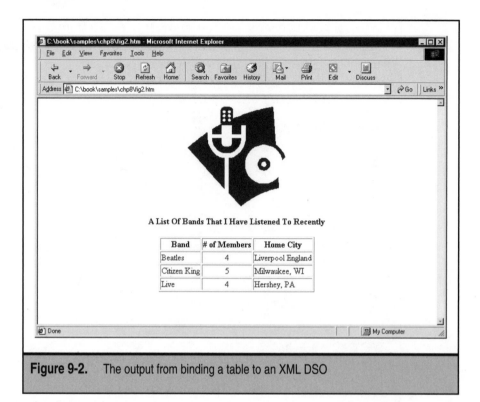

Figure 9-2. The output from binding a table to an XML DSO

As you can see, the table displays a row for each of the child elements of the root. However, there might be cases where you would like to display one record at a time or a subset of the elements. To support this functionality, an additional attribute has been added to the table tag called DATAPAGESIZE. This attribute allows you to specify the number of rows to display at one time. Figure 9-3 shows the results of our prior example with the DATAPAGESIZE attribute set to 1.

Dynamically Binding Elements

HTML elements can also be bound to a data source at runtime using the dataSrc and dataFld properties of the particular element. For

Figure 9-3. The results of setting the DATAPAGESIZE attribute to 1

example, if you wanted to dynamically bind a div element to a data source, you could do it as shown in the following code snippet:

```
<html>
<script Lanugage="JavaScript">
function bindDiv(){
  consumer.dataSrc="bandList";
  consumer.dataFld="Name";
}
</script>
...
<xml ID="bandList" ...></xml>
<div ID="consumer"></div>
...
</html>
```

To modify the binding for an existing element, you can simply set the dataSrc or dataFld properties to point to the new data source or data field. To remove an element's binding, you simply set the dataSrc and dataFld properties equal to empty strings (""").

The process of dynamically binding table elements is similar to binding any of the single-valued elements. You can use the dataSrc and dataFld properties to change or add bindings for a table. When adding binding to a table element that does not currently have any binding, you can add binding to the table and the columns in any order you wish. When modifying the binding of a table that is currently bound, there are a few steps that need to be followed:

1. Remove the binding from the HTML table by setting the dataSrc property for the table to an empty string (""").

2. Modify the data bindings of the template elements (the elements that make up the columns) by setting the dataFld to the appropriate field.

3. Rebind the table to the new data source object by setting the dataSrc property.

It is important to note that if you are changing any of the bindings of the template elements, you are required to remove the binding of the entire table from the DSO, which is done by setting the dataSrc tag to an empty string for the table.

If you wish to change the number of the rows that are visible at one time for a table, you can simply set the dataPageSize property to the number of items you wish to display. Changing the dataPageSize property does not require unbinding and rebinding to be implemented.

Navigating through a Subset of Data

So far we have shown you how to bind a single-valued consumer and how to display a limited set of data in a table. But what if you want to navigate to another record or, in the case of a table, another page of records. By *a page of records* we are describing the situation where you have set the DATAPAGESIZE attribute to a value that is less than the total number of records in the recordset. In this case, we want to be able to navigate through the records, and this can be accomplished using one of two methods. The type of method you use depends on your binding technique: single valued or set binding.

How to Navigate Through Records Using the Set-Bound Element

The following methods are available on table elements (set binding): nextPage, previousPage, firstPage, and lastPage. These methods allow you to easily navigate around the DSO. The call simply tells the table repeater agent to move its record pointer (forward, back, and so on) within the recordset, based on the type of call. The following example shows how to use the navigation methods to navigate through the list of different elements. Notice that we are using a table with only one record per page to display the data and that we have modified the template to display the data in rows rather than in columns. This "spin" on the template would also work if we were to display multiple records at a time. Figure 9-4 shows the results of the example.

singleRow.htm

```
<html>
<script Language="JavaScript">
function navigate(direction){
  switch(direction){
    case "next":
      tblList.nextPage();
      break;
    case "last":
      tblList.lastPage();
      break;
    case "previous":
      tblList.previousPage();
      break;
    case "first":
      tblList.firstPage();
      break;
```

```
      }}</script>
<body>

<xml ID="bandList">
<Bands>
  <Band>
    <Name>Beatles</Name>
    <NumberOfMembers>4</NumberOfMembers>
    <HomeTown>Liverpool England</HomeTown>
  </Band>
  <Band>
    <Name>Citizen King</Name>
    <NumberOfMembers>5</NumberOfMembers>
    <HomeTown>Milwaukee, WI</HomeTown>
  </Band>
  <Band>
    <Name>Live</Name>
    <NumberOfMembers>4</NumberOfMembers>
    <HomeTown>Hershey, PA</HomeTown>
  </Band>
</Bands>
</xml>
<p align="center"><img src="cd.gif"></p>
<p align="center"><b>A List Of Bands That I Have Listened To
Recently</b></p>
<table ID="tblList" DATASRC="#bandList" border="1" align="center"
DATAPAGESIZE="1">
  <tr> <td><b>Name:</b></td> <td><div DATAFLD="Name"></td></tr>
  <tr><td><b># of Members:</b></td><td><div
DATAFLD="NumberOfMembers"></td>
</tr>
  <tr><td><b>Home Town:</b></td><td><div DATAFLD="HomeTown"></td></tr>
</table>
<p align="center">
<input type="button" value="<<" onClick="navigate('first')"><input
type="button" value="<" onClick="navigate('previous')">
<input type="button" value=">" onClick="navigate('next')"><input
type="button" value=">>" onClick="navigate('last')">
</p></body></html>
```

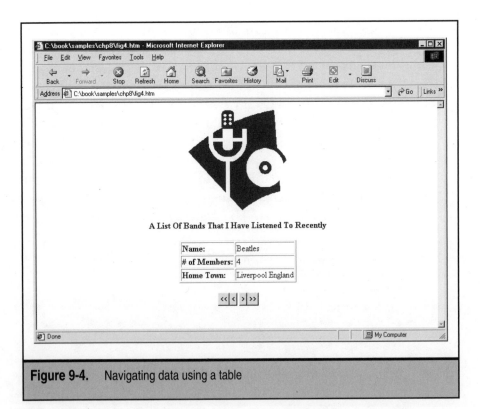

Figure 9-4.   Navigating data using a table

How to Navigate with Single-Value Bound Elements

Unfortunately, single-value bound elements don't have an HTML
element like the table that represents the complete recordset object.
However, there is another object that is exposed as part of the DSO
that allows us to navigate. The object is the *recordset object*, which is
an ADO (ActiveX Data Object) recordset object, and it is available
from the DSO using the recordset property. We will not be covering
all of the functionality of the recordset object in this book, because
there is a lot there, but rather we're concentrating on the pieces that
are applicable. We will be covering more about the recordset object
later in this chapter, but for now we want to talk about the
moveNext, movePrevious, moveFirst, and moveLast methods.

Calls to these four methods are essentially the same as the calls we made to the table element. There is one thing that the table's methods are taking care of automatically, and that is what to do at the end and beginning of the recordset, if we try to navigate beyond the start or end. So what we need to do is check to see if we are at the beginning, before we navigate to the previous record, or if we are at the end, before we navigate to the next record. To help us with this, the recordset has two properties: eof (end of file) and bof (beginning of file), which make this easy to check. The following snippet shows the code to handle navigating using the recordset's methods and trapping for the end and beginning of the recordset.

```javascript
<script Language="JavaScript">
function navigate(direction){
  var recordset = bandList.recordset;
  switch(direction){
    case "next":
      recordset.moveNext();
      break;
    case "last":
      recordset.moveLast();
      break;
    case "previous":
      recordset.movePrevious();
      break;
    case "first":
      recordset.moveFirst();
      break;
  }
  if (recordset.eof) {
    recordset.movePrevious();
    alert("Cannot navigate. You are already at the end of the recordset.");
  }
  else if (recordset.bof) {
    recordset.moveNext();
    alert("Cannot navigate. You are already at the beginning of the
recordset.");
  }
}
</script>
```

Rules for Converting XML to a Recordset

One of the issues involved with the XML DSO is determining how to convert a tree structure into the table structure of a recordset. To model the hierarchy of the XML, the DSO creates a hierarchical recordset, or, in other words, it creates recordsets inside of recordsets. The methodology implemented by the DSO is that it converts the subelements, not the top-level element, to a recordset. The DSO object converts every XML subelement and attribute to a column in one of the recordsets in the hierarchy. The name of the recordset's column maps to the name of the subelement or attribute, unless the parent element has an attribute or subelement with the same name. In these cases, the name of the subelement or attribute is prefixed with an exclamation point (!). In the recordset, each column is either a simple column with a text value or another recordset. Here are reasons why a subelement would contain a recordset rather than simple text:

▼ If the subelement contains subelements or if the subelement has an attribute, a recordset will be created.

■ If the subelement's parent contains more than one instance of the subelement as a direct child, a recordset will be created.

▲ If there are multiple instances of the subelement (even if they are under different parents), and any of the instances require the creation of a recordset, this subelement will also create a recordset.

In addition to the columns that are created by the XML elements and attributes, the XML DSO creates an additional column in the recordset named $Text. The $Text column concatenates all of the column's values for the row.

Displaying Data from Lower Levels in the XML Document

Now that you understand how the DSO object builds the recordset to hold the XML data, the next thing to do is to figure out how to actually display the data in the lower-level recordsets. For example, if we were to take our prior example that listed the bands I had listened to recently, and under that we wanted to list the actual CDs that I had listened to, we might have an XML document that looks similar to this:

```
<Bands>
  <Band>
    <Name>Live</Name>
    <NumberOfMembers>4</NumberOfMembers>
    <HomeTown>Hershey, PA</HomeTown>
    <CD>
      <Name>Throwing Copper</Name>
    </CD>
    <CD>
      <Name>The Distance To Here</Name>
    </CD>
  </Band>
</Bands>
```

The prior examples showed how to display the information for the band (the master data), but now we want to show the detail or the list of CDs for the band. To do this, you need to create a table, which will be used to display the child data. You set the DATASRC attribute to your XML DSO, and you also set the DATAFLD attribute for the table to the name of the element with the child recordset. So in our example we would set the DATAFLD attribute to CDList, and by setting that property we bind the table to the child recordset. We can then bind to the individual columns of the recordset the same way we bind to columns in a normal table. You can bind the detail data using either a table or a single-valued consumer as the master portion of the data; however, there is a bug if you navigate from record to record using a table (the detail data does not get updated); because of this we will only show the single-valued technique. The following code shows how we would create the detail using single-valued consumers for the master data. Figure 9-5 shows the results of the example.

detail.htm

```
<html>
<script Language="JavaScript">
function navigate(direction){
  var recordset = bandList.recordset;
  switch(direction){
    case "next":
      recordset.moveNext();
      break;
    case "last":
      recordset.moveLast();
      break;
    case "previous":
      recordset.movePrevious();
      break;
    case "first":
      recordset.moveFirst();
      break;
  }
  if (recordset.eof) {
    recordset.movePrevious();
    alert("Cannot navigate. You are already at the end of the recordset.");
  }
  else if (recordset.bof) {
    recordset.moveNext();
    alert("Cannot navigate. You are already at the beginning of the
recordset.");
  }
}</script>
<body>
<xml ID="bandList">
<Bands>
  <Band>
    <Name>Beatles</Name>
    <NumberOfMembers>4</NumberOfMembers>
    <HomeTown>Liverpool England</HomeTown>
    <CD>
        <Name>Yellow Submarine</Name>
    </CD>
  </Band>
```

```
    <Band>
      <Name>Citizen King</Name>
      <NumberOfMembers>5</NumberOfMembers>
      <HomeTown>Milwaukee, WI</HomeTown>
      <CD>
         <Name>Brown Paper Bag</Name>
      </CD>
      <CD>
         <Name>Better Days</Name>
      </CD>
    </Band>
    <Band>
      <Name>Live</Name>
      <NumberOfMembers>4</NumberOfMembers>
      <HomeTown>Hershey, PA</HomeTown>
      <CD>
         <Name>Throwing Copper</Name>
      </CD>
      <CD>
         <Name>The Distance To Here</Name>
      </CD>
    </Band>
</Bands></xml>
<p align="center"><img src="cd.gif"></p>
<p align="center"><b>A List Of Bands That I Have Listened To
Recently</b></p>
<table border="1" align="center">
  <tr>
    <td><b>Name:</b></td>
    <td><div DATASRC="#bandList" DATAFLD="Name"></div></td>
  </tr>
  <tr>
    <td><b>Number of Members:</b></td>
    <td><div DATASRC="#bandList" DATAFLD="NumberOfMembers"></div></td>
  </tr>
  <tr>
    <td><b>Home Town:</b></td>
    <td><div DATASRC="#bandList" DATAFLD="HomeTown"></div></td>
  </tr>
</table>
<p align="center">The CD(s) I Listened To</p>
<table DATASRC="#bandList" DATAFLD="CD" border="1" align="center">
<thead><th>CD Name</th></thead>
  <tr>
    <td><div DATAFLD="Name"></td>
  </tr>
```

```
</table>
<p align="center">
<input type="button" value="<<" onClick="navigate('first')"><input
type="button" value="<" onClick="navigate('previous')">
<input type="button" value=">" onClick="navigate('next')"><input
type="button" value=">>" onClick="navigate('last')">
</p></body></html>
```

You might be thinking, "That's pretty cool, but my data is more complex and has more levels in the hierarchy." Well, this, too, can be handled using the DSO. Let's take our prior example and add another level under the CD element to include my favorite songs from that CD. The format may look like this:

```
<CD>
    <Name>Yellow Submarine</Name>
    <FavoriteSongs>
      <Song Title="Yellow Submarine"/>
      <Song Title="With A Little Help From My Friends"/>
    </FavoriteSongs>
</CD>
```

Figure 9-5.   Binding to details of the XML document

To handle this, we need to create two new tables setting the attributes as we did before, but this time it is safe (there aren't any bugs) to put the new table inside of the template for the detail records. The reason we need to create two new detail tables is that, if you remember, the rule that states: *if there are two or more subelements with the same name, a recordset is created*. In this case, there are two song subelements, which cause an additional recordset to be created. So now we can create details for the details and navigate in the master records and the details change automatically. The following code shows what the template would look like to now include our favorite songs, and Figure 9-6 shows the results. Note: you can continue with this technique (placing tables inside of tables) until you have navigated down to the level of the XML tree for which you wish to display data.

```
<table DATASRC="#bandList" DATAFLD="CD" border="1" align="center">
  <thead><th>CD Name</th><th>Favorite Songs</th></thead>
  <tr>
    <td><div DATAFLD="Name"></td>
    <td>
      <table DATASRC="#bandList" DATAFLD="FavoriteSongs">
        <tr><td>
          <table DATASRC="#bandList" DATAFLD="Song">
            <tr><td><div DATAFLD="Title"></div>
            </td></tr>
          </table>
        </td></tr>
      </table>
    </td>
  </tr>
</table>
```

Modifying DSO Data

Everything that we have shown you thus far using the XML DSO has involved working with displaying data. Beyond this, the XML DSO also provides a nice mechanism to modify XML data. Editing data is built into the single-valued consumers such as an input or a select

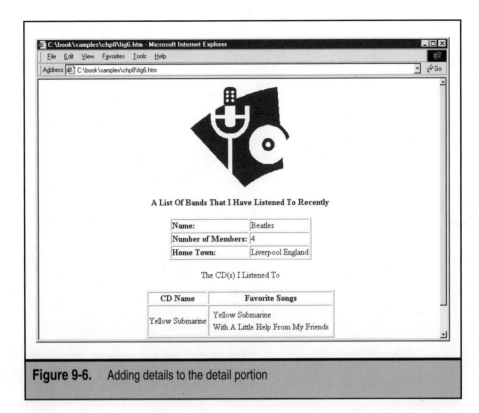

Figure 9-6. Adding details to the detail portion

element. Once the element loses focus on an updatable single-valued consumer, the underling XML is updated.

Adding and deleting data involves working with the recordset object of the DSO, rather than with the DSO directly. To add a new record to the recordset, you can simply call the addNew method on the recordset; to delete a record, you call the Delete method. One important thing to remember about the addNew method is that the new record is added at the end of the recordset. The newly added record does not become the active record; however, you can easily make the record active by calling either the lastPage method (if you are using a table for binding) or the moveLast method (if you are using a single-valued consumer) of the recordset. The following example takes our simple navigational example and extends it to support adding, updating, and deleting data from the XML tree. Figure 9-7 shows the results of our new editing capabilities.

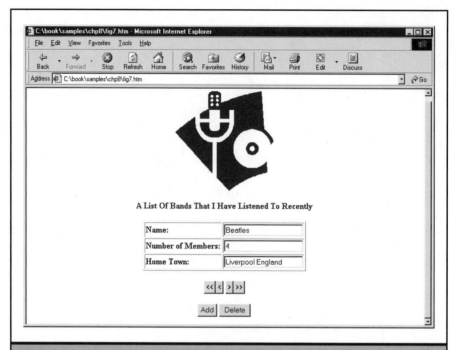

Figure 9-7. The sample application with data editing support

edit.htm

```
<html>
<script Language="JavaScript">
function navigate(direction){
  switch(direction){
    case "next":
      tblList.nextPage();
      break;
    case "last":
      tblList.lastPage();
      break;
    case "previous":
      tblList.previousPage();
      break;
    case "first":
      tblList.firstPage();
      break;
  }}
```

```
function addBand(){
  bandList.recordset.addNew();
  tblList.lastPage();
}
function deleteBand(){
  bandList.recordset.Delete();
}</script>
<body>
<xml ID="bandList">
<Bands>
  <Band>
    <Name>Beatles</Name>
    <NumberOfMembers>4</NumberOfMembers>
    <HomeTown>Liverpool England</HomeTown>
  </Band>
  <Band>
    <Name>Citizen King</Name>
    <NumberOfMembers>5</NumberOfMembers>
    <HomeTown>Milwaukee, WI</HomeTown>
  </Band>
  <Band>
    <Name>Live</Name>
    <NumberOfMembers>4</NumberOfMembers>
    <HomeTown>Hershey, PA</HomeTown>
  </Band>
</Bands></xml>
<p align="center"><img src="cd.gif"></p>
<p align="center"><b>A List Of Bands That I Have Listened To
Recently</b></p>
<table ID="tblList" DATASRC="#bandList" border="1" align="center"
DATAPAGESIZE="1">
  <tr>
    <td><b>Name:</b></td>
    <td><input type="text" DATAFLD="Name" onblur="alert(bandList.xml)"></td>
</tr>
  <tr>
    <td><b>Number of Members:</b></td>
    <td><input type="text" DATAFLD="NumberOfMembers"></td>
  </tr>
  <tr>
    <td><b>Home Town:</b></td>
    <td><input type="text" DATAFLD="HomeTown"></td>
  </tr></table>
<p align="center">
<input type="button" value="<<" onClick="navigate('first')"><input
```

```
type="button" value="<" onClick="navigate('previous')">
<input type="button" value=">" onClick="navigate('next')"><input
type="button" value=">>" onClick="navigate('last')"></p>
<p align="center"><input type="button" value="Add" onClick="addBand()">
<input type="button" value="Delete" onClick="deleteBand()"></p>
</body></html>
```

Events That Are Raised in Data Binding

The DSO object and the bound elements expose a number of events that allow us to be notified of the state of the data binding and data modification. These events are particularly useful when the page is used for data entry or modification. Let's look at each of the events and discuss any interesting characteristics of the data-binding events. While doing so, you should be aware that when we say that an event is cancelable, we are saying that we can cancel the action that caused the event to occur.

Data Source Object Events

The events for the XML DSO object can be trapped directly on the XML element or can be trapped using the following syntax:

```
<script For="xmlDSO" Event="onSomeEvent">
...Code....
</script>
```

The following is a discussion of events for the DSO.

EVENT: oncellchange CANCELABLE: FALSE   Fires whenever the data changes in the data provider.

EVENT: ondataavailable CANCELABLE: FALSE   Fires when additional data has been made available from the DSO, if the data is downloaded asynchronously. Could be used for user status messages.

EVENT: ondatasetchanged CANCELABLE: FALSE   Fires after a new data set has been requested. Also fires for other non–XML DSO that support sorting when the sorting has completed.

EVENT: ondatasetcomplete CANCELABLE: FALSE PROPERTY: REASON   Fires when the DSO has brought all of the data to the local machine. The Reason property indicates whether the download was (0) Successful, (1) Aborted, or (2) Failure.

EVENT: onreadystatechange CANCELABLE: FALSE   Determines when it is safe to access the properties of the DSO, when the readState equals complete you can access the properties. Note: this event is not specific to data binding, but it can be useful.

EVENT: onrowenter CANCELABLE: FALSE   Fires when the data provider's current row pointer is changed to point at a new row.

EVENT: onrowexit CANCELABLE: TRUE   Fires prior to the data provider changing the current row pointer. Reasons for the event to fire include calling a method of the DSO such as nextPage or the moveNext on the recordset object, deleting the current record, leaving the current page. This event can be useful to provide validation of data before moving to another record in the recordset.

EVENT: onrowsdelete CANCELABLE: FALSE   Fires when the data is about to be deleted.

EVENT: onrowsinserted CANCELABLE: FALSE   Fires after a new row has been inserted into a recordset. Can be useful to set the default values for the recordset.

Bound-Element Events and Window-Level Events

The following is a discussion of the events of bound elements.

EVENT: onafterupdate CANCELABLE: FALSE AND EVENT: onbeforeupdate CANCELABLE: TRUE   These events are fired when the data in the element has changed and is about to lose focus. One important thing to be aware of is that the events are not fired if the element's value is changed programmatically. The onbeforeupdate event is useful to validate the data and can be compared with the current value in a field by accessing the value in the following manner:

xmlDSO.recordset.Fields("ColumnName").value. If the update is not canceled in the onbeforeupdate, the onafterupdate is fired after the data has been transferred to the data provider.

EVENT: onerrorupdate CANCELABLE: TRUE   Fires if there is an error in transferring the data from the data consumer to the data provider. If the event is canceled, then any system-level messages will not be displayed.

There is only one event that is important to data binding for the window object, which is discussed next.

EVENT: onbeforeunload CANCELABLE: FALSE   The event is raised when any attempt is made to navigate off of the current page, such as clicking on a hyperlink, using the back button or a programmatic navigation. The event can be useful to inform the user that the changed data has not yet been saved to the server. You cannot cancel the navigation though code; however, you can have the browser display a message box with your message. This message box will allow the user to cancel the navigation and remain on the current page. This can be done using the following code; Figure 9-8 shows what this message box would look like.

```
<script for="window" event="onbeforeunload">
if (dataHasChanged)
  event.returnValue = "The data has changed, but you have not
saved the data to the server.";
</script>
```

SUMMARY

In this chapter, we have covered the XML DSO object, which provides a simple mechanism to create data maintenance screens for

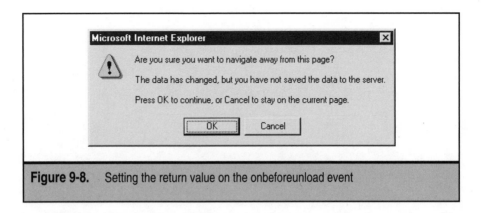

Figure 9-8.   Setting the return value on the onbeforeunload event

XML documents. The data binding mechanism makes it a little difficult to navigate into documents with a large number of levels in the tree. However, we recommend using it as a simple mechanism to build XML data maintenance pages.

CHAPTER 10

Using XSL to Query XML Data

In our discussion of working with XML data, one thing you may have noticed missing is the ability to search for a particular XML element based on its value or the value of an attribute. Moreover, it would be nice if you could limit or filter the XML data and sort the data based on a particular element. This is where a new piece of functionality, Extensible Stylesheet Language (XSL), comes into play. In addition to searching, sorting, and filtering, XSL allows us to create templates that describe how the XML data should be displayed as an HTML document or to translate the data into the format of another XML document. In general, XSL provides some great functionality and, similar to XML, is an outstanding implementation given its relative youth.

In this chapter we will cover XSL and show you how to

▼ Use XSL to create templates to transform XML to HTML.

▲ Retrieve nodes from an XML document using XSL pattern matching

Before delving into these topics, however, it would be helpful to give you an overview of XSL.

XSL describes the presentation of an XML document. Its capabilities are broken down into two major areas of functionality: transforming XML documents and an XML vocabulary used for specifying the formatting semantics.

XSL was first commercially supported in IE 5.0, and this version does include some minor conformance issues, because it was written prior to the final specification for XSL being released. In general the few conformance issues won't cause you any problems, and most of the issues relate to functions that are not yet supported, rather than incorrectly supported.

The functionality in XSL is similar to that of cascading style sheets (CSS). CSS are used to describe the formatting of an HTML document, and the XSL can be used to describe the formatting of an XML document. However, there are differences between the two, and don't look for XSL to replace the simple, declarative nature of CSS anytime soon. XSL uses XML-style notation and is well suited for complex transformations, such as taking a source XML document and converting it to an output format that is greatly different from the source. Declarative cascading style sheets, on the other hand, are designed to dynamically change the formatting of documents and enhance (not transform) the existing document tree.

The main purpose of XSL is to provide an easy-to-use mechanism whereby authors can transform the data from an XML document to the viewable format of HTML. As opposed to some other techniques to access XML data, XSL provides the ability to work with highly irregular data and create data-driven applications. With this functionality, XSL

▼ Enables the display of XML documents through XSL's transformation language.

■ Allows direct browsing of XML files. In IE 5.0 there are built-in XSL style sheets, which automatically convert the XML to HTML.

■ Provides the ability to use non–XML-aware browsers by applying the transformation on the server and generating HTML output for these browsers.

▲ Enhances the ability in script to convert XML to HTML by providing searching, sorting, and filtering functionality.

TRANSFORMING XML USING TEMPLATES

XSL provides the ability to create a style sheet template, which is merged with data from an XML document. This model is referred to as the *template-driven model*, and in its most basic form resembles a sort of mail-merge functionality. The template defines the result structure and identifies the data that should be inserted into the result document. A great feature of the template is that we are separating the functionality that handles the displaying of XML from the XML itself.

The template is composed of two types of tags: standard HTML and XSL tags. The complete document is actually an XML document and needs to follow the rules for a well-formatted XML document. Not only does the syntax of the XSL need to be well formed but also the HTML. Because of this, we cannot follow some of the shortcuts we normally do in HTML. Here is a short list of rules that you need to follow (for more details of each of the items, see Chapter 8):

▼ All of the HTML tags need a matching closing tag. (For example, you cannot just use the <BR> tag without </BR>.)

■ No overlapping tags are allowed.

■ Case matters in tag names: to match a tag, the name and the case must be the same.

■ Attributes must be enclosed in quotes.

■ All of the elements must be children of a single top-level element.

▲ If you are going to have script inside of the document, you should use escape blocks to hide unparsable characters, such as <, >, or &. The following is an example of using an escape block to hide script:

```
<script><![CDATA[
function X(){
...
}
]]></script>
```

Getting Started with Transformations

An XML document is transformed by one of two methods that are available on any of the XML elements and also the XML document itself. The two methods are transformNode and transformNodeToObject. Each of these methods processes the node it is called from and all of the children under the node using the specified XSL style sheet.

Before we can go into the details of the parameters and the results of the two calls, we need to talk about how we load the style sheet. If you remember, in the previous section we stated that an XSL style sheet is actually an XML document. Because of this, to work with the style sheet we must load the style sheet into an XML document object the same way we would load a normal XML document. We can use any of the methods to load the style sheet, such as an XML data island or creating the document object in script.

The transformNode method takes one parameter, which is an XML document object or XML element that contains the XSL style sheet. The result of the transformation is returned as a string. This string can be an XML fragment or raw text, which can be processed by the browser (such as an HTML fragment) or another application. The following is an example of the transformNode call:

```
resultString = xmlElement.transformNode(xslStyleSheet.XMLDocument);
```

The transformNodeToObject method takes two parameters: one is the XML document or element that contains the style sheet, and the other parameter is a result XML document object that is loaded with the results from the transformation. The following is an example of a transformNodeToObject call:

```
xmlElement.transformNodeToObject(xslStyleSheet.XMLDocument, resultObject);
```

Creating Your First XSL Style Sheet

Now that you are aware of how to invoke a transformation, it is time to learn the syntax of an XSL style sheet. To start with, XSL style sheets are generally saved in external files with an .xsl extension, but they can be included in the HTML file or can be dynamically generated just as you would any other XML file. Most of the functionality of XSL style sheets is built into a set of elements that are included in the style sheet. Table 10-1 lists each of the XSL elements and has a quick description of each; we will be covering these elements in more detail in the next couple of sections.

The first XSL element you need to be aware of is the <xsl:stylesheet> element. The stylesheet element serves as the document element for the XSL document and has a set of attributes that allow you to set defaults for the style sheet. Table 10-2 lists the attributes; however, most of the attributes are not changeable in IE 5.0.

There is another item to note with the stylesheet element: you need to define the name space (xmlns:xsl) for XSL, which is http://www.w3.org/TR/WD-xsl. The following is an example of the element with the name space defined.

```
<xsl:stylesheet xmlns:xsl="http://www.w3.org/TR/WD-xsl">
```

XSL Element	Description
xsl:apply-templates	Tells the XSL processor to search for the appropriate template and apply the template based on the type and context of the selected nodes.
xsl:attribute	Creates an attribute node and automatically attaches it to an output element.
xsl:choose	Provides the ability to have multiple condition testing when used with the xsl:otherwise and xsl:when elements.
xsl:comment	Generates a comment in the output document.
xsl:copy	Provides a mechanism to copy the current node from the source to the output documents.
xsl:element	Creates an element with a particular name in the output document.
xsl:eval	Executes a single line of script to generate a text string.
xsl:for-each	Loops through a set of nodes and applies a template repeatedly.
xsl:if	Applies a single conditional check of whether to apply a template fragment.
xsl:otherwise	Provides the ability to have multiple condition testing when used with the xsl:choose and xsl:when elements.
xsl:pi	Generates a processing instruction in the output document.
xsl:script	Defines a script section that contains functions or variables, which can be accessed from the XSL elements.

Table 10-1.   XSL Elements

XSL Element	Description
xsl:stylesheet	Functions as the document element and wraps one or more xsl:template and xsl:script elements.
xsl:template	Defines the output for nodes of a particular type and context.
xsl:value-of	Retrieves the value of a node and inserts it into the document as text.
xsl:when	Provides the ability to have multiple condition testing when used with the xsl:choose and xsl:otherwise elements.

Table 10-1.   XSL Elements *(continued)*

Attribute	Description
default-space	Whether to preserve the white space in the document. The only value supported in IE 5.0 is *default*.
indent-result	Whether to preserve the white space that appears in the style sheet. Only the value *yes* is supported in IE 5.0.
language	The scripting language to use in the style sheet. The default is JScript, and it also accepts the same values as the HTML script tag's language attribute.
result-ns	Determines what type of output should be returned from the transformation. IE 5.0 only supports XML, so this value is ignored.

Table 10-2.   Attributes for the stylesheet Element

The next element in the style sheet document tree is the <xsl:template> element. The template element is a very important element that defines the output for nodes of a particular type based on its context. The template element has two attributes: the language attribute and the match attribute. The language attribute defines the scripting language to use for the template; if you do not specify the attribute, the default language is JScript. The match attribute is an XSL pattern, which is used to define the context for the template; it provides an easy way to navigate into the document tree. By *context*, what we are saying is the location or level in the XML document to use. We will discuss this attribute in more detail later, but for now we will use the / (forward slash) value, which sets the context to the document level.

Now that we have defined our style sheet and defined the context of where to get the data, let's get the value of an XML element. To do this, we use the <xsl:value-of> element, that has one attribute, which is select. The select attribute takes a string, which is an XSL pattern that defines the value to retrieve. One very useful thing to be aware of is that if you do not set the select attribute or if you set the value to . (period), the value of the current node will be inserted. The XSL pattern syntax has a lot of functionality, but for now we will focus on how to retrieve an element in the current context. To retrieve an element's value, you can use the following element:

```
<xsl:value-of select="elementName">
```

Before we introduce you to any other functionality, let's put together a simple page to enforce what we have gone over thus far. There are a couple of minor things that are in the example that we want to point out. The first thing you should notice is that we have well-formed HTML included directly with our XSL elements. Another important item to note is the xsl:template element's select attribute, which is set to "Bands/Band". What we are doing here navigating from the document level to the root element (Bands), and we are telling the XSL parser that we want to retrieve the value of the Band element. The following example shows a simple XSL style sheet. An important thing to note is that in this chapter we will show the calling HTML, the XML, and the XSL style sheet all in one file. You will probably want to have an external source for the XML and XSL style sheets in real applications to aid in re-usabiltiy.

simpleXSL.htm

```
<html>
<script language="JavaScript">
function transform(){
  var transformResult =
bandList.transformNode(xslStyleSheet.XMLDocument);
  xmlValue.innerHTML = transformResult;
}</script>
<xml ID="bandList">
<Bands>
  <Band>Citizen King</Band>
</Bands></xml>
<xml ID="xslStyleSheet">
  <xsl:stylesheet xmlns:xsl="http://www.w3.org/TR/WD-xsl">
    <xsl:template match="/">
      Band Name:<b><xsl:value-of select="Bands/Band" /></b>
    </xsl:template>
  </xsl:stylesheet></xml>
<body onLoad="transform()">
<div ID="xmlValue"></body></html>
```

Handling Multiple Child Elements

In our example we had only one element under the root element. If there were multiple elements under the root, the data from the other child elements would not be retrieved. To apply the template repeatedly to multiple nodes you would use the <xsl:for-each> element. The for-each element has two attributes: the select attribute, which determines the set of nodes to iterate over, and the order-by attribute, which is a semicolon-separated list of items to sort by. One item to note about the order-by attribute is that in the latest version of the XSL specification it has been superseded by the sort attribute. Microsoft has noted that with the next release of IE, support will be added for the sort attribute. The individual sort criteria are expressed as an XSL pattern relative to the select attribute. The first non–white-space character of each sort item allows you to specify the direction by which the data should be ordered (+ means ascending, – descending). The following is a sample snippet that contains the XML and the XSL style sheet that loops though multiple elements. (Note: we are using . (period) in the order-by attribute to tell the processor to sort the data by the Band name.)

```
<xml ID="bandList">
<Bands>
  <Band>Citizen King</Band>
  <Band>Beattles</Band>
</Bands></xml>
<xml ID="xslStyleSheet">
  <xsl:stylesheet xmlns:xsl="http://www.w3.org/TR/WD-xsl">
    <xsl:template match="/">
      <xsl:for-each select="Bands/Band" order-by=".">
        Band Name:<b><xsl:value-of/></b><br/>
      </xsl:for-each>
    </xsl:template>
  </xsl:stylesheet></xml>
```

Moving beyond Your First XSL Style Sheet

With a basic understanding of the format and syntax of XSL style sheets, we can now move to some more advanced topics. The first item we will cover is how to navigate into the deeper levels of the XML tree. Later we will cover some of the more advanced elements of the XSL syntax.

Navigating Deeper into the Tree

As we have shown in our prior example, to navigate down a known path to retrieve a value from the XML document, you can put the path directly into the select attribute of the value-of element. However, it would be nicer to be able to navigate to a specific level and retrieve all the data from the level without the need to hard-code the paths in all of the elements. In addition to this, there are cases where we might not know the complete path, or you may have recursive data that you need to handle. The xsl:apply-templates element allows us to implement this type of functionality. This element directs the XSL processor to apply a template that matches the type and context of the selected nodes. For each of the selected nodes, the xsl:apply-templates element tells the XSL processor to try to find an xsl:template that has a matching match attribute. In one sense the xsl:apply-templates equates to a function call to process the selected nodes. To determine the selected nodes, this element has a select attribute, which is similar to the template's select attribute, where you set an XSL pattern string. If you do not specify the select attribute, then all of the child elements of the current element are selected.

The next thing to do is to create another xsl:template element with the select attribute set to match the select attribute of the xsl:apply-templates element. The following snippet, which is the XSL style sheet, will help us illustrate the xsl:apply-templates element's use. We take our prior simple example and expand on it to use this new element.

apply.xsl

```
<xml ID="xslStyleSheet">
  <xsl:stylesheet xmlns:xsl="http://www.w3.org/TR/WD-xsl">
    <xsl:template match="/">
      <xsl:apply-templates select="Bands" />
    </xsl:template>
    <xsl:template match="Bands">
      <xsl:for-each select="Band" order-by=".">
        Band Name:<b><xsl:value-of/></b><br/>
      </xsl:for-each>
    </xsl:template>
  </xsl:stylesheet></xml>
```

There are a few rules that apply to how the parser determines which template to use if there are multiple templates that match. Because you can place templates inside of the xsl:apply-templates element, if one of the matching templates is contained inside of the xsl:apply-templates element, then this child template is the template that is processed. The templates that are inside of the xsl:apply-template element are not visible outside of the containing element, and because of this you can create locally scoped templates. If one of the matching templates is not a child element, then the template located last in the style sheet is used.

Because we feel the xsl:apply-template element is very important, and to help further illustrate the functionality in the xsl:apply-templates element, we will now go over a slightly more complex example using this element. In addition, we want to show you an example of the multiple matching template rules. Figure 10-1 shows the results of the transformation.

apply.htm

```
<html>
<script language="JavaScript">
function transform(){
  var transformResult = bandList.transformNode(xslStyleSheet.XMLDocument);
  xmlValue.innerHTML = transformResult;
}</script>
<xml ID="bandList">
<Bands>
  <Band>
    <Name>Beatles</Name>
    <NumberOfMembers>4</NumberOfMembers>
    <HomeTown>Liverpool England</HomeTown>
    <CDList>
      <CD>
        <Name>Yellow Submarine</Name>
      </CD>
    </CDList>
  </Band>
  <Band>
    <Name>Citizen King</Name>
    <NumberOfMembers>5</NumberOfMembers>
    <HomeTown>Milwaukee, WI</HomeTown>
    <CDList>
      <CD>
```

```xml
        <Name>Brown Paper Bag</Name>
      </CD>
      <CD>
        <Name>Better Days</Name>
      </CD>
    </CDList>
  </Band>
</Bands></xml>
<xml ID="xslStyleSheet">
  <xsl:stylesheet xmlns:xsl="http://www.w3.org/TR/WD-xsl">
    <xsl:template match="/">
      <table border="1">
        <thead><th>Band</th><th># of Members</th><th>Home
City</th><th>CD(s)</th></thead>
        <xsl:apply-templates select="Bands" />
      </table>
    </xsl:template>
    <xsl:template match="Bands">
      <xsl:for-each select="Band" order-by=".">
        <tr>
          <xsl:apply-templates select="Name" />
          <xsl:apply-templates select="NumberOfMembers" />
          <xsl:apply-templates select="HomeTown" />
          <xsl:apply-templates select="CDList" />
        </tr>
      </xsl:for-each>
    </xsl:template>
    <xsl:template match="CDList">
      <td><table>
      <xsl:for-each select="CD">
        <tr><td>
          <xsl:apply-templates select="Name">
            <xsl:template match="Name">
              <td style="Font-Size:8pt"><xsl:value-of /></td>
            </xsl:template>
          </xsl:apply-templates>
        </td></tr>
      </xsl:for-each>
      </table></td>
    </xsl:template>
    <xsl:template match="Name">
      <td><xsl:apply-templates /></td>
```

```
    </xsl:template>
    <xsl:template match="NumberOfMembers">
        <td><xsl:apply-templates /></td>
    </xsl:template>
    <xsl:template match="HomeTown">
        <td><xsl:apply-templates /></td>
    </xsl:template>
    <xsl:template match="text()"><xsl:value-of /></xsl:template>
</xsl:stylesheet></xml>
<body onLoad="transform()">
<p align="center"><img src="cd.gif"></p>
<p align="center"><b>A List Of Bands That I Have Listened To
Recently</b></p>
<div ID="xmlValue" align="center"></body></html>
```

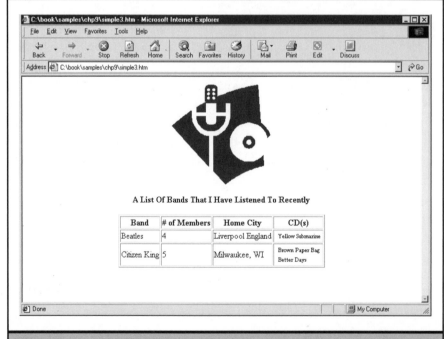

Figure 10-1.   The results of the apply-templates example. Notice the smaller font on the CD names, which shows the resolution of multiple matching templates.

Scripting inside of the XSL Style Sheet

In all of the examples we have shown so far, we simply took the data out of an XML element and placed it into the result document. This functionality is great, but there may be cases when you need to manipulate the node or execute script based on the node's value to further transform the data. There are two elements available in XSL to support calling script: the xsl:eval and xsl:script elements. The xsl:eval element executes a single line of script and inserts the results of the script into the result document. The eval element has one attribute that sets the scripting language to use, which defaults to JScript, but can be set to any of the script languages supported by the HTML script tag's language attribute. The scripting syntax is the same as if you were creating a script block inside of an HTML page with the exception of the reserved characters <,>, and &. If you are going to use any of these characters in the eval element, you must use the escaped version—<, >, and &—so that the XSL processor does not interpret the characters as part of the style sheet.

The xsl:script element allows you to define global variables and functions that can be called during the transformation. The xsl:script element can be placed inside of an xsl:stylesheet or xsl:template element and becomes visible from anywhere in the style sheet. If there are multiple global variables or functions with the same name, the last variable or function in the style sheet is used. The following is a style sheet that uses the script and eval elements to dynamically build a counter for each item in a table. The example builds off our prior example and could be used with the same XML file as shown earlier.

```
<xml ID="xslStyleSheet">
  <xsl:stylesheet xmlns:xsl="http://www.w3.org/TR/WD-xsl">
    <xsl:template match="/">
      <table border="1">
        <thead><th>#</th><th>Band</th><th># of Members</th><th>Home
City</th></thead>
        <xsl:apply-templates select="Bands" />
      </table>
    </xsl:template>
    <xsl:template match="Bands">
```

```
<xsl:script>
  var counter = 0;
  function getPosition() {
    return ++counter;
  }
</xsl:script>
<xsl:for-each select="Band" order-by=".">
  <tr>
    <td><xsl:eval>getPosition()</xsl:eval></td>
    <xsl:apply-templates select="Name" />
    <xsl:apply-templates select="NumberOfMembers" />
    <xsl:apply-templates select="HomeTown" />
  </tr>
</xsl:for-each>
</xsl:template>
...
</xsl:stylesheet></xml>
```

In addition to being able to use standard script inside the script
element, XSL provides a few new features that are available to us
inside both of the scripting elements. For example, inside the xsl:eval
and xsl:script elements you can access the current node that is being
processed using the *this* pointer. The this pointer is a reference into
the XML tree, and from here you can access any of the elements in the
XML tree using the XML document object model (see Chapter 8 for
more information on the XML DOM). Besides the ability to access the
XML DOM, there are a few methods exposed by the XSL processor,
which give us either more information about an XML element or
provide us with some useful data formatting functionality. Here is
a list of built-in XSL methods and their descriptions.

absoluteChildNumber(xmlNode)   Returns the number of the
node relative to all of its siblings. The first child of an element is
assigned a value of 1.

ancestorChildNumber(nodeName, xmlNode)   Navigates back
up the tree (from the nodeName element) to find a node that
matches the nodeName parameter and returns the child number
of that element. If a match is not found it returns a null.

childNumber(xmlNode)   Returns the number of the node relative to the siblings with the same name. The first child of an element is assigned a value of 1.

depth(xmlNode)   Returns the depth of the node in the document tree. The root node is 0, the first child of the root is 1.

formatDate(dateValue, formatString, locale)   Returns the date value formatted based on the format string and locale. The format string supports the following values:

Format	Result
m	Returns month values as 1–12
mm	Returns month values as 01–12
mmm	Returns month values as Jan–Dec
mmmm	Returns month values as January–December
mmmmm	Returns month values as the first letter of each month
d	Returns the days as 1–31
dd	Returns the days as 01–31
ddd	Returns the days as Sun–Sat
dddd	Returns the days as Sunday–Saturday
yy	Returns the years as 00–99
yyyy	Returns the years as 1900–9999

The locale is used to determine the order in which the date values should be returned. If unspecified, month-day-year is assumed. (Note: to use the formatDate function, the date value passed in must come from an XML file that is using a schema that defines the field as a DateTime type.)

formatIndex(integerValue, formatString)   Returns the integer formatted based on the formatString, in the following numbering systems:

Format	Result
1	Standard numbering
01	Numbering with leading zeros
A	Numbering following uppercase character sequence A–Z, AA–ZZ, and so on
a	Numbering following lowercase character sequence a–z, aa–zz, and so on
I	Numbering using uppercase roman numerals (I, II, III, and so on)
i	Numbering using lowercase roman numerals (i, ii, iii, and so on)

formatNumber(numericValue, formatString) Returns the number formatted based on the formatString, in the following numbering systems:

Format	Result
#	As a numeric place holder, returns only significant digits; does not return insignificant zeros
0	As a numeric place holder, returns zero if there are not that many digits in the number passed in
?	Adds spaces for insignificant zeros on either side of a number to align the numbers
.	Specifies the location of the decimal point in the number
,	Displays a comma as a thousands separator or scales a number by multiples of one thousand
%	Displays a number as a percentage
E- or e-	Displays a number in scientific notation
E+ or e+	Displays a number in scientific notation and places a plus or minus sign by the exponent

The following is an example of formatting a number to have a currency-like format with a comma separator and two decimal places:

```
formatNumber(someValue, "#,###.00");
```

formatTime(timeValue, formatString, locale)   Returns the time value formatted based on the format string and locale. The format string supports the following values:

Format	Result
h	Hours in 0–23 format
hh	Hours in 00–23 format
m	Minutes in 0–59 format
mm	Minutes in 00–59 format
s	Seconds in 0–59 format
ss	Seconds in 00–59 format
AM/PM or am/pm	Displays time with AM/PM or am/pm. Hours are displayed based on a 12-hour clock
A/P or a/p	Displays time with A/P or a/p. Hours are displayed based on a 12-hour clock
ss.00	Displays the fractions of a second

The locale is used to determine the order in which the time values should be returned. (Note: to use the formatTime function, the time value passed in must come from an XML file that is using a schema that defines the field as a DateTime type.)

uniqueID(xmlNode)   Returns a unique identifier for a particular node. Can be useful if you need to generate a unique ID for an HTML element or a unique identifier for an XML element.

Conditional Elements

The scripting functionality offers us a lot of flexibility, but in some cases you may wish to test the value of the data, and, based on the value, change the output or structure of the document that is generated. XSL supports this type of functionality in two different forms: a simple single-condition check or a multicondition check. You can implement a single-condition check using the xsl:if element. The if element allows you to evaluate the value of a script expression or the value of an XML item. To support script expressions, the xsl:if element has an expr attribute and a language attribute, which is used to define the scripting language of the expression. By *script expressions*, we are talking about a line of script that returns a true or false value. If the script in the expr attribute returns true, then the contents of the xsl:if element is inserted into the document. To support checking the value of an XML item, the xsl:if element has a test attribute. Inside of the test attribute, you specify a select pattern, and if the pattern returns one or more nodes from the document, the contents of the xsl:if element is inserted into the document. Inside of the xsl:if element you can place any output elements or other XSL elements (except for xsl:script, xsl:stylesheet, or xsl:template elements).

If you need to support multiple-part selections, such as if condition…else if condition …otherwise, you can use the xsl:choose, xsl:when, xsl:otherwise combination of elements. The xsl:choose defines the start and end of the selection criteria; the xsl:when allows you to define the individual conditional tests; and the xsl:otherwise provides the default condition if none of the other conditions are met. As soon as one of the xsl:when elements or the xsl:otherwise is chosen, the choose block is executed (you do not need to break out of the condition test). Similar to the xsl:if element, the xsl:when supports the expr, language, and test attributes to support script expressions and XML pattern matching.

The following code snippets show using both a single-condition (xsl:if) and multicondition (xsl:choose) selections. The samples check a global script variable, quantityOnHand, and adds the output to the document in the form of a re-order message based on the results.

Here is the xsl:if sample:

```
<xsl:if expr="quantityOnHand &lt; 5"><B>Re-Order Immediately</B></xsl:if>
```

And here is the xsl:choose sample:

```
<xsl:choose>
  <xsl:when expr="quantityOnHand &lt; 5">
```

```
   <B>Re-Order Immediately</B>
 </xsl:when>
 <xsl:when expr="quantityOnHand &lt; 10">
   Re-Order In Next 2-3 days
 </xsl:when>
 <xsl:when expr="quantityOnHand &lt; 15">
    Re-Order In Next 5-10 days
 </xsl:when>
 <xsl:otherwise>
   Inventory is adequate
 </xsl:otherwise>
</xsl:choose>
```

Creating Elements and Attributes Dynamically

XSL style sheets also provide us with the ability to create or copy elements and their attributes. These newly created items are included in our result document, which seems like something we could have done before. There are, however, some special considerations that these elements address. For example, what if you were trying to have the output of an XSL style sheet be an XSL style sheet itself or do something as simple as create an attribute in the output without breaking the well-formatted rules of the style sheet? The helper elements we are going to discuss next will solve the inherent problems associated with these tasks.

In our prior discussions about XSL, we placed the text inside of a block element such as an HTML div or span or an XML element. You may have tried to take an xsl:value-of element and use it to set or create an attribute, which does not work because it does not follow the well-formed rules. So to support creating attributes of elements, XSL has another element, which is xsl:attribute. The xsl:attribute element has one attribute, the name attribute, that contains the name of the new attribute to create. The xsl:attribute element contains the value of the new attribute. We realize that these last two sentences may have had one too many attributes and elements to be perfectly clear, so here's a little code snippet to show how you would create a value attribute for an HTML input element:

```
<input type="text"><xsl:attribute name="value"><xsl:value-of />
</xsl:attribute></input>
```

There may be cases (probably not very often) when you would like an XSL style sheet to generate another XSL style sheet as its output document. If you need to accomplish this, you can use the xsl:element to create an element in the output document. You need the xsl:element element because once the XSL processor sees the XSL instruction it processes it as part of the document. For example, if we wanted to generate an XSL instruction element from our XSL, we would use the xsl:element element and set the name attribute to the element name we wish to generate. For example, if we wanted to generate an xsl:template tag that has a match attribute equal to "Name," we would use the following XSL fragment:

```
<xsl:element name="xsl:template">
  <xsl:attribute name="match">Name</xsl:attribute>
</xsl:element>
```

If you would like to take a node from the source and copy it directly to the output document, you can use the xsl:copy element. The xsl:copy element copies the current element to the document; however, it does not copy the attributes or children of the element (because of this the value of the element is also not copied).

The final two elements that make up the XSL syntax are used to insert comments and processing instructions into the result document. The xsl:comment element takes text between the start and end tags and places it between the starting (<!—) and ending characters (—>) to create a comment in the result document. The xsl:pi element has one attribute, which is the name of the processing instruction, and it creates processing instructions from the text value between the start and end tags. If you are unfamiliar with what processing instructions are, they are elements that help the parser or processor know the format of the document. For example, a common XML processing instruction would be <? Xml version="1.0" ?>. It tells the XML parser that the syntax of the document should conform to the version 1.0 standard of XML. The following is an example of how you would create the previous instruction from inside an XSL style sheet:

```
<xsl:pi name="xml">version="1.0"</xsl:pi>
```

Trapping When a Node Is Being Transformed

There is a pretty useful event exposed by the data source XML document that fires each time a node of the XML source is about to be transformed to the output document. This event is the ontransformnode event, and setting the ontransformnode property of the XML document to an event handler can specifically set up an event handler. The event handler will be passed in two properties, the first of which is the node from the XSL style sheet that will transform the data and the other parameter is the XML node, which is about to be transformed. The event can be useful for two purposes, one of which is to stop the transformation if a specific node is reached, and the other is to aid in debugging. To stop transforming at a specific node, you can return a false value from the event handler function. The event can also be used as a debugging aid by looking at the XML property of the two parameters, and you can make sure that your nodes are being processed as you had planned. The following is a code snippet showing how you would set up and use the event handler from inside of an HTML page.

```JavaScript
<script language="JavaScript">
function transform(){
  bandList.ontransformnode = trapTransformation;
  var transformResult =
bandList.transformNode(xslStyleSheet.XMLDocument);
  xmlValue.innerHTML = transformResult;
}
function trapTransformation(xslNode, xmlNode){
  alert("XSL Code: " + xslNode.xml + "\n\n XML Node:" + xmlNode.xml);
  if (xmlNode.value == "Beattles")
    return false;
}</script>
```

Tips on Debugging XSL Style Sheets

One of the difficulties of using any style sheet, cascading or XSL, comes in trying to debug them. This becomes even more pronounced with XSL because of the conditional and script execution. Unfortunately, there isn't a perfect tool to debug XSL style sheets; you need to use a couple of different tools to help you figure out the bug. We have already talked about using the ontransformnode event to look at which nodes are being transformed by what XSL. Microsoft has a set of sample HTML pages/XSL style sheets available to download from its Web site, which it calls an XSL debugger. This is a nice tool that puts a user interface around the ontransformnode and allows you to set break points and watch the execution of the code. We won't go into great detail about the debugger, because it is pretty simple and self-explanatory. Figure 10-2 shows the debugger in action.

In addition to using the XSL Debugger, you can also create script blocks and call a scripting debugger from inside of script in the XSL style sheet. You can use the *debugger* method from JavaScript and use the pointer to interrogate the current node (for more information on debugging scripts, see Chapter 5).

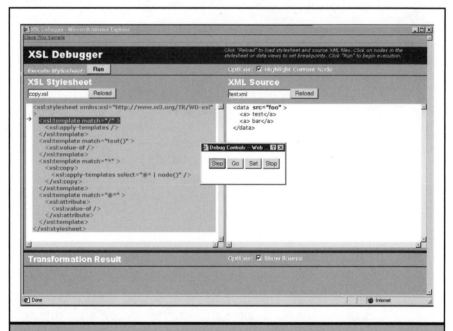

Figure 10-2.   The Microsoft XSL Debugger is a simple but useful debugging tool.

TIP: If we could give you only one tip for debugging XSL style sheets, it would be this: If you are not getting any results from your transformation or if unexplainable things are happening, open the style sheet in Internet Explorer. If your style sheet is embedded in your HTML page, save it to a separate file and open that file in IE. IE will show you any bad syntax that you may have in the style sheet. More likely than not, you have a syntax problem in your style because you are not familiar with the stringent requirements of writing well-formed HTML, or you simply forgot an end tag. In a recent project using complex XSL style sheets, IE became our best debugging asset.

XSL PATTERNS—THE STUFF THAT MAKES XSL CLICK

Up to this point, we have shied away from going over the full functionality of XSL patterns because it's a big subject, and we wanted to introduce you to the functionality of XSL first. But the time has come to take the plunge. XSL patterns are declarative in nature, rather than procedural, and you will notice that the pattern describes the types of nodes to match, based on the hierarchical relationship between the different nodes. You can think of XSL patterns as a type of query language that is a hybrid between SQL, DOS commands (such as dir and cd), and simple URL mapping. The reason we say this is because there is syntax to filter data, similar to a where clause, that deals with conditions and comparisons. However, because we are dealing with a hierarchical structure that is similar to a file system, we need to change the context (move up or down in the tree) and retrieve nodes based on the new context (similar to what you would do in DOS). You will see some similarities to both syntaxes in XSL patterns, and you will also see a new syntax to support XML.

One thing we need to remind you of is the notion of the current context. The context is the current node you are working from or, as in the case of XSL style sheets, the current node being processed. The reason we bring this up is because all of the syntax of the XSL pattern is relative to the current context.

The basic idea of an XSL pattern is to specify the path by which to change the context and then find the nodes that match a given filter or condition. The XML element names are critical in the navigation and retrieval of nodes. As you have seen in the XSL style sheet section, an XML element's name is inserted directly into the XSL pattern string to retrieve nodes or to navigate to a certain path.

The following is an XML file that will serve as our sample data to show you the pattern syntax. The design of this document is intended to easily illustrate the functionality, not to be the best XML design.

transactions.xml

```
<SalesTransactions>
  <Year Value="1999">
    <January>
      <Transaction Type="Cash" Day="1">
        <Processor>Beth</Processor>
        <Processor>Elle</Processor>
        <Sale>
           <Amount>100</Amount>
           <Customer>Acme Imports</Customer>
        </Sale>
      </Transaction>
      <Transaction Type="Credit" Day="10">
        <Processor>Sara</Processor>
        <Approved>Beth</Approved>
        <Credit>
           <Amount>500</Amount>
           <Customer>Premier Business Software</Customer>
        </Credit>
      </Transaction>
      <Transaction Type="Credit" Day="11">
        <Processor>Beth</Processor>
        <Credit>
           <Amount>5</Amount>
           <Customer>Premier Business Software</Customer>
        </Credit>
```

```
      </Transaction>
    </January>
  </Year>
</SalesTransactions>
```

The first operator you need to be aware of is the / (forward slash). The / (as is the case in a URL) tells the processor to move the context to the child, in this case, elements (in the case of a URL, a directory). If the / is the first character in the pattern, it indicates that the context of the query is the root node. For example, if we wanted to find all of the Year elements that were children of the root element, our XSL pattern would look like

```
/Year
```

If we just wanted to find the Transaction elements of the current node, the pattern would simply be

```
Transaction
```

But what if we didn't care if the elements were direct descendants of the current context? Well, in this case we can use the // operator. The // operator tells the processor to look through all of the descendants of the current node. Once again, similar to the / operator, if the // operator makes up the first characters in the pattern, the context will be the root node. The following sample pattern shows how you can start to build on your pattern by combining operators; it would find Customer elements anywhere inside of Transaction elements, where the Transaction elements were children of the current node.

```
Transaction//Customer
```

The . (period) character indicates the current context, and it is used only in situations such as the following request: I want all of the Customer elements that are one or more levels deep. In this case, the pattern would be

```
.//Customer
```

It is important to note that we don't need to use this operator if we are looking for direct descendants of the current context because the current context is implied if we simply use the element name. The following two patterns return the same results:

```
Customer
./Customer
```

There may be cases where you wish to return all of the children of an element, regardless of the element name. To do this, you can use the * (asterisk) character (also known as the wildcard character) to return all of the child elements. For example, if you wished to return all of the elements of a Transaction element, you would use the following pattern:

```
Transaction/*
```

In addition to this, the wildcard character can be used to find a certain type of grandchild element in any of the child nodes. For example if we wanted to find all of the Customer elements that were grandchildren of a Transaction element, we would use the following:

```
Transaction/*/Customer
```

If you wish to change the context to the parent element of the current element, you can use the .. operator. For example, if the current context was one of the transactions, and we wanted to return the entire set of sibling Transactions, we could use the following syntax:

```
../Transaction
```

Up to this point, all of our focus has been on elements and their values; however, XSL patterns also contain syntax operators to support working with attributes of elements. The @ character is used to specify to the processor that the following name is an attribute. So if we wanted to return the Type attribute from the Transaction element, the pattern would look like the following:

```
Transaction/@Type
```

In addition to this, the attribute also supports the wildcard character. So if you wanted to return all of the attributes of the Transaction element, you would use the following:

```
Transaction/@*
```

Working with Collections of Elements

The collection of elements returned from your XSL query preserves the order that elements were defined in within the source document. Because of this, there may be instances where you wish to return only a specific item from the collection of matching elements, such as the first element that matches my pattern. In addition to this, you can also work with a collection of elements from the source document to return a specified element in the collection, such as returning only the second transaction from every month for this year.

To retrieve a specific element, you use the bracket characters ([ ]) with the index of the item you wish to have returned inside the brackets. (Note: the first element in the collection has a position of zero.) The pattern syntax for the two different types of queries is nearly the same; the only thing that is different is the order in which the operators are performed. It is important to note that to explicitly specify the order of operations, you use brackets around the item you wish to execute first. The bracket operators have higher precedence than either the / or // operators. Because of this, if we had the following pattern

```
//Transaction[0]
```

we would be returned all of the Transactions where the Transaction was the first Transaction element relative to its parent anywhere in the document. If we wanted to return the first Transaction element that was found in the document, we would use the following syntax:

```
(//Transaction)[0]
```

If we interpret the prior pattern's syntax, it is telling the processor to find all of the transactions and then, based on that collection, return the first element.

In addition to specifying the ordinal position, the pattern syntax exposes an end() method, which returns the last item in the collection. So if we wanted the last Transaction found anywhere in the document we would use the following syntax:

```
//Transaction[end()]
```

Filters—The Where Clause Of Patterns

The ability to add filters or constraints to an XSL pattern makes XSL a very powerful tool. Because of this functionality, you have the ability to find elements based on their value or attribute, and you can turn XML documents into a type of database system. We do not recommend that you throw away your database server and use XML files; however, for small-scale data look-ups and client-side filtering, this could be what you're looking for.

A filter is defined by using the bracket ([ ]) characters and contains a special pattern inside the characters called a *filter pattern*. A filter pattern is tested against each item in the collection, and if the item does not pass the filter test, it is excluded from the result collection.

One of the simplest filters is to test for the existence of a subelement of a given element. For example if we wanted to find all of the Transaction elements, in the current context, with a Credit element, we could use the following syntax:

```
Transactions[Credit]
```

To expand a bit on using filters, if we wanted to find all of the Transactions in the current context where the first Processor element equaled Beth, we would use the following filter:

```
Transactions[Processor="Beth"]
```

It is important to note that we can use either single or double quotes around the value. This is important if you are passing the value from inside of a scripting language where you need to use either the single or double quote as the string identifier. So the prior filter could also be expressed as

```
Transactions[Processor='Beth']
```

In cases like the Processor element, where we can have multiples of the same child element, we might want to search all of the child elements for a matching value rather than just the first one. To do this, we use the any keyword prior to our search criteria. Going back to our previous pattern, now if we search for transactions where the Processor was "Elle" (which is the value of the second processor element), we will have elements returned. The following is the syntax for this filter:

```
Transactions[$any$ Processor="Elle"]
```

In cases where you know there will only be one child element, we recommend that you do not put the any keyword into the filter pattern for performance reasons.

   In addition to checking if the value matches any of the multiple elements, you can also check to see if the value matches all of the elements by using the all keyword. In the following pattern, the filter looks at all of the Processor elements and returns only the Transactions where all the Processor elements equal Beth.

```
Transactions[$all$ Processor="Beth"]
```

Advanced Comparisons

In addition to simply checking to see if a value or attribute is equal, your filter pattern can contain other comparison operators. The method of using the alternate operators is the same as using the equal operator. So if we wanted to find all of the Transactions where any of the processors were not Beth, we would use the following syntax:

```
Transactions[$any$ Processor!="Beth"]
```

The other supported operators are shown in Table 10-3.

   There is one important feature that you need to be aware of with the new operators and that is how the less-than and greater-than operators work with string values. Because all of the values from elements and attributes are returned as strings, the processor converts the text strings that contain numeric values to long or double types depending on the value. If the value is a string, however, the processor does a direct comparison. So if we wanted to return all of the Transactions in the current context where the value of the transaction (either a sale or credit) was greater than 200, we would use the following syntax:

```
Transaction[*/Amount > 200]
```

Operator	Alternate Syntax	Description
=	eq or ieq	Checks for equal values. The ieq checks for case-insensitive equality.
!=	ne or ine	Checks for not-equal values. The ine checks for case-insensitive inequality.
<	lt or ilt	Checks for less-than values. The ilt checks for case-insensitive less-than values.
<=	le or ile	Checks for less-than-or-equal values. The ile checks for case-insensitive less-than-or-equal values.
>	gt or igt	Checks for greater-than values. The igt checks for case-insensitive greater-than values.
>=	ge or ige	Checks for greater-than-or-equal values. The ige checks for case-insensitive greater-than-or-equal values.

Table 10-3.   Supported XSL Pattern Operators

To help further illustrate the pattern syntax, if we wanted to return all of the Transaction elements in the current context where the Day attribute was greater than or equal to ten (that is, return all the transactions from the tenth of the month and beyond), we would use the following pattern:

```
Transaction[@Day >= 10]
```

In addition if you use any of the greater-than or less-than comparison operators (<, >, <=, >=) against a string, the processor returns elements where the string values begin with the value that is greater than or less than the condition. In other words, if we wanted to return the Transactions where the Customer began with an M or greater, we would use the following pattern:

```
Transaction[*/Customer >= 'M']
```

Using Logical And and Or with Filter Patterns

In addition to single expression comparisons, XSL filter patterns support the ability to perform logical *and* and *or* operations. This is done using the *and* and *or* operators between two filter patterns. So, for example, if we wanted all of the Transaction elements for the current context where the Day attribute for the Transaction is greater than 9 and the Customer value began with an M or greater, we would use the following pattern:

```
Transaction[@Day >= 9 and */Customer >= 'M']
```

The following would be the syntax if we wanted Transaction elements that met either of the criteria:

```
Transaction[@Day >= 9 or */Customer >= 'M']
```

To move along with the same line of thinking, how would we handle a case where we wanted to have the opposite of the value of one of the expressions? To put this into our sample's terms, let's say, for example, that we wanted to find all of the Transactions for a month where the transaction has a Credit element but does not have an Approved element. To handle this type of situation, filter patterns have the not() operator, which negates the value of an expression within a filter pattern. The following shows what our pattern would look like, assuming that the current context was at the month level:

```
Transaction[Credit and not(Approved)]
```

Unioning Results

There may be cases where you simply cannot retrieve all of the elements you want from a single query. In these cases, you can use the union operator (|) to return a collection of elements that is a combination of results from two or more queries. The union operator preserves the source document order and does not return duplicate elements. There are a few limitations to how the union operator can be used, as far as the context of the different queries goes. The limitations are that all of the queries that are combined by the union operator must be from the same subtree and that they must have the same root element. These limitations prevent us from executing queries that start from a different context; we can return elements from different contexts, but we cannot, for example, use the .. operator in one query and not in the other, or use the / as the first character in a query and not in another.

You may be thinking that you would never have the need for such a query, but we will take our simple XML file and show you where the union operator can be useful. Let's say, for example, that you wanted to return a collection of elements from our sales file that contain all of the employees who dealt with transactions for the month, no matter if they were the person who processed the transaction or approved it. To do this, we would want a union of all of the Processor and Approved elements. If the current context were the month (January) node, we would use the following query to return all of the elements:

```
Transaction/Processor | Transaction/Approved
```

It is important to note that using our sample XML document we would be returned two nodes with the value of "Beth." The reason for this is because the two node types are different: one is a Processor node and the other is an Approved node. The union does eliminate the duplicate elements, as is the case with the multiple Processor nodes that have a value of "Beth." What the union is comparing to eliminate the duplicates is the element-value combination.

Context Changing Methods

We have already covered some of the concepts of context changing when we talked about the context changing operators (.., /, //). But now we want to take these operators to another level, one that allows you to actually change the context by using a pattern string. Both the context changing operators and methods are always first in a filter pattern and allow you to specify where in the document the current element is pointing. There are three context changing methods: *ancestor*, *context*, and *id*. The id method returns the element or elements referenced by the given ID (you can specify multiple IDs by passing in a space-delimited string) or pattern. The ID is specified in an XML schema, which we will be talking about in Chapter 11; we will cover this method in a little more detail there.

The ancestor method is used to change the context of a query or filter to the nearest ancestor (such as the parent, grandparent, great-grandparent, and so on) that matches a specified pattern based on the current context. The pattern is tested against the current element's parent for a match; if a match is found, then the parent is returned. If a match is not found, the grandparent is tested against the pattern returning the grandparent if a match is found. The method continues to test each of the ancestors until a match is found or there aren't any more ancestors. If a match is not found, the context cannot be changed and the query will not return any matching elements. As we noted earlier, the ancestor method can be used inside of a filter; however, the method cannot appear after a / or // in the filter pattern.

Let's apply the ancestor method to our sample XML document. If the current context was way down at the customer level and we wanted the Transaction element that this Customer was part of, we could simply use the following pattern to return the Transaction element:

```
ancestor(Transaction)
```

The context method allows you to change the context relative to where the query started. The context method has one parameter that indicates the relative positions upward or downward in the tree. If you do not pass any value in or you pass in a value of 0, the context method returns the element from which the query was called (the current context prior to any changes). If you pass in a negative number to the method, the method returns an ancestor that is the parameter's position higher in the tree. So, for example, if we passed in –1, we would be returned the parent of the element; –2 would return us the grandparent of the element. If you pass in a positive number to the method, it returns elements based on the context-switching elements in the style sheet. To explain this, let's create a simple style sheet for our sample XML document. The syntax of the style sheet follows:

context.xsl

```
<xsl:stylesheet xmlns:xsl="http://www.w3.org/TR/WD-xsl">
    <xsl:template match="/">
       <xsl:apply-templates select="SalesTransactions" />
    </xsl:template>
    <xsl:template match="SalesTransactions">
       <xsl:apply-templates select="Year" />
    </xsl:template>
    <xsl:template match="Year">
       <xsl:apply-templates select="January" />
    </xsl:template>
    <xsl:template match="January">
       <xsl:for-each select="Transaction">
         <P><xsl:value-of select="@Day" /></P>
       </xsl:for-each>
    </xsl:template>
</xsl:stylesheet>
```

So what we have is a very simple, some might say worthless, XSL style sheet. To fully understand this concept, you need to know what a context-switching element is. A *context-switching element* is any XSL element that changes the current context to a different location in the document. In our example, the switching elements are the xsl:template elements and the xsl:for-each element. For every time we hit one of these context-switching elements, another level becomes available to the context method. So, in the example above, if you were to pass in the following values, this is what element would be returned:

Value	Element
1	The document root—context–switching element <xsl:template match="/">
2	The SalesTransaction element—context–switching element <xsl:template match=" SalesTransactions ">

Value	Element
3	The Year element—context–switching element <xsl:template match=" Year">
4	The January element—context–switching element <xsl:template match="January">
5	The current transaction element—context–switching element <xsl:for-each select="Transaction">

If you are currently in the context of one of the higher-level elements, you cannot use the context method to retrieve a lower-level element. For example, inside of the template for the sales transactions, if you try to access the January element using the context method and passing in a value of 4, you will not be returned any elements.

Now that we are aware of how the parameter works for dealing with the context method, let's put together a very simple example of using the method. If the current context was at the customer level, and you wanted the Day attribute for the containing transaction, you would use the following pattern:

```
context(-2)/@Day
```

XSL Pattern Methods

In addition to all of the functionality we have covered so far, XSL patterns also expose a number of methods to gather information about a particular node and to retrieve various types of nodes from a document. The syntax you use to execute a method for a particular context is to append an ! (exclamation point) character followed by the method name. Because most of the method's functionality is available using different techniques in the XSL pattern syntax, we will just list the different methods, their parameters, and a brief description about each method.

Here's a list of informational methods available in XSL patterns:

date(dateFormat)   Converts the value to the specified date format that was passed into the method. Similar to the formatDate function. To use this method, the date value passed in must come from an XML file that is using a schema that defines the field as a DateTime type.

end()   Returns a match for the last element of a collection.

index()   Returns the position of the element within the parent.

nodeName()   Returns the tag name of the element, including the name space.

nodeType()   Returns the type of node. The value is an integer that maps to the following table:

Node Type Value	Actual Node Type
1	Element
2	Attribute
3	Text, represents the text content of an element
4	CDATA section
5	Entity reference
6	Entity
7	Processing instruction
8	Comment
9	Document object
10	Document type
11	Document fragment
12	Notation

number()   Converts the value to a number format.

value()   Returns the typed version of the value based on the schema. If there isn't a schema, it simply returns the text value for the element.

Here's a list of collection methods available in XSL patterns:

attribute([name])   Returns a collection of attributes with the matching name for the current context. The name parameter is optional and if it is not passed in, returns all of the attributes for the context.

cdata()   Returns a collection of all of the CDATA nodes for the current context.

comment()   Returns a collection of comments in the document based on the current context.

element([name])   Returns a collection of elements with the matching name for the current context. The name parameter is optional and if it is not passed in, returns all of the elements for the context.

node   Returns a collection of all the nodes with the exception of attribute nodes and the document node for the current context.

pi([name])   Returns a collection of processing instructions with the matching name for the current context. The name parameter is optional and if it is not passed in, returns all of the processing instructions for the context.

text()   Returns a collection of all of the text nodes and CDATA nodes for the current context.

textnode()   Returns a collection of all of the text nodes for the current context.

XSL Syntax Order of Precedence

One final thing you need to be aware of is the precedence of all of the different XSL pattern operators we have gone over. The following table lists the precedence order from the highest precedence (executes first) to the lowest (executes last):

Operator	Operator Description
()	Grouping
[]	Filters
!	Method invocation
/, //	Path operators
any, all	Set operators
=, !=, lt, le, gt, ge, eq, ne, leq	Comparison
|	Union
not()	Boolean not
and	Boolean and
or	Boolean or

SEARCHING FOR ITEMS IN AN XML DOCUMENT

Now that you have learned about XSL style sheets and all of that great XSL pattern syntax, you may be thinking, "Sure, that pattern stuff is cool, but do I have to use the style sheets to take advantage of the functionality?" Luckily for all of us, the answer is no—we can query the data in the XML document directly using the selectNodes and selectSingleNode functions. Because you have put all of that hard work in to learning XSL patterns, these two calls will be a piece of cake. However, just because this section is short, don't underestimate the capabilities covered. We have found ourselves using these two methods more frequently than we use XSL style sheets.

Both of the methods are available from the XML Document node or from any element in the document tree. The element from which you are calling the method serves as the current context for the pattern. All of the syntax of the patterns can be used, with the exception of the context method, simply because the functionality is tied directly to XSL style sheets. Both the selectNodes and selectSingleNode methods take a single parameter, which is an XSL pattern. The selectNodes method returns an object that you might remember from our discussion of the XML DOM, the XMLDOMNodeList Object. (For more information about the functionality of this object, we refer you back to Chapter 8.) The selectSingleNode method returns a single node; if there are multiple nodes that match the criteria of the pattern, the first item in the document that matches the pattern is returned.

To show the power of these methods, we will create a simple code snippet that once again goes back to our sample XML document and builds a table of transactions and displays a sum of the total sales (less the total credits). One thing you should think about is how you would have accomplished this same functionality using the non-XSL portion of the XML document object model—it will make you appreciate XSL. This is a simple implementation, and if we were doing something more complex the power would be even more evident.

```
function buildTable(){
  var customer;
  var amount=0;
  var totalAmount=0;
  var saleCreditNode;
  var transactions = sales.documentElement.selectNodes("Year[@Value=
'1999']/January/Transaction")
;
  var transaction = transactions.nextNode();
  var tableString = "<table border='1'><thead><th>Day</th>";
  tableString += "><th>Customer</th><th>Payment
Method</th><th>Amount</th></thead>";
  while (transaction != null){
    //get the day
    tableString += "<tr><td>" + transaction.getAttribute("Day") + "</td>";
    //get the customer
    tableString += "<td>" + transaction.selectSingleNode("*/Customer").text
+ "</td>";

    //get the payment type
    tableString += "<td>" + transaction.getAttribute("Type") + "</td>";
    //get the dollar amount
    saleCreditNode = transaction.selectSingleNode("Credit | Sale");
    amount = parseFloat(saleCreditNode.selectSingleNode("Amount").text);
    if (saleCreditNode.nodeName == "Credit")
```

```
        amount = -(amount);
    tableString += "<td>" + amount  + "</td>";
    totalAmount += amount;
    transaction = transactions.nextNode();
  }
  tableString += "<tr><tdcolspan='3'align='right'>
  <B>Total:</B></td><td><B>"
  tableString += totalAmount + "</B></td></tr></table>";
  tableResults.innerHTML = tableString;
}
```

SUMMARY

We have covered a lot of ground with XSL, and there is a lot to the specification, but when you see the usefulness and flexibility and start implementing applications using XSL, we think you will agree that XSL is phenomenal. The syntax covers everything from adding style to XML to providing a SQL-like query language. It is our feeling that XML is a great specification, but with XSL the specification becomes truly viable as a development tool and adds much-needed functionality to the extremely popular tool.

CHAPTER 11

Describing Data with XML Schemas

In our prior discussions about XML, we assumed that the application that is dealing with the XML document knows about the layout of the document. This assumption is probably valid when you are using XML internally in a company, but it's a different situation if you want to use XML to share data across the Internet with different companies. In that case, you would need to describe the format of the document so that anyone can understand how it is laid out, the relationship between elements, and the data types that are used in the document. To do this, you need another mechanism to describe the content of the document. This is where XML schemas come into play.

You might be thinking, "I am not going to share my data with other people, so schemas are useless to me." However, in addition to describing the format of the data, XML schemas allow you to set up relationships and format data based on the data type. We feel that schemas have a little to offer everybody and will grow in importance as their specification matures.

In this chapter we will cover the following topics:

▼ Why to describe your data.

■ Working with schemas and building your first schema.

▲ Advanced uses of schemas, including cross-referencing data and showing the extensibility feature of schemas.

DESCRIBING YOUR DATA

Many people have a lukewarm feeling, at best, about creating documents that simply validate the contents of another document. They think, "I know the data is in the correct format so I don't need to create another document to validate its structure," but what we are really doing is describing, not just validating, the layout of the document. Yes, we are validating the document, but we are also defining relationships and data types within the data. One of the reasons we need to describe the data is so that different developers can understand the structure of the data. With XML we have moved from passing comma-delimited or size-defined data to describing the data in elements. Now we are taking the next step and describing the relationships between the different elements. Once you see the benefits of describing the data, you will likely warm up to the concept much more.

There are two different mechanisms to describing XML data: one is document type definitions (DTD), and the other is XML schemas. Based on the fact that this chapter is not called "Describing Data with Document Type Definitions," you can figure out which one we prefer. DTDs have been around since the release of the XML Specification (in XML terms, a long time) and use their own unique syntax to describe documents. The newer schema syntax takes the concepts of DTDs and extends them to support improved data typing, a more flexible open content model and name space integration, all from an XML document that describes the format rather than another new unique syntax, as is the case with DTDs. The only drawback with schemas is that their specification is very new and isn't even fully supported in IE 5.0. This will very quickly change, however.

Because of the added features and better syntax of XML schemas, coupled with the fact that all the forthcoming standards (W3C, Microsoft, IBM) are based primarily on schemas and not DTDs, we highly recommend learning and using XML schemas right now.

Working with Schemas

As stated earlier, XML schemas use XML syntax, which makes learning how to use them a simple matter of learning how to declare the elements and attributes. A schema is usually stored in a file with the .xml extension, but it can be dynamically generated just as any XML document can be. The first thing you need to know is just how to tie a schema to a particular XML document. This is done by adding an XML name space to the root node of the XML document, thereby telling the processor to point at the XML schema's source. The syntax to add an XML schema named sampleSchema.xml, which in this case is in the same path on the server as the XML document, is shown below:

```
<rootNode xmlns="x-schema:sampleSchema.xml">
...
</rootNode>
```

The x-schema is used to indicate to the XML parser that there is a schema corresponding to this name space. If the schema is not in the same path as the XML file, you can use the standard URL relative syntax (for instance, /xmlschemas/sampleSchema.xml) to get the file.

Building Your First Schema

Building a schema is similar to building a database, and, as with building a database, the first place to begin the creation of your schema is with a good design. We realize that the structure may need to change as new features are introduced, but it is important to have a good idea about what needs to be in the document and how the data is related before you sit down and design your schema. With that said, we must note that changing the schema's layout is actually relatively easy, but the more time you put in up front, the better off you will be.

Well, it is time for us to get off of our soapbox and move on to showing you how to build a schema. The first element in a schema, appropriately enough, is the Schema element, which serves as the root element of the document. The Schema element has two attributes: the name of the schema (attribute: name) and the name space(s) for the schema (attribute: xmlns). The xmlns attribute can include one or more name spaces to be used in the schema. One of the name spaces must be the name space for the schema-defining elements that will be used later on to define the layout of the XML document. In addition to this, you might want to include other name spaces for other definitions or if you are going to be defining data types you will need to add the name space for the data type definitions. The following is a code snippet for a Schema element, which defines two name spaces—the schema and data type name spaces—and makes the schema the default name space (the elements do not have a prefix) and gives the data type's name space a prefix of dt.

```
<Schema name="sample"
xmlns="urn:schemas-microsoft-com:xml-data"

xmlns:dt="urn:schemas-microsoft-com:datatypes">
...
</Schema>
```

Defining Elements and Attributes

Now that we have defined our root element and told the processor that we are working with schemas, it is time to start building the rules of the document. The general concept of a schema's layout is similar to how you create your own objects in script code. The first thing you do in script is to define your object; in schemas we define our elements and attributes. The next thing done in script is to use the object definitions and instantiate the object; in schemas we use the elements and attributes to define the structure of the document.

The way that we define an XML element is to use the ElementType schema element. The ElementType schema element has five attributes (content, dt:type, model, name, order) that define the rules for that particular element. We will go over the remainder of the attributes later; for now we will just use the name attribute, which simply defines the name of the element and is a required attribute. Similar to elements, attributes are defined using the AttributeType element. Like the ElementType, the AttributeType has five attributes (default, dt:type, dt:values, name, required), of which we will just use the name attribute for now. The name defines the name of the attribute and is required.

The way that we instantiate the element or attribute is by using the element or attribute element, respectively. A parent ElementType schema element contains the instantiated elements and therefore defines the relationship between the elements. Both of these elements contain a required attribute called type, which is used to specify what ElementType or AttributeType to instantiate. Before we go any farther, let's put together a very simple schema so you can get the feel for the structure and elements. The examples for this chapter will expand and improve on our example that we used from the prior XSL chapter. Let's start by defining a schema for a customer element that has the basic (Name, Address, City, State) contact information and that has a customer ID that uniquely identifies the customer. Our simple schema example follows; an XML file fitting the schema is shown after the definition.

sampleSchema.xml

```
<Schema xmlns="urn:schemas-microsoft-com:xml-data"
        xmlns:dt="urn:schemas-microsoft-com:datatypes">
<ElementType  name="Name" />
<ElementType  name="Address" />
```

```
<ElementType  name="City" />
<ElementType  name="State" />
<ElementType  name="Zip" />
<ElementType  name="Phone" />
<AttributeType name="ID" />
<ElementType  name="Customer">
  <element type="Name" />
  <element type="Address" />
  <element type="City" />
  <element type="State" />
  <element type="Zip" />
  <element type="Phone" />
  <attribute type="ID" />
</ElementType>
</Schema>
```

sample.xml

```
<Customer ID="1234" xmlns="x-schema:sampleSchema.xml" >
  <Name>Beth Camera</Name>
  <Address>113 Lead</Address>
  <City>New York</City>
  <State>NY</State>
  <Zip>23412</Zip>
  <Phone>123-345-6789</Phone>
</Customer>
```

Defining the Content Model with Elements

Now that you understand the basic layout of a schema, we can move forward to discuss some of the other attributes of the element and ElementType schema elements that we previously identified. To start with, we'll discuss the ElementType schema element and the model attribute. The model attribute allows you to specify whether the XML documents can contain other elements and attributes or just the elements and attributes you have defined. If you wish to allow other content inside the element (the default), you can set the model attribute to open.

Otherwise, set the model attribute to closed; this allows only the content that you have defined in the schema in the XML document. It is important to note that just by setting the model attribute to open does not automatically permit additional content. Setting the model attribute to open simply allows you to add elements or attributes from other name spaces that are not part of the schema. So, for example, if we wanted to have an XML document that had customer elements that were not defined in the schema, we would need to create a name space for the elements not in the schema and then prefix the elements with the new name space. The following example shows how to add to an XML document the PreferredDiscount and Contact elements even though they are not declared in the schema:

additional.xml

```
<Customer ID="1234" xmlns="x-schema:sampleSchema.xml"
                    xmlns:additional="myElements">
  <Name>Elizabeth's Camera</Name>
  <Address>113 Lead</Address>
  <City>New York</City>
  <State>NY</State>
  <Zip>23412</Zip>
  <Phone>123-345-6789</Phone>
  <additional:PreferredDiscount>7% on purchases over
$300</additional:PreferredDiscount>
  <additional:Contact>Beth</additional:Contact>
</Customer>
```

This functionality is a little different from what is documented by Microsoft. We actually wish it worked the way their documentation reads, which is that simply setting model equal to open allows you to add any elements or attributes you want, without regard for the name space. The following is an example of completely disabling the ability to add user-defined elements:

```
<ElementType name="Customer" model="closed">
...
</ElementType>
```

The next attribute we'll cover from the ElementType schema element is the content attribute. The content attribute allows you to specify what types of information should be contained inside the element. For example, should the element contain text, other elements, or nothing at all? Table 11-1 lists the different values for this attribute.

The following is an example of creating an ElementType that can contain only text:

```
<ElementType  name="Name" content="textOnly" />
```

The last attribute of the ElementType schema element used in defining the content model is the order attribute. The order attribute allows us to specify the order in which subelements are to appear and also to note if only one of the subelements should appear. The attribute has three valid values: seq, one, or many. The seq value (the default value if content attribute is eltOnly) indicates that all of the subelements must appear, and they must appear in the order that they are listed in the schema. The one value indicates that only one of the subelements in the list can be used. The many value (the default if content attribute is mixed) specifies that the subelements may appear in any order and can appear multiple times. It is important to note that if you wish to use the one or seq value for the order attribute, you

Value	Description
empty	The element cannot contain anything.
textOnly	The element can contain only text and not any elements. If the model attribute has a value of open, then the element can contain other elements as well.
eltOnly	The element can only have the specified elements and not any text.
mixed(default)	The element can contain both text and elements.

Table 11-1. Values for the content Attribute

must set the content attribute equal to eltOnly (this is not the default value). So for example, if we wanted to specify a transaction element that could contain either a sale or a credit, we could use the following:

```
<ElementType name="transaction" order="one" content="eltOnly">
  <element type="sale" />
  <element type="credit" />
</ElementType>
```

There are also a couple of attributes on the element element that allow you to further define the content model. The minOccurs and maxOccurs attributes allow you to define the minimum and maximum number of times the reference element type can occur in this particular element. The minOccurs has two accepted values: 0 (default) or 1. If you set the attribute to 0, the specified element is not required. If you set the attribute to 1, the specified element must occur at least once. The maxOccurs also has two acceptable values: 1 or * (default). A value of 1 indicates that the element must occur at most once. A value of * indicates that the element can occur an unlimited number of times. We feel that in the maxOccurs you should be able to specify a specific number of occurrences, not just 1 or many, but unfortunately this is not part of the specification. The following is an example of setting the minOccurs and maxOccurs attributes for an element:

```
<element type="Address" minOccurs="1" maxOccurs="*" />
```

Defining the Content Model with Attributes

Before we can go into the attributes of the AttributeType and attribute elements, we need to discuss the definition of AttributeType elements. Unlike ElementType schema elements, AttributeType elements can be defined within an ElementType schema element, allowing us to create attributes that have the same name but a potentially different meaning (attribute settings), based on the current scope. For example, let's say we wanted a global attribute called Type that is used in most elements, but we need a custom Type attribute for the Phone element. We can do so as follows:

```
<Schema xmlns="urn:schemas-microsoft-com:xml-data"
        xmlns:dt="urn:schemas-microsoft-com:datatypes">
```

```
...
<AttributeType name="Type" />
<ElementType  name="Phone"
  <AttributeType name="Type" />
  <attribute type="Type" />
</ElementType>
...
</Schema>
```

This example may not mean much to you right now, but you will see its usefulness later on when we introduce some of the remaining attributes.

The AttributeType and attribute elements expose only one property that allows us to define the content model. The attribute is the required attribute, which simply takes a yes or no value. The required attribute, as you might expect, defines whether the attribute is required for the element. It is important to note that both the AttributeType and attribute elements expose this attribute. If the value is set in the AttributeType, the attribute does not need to specify the value, and setting it does not override the value in the AttributeType element. The following shows an example of requiring the ID attribute from our original example:

```
<Schema xmlns="urn:schemas-microsoft-com:xml-data"
        xmlns:dt="urn:schemas-microsoft-com:datatypes">
...
  <AttributeType name="ID" required="yes" />
...
</Schema>
```

Defining the Content Model with the Group Element

The group element allows us to define subsets of elements that we can apply constraints to. This can be useful if you wish to apply the order functionality of the ElementType schema element or the min and max occurrences functionality found in the element element to a group of elements.

The group element supports three attributes: maxOccurs, minOccurs, and order. Just like the element element, the minOccurs attribute specifies the minimum number of times the group should occur and has two acceptable values: 0 (the specified group of elements are not required) and 1 (the specified group of elements must occur at least once). The maxOccurs attribute defines the maximum number of times the group should occur and also has two acceptable values: 1 (indicates that the group of elements must occur at most once) or * (indicates that the group of elements can occur an unlimited number of times). Similarly, the order attribute allows us to specify the order in which subelements are to appear in a group and also to note if only one of the subelements should appear. The order attribute has three valid values: seq (indicates that all of the subelements must appear, and they must appear in the order that they are listed in the schema), one (indicates that only one of the subelements in the list can be used), or many (indicates that the subelements may appear in any order and can appear multiple times).

The following is an example of using the group element to define a subset of elements and setting the group element's attributes. The example shows us a schema snippet for a situation where we want to specify a transaction element that can contain either a sale or a credit element (you must have one but not both) and still contain other elements.

```
<ElementType name="transaction" content="eltOnly">
  <group order="one" minOccurs="1" maxOccurs="1">
    <element type="sale" />
    <element type="credit" />
  </group>
  <element type="timeOftransaction" />
</ElementType>
```

How Do I Put This Together and Test My Schema?

The best way to test your schema is by applying it against a sample XML document, making sure that the sample document tests and conforms to all of your rules. The unfortunate part of doing this is that if you load the XML document in IE and there is a conformance issue, no error is reported back, as IE thinks everything is fine. So the proper way to test for conformance issues using a browser is to create a simple HTML page that loads the XML document and then checks the XML document object's parseError property to return the parse error object and investigate any errors. The following example code is a very simple document we use to check for conformance. You may wish to expand on it to suit your own requirements.

handleError.htm

```
<html>
<script language="JavaScript">
function loadXML(){
  testXML.load("test.xml");
  if (testXML.parseError != 0)
    alert(testXML.parseError.reason);
  else
    alert("Looks good.");
}</script>
<xml ID="testXML"></xml>
<input type="button" onClick="loadXML()" value="Test
Conformance">
</html>
```

MOVING BEYOND YOUR FIRST SCHEMA

Before we can move beyond defining the content model of an XML schema, we want to make sure that you understand how to define more complex structures. We've shown how to create simple hierarchies, but we want to make sure you understand how to create more complex implementations. You already have all of the building blocks you need, but now we want to walk you through building a slightly more complex example. This example is based on an XML document that looks like the following:

sales.xml

```
<SalesTransactions>
  <Year Value="1999">
    <Month Name="January">
      <Day Value="1">
```

```
    <Transaction Type="Cash">
      <Processor>Beth</Processor>
      <Processor>Elle</Processor>
      <Sale>
         <Amount>100</Amount>
         <Customer>Acme Imports</Customer>
      </Sale>
    </Transaction>
  </Day>
  <Day Value="2">
    <Transaction Type="Credit">
      <Processor>Sara</Processor>
      <Approved>Beth</Approved>
      <Credit>
         <Amount>500</Amount>
         <Customer>Premier Business Software</Customer>
      </Credit>
    </Transaction>
    <Transaction Type="Cash">
      <Processor>Beth</Processor>
      <Sale>
         <Amount>5</Amount>
         <Customer>Premier Business Software</Customer>
      </Sale>
    </Transaction>
  </Day>
</Month></Year></SalesTransactions>
```

The method you use to generate your XML schema is to start from
the lowest level and create your ElementType schema elements for that
level first; then work your way up the hierarchy. What you end up with
is a bunch of little definitions that are used in the higher level, then the
higher level is used in the next level, and so on until you have the
completed definition. It is also our recommendation to test each piece of
the schema as you build it so you can isolate any errors more easily.

We will now build the schema for the sample XML document. In
addition to the layout of the document we also have a few additional

rules that we want to enforce. For our sample document, these rules are as follows:

▼ We must have a value for the year, and we must have a name for the month.

■ We must have a value for the day.

■ We can have only one credit or one sale element.

■ We must have a processor.

■ We need a credit or sale for a transaction.

■ We must have an amount.

▲ We must have a customer for a credit or debit.

One thing you will notice is that all of the AttributeType definitions are locally scoped (inside of the ElementType); this is a personal preference, but it makes it easier to tell which attributes belong to which elements. The following is our schema definition for the sales XML document:

salesSchema.xml

```xml
<Schema xmlns="urn:schemas-microsoft-com:xml-data"
        xmlns:dt="urn:schemas-microsoft-com:datatypes">
<ElementType name="Amount" />
<ElementType name="Customer" />
<ElementType name="Sale" model="closed" order="seq"
content="eltOnly">
  <element type="Amount" />
  <element type="Customer" />
</ElementType>
<ElementType name="Credit" model="closed" order="seq"
content="eltOnly">
  <element type="Amount" />
  <element type="Customer" />
</ElementType>
<ElementType name="Processor" />
<ElementType name="Approved" />
```

```
<ElementType name="Transaction" content="eltOnly"
model="closed">
  <element type="Approved" minOccurs="0"/>
  <element type="Processor" maxOccurs="*"/>
  <group order="one">
    <element type="Credit" />
    <element type="Sale" />
  </group>
  <AttributeType name="Type" />
  <attribute type="Type" />
</ElementType>
<ElementType name="Day" model="closed">
  <AttributeType name="Value" required="yes"/>
  <attribute type="Value" />
  <element type="Transaction" />
</ElementType>
<ElementType name="Month" model="closed">
  <AttributeType name="Name" required="yes"/>
  <attribute type="Name" />
  <element type="Day" />
</ElementType>
<ElementType name="Year" model="closed">
  <AttributeType name="Value" required="yes"/>
  <attribute type="Value" />
  <element type="Month" />
</ElementType>
<ElementType name="SalesTransactions" model="closed">
  <element type="Year" />
</ElementType>
</Schema>
```

Putting Comments into Your Schema

There may be cases where you would like to add a human-readable or
machine-readable description about one or more of the elements or
attributes in a schema. To do this you can use the description element
to define your comment. The information inside of the description

element is not used for validation, but it can be useful for automated tools. The following is a snippet that uses the description element:

```
<Schema xmlns="urn:schemas-microsoft-com:xml-data">

...

<description>The transaction can only be a sale or a credit not
both</description>
  <group order="one">
    <element type="Credit" />
    <element type="Sale" />
  </group>

...

</Schema>
```

Setting Default Values for Attributes

In addition to defining the content model for attributes, schemas allow you to define default values for attributes. Through the use of the default attribute, which is available in both the AttributeType and attribute elements, you can define the value for the attribute when a value is not defined for an element. This, of course, applies to elements that are not required, because the value from the XML document will override the default. Unlike a required attribute, if you set the default value on both the AttributeType and attribute elements, the attribute elements will override the default value that is specified in the AttributeType element. The following is an example of setting the default for an AttributeType element.

```
<AttributeType name="Type" default="Cash" />
```

It is important to note that if you use the XML DOM and look at the XML property for the document, the default attribute value will not be there, but if you query the actual attribute value, the default will be set.

The XML DOM exposes the specified property of attribute nodes that tells us if the default value is being used or if a value was specified for the attribute. The specified property returns a true or false value indicating whether the attributes value was actually specified in the XML document (true) or if the default value in the schema was used to fill in the value (false). The following script code snippet shows an example of using the specified property:

```
var transaction = testXML.selectSingleNode("//Transaction");
var transType = transaction.getAttributeNode("Type");
  if (transType.specified == false)
    alert("You did not specify the transaction type.");
```

Working with Data Types

In addition to simply defining the content that is in a document, XML schemas allow you to specify the appropriate types of data that can be stored in elements and attributes. By specifying the data type, it allows us to take advantage of the XML processor's ability to validate the data and enables data-type–specific functionality in the XML document object model, making your XML documents *strongly typed*, as you find in most database structures and programming languages. A wide range of data types are supported, from the primitive data types of string to the more advanced date-time data type. We will just use the primitive data type of integer here to show you the basic functionality; we will go over some special data types later. For a complete list of supported XML data types, see Appendix E.

Specifying Data Types

The first step in specifying the data types in your schema is to set up the name space for the data types as shown below:

```
<Schema name="sample"
xmlns="urn:schemas-microsoft-com:xml-data"

xmlns:dt="urn:schemas-microsoft-com:datatypes">
...
</Schema>
```

Now we can start to unleash the power of data types by using the dt:type attributes in the ElementType and AttributeType elements or by using the datatype element. To set the data type using the dt:type attribute, you simply set the attribute to the appropriate data type as shown below:

```
<ElementType name="sample" dt:type="int" />
```

The datatype element is simply placed inside of an ElementType or AttributeType element and has one attribute, which is dt:type. The functionality that is available using the datatype element is the same as specifying the dt:type in the ElementType and AttributeType elements. We prefer using the dt:type on the ElementType or AttributeType elements, but here's an example of using the datatype element, in case you prefer this syntax:

```
<ElementType name="sample">
  <datatype dt:type="int" />
</ElementType>
```

The XML DOM exposes a few properties that give us information about the elements and attributes and their interaction with the data types of the XML schema. For example, both XML elements and attributes have a dataType property that returns a string representation of the data type that was specified in the schema, if one has been specified. The following shows a script code snippet of using the dataType property.

```
...
var scoreElement = testXML.selectSingleNode("//Score");
if (scoreElement.dataType == "int")
...
```

Another even more useful property that is exposed by elements and attributes in the XML DOM is the nodeTypedValue. The nodeTypedValue returns the value of the attribute or element in the specified data type format from the schema. For example, if we defined an element as an integer in the schema, the value would be returned to us in integer format, not in text format. The following snippet shows an example of calling the nodeTypedValue property.

```
var score = scoreElement.nodeTypedValue;
```

Defining a Value List for Attributes

XML schemas also allow you to define a list of possible acceptable values for an attribute. The method for doing this involves setting the dt:type for the AttributeType element equal to the special data type enumeration and then using the dt:values attribute to specify the list of possible values. The dt:values attribute contains a list of space-delimited possible values. This can be very useful if you have a small set of acceptable values that you wish to define as acceptable values, providing simple data validation. For example, if we wanted to define a list of acceptable values for the name attribute of our month element, we can. Anyone else who uses the schema must then follow our naming standards for the month, rather than some people having "Jan." and others "January," and so on. The following shows the schema snippet for setting a list of values.

```
<AttributeType name="Name" required="yes"
dt:type="enumeration"
dt:values="January February March April May June July August
September October November December"/>
```

It is important to note that if we define a default value in the AttributeType or attribute elements, the value must be a member of our value list, if a list has been defined.

Cross-Referencing Data

Up to this point, all of our XML examples have contained simple hierarchical data, such as our transaction examples. But as we alluded to in the beginning of the chapter, there may be situations when we want to store more information about the customer than just their name. For example, we might want to save their address, city, state, and so on. We could simply repeat that information for every transaction for each customer, but that wouldn't be efficient and would result in needlessly longer downloads. Instead, we want to store all of the customers in one section of the document and point to the appropriate customer from inside of the transaction. You might be thinking,

"Yeah that sounds great, but XML is hierarchical not relational."
Well, that is true, but through the use of two special data types you
can create references from one part of the hierarchy to another.

To help show how this works, we will go back to our transaction
example and add the additional customer information. However, we
are going to simplify the layout of the XML document a little to make
it easier to understand. We want you to concentrate on the referencing
method, not the extra stuff going on. Shown below is a sample of the
simplified format (no more credit and sales, day, month, or year
elements):

```
<SalesTransactions>
    <Transaction>
        <Amount>100</Amount>
        <Customer>
          <Name>Acme Imports</Name>
          <Address>112 N.W. Angles</Address>
          <City>Camera</City>
          <State>WI</State>
        </Customer>
    </Transaction>
    <Transaction>
        <Amount>300</Amount>
        <Customer>
          <Name>Acme Imports</Name>
          <Address>112 N.W. Angles</Address>
          <City>Camera</City>
          <State>WI</State>
        </Customer>
    </Transaction>
<SalesTransactions>
```

You can see from this simple example how much extra data is
in the document when we have the same customer in multiple
transactions. Ideally, what we want to do is remove the repeated
customer data and separate it into its own hierarchy, simply having
a pointer to the detailed customer data. The XML below shows what
we would like to achieve:

salesRef.xml

```
<SalesTransactions >
  <Customer id="C1">
    <Name>Acme Imports</Name>
    <Address>112 N.W. Angles</Address>
    <City>Camera</City>
    <State>WI</State>
  </Customer>
  <Transaction>
    <Amount>100</Amount>
    <Customer referToID="C1" />
  </Transaction>
  <Transaction>
    <Amount>300</Amount>
    <Customer referToID="C1" />
  </Transaction>
</SalesTransactions>
```

In the above example what we have done is to remove the customer information from the transaction and given the customer an id attribute that can be used to reference the customer. Then in the transaction's customer element, we use the attribute referToID to point us to the actual customer data.

The links or references are pretty easy to follow from our standpoint, but we must decide how we are going to alert the processor of these references. From a high level, what we need to do is create two schemas: one that defines the layout of the Transactions, saying the Customer element actually points to another location; and another that defines the layout for the customer, saying that I am the target for customer references.

Let's get into the details by starting with the Transactions definition. What we need to do is create our schema the same way we normally would build a schema. When we get to the Customer element, we want to create the referToID AttributeType and add that attribute to the Customer element. In the referToID AttributeType, you need to set the dt:type equal to the primitive data type "idref". This data type alerts the parser that the data for this element is actually stored elsewhere in this document. The schema below shows how we would set up the link to the customer.

transSchema.xml

```
<Schema xmlns="urn:schemas-microsoft-com:xml-data"
        xmlns:dt="urn:schemas-microsoft-com:datatypes">

<AttributeType name="referToID" dt:type="idref" />
<ElementType name="Customer" content="eltOnly">
  <attribute type="referToID" />
</ElementType>

<ElementType name="Amount" />
<ElementType name="Transaction" content="eltOnly">
  <element type="Amount" />
  <element type="Customer" />
</ElementType>
</Schema>
```

The next thing we need to do is to create our Customer schema, which, similar to the Transaction schema, looks like the other schemas we have built with one exception. Once again we need to define a special attribute, which this time will be the recipient of the link. In this schema, we will create an AttributeType element with a name of id, and we will set the dt:type equal to the special primitive type "id". This data type alerts the parser that this element will be a recipient of links from other places in the document. The schema below shows how we would set up the customer schema.

custSchema.xml

```
<Schema xmlns="urn:schemas-microsoft-com:xml-data"
        xmlns:dt="urn:schemas-microsoft-com:datatypes">

<AttributeType name="id" dt:type="id" />
<ElementType name="Name" />
<ElementType name="Address" />
<ElementType name="City" />
<ElementType name="State" />

<ElementType name="Customer">
```

```
      <attribute type="id" />
      <element type="Name" />
      <element type="Address" />
      <element type="City" />
      <element type="State" />
   </ElementType>
</Schema>
```

Now that we have all of the definitions in place, we just need to
tell our XML document to use the two schemas and then begin using
our referenced data. There is one important issue you need to contend
with here. If we include both schemas, there is a conflicting definition
of what a customer is. How will the parser know which one to use?
By using name spaces, we can easily resolve this problem by telling
the parser which schema to use. So in our example, in our root node
of the XML document we include the two schemas and give the
transaction schema a name space of referTo and the customer schema
a name space of target. Then on the Customer XML elements that
should use the transaction's schema, we prefix the Customer element
with referTo:, as shown below:

```
<referTo:Customer referToID="C1" />
```

And we prefix the Customer elements that should use the customer
schema with target:, as shown below:

```
<target:Customer id="C1">
...
</target:Customer>
```

Let's take a look at what our sample XML document would look
like with the schemas and name spaces in place:

salesRef.xml

```
<SalesTransactions xmlns:target="x-schema:custSchema.xml"
                   xmlns:referTo="x-schema:transSchema.xml">

   <target:Customer id="C1">
      <Name>Acme Imports</Name>
      <Address>112 N.W. Angles</Address>
      <City>Camera</City>
```

```
    <State>WI</State>
  </target:Customer>

  <Transaction>
    <Amount>100</Amount>
    <referTo:Customer referToID="C1" />
  </Transaction>
  <Transaction>
    <Amount>300</Amount>
    <referTo:Customer referToID="C1" />
  </Transaction>
</SalesTransactions>
```

Well, we have almost done it: we have almost turned XML into a relational, hierarchical system. All that is left to do is to follow the links and return the data. The method that is used to follow the links varies, depending on what you are using to retrieve data from the XML document: the XML DOM itself or XSL.

To follow the link using the XML DOM, you use the nodeFromID method that is available from the document object. The nodeFromID method simply takes one parameter, which is the ID of the element you wish to find, and it returns the matching node. The only somewhat disappointing thing about this method is that there isn't an automatic way to jump to the referenced node. What you need to do is get the referToID (in our example) attribute's value and then pass it in to the method, but this is still a very cool functionality. The following example builds a table with the transactions and the associated customer information. The one important thing to note is that when we go to find the referring customer element, we need to prefix the element's name (customer) with the name space (referTo:Customer).

salesref.htm

```
<html>
<script language="JavaScript">
function buildTable(){
  sampleXML.async = false;
  sampleXML.load("salesRef.xml");
  if (sampleXML.parseError != 0)
    alert(sampleXML.parseError.reason);
```

```
    else {
      transactions = sampleXML.selectNodes("//Transaction");
      var transactions;
      var referCustomer;
      var actualCustomer;
      var custID;
      var transaction = transactions.nextNode();
      var tableString = "<table border='1'><thead>";
      tableString +=
"<th>Customer</th><th>Address</th><th>City</th><th>State</th><th>Amount</th>
</thead>";
      while (transaction != null){
        referCustomer =
transaction.selectSingleNode("referTo:Customer");
        custID = referCustomer.getAttribute("referToID")
        actualCustomer = sampleXML.nodeFromID(custID);
        tempNode = actualCustomer.selectSingleNode("Name");
        tableString += "<tr><td>" + tempNode.text + "</td>";
        tempNode = actualCustomer.selectSingleNode("Address");
        tableString += "<td>" + tempNode.text + "</td>";
        tempNode = actualCustomer.selectSingleNode("City");
        tableString += "<td>" + tempNode.text + "</td>";
        tempNode = actualCustomer.selectSingleNode("State");
        tableString += "<td>" + tempNode.text + "</td>";
        tempNode = transaction.selectSingleNode("Amount");
        tableString += "<td>" + tempNode.text + "</td></tr>";
        transaction = transactions.nextNode();
      }
      tableString += "</Table>";
      tableResults.innerHTML = tableString;
  }}</script>
<body onLoad="buildTable()">
<xml ID="sampleXML"></xml>
<div ID="tableResults"></div>
</body></html>
```

NOTE: It is important to note that the ID values need to be unique across all of the XML elements in the document. For example if we were to add IDs to two different types of elements, each of the ID values must be unique throughout the document, not just all of the IDs for a particular element type.

TIP: The id data type is not limited to cross-references; you can also use it to jump quickly to a specific element in a document, if you know its ID. This can be useful if you are displaying data from an XML document on an HTML page and based on the user interaction, such as clicking on a piece of the data, you want to jump to an XML element and display more data or take action based on the data in the element.

USING THE ID() CONTEXT CHANGING METHOD IN XSL   In addition to jumping to a node using the nodeFromID method, you can also use the id() method of XSL. The id method allows you to pass in a list of space-delimited ID values for which you wish to return the nodes, or you can use an XSL pattern. By passing in a list of IDs, you are simply returned a collection of matching nodes. This functionality is similar to using the nodeFromID method, except that you can return multiple elements. So, for example, if we wanted to return the elements in a document that have an ID of C1 or C2, we could use the following code snippet:

```
elements = xmlDoc.selectNodes("id('C1 C2')");
```

This is nice functionality, but the true power of the id method comes when using the id method in an XSL pattern to retrieve subnodes of the linked element. (For more information on XSL patterns, see Chapter 10.) For example, if we wanted to retrieve the Name element from the Transactions Customer element, we could use the following code and pattern syntax:

```
nameElement =
transaction.selectSingleNode("referTo:Customer/id(@referToID)/Name");
```

Extensibility of XML Schemas

One of the nice features afforded by XML schemas is that an author can extend the default functionality. What this means is that if a piece of functionality is not built into XML schemas, you can add the feature yourself without disturbing the standard XML schema functionality.

For example, if we wanted to add a range that an element must fall into, we could extend the base functionality to support this behavior. Let's say we had an element that we typed as an integer (dt:type="int") value; we could further define the value to say it must be between 0 and 100. To make the XML processor not only verify that value is an integer but also within the range, from inside of your application (Web page, Active Server Page, and so on) you could retrieve the limits and validate that the value meets your criteria. To do this, you need to create a name space for your elements and then simply prefix your new elements with this name space in your schema and your XML document. The following is a simple schema that defines min and max values for an element.

minMaxSchema.xml

```
<Schema xmlns="urn:schemas-microsoft-com:xml-data"
    xmlns:dt="urn:schemas-microsoft-com:datatypes"
    xmlns:minMax="urn:minMax-extensions">
<ElementType name="Score" dt:type="int">
  <minMax:min>0</minMax:min>
  <minMax:max>100</minMax:max>
</ElementType>
<ElementType name="Test">
  <element type="Score" />
</ElementType>
</Schema>
```

Now that you have extended the schema, you can retrieve the values from the XML DOM for the element you applied them to. So for example, if we had an XML document like the one that follows, we could retrieve the definitions from the Score element.

```
<Test xmlns="x-schema:minMaxSchema.xml">
 <Score>33</Score>
</Test>
```

In this instance of using the Score element, to retrieve the extended definitions we would use the definition property of an XML element. The definition property returns the ElementType schema element for an element and returns the AttributeType element for an attribute. But what is really important to remember is that because a schema is itself an XML document, we can use the childNodes property of the element, returned from the definition property, to get access to the extended schema elements, which in our sample are the min and max elements. To show how this works we created the following sample HTML page that loads the XML and verifies that the Score falls in between the acceptable range.

testMinMax.htm

```
<html>
<script language="JavaScript">
function loadXML(){
  testXML.load("minMax.xml");
  if (testXML.parseError != 0)
    alert(testXML.parseError.reason);
  else{
    var scoreElement = testXML.selectSingleNode("//Score");
    var scoreDefinition = scoreElement.definition;
    var score = scoreElement.text;
    var minVal = new
Number(scoreDefinition.childNodes(0).text);
    var maxVal = new
Number(scoreDefinition.childNodes(1).text);
    if (minVal < score && maxVal > score)
      alert("Looks good.");
    else
      alert("The score value is out of range.");
  }
}</script>
<xml ID="testXML"></xml>
<input type="button" onClick="loadXML()" value="Test
Conformance">
</html>
```

SUMMARY

In this chapter we covered a lot of information about designing XML schemas. We think that now that you have seen some of the features that are available when using schemas, you may agree that there are good reasons to use them, besides just to describe your data to the outside world. Despite the fact that the specification is still being developed, XML schemas are becoming an increasingly popular method of describing the format of shared data and are worth learning.

CHAPTER 12

Building a Real-World XML Solution

In the previous chapters about XML, we introduced you to the basic concepts of XML and showed you how to work with the XML object model and how to work with the data in the XML document. In this chapter we will take these concepts and begin to apply them to a real-world example. It is important to note that the complete example is included on the Osborne Web site; however, we have included some of its more interesting and important parts in this chapter to help you understand the example. The example utilizes most of the techniques we have covered relating to XML, and it takes you through a practical use scenario.

In this chapter we will cover the following situations and technologies:

▼ Using XML on the client for an advanced browsing experience.

■ Using XML on the server for non–XML-aware clients.

▲ Using the XML DSO object to edit data.

THE SAMPLE APPLICATION

The sample application creates a simple online catalog that includes a categorization of the store and an XML shopping cart. In addition to this, we create a catalog maintenance piece to add, delete, or update items. Once the users have completed their shopping experience, the items selected for purchase are in an XML format that can be exchanged with business partners or can be processed in a credit card transaction.

The application is designed to dynamically define different categories or shopping areas and can be used for any type of business. In our implementation, we are creating an online office supply store with a very simple set of shopping areas. However, simply by adding more categories and data to the XML documents, you can easily expand on it or can change the whole catalog and types of products in the store.

The application was designed to show how XML can be used on both the server and the client with minor changes—doing so does not require a complete rewrite of the application. On the server side, we are using Active Server Pages (ASP); however, if you wanted to use some other technique (Java Servlets or CGI for example), you could.

But one of the nice features of using ASP is that we can easily take the code (JavaScript) we used on the client and use it on the server. We feel it is important to show how to use XML on the server, because on the real-world Internet not everyone will have an XML-enabled browser such as IE 5.

GETTING STARTED WITH THE IMPLEMENTATION

We begin the project (as we should begin any project) by defining the requirements for what we want to accomplish. We have two major requirements for the application: to make sure that the application can handle multiple levels of shopping areas and to show how to support other browsers besides IE 5. Multiple levels of shopping areas means that, for example, in our office supply store we can place general office items into a category, and then if we want we can add a subcategory, such as paper clips. Then if we have a lot of paper clips, we can subdivide that category into clamp type and simple paper clips categories. In addition to simple subdivisions, we also want to support situations in which some categories can have three levels of subcategories, while other categories only have one. Then, based on this categorization, users can drill down into different levels of the store.

Besides the basic requirements, we also want to be able to display special products that are on sale or that we want to draw special attention to as the user navigates down into the subcategories. Our final requirement is to save the shopping cart's resultant data in an XML format that can be sent to business partners to confirm what was ordered rather than sending a paper invoice. By doing this we are ready for business-to-business transactions whenever we want to implement this with business partners.

DESIGNING THE SCHEMAS

Now that we have defined our application's requirements, it is time to get to work on designing the structure of the XML documents we are going to use. To define the structure and establish the rules for the document, we create a set of XML schemas. The overall concept of the design is to have one XML document that contains all of the categorization information and special items and another set of documents that contains all of the catalog items. By not putting the entire set of catalog items into a single document, we minimize the risk of having a huge XML document that needs to be downloaded and parsed both on the server and client. In addition to these documents, there will be one XML document that represents the cart containing all of the items a user had chosen.

The Category Schema

The first item we need to tackle is defining the structure of the categorization menus (defining the different shopping areas). One of the requirements, as we stated earlier, is to create variable-depth subcategories, so we will have categories inside of categories. Because of this structure, we need an easy way to find particular categories because we cannot depend on the names or the structure of the elements to be able to find elements. Therefore, we want each category to have a unique ID we can reference it by.

The other item we need to handle in the schema is the requirement to support featured items (those on sale and so on) that are tied to each category and will be shown as the user navigates down into the subcategories. Because the same featured item can be tied to more than one category, we want to simply reference the item in the category and not store the entire feature item's data inside of the category itself. To do this we need to create id/idrefs (for more information see Chapter 11) in our schema and use name spaces in the XML document to point to the featured item's subdocuments.

Because we are using the id/idref architecture, we will need two schemas: one to define the items and another to define the categories. The schema for the categories is shown as follows; Table 12-1 defines what each of the elements and attributes are used for.

menuSchema.xml

```
<Schema xmlns="urn:schemas-microsoft-com:xml-data" xmlns:dt="urn:schemas-
microsoft-com:datatypes">
<AttributeType name="catID" required="yes" />
<AttributeType name="referToItem" dt:type="idref" required="yes" />
<AttributeType name="products" required="yes" />
<AttributeType name="source" />
<ElementType name="item" content="eltOnly">
  <attribute type="referToItem" />
```

```
    </ElementType>
    <ElementType name="featureItems" content="eltOnly">
      <element type="item" />
    </ElementType>
    <ElementType name="category" content="eltOnly">
      <attribute type="catID" />
      <attribute type="products" />
      <attribute type="source" />
      <element type="featureItems" />
    </ElementType>
    <ElementType name="categories" content="eltOnly">
      <element type="category" />
    </ElementType>
    <ElementType name="itemList" content="eltOnly" />
    <ElementType name="catalogMenu" content="eltOnly">
      <element type="categories" />
      <element type="itemList" />
    </ElementType>
    </Schema>
```

Element/Attribute	Function
catalogMenu	The root element of the document
itemList	A list of featured items
categories	The list of category elements
category	A list of feature items, details about the category, and optionally categories elements (which are subcategories)
catID	Unique identifier for the category
product	The text for a category that is displayed on screen
source	Used only on the lowest-level category elements to point to the subcategories XML document
featureItems	A list of item elements
item	The featured items: contains a pointer to the item in the item list
referToItem	Reference to the item's data stored in the itemList portion of the document

Table 12-1. Elements in Our Category Schema

The following schema defines the feature items; Table 12-2 defines what the elements and attributes are used for.

featureItemSchema.xml

```
<Schema xmlns="urn:schemas-microsoft-com:xml-data" xmlns:dt="urn:schemas-
microsoft-com:datatypes">
<AttributeType name="id" dt:type="id" required="yes" />
<ElementType name="shortDesc" content="textOnly" />
<ElementType name="longDesc" content="textOnly" />
<ElementType name="price" dt:type="number" />
<ElementType name="imagePath" content="textOnly" />
<ElementType name="item" content="eltOnly" order="many">
  <attribute type="id" />
  <element type="shortDesc" />
  <element type="price" />
  <element type="longDesc" />
  <element type="imagePath" />
</ElementType>
</Schema>
```

Element/Attribute	Function
item	Details about an item
id	Unique identifier of the featured item
shortDesc	A short description that will identify the item in the cart
price	The price for the featured item
longDesc	A complete description for the featured item (only shown when viewing details about the item)
imagePath	A path to the image on the server for the featured item

Table 12-2. Elements in Our Featured Item Schema

The following is a snippet of what our menu structure looks like. It is important to note that with this layout, we can add subcategories (categories elements) inside of a category to create the drill-down structure to a shopping area.

```xml
<catalogMenu xmlns:referTo="x-schema:menuSchema.xml" xmlns:target="x-schema:featureItemSchema.xml">
  <categories>
    <category products="Home" catID="ROOT">
      <featureItems>
        <referTo:item referToItem="H23199" />
      </featureItems>
      <categories>
        <category products="Calendars and Planners" catID="C1">
          <featureItems>
            <referTo:item referToItem="H23199" />
          </featureItems>
          <categories>
            <category products="Calendars" source="subcatalog1.xml"
catID="C3" />
            <category products="Planners" source="subcatalog2.xml"
catID="C4" />
          </categories>
        </category>
...
...More categories/subcategories
...
      </categories>
    </category>
  </categories>
  <itemList>
    <target:item id="H23199">
      <shortDesc> At-A-Glance Daily Desk Calendar Refills - 2000
Dated</shortDesc>
      <price>2.99</price>
      <longDesc> Don't forget to refill your old calendar with this twelve
month (January-December) year 2000 replacement. Keep Appointments by the
half hour, two pages per day. Includes prior, current, future month
reference. Fits standard 17-style bases.</longDesc>
      <imagePath>image/img1.gif</imagePath>
```

```
      </target:item>
    </itemList>
  </catalogMenu>
```

As you may have noticed, XML is ideal for our recursive hierarchical type of data. It allows us to easily keep adding additional subcategories until we have reached an acceptable level of detail. We think this works in a very cool way and allows us to quickly build a menu-based (categories/subcategory) system, as you will soon see.

The Subcatalog Schema

In comparison to the menu schema, the subcatalog schema is very simple. The structure of the subcatalog schema is very similar to that of the item list in the menu schema. The following code is the schema for the subcatalog. Because it is simple, we refer you to Table 12-2 for a discussion of any of the elements.

subCatalogSchema.xml

```xml
<Schema xmlns="urn:schemas-microsoft-com:xml-data" xmlns:dt="urn:schemas-microsoft-com:datatypes">
<AttributeType name="id" dt:type="id" required="yes" />
<ElementType name="shortDesc" content="textOnly" />
<ElementType name="longDesc" content="textOnly" />
<ElementType name="price" content="textOnly" dt:type="number" />
<ElementType name="imagePath" content="textOnly" />
<ElementType name="item" content="eltOnly">
  <attribute type="id" />
  <element type="shortDesc" />
  <element type="price" />
  <element type="longDesc" />
  <element type="imagePath" />
</ElementType>
<ElementType name="itemList">
  <element type="item" />
</ElementType>
<ElementType name="subcatalog">
  <element type="itemList" />
</ElementType>
</Schema>
```

The Shopping Cart and Invoices

Because the shopping cart is built entirely in code from the catalog and menu list, it is not too important to have a schema for the application itself. However, the cart or an invoice would be very important if you wished to exchange the data with business partners. Because of this, we developed a very simple schema for an invoice that simply contains all of the items the user has chosen and put in their cart, along with some general billing information. Rather than showing the complete schema here (because it is a little lengthy), we refer you to invoiceSchema.xml. Instead, we'll show you an example XML document that conforms to the schema:

```
<invoice xmlns="x-schema:invoiceSchema.xml" subTotal="5.98" discount=".88"
invoiceTotal="5.10" date="1/11/2000">
  <items>
    <item id="H23199">
      <shortDesc> At-A-Glance Daily Desk Calendar Refills - 2000
Dated</shortDesc>
      <price>2.99</price>
      <longDesc>Don't forget to refill your old calendar with this twelve
month (January-December) year 2000 replacement. Keep Appointments by the
half hour, two pages per day. Includes prior, current, future month
reference. Fits standard 17-style bases.</longDesc>
      <quantity>2</quantity>
      <itemTotal>5.98</itemTotal>
    </item>
  </items>
  <customer customerID="101" purchaserID="C101P001">
    <shipToAddress_1>1111 N. Main St.</shipToAddress_1>
    <shipToAddress_2>Suit 2020</shipToAddress_2>
    <shipToCity>Manchester</shipToCity>
    <shipToState>KY</shipToState>
  </customer>
</invoice>
```

With regard to the schema for this example, it is important to note that if we were to actually exchange this XML document with a customer, you might want to put the full URL for the schema in the document; your decision depends on the delivery mechanism of the

XML document. If our business partner retrieves the invoices from us, the document is fine as is because the schema's path is relative to our document. However, if we send our partner data by e-mail or post it to one of their servers, they will need access to the schema, and because of this we would need to include the complete URL.

MOVING ON TO THE APPLICATION

After designing the structure of our XML documents and their associated rules, we move on to the design and development of the application. One of the primary requirements for the client application is the ability to run the application both on Internet Explorer 5.x (using XML on the client) and other browsers (using XML on the server). By using XSL templates and a few minor changes to the code, this problem actually isn't too difficult to solve. (One thing you will notice about the pages is a general lack of graphics or fancy formatting; we are more concerned about showing the concept of the application. If you would actually like to use this as a base for an application, it would be very easy to add graphics and advanced formatting.)

The general concept of the application is to present the user with a page with two horizontally divided frames. The top frame can have advertising or company information, and the bottom frame is for navigation and the catalog display. For our implementation, the top frame is a very simple, static HTML page (banner.htm). The first page (choice.htm) that is displayed in the bottom frame is a page that allows you to decide which version of the application you want to run (XML on client or XML on the server). Figure 12-1 shows what the application looks like with the initial page loaded.

Once you click on the Start Shopping button, a very simple Active Server Page is called (choose.asp) that simply redirects the user to the appropriate version of the application. Next we will cover each version of the client and show how we put our XML designs to work.

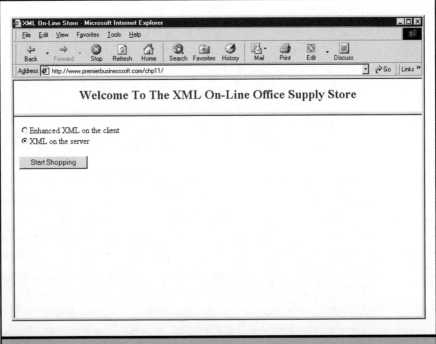

Figure 12-1.   The initial page that allows you to choose which version of the application to run

Using XML on the Client

The first part of the application we designed and developed was the piece that used XML on the client. The way we decided to implement this design was to have one page in the catalog area that would do all of the work of displaying the catalog. All of the navigation and catalog display was handled from this one page; we never go back to the server for additional HTML pages, only to retrieve data and other files such as images and XSL templates. So essentially what we created was a one-page application. You may be thinking that this controlling page must be quite large in size and require a lengthy download, but it isn't because the logic for displaying the data and the data itself were not contained in this page. All of the data formatting is handled in XSL templates, which are a crucial part of the implementation.

The Structure of the Controlling Page

In the controlling page (product_catalog.htm), we have three div elements that are used to display the current cart status, the navigation path into the subcategories of the store, and a working area where the catalog and navigation items are displayed. Essentially these div elements act as a place to hold the results from an XSL transformation or application-generated data.

To work with the different data, we have defined four XML elements that contain the following data: the category or menuing document (menu.xml), the XSL template to format the data (menu.xsl), the subcatalog documents (multiple documents), and the cart of selected items (document built-in code). As the user navigates to the different subcatalogs in the store, we simply replace the catalog that was previously stored in the element rather than holding onto the document. This is potentially an area whose performance we might improve. We might do so by holding onto the subcatalog's XML documents in an array and simply substituting the document that is in the array if the subcatalog has already been visited, rather than always getting the document from the server.

Beyond the elements to display and retrieve the data, we have two other elements: one that we use in persisting data and another that is a hidden text element that is used to send the cart to the server when the user has finished shopping. The element we use to persist data uses an intrinsic DHTML behavior to store the data if the user leaves our site and goes to another Web site. The element uses the userData behavior, which allows us to define the data we want to save (in this case, the XML from the document). For more information about the userData behavior, see Chapter 3 on the default behaviors of IE.

The Code of the Controlling Page

The application's functionality can be broken down into the following major pieces: building and navigating categories and feature items, displaying details of feature items or subcatalogs, adding items to the cart, and displaying and updating the cart.

Because the functionality of the application is implemented in one page, we will cover the functions in the controlling page based on the different pieces of functionality, as well as the more complex and interesting sections of code.

When building the navigation functionality, we further subdivide the working area into two areas: one for navigation and one for displaying feature items. The navigational area is a simple table with the entire list of associated subcategories for the current category. The feature items section is also a table that lists the short description of the feature item, its price, and the associated image. The code to build categories and feature items is the first functionality that is executed for the page. Because of this, there is some special processing that we need to do, so we separated this functionality out.

The first thing we do is to check if there are any items in the cart that have been persisted for the application from a prior visit. Whenever the user puts items into their cart and navigates away from the application, we save the XML on the client side using the userData behavior. Because of the fact that we are persisting the raw XML, we can simply load the persisted data into the cart's XML document. The last setup item we handle is to find the starting point for the categories in the XML menu document.

Now that we have completed the setup, we can go ahead and build the output for the page by calling the buildNavPage function. The buildNavPage does two XSL transformations to build the navigational section and to build the feature items. The power of the transformation comes from the transformNode function. As we briefly discussed in our chapter about XSL (Chapter 10), the transformNode function of an XML node allows you to pass in either the complete XSL template or just specific nodes. Because we don't know how many levels there will be in our document, it would be very difficult to build a single XSL style sheet that would handle the display. However, what we can do is to build a set of nonrelated templates and put them in the style sheet, finding the XSL template we want to apply to our set of nodes and passing the XSL node into our transformNode function. The buildNavPage finds the template for the categories, transforms the nodes, finds the template for the feature items, and transforms those nodes. The following is the code listing for the buildNavPage:

```
function buildNavPage(transformStart){
    var xslNode =
menuTransform.selectSingleNode("//xsl:template[@match='categories']");
    var result = "<table><tr><td width='40%' valign='top'>";
    var transformCategories;
    var transformFeature;
    transformCategories = transformStart.selectSingleNode("categories");
    result += transformCategories.transformNode(xslNode);
    result += "</td><td width='60%'>"
    xslNode =
menuTransform.selectSingleNode("//xsl:template[@match='featureItems']");
    transformFeature = transformStart.selectSingleNode("featureItems");
    result += transformFeature.transformNode(xslNode);
    result += "</td></tr></table>";
    workArea.innerHTML = result;
}
```

The following are the XSL templates used to transform both the *categories* and the *feature items* XML elements.

```
<xsl:template match="categories">
  <table BGCOLOR='#00FFFF'>
  <thread><th colspan="2">Shoping Areas</th></thread>
  <xsl:for-each select="category">
    <tr>
      <td width="15px"><img src="image/arrow.gif" /></td>
      <td class="nav">
        <xsl:attribute name="onClick">buildNextPage('<xsl:value-of
select="@catID" />')</xsl:attribute>
        <xsl:value-of select="@products" />
      </td>
    </tr>
  </xsl:for-each>
  </table>
</xsl:template>
<xsl:template match="featureItems">
  <table>
  <thread><th colspan="2">Featured Items</th></thread>
  <xsl:for-each select="referTo:item">
    <tr>
      <td rowspan="2"><img>
        <xsl:attribute name="src"><xsl:value-of
```

```
select="id(@referToItem)/imagePath"/></xsl:attribute>
        </img></td>
        <td class="nav">
          <xsl:attribute name="onClick">buildSingle('<xsl:value-of
select="@referToItem" />', '<xsl:value-of select="ancestor(category)/@catID"
/>' )</xsl:attribute>
          <u><xsl:value-of select="id(@referToItem)/shortDesc" /></u>
        </td>
    </tr>
    <tr>
        <td>Price:
          $<xsl:value-of select="id(@referToItem)/price" />
        </td>
    </tr>
  </xsl:for-each>
  </table>
</xsl:template>
```

One important thing you may have noticed with the templates is that we are creating an onClick attribute for the table cell. What we are doing is setting up the event handler to call into our function when the user clicks on either the category (calls buildNextPage) or feature item (calls buildSingle). We are then passing the function either the category ID or the item ID, respectively, so we can easily navigate to that portion of the document. Figure 12-2 shows the results from the initial transformations.

The buildNextPage function is called when the user clicks on one of the categories to display its subcategories or subcatalog. We will discuss what happens when the user clicks on one of the navigational aids (also calling the buildNextPage function) shortly. The function is passed the category ID of the clicked item and uses that ID to find the corresponding category element in the XML document. Next the function checks to see if there are any additional categories underneath that category. If there are more child categories, it calls the buildNavPage function to build the subcategories page. If there are no more child categories, we are at the end of the subcategories and need to build the list for the subcatalog. One final thing that buildNextPage does is build a navigational aid. The navigational aid is nothing more than a single-row table that allows the user to see the path they have navigated in the catalog to get to the current category, providing a way to quickly jump to one of the higher-level categories.

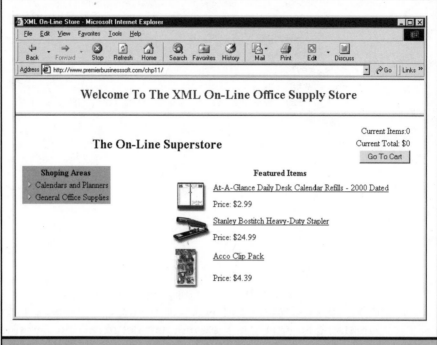

Figure 12-2. The first view of the online catalog

The code simply uses the ancestor XSL pattern to find the parents of the current element. The following is the code for the buildNextPage function:

```
function buildNextPage(id){
  var menuItem = catalogMenu.selectSingleNode("//category[@catID='" + id +
"']");
  var subElement = menuItem.selectSingleNode("categories");
  var parentElement ;
  var navigatePath = "";
  var seperator="";
  if (subElement != null)
    buildNavPage(menuItem);
  else
    buildListPage(menuItem, id);
  parentElement = menuItem.selectSingleNode("ancestor(category)");
  while (parentElement != null){
```

```
    navigatePath = "<td class='nav' onClick=buildNextPage('" +
parentElement.getAttribute("catID") + "')><u>" +
parentElement.getAttribute("products") + "</u>" + seperator + "</td>" +
navigatePath;
    parentElement = parentElement.selectSingleNode("ancestor(category)");
    seperator=" :";
  }
  if (navigatePath != "")
    navigatePath = "<table><tr><td>Navigate To:</td>" + navigatePath + "<td>
: " + menuItem.getAttribute("products") +
"</td></tr><tr><td> </td></tr></table>";
  navArea.innerHTML = navigatePath;
}
```

Displaying Items

After the user has chosen a feature item or has reached the end of
the subcategories, the detail for the feature item or subcatalog is
displayed. This view is a simple table, with one or more items from
the list and an input field where the user can indicate the quantity of
the item they wish to purchase. We set the ID of this input field to be
the ID of the product so we can easily reference the product in either
the subcatalog or the featured item list. The one thing you may notice
that is a little interesting is that we pass around the current category
ID into the listing pages. The reason for this is so we can easily return
to the category page if the user clicks on the Return button. Beyond
that, this functionality is made pretty straightforward through our
use of XSL templates. Figure 12-3 shows a listing page.

Working with the Shopping Cart

Once the user has entered the number of items they wish to purchase,
either for a feature item or from a subcatalog, we need to retrieve the
values for the selected items and add the items to the cart. The only
difference between the single-item and multiple-item subcatalog is
which XML document we use to retrieve the item's data. Because of this
difference, we call the addToCartSingle function for a feature item or the
addToCartSingle function from a subcatalog. These functions simply pass
the appropriate XML document to the addToCart function. Additionally,
we pass addToCart the category ID, so from the cart page, we can easily
navigate back to the previous location in the catalog.

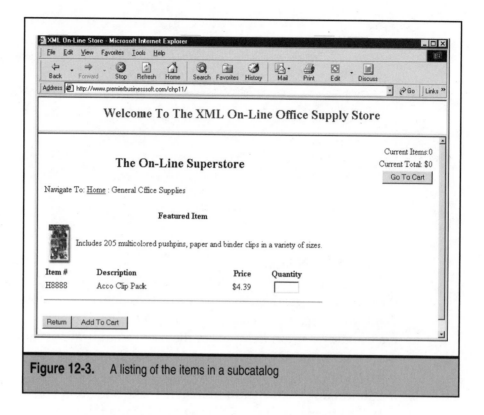

Figure 12-3. A listing of the items in a subcatalog

The addToCart function loops through all of the input elements for the page. Because there could also be input elements that are buttons, the function processes only the text elements. Next, addToCart checks to make sure the data entered is a number. If it is, addToCart then checks to see if the item is already in the cart. If the item is in the cart, the quantity is just added to the existing quantity. If it is not in the cart, a new XML item element is created, and we copy all of the detail elements (price, short description, and so on) for the particular element into the cart. We don't use the cloneNode method for the XML element because of name spaces. Remember, we are also handling items that are coming from the product list in the menu.xml document. These items have a name space associated with them, and we don't want those name spaces carried over to the cart, just simple item elements. We therefore create new elements and set the text and attributes for those elements.

After we have added the items to the cart, we display the contents of the cart and update the cart status. Figure 12-4 shows the cart and the cart status.

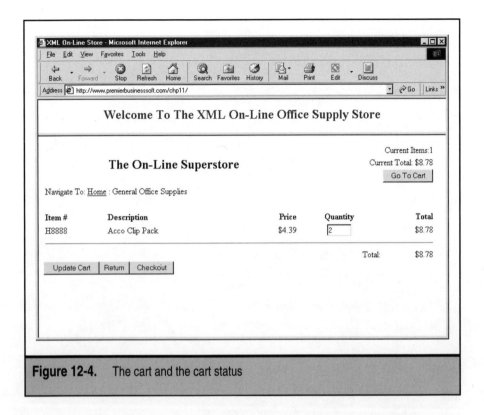

Figure 12-4.   The cart and the cart status

To set the cart status we simply loop through all of the elements in the cart and calculate the total cost and number of items in the list. We then display these values, along with a button to return to the cart. The cart list is a table of all of the elements that are in the cart, with a subtotal for each element and a total value for the complete cart. Additionally, the quantity values for the cart are displayed in input text boxes so that the user can easily change the order quantity and click the Update Cart button to update the cart. All of the calculations for the cart listing are done in the following XSL template:

```
<xsl:template match="cart">
  <xsl:script>
    var cartTotal = 0;
    function calculateTotal(){
      var qty = this.selectSingleNode("quantity").text;
      var price = this.selectSingleNode("price").text;
      var total = qty * price;
      cartTotal += total;
      return total;
```

```
      }
    </xsl:script>
    <table width="100%">
    <thread><th align="Left">Item #</th><th align="Left">Description</th><th
align="Right">Price</th><th>Quantity</th><th align="Right">Total</th>
    </thread>
      <xsl:for-each select="item">
        <tr>
          <td>
            <xsl:value-of select="@id" />
          </td>
          <td>
            <xsl:value-of select="shortDesc" />
          </td>
          <td align="Right">
            $<xsl:value-of select="price" />
          </td>
          <td align="Center">
            <input type="text" maxlength="5" size="5">
              <xsl:attribute name="itemID"><xsl:value-of select="@id"
/></xsl:attribute>
              <xsl:attribute name="value"><xsl:value-of select="quantity"
/></xsl:attribute>
            </input>
          </td>
          <td align="Right">
            $<xsl:eval>calculateTotal()</xsl:eval>
          </td>
        </tr>
      </xsl:for-each>
    <tr><td colspan="5"><hr/></td></tr>
    <tr><td colspan="4" align="right">Total:</td><td align="Right"
>$<xsl:eval>cartTotal</xsl:eval></td></tr>
    </table>
</xsl:template>
```

As stated earlier, the user can update the quantity of items they wish to purchase from the cart page. When the user makes changes and clicks the Update Cart button, the updateCart function is called. Similar to the addToCart function, the updateCart function loops through all of the input elements and updates the values for the cart. The only thing that is slightly different is that if the user clears or puts a 0 (zero) in the quantity field, the item is removed from the cart. After updating the cart, we redisplay the new cart's contents and update the current cart status.

The final piece of the application's functionality is the submission of the cart to the server for invoicing. We use an HTML form and a hidden input box to accomplish this. When the user clicks the Checkout button, we move the contents of the cart's XML document into the hidden field and then submit the form to the server. In our simple implementation, after the cart has been submitted to the server, we use an Active Server Page to write out the contents of the cart back to the client. The only other thing that we do is to set the submittedToServer flag to true because when we submit this page, it will fire the onbeforeunload event for the page. In most cases this event would be fired because the user is navigating away from our site, and we would want to persist the cart on the client machine. However, in this case we want to clear the cart that is on the client machine because the user has decided to purchase the items. In the event handler for the onbeforeunload event, we check the submittedToServer flag. If it is true, we clear the persisted version of the cart on the client.

Using XML on the Server

Fortunately the majority of the work we did using XML on the client can easily be transferred to run on the server. As we stated earlier, our server implementation uses Active Server Pages, and we can therefore use the same JavaScript scripting language for the server implementation as we did for the client implementation. Because the entire client-based functionality revolves around the XSL transformation and the creation of a new page based on that transformation, it is relatively easy to map the client side functions to Active Server Pages with only minor coding changes required. (One thing you will notice is that we tried to change as little code as possible when we moved from the client environment to the server environment.)

The first major change we need to make is to move from the stateless implementation of having HTML elements that hold onto the XML documents to a state-based Active Server Page implementation. Essentially we move the XML documents into Application-level (menu.xml, menuServer.xsl) and Session-level (the cart and the subcatalog documents) variables and then create local variables in our Active Server Pages that match the IDs of the HTML elements from our client-based implementation.

The next major change we need to make is to move away from using table cells to handle capturing the click events and, instead, create HTML hrefs to call back to the server. To handle this, we need to create another version of the XSL template that produces HTML that is supported by lower-level browsers (such as Netscape 4.x and IE 4.x). Additionally, we try to minimize or remove all of the client-side JavaScript that is not an absolute requirement. The final major change that we need to make is in how we display the output. In the client implementation, we take the results of the transformation and set the innerHTML of a DIV element; in the server implementation we remove the DIV elements (Netscape does not support DIVs) and simply merge the output of the transformation into the page output using the Active Server Page's Response.Write method.

The Active Server Page Code

Because the code is designed to be nearly identical and the purpose of this chapter is to go over XML (not Active Server Pages), we will not go over all of the details of the server code. However, we would like to go over some of the code to give you a feel for the implementation as well as an understanding of how the application works. One generalization we can make is that for every action non-helper (functions that capture click events), there is a corresponding Active Server Page with nearly the same code that is used on the client.

The first time the application is run, we load the categories and the XSL template, re-using those documents for all of the application users. It is important to remember that when you create variables that are used in Application- and Session-level variables, you create free-threaded XML document objects. When a user starts a new session, we set the session-level variable that contains the cart document to null, allowing us to easily check whether the cart already exists. We also create an XML document object for the session-level variable that will hold onto the subcatalog documents, but we do not load an XML document into the object. The following code is from the global.asa file, which is used to initialize Applications and Sessions in the Active Sever environment. It is important to note that all of our Active Server Page code is in JavaScript and not VBScript.

global.asa

```
<Script LANGUAGE="JavaScript" RUNAT="Server">
function Session_OnStart(){
  Session("Cart") = null;
  var subcatalogList = new
ActiveXObject("Microsoft.FreeThreadedXMLDOM");
  Session("subcatalogList")= subcatalogList;
}
function Application_OnStart(){
  var newXMLDoc =
Server.CreateObject("Microsoft.FreeThreadedXMLDOM");
  newXMLDoc.async = false;
  newXMLDoc.load(Server.MapPath("menu.xml"));
  Application("catalogMenu")= newXMLDoc;
  var newXMLDoc2 =
Server.CreateObject("Microsoft.FreeThreadedXMLDOM");
  newXMLDoc2.async = false;
  newXMLDoc2.load(Server.MapPath("menuServer.xsl"));
  Application("menuTransform")= newXMLDoc2;
}
</Script>
```

Many of the functions in our client-side example provide the common functionality needed in several different functions. We now need that common functionality across multiple Active Server Pages. We therefore create an include file (commonSource.inc) that contains this common source, and we simply include that file at the beginning of all of our ASP pages. This allows us to maintain a single copy of these common pieces rather than having to find all the locations where a certain piece of code is used when we need to make changes to a particular function. So, toward the beginning of every page, you will see the line

```
<!-- #include file=commonSource.inc -->
```

To give you a feel for what the code looks like, we will go over the first page that is displayed (firstPage.asp). Similar to the client-based version, we have special code to handle the setup of the cart for the pages. We will show the code next and then talk about the details.

firstPage.asp

```
<%@ LANGUAGE=JavaScript %>
<!-- #include file=commonSource.inc -->
<html>
<head>
<title>Product Catalog</title>
<base target="_self">
</head>
<body>
<%var cart = Session("cart");
  if (cart == null){
    cart = new ActiveXObject("Microsoft.FreeThreadedXMLDOM");
    Session("cart")= cart;
    cart.loadXML("<cart></cart>");
  }
  var catalogMenu = Application("catalogMenu");
  var menuTransform = Application("menuTransform");
  var subcatalogList = new ActiveXObject("Microsoft.FreeThreadedXMLDOM");
  Session("subcatalogList")= subcatalogList;
buildNavigate();setCartStatus('ROOT');
  var transNode =
catalogMenu.selectSingleNode("//category[@catID='ROOT']");
  buildNavPage(transNode);
%>
</body></html>
```

The first thing we do is to check if there is already a cart object in the Session-level variable. If not, we build the cart with only the document nodes. Additionally, before we can call any of our functions that perform the transformation, we need to create local variables that contain the XML documents from our Session and Application variables so we don't need to change the code from the client. For example, on the client we had an XML element with the ID of menuTransform. So to simulate the element in our ASP code, we create a local variable that contains the XML document containing the XSL style sheet. By doing this we don't need to change all the code to point at the Application("menuTransform").

There are cases in our server example where we need to navigate to a page with a button click but we don't need to submit a form. To support this, we created a function (buildNavigate) in the commonSource.inc that simply inserts the JavaScript code required to navigate to the location that is passed in. It is important to note that this is the only client-side JavaScript we use, thereby avoiding the need to worry about the syntax and capabilities of different browsers.

Now that we have all of our setup done, we can set our cart status (setCartStatus) and call the buildNavPage just as we did from the client. We changed only one line of code for the server version, so we're just showing you that line. The only thing that needs to change is how we output the results of the transformation.

Client version:

```
workArea.innerHTML = result;
```

Server version:

```
Response.Write(result);
```

As you can see, there isn't much to change. The bigger changes (if you can call them big) are in the XSL template where we need to change from capturing the click on the table cell to creating an <a href > HTML element. The following is the XSL template code for the categories and featured items.

```
<xsl:template match="categories">
  <table  BGCOLOR='#00FFFF'>
  <thread><th colspan="2">Shoping Areas</th></thread>
  <xsl:for-each select="category">
     <tr>
       <td width="15px"><img src="image/arrow.gif"></td>
```

```xml
      <td>
        <a>
          <xsl:attribute name="href">navPage.asp?catID=<xsl:value-of
select="@catID" /></xsl:attribute>
          <xsl:value-of select="@products" />
        </a>
      </td>
    </tr>
  </xsl:for-each>
  </table>
</xsl:template>
<xsl:template match="featureItems">
  <table>
  <thread><th colspan="2">Featured Items</th></thread>
  <xsl:for-each select="referTo:item">
    <tr>
      <td rowspan="2"><img>
        <xsl:attribute name="src"><xsl:value-of
select="id(@referToItem)/imagePath" /></xsl:attribute>
      </img></td>
      <td><a>
        <xsl:attribute
name="href">singleItem.asp?itemID=<xsl:value-of
select="@referToItem" />&amp;catID=<xsl:value-of
select="ancestor(category)/@catID" /></xsl:attribute>
        <xsl:value-of select="id(@referToItem)/shortDesc" />
      </a></td>
    </tr>
    <tr>
      <td>Price:
        $<xsl:value-of select="id(@referToItem)/price" />
      </td>
    </tr>
  </xsl:for-each>
  </table>
</xsl:template>
```

We continued mapping all of the functionality to the server version with very few changes required to the code. The biggest issues were in creating HTML that was supported by all the browsers, rather than in the XML or XSL implementation. The result is an application that allows you to support many different browsers and provides functionality that is similar to that of the version that uses the XML on the client side.

Editing the Catalog

Now that we have this cool XML catalog system, we want to build a simple module that will allow us to add items to the catalog. Because this administrative module would run only within the company, we do not have to worry about supporting different versions of browsers, and we can rely on the functionality built into IE 5. To build the editor, we again turn to XSL transformations and the XML data source object (DSO). Because most of the editing functionality is already built into the DSO, this task is pretty straightforward.

We create a simple HTML page (hier.htm) that uses transformations (cat.xsl) to allow the user to drill down into the subcatalog they want to modify. Then once they reach the lowest subcatalog level, we navigate to a different page (which is actually an Active Server Page: modifySubCatalog.asp) where they can edit the associated subcatalog. After making all of their changes, the user clicks the Save button and the updated document is sent to the server and saved to the server side using another Active Server Page (saveSubCatalog.asp).

To allow the user to navigate into the different levels of the document, we create a simple unnumbered list and list item HTML elements that represented the different levels of categories. Figure 12-5 shows the look of the drill-down page.

When the user clicks on a list item, it calls the loadNextLevel function, which performs the transformation for the children of the element that was clicked. If there aren't any children, it navigates to the modifySubCatalog.asp, passing in the name of the category and the file name to edit on the query string.

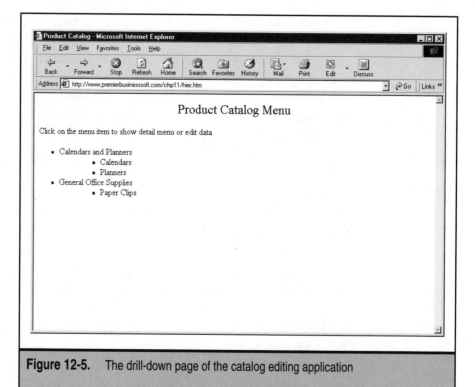

Figure 12-5.   The drill-down page of the catalog editing application

The user is then presented with a very simple data editing screen that allows them to make modifications to the existing data or add new elements. This simple editing screen is shown in Figure 12-6.

Once the user has completed all of their changes, they click the Save button to send the changes to the server. The data editing page has a hidden text box (xmlSource) inside of a form that is used to submit the data to the server. The Active Server Page gets the data from the form and loads it into an XML document object and then uses the save method of the document object to save the data. One thing to note is that we turn off the resolve externals for the newly loaded document. The reason for this is because the parser is looking for the subCatalogSchema.xml. Because the path is relative to the location of the file, and the file has not yet been saved, the parser cannot find the schema. So to stop an error from occurring, we turn off this validation. In a production environment, you would need to give the complete schema URL to avoid this error and allow the validation to occur.

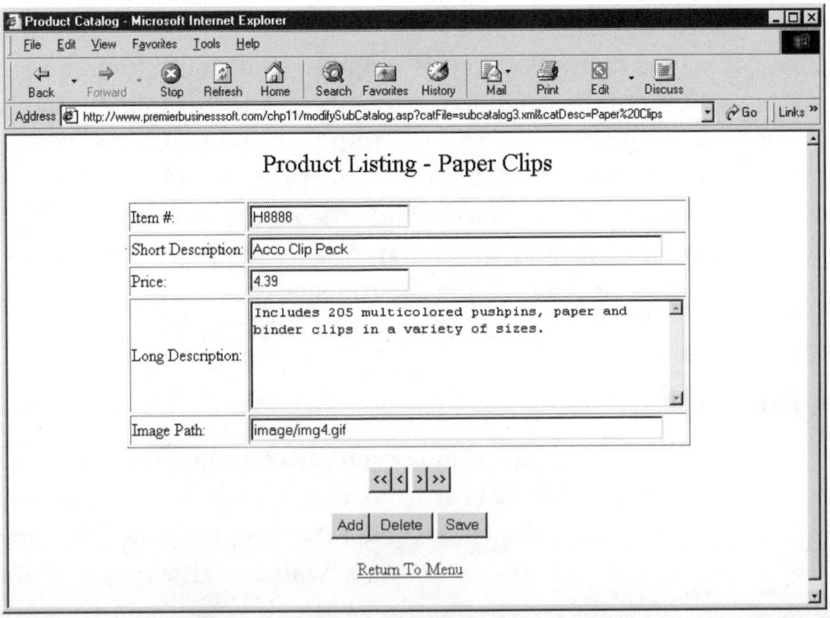

Figure 12-6. The data editing page of the catalog editing application

What's Missing

One of the obvious questions you might be asking is, "What is missing from this implementation if I want to use it?" One thing that is missing is some nice formatting, as well as images in the client application. As we stated earlier we didn't spend too much time on the aesthetics, but rather we concentrated on the functionality. The good news is that adding some window dressing is quite easy to do and won't affect the current implementation. You would also want to query the user's browser type and version, sending them to the correct application implementation without their having to choose the correct version themselves. Our example lacks this simple functionality, so you can choose the version you want to work with for testing purposes.

Another thing that is missing is an integration of the cart into your existing database system for invoicing or your credit approval system. Currently all the application does is generate an XML document that has all of the items the user wants to purchase; once the user leaves, the document is not saved.

One final thing that is lacking is the ability to do more advanced editing of the catalog documents or, for that matter, maybe even retrieving the catalog data from an existing database system. If you were to use the existing XML documents and the editing program as is, you would need to include the ability to add subcategories and feature items and a transparent way to upload the images for the items rather than doing the transfer manually.

SUMMARY

Overall, the application is pretty cool and meets the basic requirements we set forth. As noted, there are some things that are missing, but it shows the general concept of how you can put XML to use today. You don't need to wait until the majority of the world has XML support in their browsers. If you design your application correctly, you can pretty easily move your application from using XML on the client to having the server perform all of the XML operations.

PART IV

Advanced
Internet Explorer
Functionality

CHAPTER 13

HTML Applications

One of the problems with traditional client/server applications is the burden of installing the client application on all of the client machines. Added to this burden, whenever any client application's components, such as a DLL and ActiveX controls, need to be updated, a new install program must be created and again installed on the client systems. This is where the new Web architecture improves on the old client/server architecture because the client program is the browser. The browser has some client/server capabilities because it contains a DHTML object model on the client side to program its user interface. The user is responsible for installing the browser on his machine. The company who makes the browser is responsible for updates to the browser and the installation program. The Web developer is responsible for creating a Web application that will work for the target browser or browsers.

What if you wanted to combine the two architectures together? What if you wanted to build and distribute an application that doesn't look like a browser and doesn't have the headaches of a traditional client installation? Internet Explorer 5 and later make building such an application possible through the use of its HTML application technology.

HTML applications (HTAs for short) are stand-alone applications written using Internet Explorer's supported technologies (such as HTML, DHTML, DHTML behaviors, XML, XSL, and so on) that run on a Microsoft Windows development platform. In this chapter we will cover

- ▼ Features of HTAs.
- ■ How to create and execute HTAs.
- ■ Security issues of HTAs.
- ■ How to deploy HTAs.
- ■ Why, and why not, to use HTAs.
- ▲ An example of a working HTA.

THE FEATURES OF HTML APPLICATIONS

An HTA is run just like an executable, but it uses the IE browser engine. The user can double-click on an HTA from Windows Explorer or can start it from the command line. The machine on which an HTA is executed must have the application/hta MIME type installed and registered on it. This MIME type is installed by default with IE 5. Since an HTA uses the IE browser engine, it has all the functionality the browser offers. It can use such IE functionality as HTML, DHTML, the DHTML object model, cascading style sheets, any scripting language that the browser supports, DHTML behaviors, ActiveX components, XML, XSL, and any other browser-supported functionality.

HTAs provide control of the user interface design and the client system. They can be used as a number of different applications, such as create prototypes, wizards, full-fledged business applications, or whatever you need them to do. An HTA does not have to use the Internet in order to be run, but if the application calls for the use of the Internet it is at its disposal. An HTA can also use COM objects to work with the user's system. For example, when IE 5 is installed, it also installs the Scripting Runtime object, which contains the File System object. With that COM object, you can manage the user's file system. We will see how this object is used later in the chapter.

HTML APPLICATION CONSTRUCTS

It does not take much to create an HTA: just create a file and save it with an .hta extension. After saving the file, double-click it to execute it. Figure 13-1 shows what an empty HTA file looks like when it is executed. Internet Explorer does not even need <html> or <body> tags to run the HTA. If you place text into the file and execute the HTA, the HTA displays the text in the HTA window.

The <HTA:APPLICATION> tag has been add to Internet Explorer's HTML interpreter to create the HTA's window attributes. This tag must appear within the <head> tag. The majority of the

Figure 13-1. An HTML application is defined by the file extension (.hta), not by any HTML elements on the Web page

<HTA:APPLICATION> tag's attributes have default values. The syntax of <HTA:APPLICATION> is shown below with each attribute's possible values (default values in bold)

```
<HTA:APPLICATION
    APPLICATIONNAME=value
BORDER=thick | dialog | none | thin
    BORDERSTYLE=normal | complex | raised | static | sunken
    CAPTION=YES | NO
    ICON=value
ID=value
MAXIMIZEBUTTON=YES | NO
    MINIMIZEBUTTON=YES | NO
    SHOWINTASKBAR=YES | NO
    SINGLEINSTANCE=YES | NO
    SYSMENU=YES | NO
    VERSION=value
WINDOWSTATE=normal | maximize | minimize
>
```

The HTA element also has properties that match each of the tag's attributes. Table 13-1 gives a brief description of each attribute/property and its property access availability. If a property is read only, then that property can only be set as an attribute on the <HTA:APPLICATION> tag.

Attribute/Property	Description	Property Access
applicationName	Name of the HTA. If the singleInstance property is set to true, this value is used to test for an instance already running.	Read only
border	The HTA's application window border type. This property is only valid when the HTA has a title bar. Setting the border to *none* removes the HTA's title bar, program icon, and Minimize/Maximize buttons.	Read only
borderStyle	The HTA's content border style.	Read only
caption	States whether the HTA's title bar is displayed.	Read only
commandLine *	Retrieves parameters that are passed into the HTA when it is started. This property returns an empty string when the HTA is started over the HTTP protocol.	Read only

Table 13-1.   HTA Attributes and Properties

Attribute/Property	Description	Property Access
icon	A 32x32-pixel Microsoft Windows format .ico file.	Read only
id	The DHTML DOM identifier of the HTA:Application element.	Read only
maximizeButton	States whether the maximize button is displayed. The HTA must have a caption for this button to be displayed.	Read only
minimizeButton	States whether the minimize button is displayed. The HTA must have a caption for this button to be displayed.	Read only
showInTaskBar	States whether the HTA is displayed in the Microsoft Windows taskbar. This property has no effect on whether the application is displayed when the user presses Alt+Tab.	Read only
singleInstance	States whether multiple instances of the applications can run at the same time. The application's applicationName property is used to identify other running instances of the application.	Read only

Table 13-1. HTA Attributes and Properties *(continued)*

Attribute/Property	Description	Property Access
sysMenu	States whether the sysmenu button is displayed. The HTA must also have a caption for this button to be displayed.	Read only
version	Returns the application version number. The default is an empty string.	Read only
windowState	Sets or retrieves the window state of the HTA window (normal, minimize, maximize).	Read/write

Table 13-1. HTA Attributes and Properties *(continued)*

NOTE: An * next to an attribute/property value denotes that it is only a property, with no matching attribute. Also, HTA attributes and properties are the same except for the commandLine property, which is not an attribute of the <HTA:APPLICATION> tag.

CREATING SIMPLE HTML APPLICATIONS

Now we will create four simple HTAs. The first is shown in Figure 13-2. It creates an HTA that displays the properties of the HTA. The following listing creates the HTA:

WinStyle.hta

```
<html>
<head>
<title>HTA Window Style Example</title>
<HTA:APPLICATION id=HTAApp
```

```
        APPLICATIONNAME="First HTA Example"
        BORDER=thin
        BORDERSTYLE=complex
        MAXIMIZEBUTTON=No
        MINIMIZEBUTTON=YES
        SHOWINTASKBAR=NO
        VERSION="1.00"
        WINDOWSTATE=normal/>
<script language=JavaScript>
function onLoad(){
var str;
    str = "This HTA has the following properties:<br>"
    str += "<br> Application Name = " + HTAApp.applicationName;
    str += "<br> Border        = " + HTAApp.border;
    str += "<br> Border Style   = " + HTAApp.borderStyle;
    str += "<br> Caption        = " + HTAApp.caption;
    str += "<br> ID             = " + HTAApp.id;
    str += "<br> Maximize Button = " + HTAApp.maximizeButton;
    str += "<br> Minimize Button = " + HTAApp.minimizeButton;
    str += "<br> Show in Taskbar = " + HTAApp.showInTaskBar;
    str += "<br> Single Instance = " + HTAApp.singleInstance;
    str += "<br> System menu    = " + HTAApp.sysMenu;
    str += "<br> Version        = " + HTAApp.version;
    str += "<br> Window State   = " + HTAApp.windowState;
    document.body.innerHTML = str;
}
</script>
</head>
<body scroll=no onload="onLoad()" id=body>
</body>
</html>
```

There are a couple of interesting things in this listing. The purpose of this example is to show how an HTA window's attributes are set. The first item to look at is the <HTA:APPLICATION> tag in the page's <head> tag. It sets the HTA's window look and feel. The <body> tag turns scrolling off and specifies the onload event. The scrolling of the body is turned off because HTAs have a vertical scroll

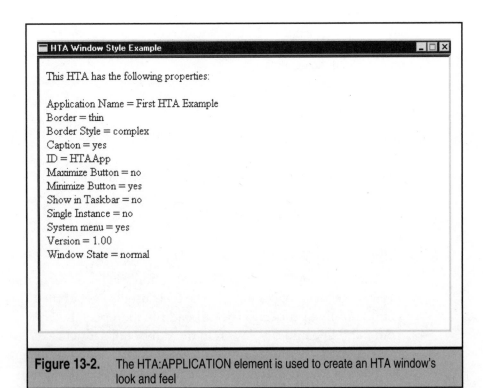

Figure 13-2.   The HTA:APPLICATION element is used to create an HTA window's look and feel

bar by default. If the HTA is large enough not to scroll, then the scroll bar is disabled. Looking at the <body> tag, notice that it contains no HTML. For its displayed content, the <body> tag's onload event calls the onLoad function when raised. The onLoad function then creates the body's HTML using the HTA's properties.

The second HTA example shows how a command-line parameter is passed to the HTA and how the HTA receives it. Figure 13-3 displays the command line that is passed to the HTA. Since parameters are being passed to the HTA, the HTA should not be started by double-clicking on it in Windows Explorer. The next code listing shows the HTA:

CmdLine.hta

```
<html>
<head>
<title>HTA Command Line Example</title>
```

```
<HTA:Application id=HTAApp>
<script language=JavaScript>
function onLoad(){
    txtCmdLine.innerText = HTAApp.commandLine;
}
</script>
</head>
<body scroll=no onload="onLoad()">
This HTA should only be run from a command line.<br>
The value of the command line is:<br>
<div id=txtCmdLine></div>
</body>
</html>
```

The only item in the HMTL application's HTA element that needs to be declared is the ID. The ID is used to get at the HTA command-line property. The onLoad function gets the HTA's command line and displays it in the <div> tag's innerText. To execute an HTA with parameters, use the Run command from the Start menu. The first item that is passed to the HTA is the directory location of the HTA, followed by the actual parameters. The command-line value is a string that must be parsed to get to the individual values.

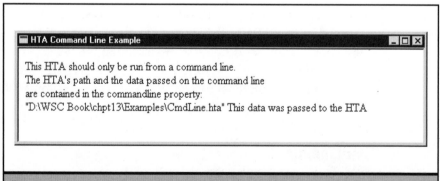

Figure 13-3. Command-line parameters can be passed to an HTA

NOTE: When an HTA is loaded via HTTP, the commandLine property always returns an empty string.

The third HTA example shows how to create a single instance of the HTML Application. The following listing shows what is needed to accomplish this:

SingleInst.hta

```
<html>
<head>
<title>HTA Single Instance Example</title>
<HTA:Application id=HTAApp
    APPLICATIONNAME=Single Instance"
    SINGLEINSTANCE=YES
>
</head>
<body scroll=no>
This HTA can only be run as a single instance.
</body>
</html>
```

There are two attributes that need to be set to prevent a second instance of the application from running at the same time: the applicationName and singleInstance attributes. The applicationName attribute is used by the HTA to identify the HTA uniquely. If the singleInstance attribute is set to Yes, then the applicationName is used to check whether there are any other applications executing using that name. If there are, the second instance of the HTA exits without ever appearing to the user.

The last HTA example shows how to display other Web pages in an HTA. Figure 13-4 shows a Web page within the HTA. Here's the code to do this:

HTAComm.hta

```
<html>
<head>
<title>HTA - Calling an URL or an HTML Page</title>
```

```
<HTA:Application id=HTAApp
    windowstate=maximize>
<script language=JavaScript>
function gotoURL(){
    document.all.frmOutputWin.src = txtURL.value;
}
function onEnter(){
    if (window.event.keyCode == '13')
        gotoURL();
}
</script>
</head>
<body scroll=no>
Enter a URL and press the Go To button:
<br>
<input type="text" size="100" id=txtURL onkeyup="onEnter()">
<input type="button" id=btnGoto value="Go To"
onclick="gotoURL()">
<br>
<iframe width="100%" height="88%"
src="http://msdn.microsoft.com/workshop/"
id=frmOutputWin>
</iframe>
</body>
</html>
```

This HTA contains a <iframe> tag that will contain the Web page
that is viewed. When the HTA is first displayed, it shows Microsoft's
Web Workshop page in the iframe element. The user can enter a URL
or local path to an .htm file in the text box and press the Go To button
to display a different Web page.

HTML APPLICATION SECURITY

HTML applications are considered to be fully trusted applications.
What that means is that they can directly read from and write to the
client's machine. An HTA will run without any warnings of what it is

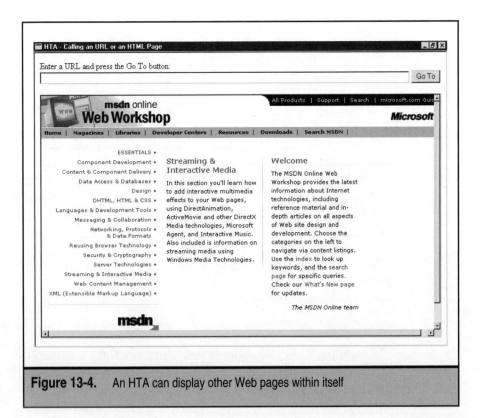

Figure 13-4.   An HTA can display other Web pages within itself

doing—unlike Internet Explorer, which has different security levels for each of its defined security zones. An example of this is the use of ActiveX components. When the browser creates an instance of an unsigned ActiveX component using client-side script, the warning in Figure 13-5 may be shown to the user (depending on their security settings for the current zone). If that same code is run within an HTA, the warning message will not be displayed, regardless of IE's security settings. The user of an HTA needs to have confidence that an HTA will not do damage to their system nor send out any unauthorized information because HTAs turn off all security. Currently, HTAs cannot be code-signed.

Cross-domain trust relationships can be set up using HTAs. To do this, the HTA uses either the <frame> or <iframe> tag and the HTA's

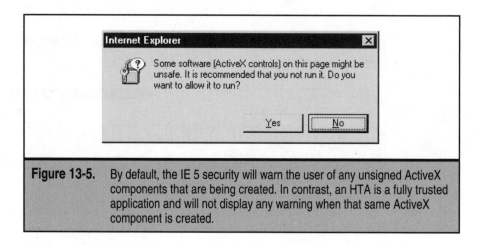

Figure 13-5. By default, the IE 5 security will warn the user of any unsigned ActiveX components that are being created. In contrast, an HTA is a fully trusted application and will not display any warning when that same ActiveX component is created.

application attribute. For example, to give a domain a trusted relationship, add the following to a <frame> tag:

```
<frame src="http://www.somedomain.com" application="yes">
```

The application attribute is used for only the <frame> and <iframe> tags and is ignored if the Web page is not an HTA. When a domain is trusted, it has script access to its HTA's window objects and cookies.

HTML APPLICATION DEPLOYMENT

HTAs can use three types of deployment: the Web model, the package model, or a hybrid of each of the models. In the Web model, the entire HTA is either opened in the browser or it is downloaded to the client machine through IE 5's download dialog box. After the HTA is launched, its components are downloaded from the server as they are needed and cached. In the package model, the HTA is installed using an installation program or a self-extracting executable. The hybrid model uses parts of the Web model and parts of the package model.

The HTA installation is transparent to the HTA. The developer needs to decide which deployment method best suits their needs. If download time is at a premium, then a hybrid approach is probably best, where only the initial page is downloaded to the client and the components that the application uses are retrieved from the server as needed. If download time is not a concern, then the package model may be a better choice. If you want to update the application automatically, possibly even without the user knowing that it is being updated, then the Web model would work best. If the application is being used both in the office and remotely, then it might be better to use the package model because the application would not have access to the server when the user is running the application remotely.

WHY AND WHY NOT TO USE HTML APPLICATIONS

There are many compelling reasons for developing an HTML application. Here are some of those reasons:

▼ It is easy to create an HTA: most Web developers already know most of the technology.

■ The browser contains software components that can be used to build robust applications.

■ If the application needs additional software components, then only those components need to be installed on the client's machine.

■ The application has access to the Internet's protocols, if needed.

■ You can use existing Web pages to create an HTA.

▲ It is easier to convert an HTA into a Web site than to convert a client/server application into a Web site.

There are, however, some drawbacks to using HTML applications:

▼ Only IE 5 and later support them.

■ The application's code is interpreted, so it will not execute as fast as a compiled application.

▲ HTAs do not use the same security model as a Web page. An HTA has read/write access to the file system on the client's machine (see "HTML Application Security" earlier in the chapter).

ANOTHER HTML APPLICATION EXAMPLE

Back in Chapter 4 we used an HTML Component Wizard application to help in the creation of an HTML component. The HTML Component Wizard is an HTML application. The Wizard is started by the HTCWiz.hta file, which is listed below.

HTCWiz.hta

```
<HTML>
<HEAD>
<TITLE>HTML Component Wizard</TITLE>
<HTA:APPLICATION ID="HTCWizard"
     APPLICATIONNAME="HTML Component Wizard"
     SINGLEINSTANCE="yes"
     WINDOWSTATE="maximize">
</HEAD>
</script>
<body topmargin="0" leftmargin="0" rightmargin="0" bottommargin="0"
scroll="no">
    <IFRAME id="frmeMain" APPLICATION="yes"
         algin="middle" name="frmeMain" frameborder="0" height="100%"
width="100%" src="component.htm">
    </IFRAME>
</body>
</HTML>
```

There is no application logic in this .hta file. The purpose of this file is to set up the applications environment. The HTA:APPLICATION element at the top of the file allows for a single instance of the Wizard and maximizes the application's window when it is created. The application uses an <iframe> tag to create a single frame in the body of the page. The frame takes the entire body's area. When the HTA is first displayed, the <iframe> tag's src attribute's value, the component.htm page, is loaded into the frame. Using the <iframe> tag in this manner causes other pages that are

navigated to within the <iframe> area also to be displayed inside
the frame. For example, in the component.htm page when the Next
button is pressed and the page is validated, the following code is
executed to go to the property page:

```
window.navigate("property.htm");
```

Normally when pages are loaded in this manner, the new
page is displayed in the entire window, which would take us out
of our HTA.

The <iframe> tag contains the application="yes" attribute because
the application uses the Microsoft's Scripting File System ActiveX
component to create the HTML component's file. For example, on the
component page (component.htm), the component file location is
entered. The value entered is validated to make sure that it is a valid
directory on the user's machine. The following code listing shows
how the Scripting File System ActiveX component is used to do this:

```
function isValidDir(dir){
  var fso;
  fso = new ActiveXObject("Scripting.FileSystemObject");
  if (fso.FolderExists(dir))
    return true;
  else
    return false;
}
```

In the isValidDir function, the dir parameter is the directory
to be validated. A Scripting File System object is created using the
JavaScript ActiveXObject function and is assigned to the variable
fso. The fso object is used to check if the directory exists by using
the FolderExists method of the Scripting File System object. The
Wizard uses other methods of the Scripting File System object
throughout the application.

The last item that we will show in the HTC Wizard is how data is
saved when a page navigates to another page. The Wizard uses IE 5's
userData default DHTML behavior to save its data. An example of
this can be found in the events.htm page. The next code listing shows
how the userData behavior is used:

```
function saveData(){
var i;
var data;
var cnt = 0;
    document.all.objUD.load("DHTMLWiz");
    for (i = 0; i < document.all.txtEventName.length; i++){
        if (! validData(i))
            return;
        if (trimText(document.all.txtEventName(i).value) != ""){
            cnt++;
            data = document.all.txtEventName(i).value;
            if (trimText(document.all.txtEventID(i).value) != "")
                data = data + '||' + document.all.txtEventID(i).value;
            else
                data = data + '||' + ' ';
            document.all.objUD.setAttribute("DWEvent" + eval(cnt), data);
        }
    }
    document.all.objUD.setAttribute("DWEventCount", eval(cnt));
    document.all.objUD.setAttribute("DWBtnAction",
    document.all.btnNext.value );
    document.all.objUD.save("DHTMLWiz");
    window.navigate("attach.htm");
}
```

The saveData function is executed when the Next button is pressed. The first thing that this function does is to load the DHTMLWiz userData area. The userData area contains all the data that is saved by the Wizard. The FOR loop cycles through each event entry on the page, validates the data in the entry, and concatenates the values into a string variable. The string is then added to userData with the name DWEvent, concatenated with the count of the entry in the loop. When the loop is finished, a count of the number of entries that were saved in the userData is saved into the userData area. The value of the action being performed is also saved in the userData area. This value is used when the page is first loaded. If the value is << Back, then the data from the userData area is loaded onto the page so it can be edited. Otherwise, the page is shown with blank entries. The last thing this function does with the userData is to write it to the client's userData area on the hard drive.

SUMMARY

This chapter introduced a new technology supported by Internet Explorer 5 called the HTML application (HTA). HTAs are applications created with an .hta file extension that uses Internet Explorer's browser engine. An HTA has all of the capabilities of the browser at its disposal, such as HTML, DHTML, XML, XSL and so on. An HTA does not use the same security model as Internet Explorer. It is a fully trusted application that has read/write access to the client's machine. An HTA can be deployed either by downloading it from a Web site, installing it on the client machine with an installation program, or by combining both methods.

CHAPTER 14

Advanced DHTML Features

With the release of Internet Explorer 5.0, Microsoft introduced advanced techniques in DHTML that simplify programming tasks and allow us to create applications that interact with the user the same way normal desktop applications do. In this chapter we will cover some of these new features and show you how they are bringing the functionality available to Web developers closer to that of normal desktop applications. We will cover these new features of DHTML:

- ▼ Dynamic properties.
- ■ DHTML data transfer, such as drag and drop.
- ▲ Capturing mouse input in a Web page.

DYNAMIC PROPERTIES

Dynamic properties provide an easy-to-use technique, which allows us as developers to improve the appearance and rendering of HTML pages. Dynamic properties, as the name implies, allow us to define a "dynamic" formula that can be used to set properties and attributes of HTML elements. So instead of just setting a property to a particular value, such as width=10, you can dynamically change the width based on an expression. Inside of our dynamic property, we can reference the values of properties for other elements, which opens up a new set of functionality to dynamically change a page more efficiently than with script.

Dynamic properties can help simplify and reduce the amount of code needed in a Web page. Prior to the release of IE 5, the functionality available in dynamic properties was available only by using script. Dynamic properties are similar in functionality and implementation to that of a formula in a spreadsheet. Formulas include references to one or more cells in the spreadsheet, whereas dynamic properties can refer to one or more properties of one or more HTML elements. One of the great features of dynamic properties is to define relationships between different elements. By setting up a relationship, you don't need to create event handlers to capture state changes in the document; rather you just set up the relationship, and all the changes are automatically handled.

HOW TO IMPLEMENT DYNAMIC PROPERTIES

Dynamic properties can be applied to an element using two different techniques: directly on the style sheet property or from script. To apply a dynamic property directly to a style block or style attribute you use the expression() method. Inside of the expression method, we pass in the formula for the dynamic property. Let's take an example where we want to center an element on a page both horizontally and vertically. We would set the left and top attributes for the element to be equal to the dynamic value of one-half of the height and width of the document, less the height and width of the element itself. The following is an example of code that would center a div element.

simpleDynamic.htm

```
<html>
<body>
<div id="centerDiv" style="position:absolute;
left:expression((document.body.clientWidth - centerDiv.clientWidth) /2);
top:expression((document.body.clientHeight - centerDiv.clientHeight) /2);
width:85px;background:yellow">Centered Div</div>
</body>
</html>
```

The really nice thing about this sample is that if we resize the browser window, the element automatically stays centered inside of the client area. We don't need to set up any event handlers for the window resizing as it is automatically handled by the dynamic properties.

There are, however, a few limitations to using the expression syntax, such as only working on style sheet values. In addition to this limitation, your expression cannot contain semicolons or quotation marks, and the expression cannot contain array references. Because of these factors, the use of the expression () syntax is somewhat limited, but in certain cases, as we have shown, this syntax can save a lot of coding.

In addition to defining dynamic properties in a style sheet, you can also set them within code using the setExpression() method. The setExpression method provides more flexibility than the expression syntax. The setExpression method allows you to define dynamic properties not only for style sheet attributes but also as read/write Dynamic HTML properties. The setExpression method has three parameters: the property to set the expression to, the expression itself, and the scripting language used in the expression (such as JavaScript or VBScript).

The calling syntax for setting a DHTML property is slightly different from the syntax for setting a CSS attribute. To set the DHTML property, you call the setExpression method directly from the element as follows:

```
element.setExpression("innerText", "body.innerHTML()", "JavaScript");
```

On the other hand, if you wanted to set an attribute for a CSS, you would call the setExpression method against the style object of the element, as in the following example:

```
element.style.setExpression("left", "document.body.clientWidth / 2",
"JavaScript");
```

In addition to being able to set DHTML properties, the setExpression method allows you to have quotes and semicolons in your expressions. However, we still are unable to reference arrays in our expression. By allowing quotes and semicolons in the expression, we can create more complex and useful dynamic properties, but it is important to remember that an expression must be a single line of script code.

Another neat feature of dynamic properties is that you can reference global script variables and other functions inside of your expression. When the values for the variables change or the output for the function changes, the dynamic property automatically updates the field. So, for instance, in the following simple code example we reference a global script variable that keeps track of the number of times a user clicks an up or down button; then we display the value in the text box. The functionality is similar to a spinner user-interface control.

spinner.htm

```html
<html>
<script language="JavaScript">
var spinValue = 0;
function setup(){
  spinText.setExpression("value", "spinValue", "JavaScript");
}
function change(changeValue){
  spinValue += changeValue;
}
</script>
<body onLoad="setup()">
<table><tr><td>
    <input type="text" id="spinText" Size="5">
  </td>
  <td>
    <input type="button" onClick="change(+1)" value="^"
style="height:20;width:20"><BR>
    <input type="button" onClick="change(-1)" value="v"
style="height:20;width:20">
  </td></tr></table>
</body></html>
```

In addition to simply adding expressions to an element, dynamic properties support three other methods (getExpression, removeExpression, and recalc) that can be useful when working with this functionality. The getExpression() method allows us to retrieve the current expression or formula that is being used to calculate a value. The getExpression method has one parameter, which is the properties expression you wish to retrieve. Similar to the setExpression method, if you want to retrieve the expression for a CSS attribute, you need to use the style object. The following is sample syntax for retrieving the expression for both a DHTML property and a CSS attribute.

DHTML property:

```
x= spinText.getExpression("value");
```

CSS attribute:

```
x= spinText.style.getExpression("left");
```

The removeExpression() method is the only way to remove a dynamic property from an element. The removeExpression method has only one parameter, which is the expression to remove. This method returns true if the expression was successfully removed. Similar to the other methods, if you want to remove the expression for a CSS attribute, you need to use the style object.

The recalc() method is used to recalculate dynamic properties in a document. You might be thinking, "Why do I need to do this? Isn't that automatically done?" While we agree, according to Microsoft there may be such cases as implicit dependencies, internal property changes, and related properties that can cause some expressions not to recalculate. In such cases you can force a recalculation of the dynamic properties by calling the recalc method for the document object. The recalc method takes one parameter, which is either a true (recalculate all dynamic properties) or false (default: recalculate only the properties that have changed since the last recalculation). The only value that is of use as a parameter is the true value, because it recalculates all of the dynamic properties. With a false, we are telling the processor to calculate values it knows it should recalculate. If it knows it needs to update the values, it will do so automatically, making the false attribute somewhat redundant. The following code snippet shows the syntax for calling the recalc method:

```
document.recalc(true);
```

DHTML DATA TRANSFER

DHTML data transfer refers to the process of implementing the transfer of data from a source to a destination (or target), such as drag-and-drop and clipboard operations. Internet Explorer 5.0 greatly improves the ability to perform these types of transfer operations and allows us to deliver functionality users have begun to expect from desktop applications. Through the use of these transfer techniques, we can exchange data inside of our browser or to other applications, even including desktop applications such as Microsoft Word. There are, for security reasons, limitations on what we can receive as a drop target. We'll cover those limitations later. Right now, let's look at the objects that are used to implement the data transfer functionality.

The Data Transfer Objects

There are two main objects that are used in the data transfer process: the dataTransfer object and the clipboardData object. The dataTransfer object is used for drag-and-drop operations and contains its own clipboard object, which is used to transfer data from the source to the destination. Once the drag-and-drop operation has completed, the clipboard is cleared. The clipboardData object is used to transfer data through operations in the edit menu or by keyboard or menu shortcuts (such as cut, copy, paste). The clipboardData object transfers its information to the global system clipboard and stays in the clipboard until another operation overwrites the data.

Working with the dataTransfer Object

Now that you have some idea about the objects that are involved with data transfer, we want to introduce you to the details of the dataTransfer object. The dataTransfer object is available through the event object and has methods and properties to specify the data that should be transferred, also providing visual feedback to the user.

The methods and properties of the dataTransfer object are generally set in the events that notify both the source and target elements about the status of the drag-and-drop operation. Table 14-1 lists the events that get fired during the drag-and-drop operation, in the order in which the events are fired.

Each of these events exposes a number of properties that are available through the event object that provide us with more

Event	Object Fired On (Source or Target)	Description
ondragstart	Source	Fires when the user starts to drag a text selection or selected object.
ondrag	Source	Fires throughout the drag operation, whether the selection being dragged is over the drag source, a valid target, or an invalid target.
ondragenter	Source and target	Fires when the user drags the object to a valid drop target. First event to be fired on the target object.
ondragover	Target	Fires continuously while the user drags the object over a valid drop target. Setting the return value to false cancels the default message handler.
ondragleave	Target	Fires when the user moves the mouse out of a valid drop target during a drag operation.
ondrop	Target	Fires when the mouse button is released during a drag-and-drop operation.
ondragend	Source	Fires when the user releases the mouse at the close of a drag operation.

Table 14-1. Events in the Order That Occur During a Drag-and-Drop Operation

information about what the user is currently doing or allows us to override the default event handlers. The following is a snippet of code retrieving a property from the event object.

```
function onDragHandler(){
if (event.altKey)
  alert("The ALT key is pressed");
}
```

Table 14-2 lists each of the properties and provides a short description of each.

Building a Drag-and-Drop Data Transfer

Now that you are aware of all of the events that get fired during a drag-and-drop operation, we can begin working on setting up our own operation. You may or may not know that IE by default has drag and drop built into the HTML elements. So to set up the simplest form of drag and drop, we really don't need to set anything up if we have an application that knows how to act as a target, such as Microsoft Word. Figure 14-1 shows this type of interaction, with Word acting as our target.

This functionality is pretty cool, as a starting point, but it is limited from the application development perspective. What we need is the ability to define the data that gets passed and retrieve the data as our target. Through the use of the dataTransfer object, we are able to do all of these things and more.

The dataTransfer object supports three methods that allow us to set, retrieve, and remove data from the object's clipboard. When a user selects data from a Web page and begins the drag-and-drop operation, the default data that will be transferred is the data that is selected. There may be cases where you want to specify the data that is to be passed to the target. The setData() method is used to specify the data that is to be transferred to the target. The setData method has two parameters: the first parameter is the format of the data to be transferred (either Text or URL), and the second is the data to be transferred. If you pass in Text as the format value, you can pass in any text string. Passing URL to the format value requires that you pass in the location for the object being transferred. The method returns true if the call was successful; otherwise it returns false.

Property	Description
altKey, ctrlKey	Retrieves the status of the Alt or Ctrl key, respectively. Returns true if pressed.
cancelBubble	Sets or retrieves whether to cancel the bubbling of the event. True cancels bubbling.
clientX, clientY	Retrieves the x coordinate or y coordinate, respectively, of the mouse cursor in pixels, relative to the client area of the window, excluding window decorations or scroll bars.
offsetX, offsetY	Retrieves the x coordinate or y coordinate, respectively, in pixels, of the mouse pointer's position, relative to the object firing the event.
returnValue	Sets or retrieves the return value from the event.
screenX, screenY	Retrieves the X or Y position of the mouse, in pixels, relative to the user's screen.
srcElement	Retrieves the object that caused the event to fire.
type	Retrieves the event name.
x, y	Retrieves the x coordinate or y coordinate, respectively, in pixels, of the mouse cursor relative to the parent element.

Table 14-2.   Available Properties from the event Object During Data Transfer Events

The setData method is usually called inside of the ondragstart event. Generally you want to set the data to be transferred as soon as the drag-and-drop operation starts so that the data is always available for the target to do pre-drop validation and the like.

To retrieve data from the dataTransfer object's clipboard, you use the getData() method. The getData method has one parameter, which

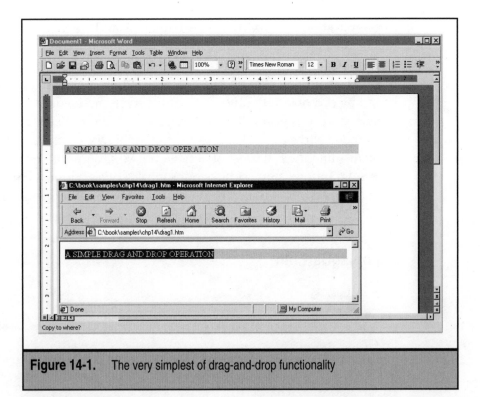

Figure 14-1. The very simplest of drag-and-drop functionality

is the data type to retrieve from the clipboard, either Text or URL, and it returns the data from the clipboard in the specified format. The getData method is generally used in the ondrop event of a target item to retrieve the data from the clipboard once the user drops the selected item.

There may be cases when you wish to remove data from the dataTransfer object. To do so you can call the clearData() method, which has one optional parameter that is the data type. If you do not pass in this parameter, all of the formats on the clipboard are cleared. The clearData method supports removing the following data types: Text, URL, File, HTML, and Image.

A perfect example of where this functionality is particularly useful is if we wanted to implement a drag-and-drop operation in a shopping cart application. A user could click on the image of a product and then drop that image into a shopping cart. To show you how this could work, we start with a simplified version of our example shopping cart application using XML from Chapter 12, and we then extend one of the pages to support the drag-and-drop shopping. What we want to put on the dataTransfer object's clipboard is the XML that identifies that item, allowing us to easily add the new item to the shopping cart object. Because we want to focus on the data transfer functionality, our example, which follows, has the XML for the item hard-coded and simply displays the XML in a DIV element, but implementing the full functionality would be straightforward. Figure 14-2 shows the results of our sample page after the item has been dropped into the cart. The complete code for this example is as follows:

shoppingCart.htm

```
<html>
<script Language="JavaScript">
function dropItem(){
  // In the real application we would add the item to the cart object
  // To make the sample easier we simply display the XML
  displayXML.innerText = event.dataTransfer.getData("Text");
}
function startDrag(itemID){
  // In the real application we would look up the item by the id
  // To make the sample easier we will hard code the XML
  var source = "<item id='H23199'>";
  source += "<shortDesc>At-A-Glance Daily Desk Calendar Refills - 2000
Dated</shortDesc>";
  source += "<price>2.99</price></item>";
  event.dataTransfer.setData("Text", source);
}
function dragOver(){
  event.returnValue = false;
}
</script>
<body>
<p align="center">
<img ID="dropTarget" ondrop="dropItem()" ondragover="dragOver()"
src="image/cart.gif">
<BR>Click on the image for the item and drop it into the cart.</p>
<p><DIV ID="displayXML"> </DIV></p>
<table><thread><th colspan="2">Featured Items</th></thread>
```

```
<tr>
  <td rowspan="2"><img src="image/img2.gif"
ondragstart="startDrag('H23199')" /></td>
  <td>
    <a href="singleItem.asp?itemID=H23199&amp;catID=ROOT">At-A-Glance
Daily Desk Calendar Refills - 2000 Dated</a>
  </td>
</tr>
<tr>
  <td>Price: $2.99
</tr>
</table>
</body></html>
```

One thing you may have noticed in our example of the
drag-and-drop functions is that IE does not support the Ctrl and
Shift keyboard modifiers. If you are not aware of the Ctrl and Shift
modifiers, they allow you to determine whether the object should be
copied (Ctrl), moved (Shift), or linked (Ctrl+Shift). This functionality

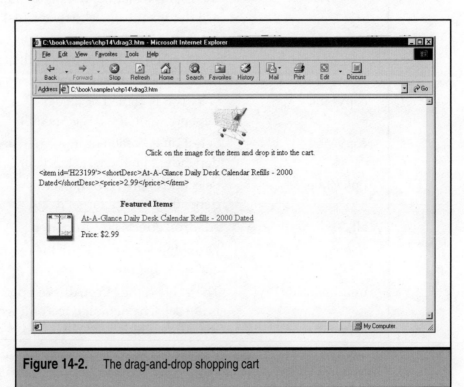

Figure 14-2.   The drag-and-drop shopping cart

is controlled through code and the effectAllowed property of the dataTransfer object. The effectAllowed property supports more values than just the standard copy, move, and link that are supported in standard applications. In general, the effectAllowed property is set in the ondragstart event handler and is used to define the types of operations supported by the source object. Table 14-3 lists the valid values for the effectAllowed property and briefly describes the functionality of each.

Valid effectAllowed Value	Description
copy	Selection is copied (default in the browser except for anchors and text fields).
link	Selection is linked to the drop target by the data transfer operation (default action for source anchor elements).
move	Selection is moved to the target location when dropped (default action for source text elements).
copyLink	Selection is copied or linked, depending on the target default.
copyMove	Selection is copied or moved, depending on the target default.
linkMove	Selection is linked or moved, depending on the target default.
all	All drop effects are supported.
none	Dropping is disabled and the no-drop cursor is displayed.
uninitialized	The value if the effectAllowed property is not set. The default effect still works. Returns uninitialized if queried.

Table 14-3. Valid Values for the effectAllowed Property

The dropEffect is used to determine which drag-and-drop operations are allowed for the target object. The dropEffect not only determines the type of operation that should occur on the target item, but it also sets the cursor to provide user feedback. The dropEffect supports four values: copy, link, move, or none (default). Setting the value to none displays the no-drop cursor. The dropEffect property can be set during the ondragenter, ondragover, and ondrop events. However, if you wish to display the chosen cursor, the default action of the ondragenter, ondragover, and ondrop events must be canceled. Otherwise, the copy cursor, move cursor, or link cursor set by this property displays only until the first valid drop target element is moved over. From then on, the cursor is replaced by the no-drop cursor for the duration of the drag operation.

To help illustrate the effectAllowed and dropEffect properties, we put together a simple example that shows the effectAllowed and dropEffect effects of some of the properties values.

dragDrop.htm

```
<HTML>
<HEAD>
<SCRIPT>
function dragStart(){
  var effect = event.srcElement.id;
  window.event.dataTransfer.effectAllowed = effect;
  window.event.dataTransfer.dropEffect = effect;
}
function drop(){
  window.event.returnValue = false;
  window.event.srcElement.innerText +=
window.event.dataTransfer.getData("text");
}
function dragOver(){
  window.event.returnValue = false;
}
function dragEnter(){
  window.event.returnValue = false;
}
function changeLinked(){
  link.innerText += " additional linked text]";
}
```

```
</SCRIPT>
</HEAD>
<BODY>
<SPAN ID="move" ondragstart="dragStart()">[Will be moved]</SPAN>
<SPAN ID="link" ondragstart="dragStart()">[Will be linked]</SPAN>
<SPAN ID="copy" ondragstart="dragStart()">[Will be copied]</SPAN>
<SPAN ID="target" STYLE="background:yellow; height:200; width:200"
ondrop="drop()" ondragover="dragOver()" ondragenter="dragEnter()">Drop
Here<BR></SPAN>
</BODY>
</HTML>
```

Working with the Clipboard Object

The functionality available in the clipboardData object is very similar, but it is a subset of the dataTransfer object. The clipboardData object is available from the window object. The clipboardData object contains the same getData, setData, and clearData methods that the dataTransfer object contains. We will briefly go over these methods, but where we will spend most of our time is on the different events that are raised on the source and target elements.

The clipboardData object and the associated events are used to create custom event handlers that extend the built-in functionality. There are a total of six events that are raised during the editing functionality: onbeforecopy, oncopy, onbeforecut, oncut, onbeforepaste, onpaste. The onbeforecut and onbeforecopy set of events are raised when the user selects text and then does one of the following: right-clicks on the selected text, clicks on the Edit menu, or with focus on a text box, presses the shortcut keys for either cut or copy (such as Ctrl+X or Shift+Del). The onbeforepaste event is raised when the user selects text and right-clicks on the element, right-clicks in a text box, or with focus on a text box, presses the shortcut keys for paste (such as Ctrl+V or Shift+Insert). The main purpose of these events is to enable cut, copy, or paste functionality on elements that do not natively support this functionality (such as DIV and SPAN elements). The oncut, oncopy and onpaste events are raised when the actual action is occurring and allows us to create custom handlers for the data that should be written to or retrieved from the system clipboard.

Similar to the events of the dataTransfer object, each of these clipboard events expose a number of properties that are available through the event object. These properties provide us with more information about what the user is currently doing and allow us to work with the default event handler. These properties are the same properties that are exposed in the events of the dataTransfer object, so we refer you to Table 14-2 for the details of the properties.

As stated earlier in the onbefore set of events, you can enable editing functions to elements that do not natively support editing, such as DIVs. To enable a particular function, you simply set the event.returnValue equal to false. By doing this we are overriding the default behavior and taking on the responsibility of handling the data transfer. This is actually quite easy to implement because, as we stated earlier, the setData, getData, and clearData methods are available on the clipboardData object. The setData method allows you to set the data that is currently on the system clipboard.

This method has two parameters: the first parameter is the format of the data to be transferred (either Text or URL), and the second is the data to be transferred. To retrieve data from the clipboard, you simply use the getData method, which has one parameter, the format of the data to retrieve (either Text or URL); it returns the specified format's data. Finally, if you want to remove data from the clipboard, you can use the clearData method, passing the format to remove (either Text, URL, File, HTML, or Image) or nothing to remove all the data from the clipboard.

To help illustrate how you can use the custom editing functionality, we created a simple little page that adds the cut functionality to a DIV element and the paste functionality to another DIV. In addition to this, we created a custom event handler for the cut method of a text box that supplies a hard-coded string rather than the value you have selected to cut. One thing to note about the handling of the text box is that in the oncut event we set the event.return value equal to false, which as we have discussed before disables the default functionality. The code for this sample is as follows:

clipboard.htm

```
<HTML>
<SCRIPT>
function beforeCut() {
   event.returnValue = false;
}
function cut() {
  var sourceData = source.innerHTML;
  window.clipboardData.setData("Text", sourceData);
  event.returnValue = false;
  source.innerText = "";
}
function cutCustom(){
  window.clipboardData.setData("Text", "Special Data Handler");
  custom.value = "";
  event.returnValue = false;  //Disable built in cut handler
}
function beforePaste() {
  event.returnValue = false;
}
function paste() {
  window.clipboardData.getData("Text");
  event.returnValue = false;
  event.srcElement.innerText = window.clipboardData.getData("Text");
}
</SCRIPT>
<BODY>
<p><DIV ID="source" onbeforecut="beforeCut()" oncut="cut()">This text can be
cut (Select & Right Click)</DIV></p>
<p><DIV ID="target" onbeforepaste="beforePaste()" onpaste="paste()">Select
this text and right click to paste</DIV></p>
<input id="custom" type="text" oncut="cutCustom()" size="50" value="Copy
and
paste from here to see custom data handler">
</BODY>
</HTML>
```

Security Considerations

Depending on where you look in Microsoft's documentation, you will get different answers as to what is supported in the data transfer environment. The reality is that currently in IE 5.0, you can copy/drag text from any desktop application or another Web site to a target container in your page. Likewise, you can copy/drag text from your page to any other page or desktop application that supports drag/drop or editing functionality. However, a user does have the option of disabling this feature by modifying the "Allow paste operations via script" radio button group in the Security Settings dialog by going into the Custom Level section, available through the Internet Options Control Panel applet. You cannot, however, accept binary content from the desktop, such as a Word Document or even a text document.

MOUSE CAPTURING

There may be cases in your DHTML applications where you wish for one object to receive all of the mouse events, even if the events do not occur inside of the particular element. By using mouse capturing, we are able to handle all of the mouse-related events for a particular document through a single element. Whether the page has been designed to incorporate a drop-down menu or to create a game, mouse capturing permits a user to better interact with a Web page.

One place where implementing mouse capturing can be very beneficial is in a drop-down menu. One of the problems with creating a drop-down menu in DHTML is to capture when the user has left the menu, which should cause the menu to be hidden. By using mouse capturing, once a user clicks on the menu we can track the user's actions from the menu object. By doing this we receive the entire set of mouse events even if the actions are not executed against the menu itself. We can therefore be alerted when the user clicks on the document or any element on the document, which should hide the drop-down menu.

HOW TO IMPLEMENT MOUSE CAPTURING

Mouse capturing is handled though two simple methods (setCapture, releaseCapture) that are available for HTML elements. The setCapture() method tells the document to send all of the mouse events to the element which the setCapture method is executed against. The setCapture method takes one parameter, which is a true/false value that indicates if the events originating within a mouse capturing–enabled container are fired (true means fired, which is the default; false means not fired). Once mouse capturing is set for an object, that object fires all mouse events for the document. The mouse events that are fired are onmousedown, onmouseup, onmousemove, onclick, ondblclick, onmouseover, and onmouseout. The srcElement property of the window event object always returns the object that is positioned under the mouse rather than the object that has the mouse capture. The following is an example of calling the setCapture method:

```
htmlElement.setCapture(true);
```

To remove the mouse event capturing, you call the releaseCapture() method. The releaseCapture method is called from the object that you specified to handle the mouse capture or from the document object. Calling the releaseCapture method on the document object releases mouse capturing without determining which object is capturing mouse events. The following is an example of calling the releaseCapture method on the document object:

```
document.releaseCapture();
```

In addition to calling the releaseCapture method, an object will also lose the mouse capture when the following events occur: opening context menus, calling the alert method, scrolling the page, or losing focus on the window. When the object specified in the setCapture method loses mouse capturing, the onlosecapture event is raised. The onlosecapture event is generally used to handle hiding or any cleaning up that needs to be done once an item loses the capture.

To help illustrate the mouse capturing methods, we created a very simple example menu. We capture the mouse when you click on the menu and then release the capture when you click on the submenu item or on another element. Once you click on the submenu, it goes away and we display a simple message box. The following is the mouse capturing sample:

mousecapture.htm

```
<html>
<script>
var activeMenu = null;
function displayMenu(){
  if (event.srcElement == menu){
    if (activeMenu == null){
      newElement = document.createElement("DIV");
      newElement.style.width = 100;
      newElement.style.backgroundColor = "lightblue";
      newElement.innerHTML = "New";
      body.appendChild(newElement);
      menu.setCapture(true);
      activeMenu = newElement;
    }
  }
  else
    if (event.srcElement == activeMenu)
      alert("The New menu has been clicked");
    else
      menu.releaseCapture();
}
function closeCapture(){
  body.removeChild(activeMenu);
  activeMenu = null;
}
</script>
<body id="body">
<p>Click on the File Menu above to see the child element</p>
<DIV id="menu" onloseCapture="closeCapture()" onClick="displayMenu()"
style="background:lightblue">File</DIV>
</body>
</html>
```

SUMMARY

In this chapter we covered some of the new and advanced features found in IE 5.0. These features make coding advanced applications much simpler and help reduce the amount of code that needs to be written. The topics covered allow us as developers to create applications that contain features that users have come to expect. Look for Microsoft and Netscape to continue adding in these types of features so that we can develop complete applications from within the browser interface.

PART V

Windows Script Components and Remote Scripting

CHAPTER 15

Windows Script Components

Using scripting languages has become popular with the advent of the World Wide Web. In the beginning, script code was used to write procedures to execute some logic. The script code was placed either on the client or the server, as was appropriate for the application.

In this early implementation, the script code was not easily scalable or reusable. If the script logic needed to be reused in other places, then the code was either cut and pasted into the required location or an include file was created and included with the main script code. The script code was still a set of functions that were procedural in nature. Today, we have a more powerful way of handling script code by making it into a *component*. This also makes the script code object-oriented and offers some of the benefits of OOP (object-oriented programming).

Microsoft's Windows Script Component (WSC) technology gives script code the capability of being a COM component. WSC COM components can be executed either on the client as a DHTML behavior or on the server as either a COM object or an Active Server Page–aware COM object. On the server, the WSC can even be used with the Microsoft Transaction Server (MTS).

This chapter will cover the following information on WSCs:

▼ Their advantages and disadvantages.

■ Types of WSCs.

■ How to install the required files to create WSCs.

■ How to create a component using the WSC Wizard.

■ The architecture of WSCs.

▲ Examples of a COM and DHTML WSC.

WINDOWS SCRIPT COMPONENTS OVERVIEW

WSCs are COM components that are created using scripting code. Any scripting language can be used to create WSCs, as long as the scripting language supports Microsoft ActiveX Scripting interfaces. Some examples of scripting languages that support these interfaces are VBScript, JScript, PERLScript, Pscript, and Python. The examples in this chapter are in JScript.

What Are WSCs?

By default, a WSC is a COM component. The Windows Script Component technology has two other built-in interfaces that it supports: DHTML behaviors and ASP. Other interface handlers can also be created to extend the script component engine. These interface handlers are usually DLLs, written using C++. The interface handlers implement specific COM interfaces. Interface handlers are beyond the scope of the book, so we won't discuss them further.

WSCs can serve a number of functions. As COM components, they can be used as middle-tier business components or utility components, act as an interface between applications and a database, or whatever other functionality is needed that can be done in script. Since they are COM components, WSCs can be hosted in other COM-aware applications. COM WSCs are best targeted for execution on the server, but they can be run on the client if the client has the WSC runtime files installed. As an ASP implementation, a WSC serves as an ASP request made to the server from a Web page. This type of WSC will only run on a Web server that supports Active Server Pages.

When a WSC is implemented as a DHTML behavior, it is attached to an element on the Web page and will run only in Internet Explorer 5.0 and later. It can have a user interface on the Web page, or it can act as a helper utility on a Web page that does not have a user interface. WSCs can also be coded to work on both the server and the client with very little effort.

The Good and the Bad of Windows Script Components

WSCs are beneficial because

▼ They are reusable as COM components.

■ They are easy to create.

■ The script code is in a component and is therefore easy to maintain within the entire application.

■ They work with Microsoft Transaction Server.

■ They work well on either client or server.

- They are small and efficient.

- They take scripting to the next level of development (from procedural to components).

- They can be written in a choice of multiple script languages.

There are, however, also reasons for not using WSCs:

- A WSC's script code is interpreted and not compiled; therefore it executes more slowly than compiled code.

- Script languages are not as robust as a full-featured programming language like Visual Basic or Visual C++.

▲ Script code cannot directly access the Win32 API.

REQUIRED WINDOWS SCRIPT COMPONENT FILES

The files required for using WSC technology come with Internet Explorer 5.x, Windows Script Hosting 2.0, and Windows 2000. (WSC is scheduled to be part of the Windows 2000 release version.) You can also download the most current version at Microsoft's Web Site.

NOTE: The location of the current version of Windows Script Component is at http://msdn.microsoft.com/scripting/ in the download area of the windows scripting component section. The location of this site may change, so we suggest that you search for windows scripting components on the Microsoft Web site if the supplied URL no longer functions.

WSC will run on Windows 95, 98, and NT 4.0. There are, however, some special requirements for running it on Windows 95. Either Windows 95/OSR2, Internet Explorer 4.0 or later, or DCOM needs to be installed.

NOTE: The DCOM installation files can be found at www.microsoft.com/com/dcom/dcom95/dcom1_3.asp, as of this writing.

After the installation has completed, a Microsoft Windows Script group is created in the Programs menu. The Windows Script Component Wizard is added to this group and is used to help in the initial creation of a WSC. The WSC installation also includes the Windows Script Component documentation, which is the WSC help file. This help file covers the WSC information very thoroughly.

WSC Run-Time Files

Running the WSC setup program installs the WSCs runtime files. The main file that runs the WSC engine is script object dynamic link library (scrobj.dll), which is the Windows Script Components runtime. The WSC runtime acts as an in-process server to WSC files, dispatching COM requests to the script (see below). This allows the WSC file to contain mainly script code and removes the need for it to deal with the complexities of COM. Each WSC file tells the runtime engine what type of COM interface (Automation, DHTML Behavior, ASP, and so on) it would like to create. (We will see how this done in "Windows Script Component Architecture" later in the chapter.)

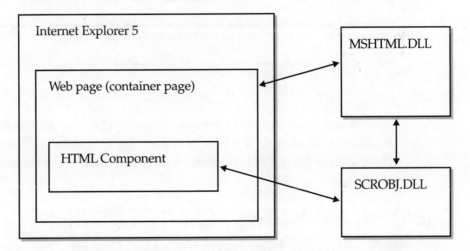

The WSC setup also installs a MIME type of "text/scriptlet" for files with a file extension of .wsc or .sct. The MIME type can be viewed

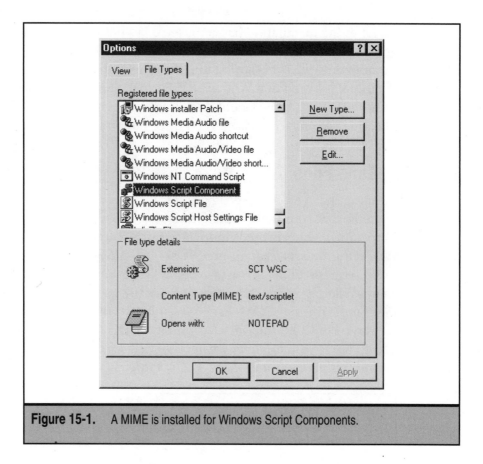

Figure 15-1.   A MIME is installed for Windows Script Components.

in the Windows Explorer's View/Options menu item's File Types tab
(see Figure 15-1). This MIME type allows a WSC file to be launched
by double-clicking on the WSC file itself. WSC files have an extension
of .wsc. The .sct is a holdover from Microsoft's Scriptlet technology.

CREATING A WINDOWS SCRIPT COMPONENT

A Windows Script Component is just a text file with a .wsc extension,
containing XML and script code. The WSC file has three major pieces:
the public interface, script section, and other supporting XML
elements. The public interface section contains the properties,

methods, and events of the component. The script section obviously contains the script that implements the public interface and component functionality. The supporting XML elements allow the WSC to be registered, include type libraries, define what type of COM to implement, and define constant values to be used by the WSC.

The Windows Script Component Wizard

The easiest way to create a WSC is by using the WSC Wizard. The Wizard, installed with the WSC installation, creates a skeleton WSC in a .wsc file. After the Wizard is finished, the only tasks left to complete the component are to add script code implementing the component's functionality and to add any supporting XML elements. Figure 15-2 shows the first page of the Wizard.

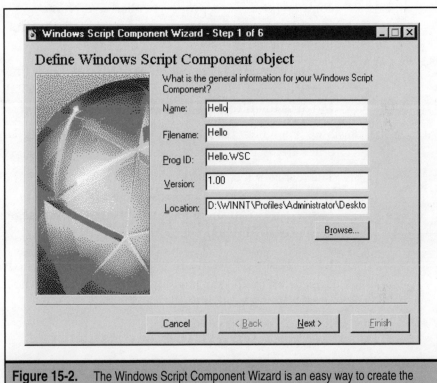

Figure 15-2.   The Windows Script Component Wizard is an easy way to create the skeleton of a WSC.

Creating a "Hello" WSC

Let's walk through the steps of using the WSC Wizard to create a very simple component.

1. Start the Wizard: it is located in the Microsoft Windows Script menu off of the Programs menu.

2. On the Step 1 page, enter **Hello** in the Name field. This entered value will propagate to the Filename and the Prog ID fields. Leave the other fields, including Location, as their defaults and press the Next button.

3. On the Step 2 page, select JScript as the language and uncheck the special implements support, error checking, and debugging checkboxes. Press the Next button to move to the third step.

4. The Step 3 page is where you enter the properties of the component. Enter a property called **userName** as type **Read/Write**, and use your name as the default value. Press the Next button.

5. In Step 4, methods are added to the component. Enter a method called **display** and give it one parameter called **text**. Move to the fifth step by pressing the Next button.

6. Step 5 is where the component can expose events. Do not enter any events for this component. Press the Next button.

7. The last step lets you confirm everything that you have entered up to this point. Press the Finish button to create the component. You should see a confirmation message verifying its successful creation.

At this time, we should have a file named hello.wsc in the location that was specified in the first step of the Wizard. Open the file in Notepad; it should look like this:

```
<?xml version="1.0"?>
<component>
<registration
    description="hello"
    progid="hello.WSC"
```

```
        version="1.00"
        classid="{db511d30-c5aa-11d3-a554-002078128f96}">
</registration>
<public>
    <property name="userName">
        <get/>
        <put/>
    </property>
    <method name="display">
        <PARAMETER name="text"/>
    </method>
</public>
<script language="JScript">
<![CDATA[
var description = new hello;
function hello(){
    this.get_userName = get_userName;
    this.put_userName = put_userName;
    this.display = display;
}
var userName = "Dan";
function get_userName(){
    return userName;
}
function put_userName(newValue){
    userName = newValue;
}
function display(text){
    return "Temporary Value";
}
]]>
</script>
</component>
```

NOTE: The classid value is generated by the Wizard and will most likely be different from what is in the hello.wsc file that you created.

Edit the hello.wsc file. (Microsoft Notepad is a .wsc file's default editor. There isn't a WSC development environment currently, and since a WSC is just a text file, Notepad does just fine.) Change the display function to look like this:

```
function display(text){
    return userName + ",\n" + text + "\nWindows Script Components";
}
```

To run this WSC, all you need to do is to create it as an ActiveX object. But before you do that, you need to register it. The easiest way to register a WSC is to right-click on the .wsc file. The menu in Figure 15-3 shows the Register menu item in the menu list.

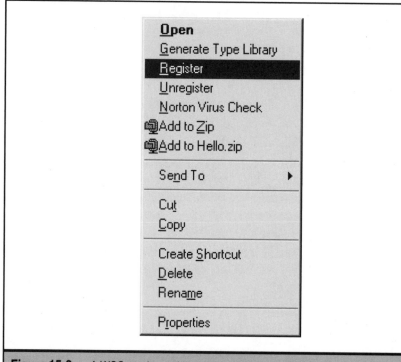

Figure 15-3. A WSC can be registered by using its context menu.

Click on that menu item; a successful message should be displayed stating that "DllSelfRegister and DllInstall" succeeded. If this message is not displayed, then there is an error in the WSC file that needs to be corrected. Once the hello.wsc file has been registered, a host application is needed to create and execute the component. Create either a Web page or HTML application. Add the following code to execute in the onload event of the <body> tag (<body onload="displayMesage();">):

```
<script language=JavaScript>
function displayMessage(){
var objHello;
    objHello = new ActiveXObject("Hello.WSC");
    document.body.innerText = objHello.display("Welcome to the world of
Windows Script Components");
}
</script>
```

If a WSC is created in Internet Explorer, you may get a warning about unsafe ActiveX controls. Just answer Yes to this warning message to run the code. The security level setting in Internet Explorer causes this warning. The output shown in Figure 15-4 is an HTML application that uses hello.wsc.

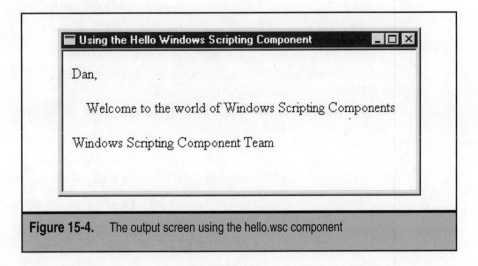

Figure 15-4. The output screen using the hello.wsc component

WINDOWS SCRIPT COMPONENT'S ARCHITECTURE

As we mentioned previously in this chapter while looking at
hello.wsc, a WSC is a text file that conforms to a specific XML
schema. In this section we will cover all the XML elements that make
up a WSC (see Table 15-1 for an overview).

XML Element	Purpose
<?component?>	Enables/disables debugging and error messages for the WSC
<?XML?>	Declares that WSC file conforms to XML standards
<component>	Defines a WSC within a file
<comment>	Denotes a comment in the WSC file
<event>	Defines a custom event that the WSC fires up to its container object
<implements>	Identifies which additional COM interfaces the WSC uses
<method>	Defines a public method for the WSC
<object>	Defines an object the WSC will use
<package>	Encloses multiple WSCs in one file
<property>	Defines a public property of the WSC
<public>	Encloses the property, method, and event XML elements
<reference>	Refers to a type library of an external object that the WSC will use
<registration>	Contains registration information used to register the WSC as a COM component
<resource>	Defines constant values that are used in the script
<script>	Defines the WSCs functionality

Table 15-1. XML Elements That Define WSC Functionality

The WSC architecture also has some functions and methods, which are shown in Table 15-2.

Now let's take a closer look at the details of WSC's XML elements, functions, and methods.

The <?xml?> and <?component?> XML Elements

The <?xml?> element states whether the WSC file conforms to strict XML formatting standards. This element is optional. If it is included in the file, then the WSC's XML must follow these strict XML guidelines: element types and attribute names are case sensitive; attribute values must be in single or double quotes; and all elements are parsed. If the declaration is not included, the compiler allows looser XML syntax. The syntax of the <?xml?> element is

```
<?xml version="version" standalone="DTDflag" encoding="encname" ?>
```

The version attribute is the XML level that the WSC file must conform to. At this time, you will always use 1.0. The optional standalone attribute is set if the WSC file refers to an external Document Type Definition (DTD). Since WSC files do not have DTDs, this value is always yes. The optional encoding attribute is a string that describes the encoding character set used by the WSC file.

WSC Function/Method	Purpose	Type
createComponent	Creates an instance of another WSC component from within same WSC package	Function
getResource	Retrieves the value of a resource element from within the WSC	Function
fireEvent	Raises an event to the WSC's container object	Method

Table 15-2.   Methods and Functions Used to Create a WSC

Though the <?xml?> element is not required, it is highly recommended. If the WSC file is edited in an XML-conforming editor, it will need this element.

The <?component?> element is also optional. If it is used in the WSC file, then it needs to be placed after the <?xml?> element. Its syntax is

```
<?component debug="flag" error="flag"?>
```

(where flag value is either true, false, yes, no, 1, or 0). The error attribute is used to display either a syntax or runtime error. If the error attribute is set to true, it will display a message box with the error and the location (line, column) in the WSC file where the error was generated. The debug attribute is used to allow debugging of the script code. Both of these flags should be turned off before the WSC is placed into production.

The <package> and <component> XML Elements and the createComponent Function

The <package> and <component> elements kind of go together. The <component> element is used to wrap all the XML elements for a given component. The <package> element is used to wrap multiple components within one WSC file. The <package> element is not needed if there is only one component in the WSC file.

The <component> element's syntax is as follows:

```
<component id="componentID">
    (the WSC is defined between these 2 elements)
</component>
```

The <component> element contains only one attribute, id. The id attribute is used to identify the component when there is more than one component within a <package> element.

The <package> element does not have any attributes. The following code shows how to create multiple components within a package:

```
<package>
<component id="FirstWSC">
(script component information here)
```

```
</component>
<component id="SecondWSC">
(script component information here)
<script language="JScript">
![CDATA[
function createFirstComp(){
    return createComponent("FirstWSC");
}
]]>
</script>
</component>
</package>
```

Assuming that the second WSC's createFirstComp function is public, then this function can be called to create an instance of the FirstWSC component. The way the container application would call this function is

```
comp2 = new ActiveXObject("component.SecondWSC");
comp1 = comp2.createFirstComp();
```

The value "component.SecondWSC" is the prog id on the <registration> element (not shown), which is covered later in the chapter. The first line creates the SecondWSC component. The second line calls the SecondWSC's createFirstComp function to create a reference to the FirstWSC component.

The <public>, <property>, <method>, and <event> XML Elements

The <public> element wraps the <property>, <method>, and <event> elements. This is where the public interface of the WSC is located. Each of the three XML elements (<property>, <method>, and <event>) have some attributes in common. The name attribute is used as the public name that the container or host will use to reference a property, method, or event of the component. The internalName attribute is used by the <property> and <method> elements to give a function name for the implementation of the particular XML element in the <script> element section.

The <property> element is used to create properties for the WSC. Properties can be defined in one of two formats: simple values and functions. Simple values are global variables within the <script> element. The difference between the two formats is that with the function format, the property can do some processing before it either sets or returns the value.

The syntax of a simple format type is

```
property name="propName" internalName="propName" />
```

The internalName attribute is used to reference a different global variable name than the property name. The following code shows a simple format with and without using an internal name attribute:

```
<property name="myProp />
<property name="yourProp" internalName="someProp" />
<script language="JScript">
![CDATA[
var myProp;
var someProp;
```

Notice that a yourProp variable was not declared, but a someProp was declared. The caller of this WSC will use the yourProp name to get to the property, but the someProp variable will be used by that property.

To declare the <property> element using the function format, use this syntax:

```
<property name="propName">
   <get internalName="getPropName" />
   <put internalName="putPropName" />
</property>
```

The <get> and <put> elements' internalName attributes are optional. If the internalName attribute is not given, then the name of the functions are get_propName and put_propName for get and put, respectively. The propName part of the function name is the value of the name attribute. If the internalName attribute is given, then the get and put functions use those names. The following code listing shows an example of both methods:

```
<property name="myProp">
    <get />
    <put internalName="setMyProp" />
</property>
...
<script language="JScript">
![CDATA[
var somePropValue;
function get_myProp(){
    return somePropValue;
}
function setMyProp(data){
    somePropValue = data;
}
```

Read-only and write-only properties can be created by using only the <get> element for read-only and using only the <put> element for a write-only property.

The <method> element creates public methods for the component. The syntax for the <method> element is

```
<method name="methodName" internalName="functionName" dispid=dispID>
<parameter name="parameterID1"/>
<parameter name="parameterID2"/>
...
</method>
```

The <method> element has a dispid attribute (dispatch ID) that is used to identify a component's method (they are also used with events). The dispid attribute for a method is an integer value from –999 to –500. The dispid attribute is compiled into a type library to bind the method or event to the host application. If a dispid attribute is not given, then one is automatically given to the XML element. If a dispid value of 0 is given to a method, that method becomes the default method of the component. A <property> element can also have a dispid of 0. Each dispid of a given component must be unique: there can only be one default property or method of a given component.

The <method> element can have zero or more parameters passed to it. The parameter name is the name used in the method's function declaration. Parameters are passed by value, so a parameter's value cannot be changed inside the method and returned to the caller. The following listing shows an example <method> element in a component:

```
<method name="addValues"
  <parameter name="value1" />
  <parameter name="value2" />
</method>
...
<script language="JScript">
![CDATA[
function addValues(value1, value2){
    return value1 + value2;
}
```

The <event> element allows the component's container (or host application) to be notified of events that the component raises. The syntax of the <event> element is very simple:

```
<event name="evtname" dispid="dispnumber" />
```

The event is raised by the component in the script code using the fireEvent method, like this:

```
<event name="onChangeofSomething" dispid="212" />
...
<script language="JScript">
![CDATA[
function doSomething(){
    fireEvent("onChangeofSomething");
}
```

When the doSomething function is called, it fires the event "onChangeofSomething" up to its container.

The <implements> XML Element

The <implements> element is used to tell which additional interfaces the WSC will be using. A WSC can implement multiple interfaces. If the <implements> element is not given, then the WSC is a COM object. WSCs have three built-in interfaces (within srcobj.dll): COM, DHTML behaviors, and ASP. We will cover the COM and DHTML behavior interfaces in this chapter. Chapter 16 will cover the ASP interface. The syntax of the <implements> element is

```
<implements type="COMHandlerName" id="internalName" default=fAssumed>
    (handler-specific information here)
</implements>
```

The type attribute is required; it specifies the interface being used. Besides the three interfaces that are built into WSC, other DLLs can be created as interfaces to WSCs. (We will not cover how to create an interface DLL in this book.) The optional id attribute is used to resolve variable names in the script. The properties, methods, and event names are contained within a global name space. The id attribute can be used to prefix a property, method, or event to resolve a naming conflict. The optional default attribute is used to assume that the script code is qualified with the internalName of the <implements> element. By default this value is set to true. Set it to false if you want to hide the members of specific <implements> elements.

Each interface can have its own set of interface handlers. Those handlers are specified within the <implements> element. We will see an example of this when we cover WSC DHTML behaviors later in this chapter.

The <reference> and <object> XML Elements

The <reference> element adds a reference to an external type library for the component. This allows the component to reference any constants that the type library defines, which helps in making the code more readable. The syntax of the <reference> element is very simple:

```
<reference object="progID" guid="typelibGUID" version="version">
```

Either the object attribute or the guid attribute must be specified. The object attribute is the program ID, and the GUID is the class ID of the type library. The optional version attribute gives the version number of the type library to be included in the component.

The <object> element defines a COM object reference for the component. The object's scope is global for the component. Also, if the component is edited in a script-aware environment, then the <object> element will help with statement completion. The syntax of the <object> element is

```
<object id="objid" classid="clsid:GUID" progid="progID"/>
```

The id attribute refers to the object within the script code. Either a classid attribute or a progid attribute is required, but not both. The classid attribute's value is the GUID of the object. The GUID must be prefixed with clsid:. The progid is the server.class name of the object, such as ADODB.Recordset. An example of how the component would use the <object> element is

```
<object id="objFS" progid="Scripting.FileSystemObject" />
...
<script language="JScript">
![CDATA[
function fileData(fileName){
var txt;
var data;
    txt = objFS.OpenTextFile("C:/temo/text.dat");
    data = txt.ReadAll();
    txt.Close();
    return data;
}
...
```

This <object> element creates a reference to the file system object. The ID of the object is objFS, and its progid is Scripting.FileSystemObject. This object is used to manipulate files. The fileData function calls the file system object's OpenTextFile method to open a file. This method returns a textstream object, which is also an object of the Scripting server. Then, all the data from the textstream object is read into a variable named data. The textstream is closed and the data variable's value is returned to the caller.

The <resource> XML element and the getResource Function

The <resource> element holds constant values. This helps keep the code clean and free of hard-coded values. The syntax of the <resource> element is

```
<resource id="resourceID">
text or number here
</resource>
```

The <resource> element contains an ID to refer to the specific resource and the value of the resource itself. The resource is either text or a number value. The getResource function is used to retrieve the resource value from the resource. Here is an example of how to use resources:

```
<resource id="MaxRtnCD">
512
</resource>
<script language="JScript">
<![CDATA[
function checkReturnCD(code)
    if (code > getResource("MaxRtnCD"))
        return false;
    else
        return true;
End Function
]]>
</script>
```

The checkReturnCD function uses a resource to check to see if the code variable's value is greater than the max return code allowed.

The <script> XML Element

The <script> element is where the functionality of the WSC is located. The familiar syntax of the <script> element is

```
<script language="language">
  (script code here)
</script>
```

The <script> element has only one attribute, the language of the script code. The only other requirement is that if the <?XML?> element is used in the WSC file, then the script code must be enclosed in a <![CDATA[...]]> element section. The CDATA section causes the XML parser not to parse text within it. If the <?XML?> element is not included in the WSC file, the CDATA section should not be used in the <script> element. If you do this by mistake, then the language's interpreter will interpret the CDATA section. The code below shows how to code the <script> element with a CDATA section:

```
<?XML?>
...
<script language="JScript">
<![CDATA[
function x(){
...
}
function y(){
...
}
]]>
</script>
```

The <registration> XML Element

Since WSCs are COM components they need to be registered with the OS. The <registration> element contains information used to register the component in the OS's registry. Once registered, the WSC can be created in an application as a COM object. The listing below shows the syntax of the <registration> element:

```
<registration progid="someprogid" classid="someclassid"
    description="somedescription" version="versionNumber" />
```

The optional progid attribute is the text name of the component that is put in the registry. The name is used by an application to refer to the component. The optional classid attribute is a globally unique identifier (GUID). If a classid is not assigned, then one is automatically assigned to the component when it is registered. It is *not* recommended to use the automatic GUID because then the component will a have different GUID every place the component is registered. If you want to generate a GUID yourself, you can do so by using the Uuidgen.exe utility program. Note that while using both the progid and classid attributes is optional, specifying at least one of them is required. The optional description attribute is a text string that is placed in the registry and is used by host applications. The optional version attribute can be used to assign the component a version and a host application can create a specific version of the component.

A WINDOWS SCRIPT COMPONENT COM EXAMPLE

Now that we've covered the architecture of a WSC, let's take a look at how it all fits together. To do so, we'll use an example of a COM WSC that maintains a contact list in an Access 97 database using ADO to communicate with the database. Figure 15-5 shows the page that maintains the contact list.

The Contact Information Object Example

We started to build the contactinfo.wsc file by using the WSC Wizard. Enter the properties and methods that are in Table 15-3 in the Wizard. Then fill in the logic behind each of the properties and methods.

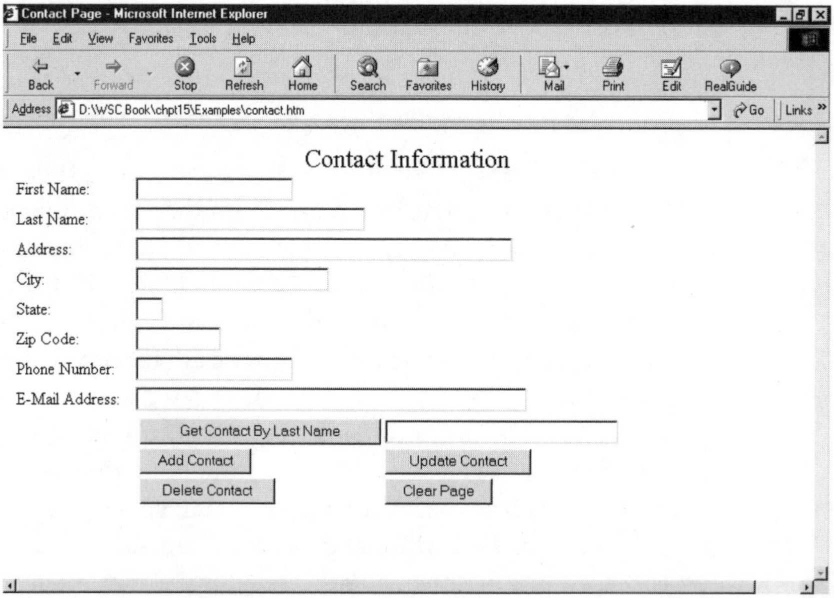

Figure 15-5.   This contact information page uses a WSC COM object to maintain the data in an Access database.

The properties are used to transport the data values in and out of the object. This code listing shows an example:

```
<property name="fName">
      <get/>
      <put/>
</property>
...
function get_fName(){
    return fName;
}
function put_fName(newValue){
    fName = newValue;
}
```

All the properties perform the same kind of process. The dbLoc property is write only and the id property is read-only.

Name	Type	Purpose
lName	Property	Contains the contact's last name
fName	Property	Contains the contact's first name
address	Property	Contains the contact's address
city	Property	Contains the contact's city
state	Property	Contains the contact's state
zip	Property	Contains the contact's zip code
phone	Property	Contains the contact's phone number
email	Property	Contains the contact's e-mail address
id	Property	Contains the contact's unique ID, which is a database-generated value
dbLoc	Property	Location of the database
retrieve	Method	Loads the object with a contact's information
update	Method	Updates the contact information
del	Method	Removes the contact from the database
add	Method	Inserts a new contact into the database
clear	Method	Removes the contact information from the object's variables

Table 15-3.   Properties and Methods Used by the contactinfo WSC

The working logic of the component is its methods. They all have the same logic except for the clear method, which resets the internal variables to their original values. The other methods set up a SQL statement, open the database connection, execute the SQL statement, and close the database connection. The following listing shows how the retrieve method works:

```
<object id="cnn" progid="ADODB.Connection"/>
<object id="rs" progid="ADODB.Recordset"/>
...
function retrieve(){
    cnn.Open("provider=Microsoft.Jet.OLEDB.4.0;Data Source=" + dbLoc +
"contact.mdb;Persist Security Info=False");
    rs.Open("select * from contact where lastname = '" + lName + "'", cnn,
3, 1);
    if (rs.EOF && rs.BOF){
        clear();
        rs.Close();
        cnn.Close();
        return;
    }
    if (rs(0).value != null)
        fName = rs(0).value;
    else
        fName = "";
...
    if (rs(8).value != null)
        id = rs(8).value;
    else
        id = "";
    rs.Close();
    cnn.Close();
}
```

NOTE: The entire retrieve function was not shown because it would take up too much room. The items that were not displayed assign the values from the database to the object's variables, like the fName and the id properties shown.

The first two items in the code listing are the declaration of the ADO Connection and Recordset objects. These are global objects that the component uses to communicate with the database. The first two lines in the retrieve function use these objects by their IDs. The first line opens the database connection, and the second line opens a recordset. The record is retrieved using the lastname column in the contact table. If an empty recordset is returned (indicated by the recordset's BOF and EOF value being true), the recordset and the connection are closed, the object's variables are cleared, and the function returns to its caller. Otherwise the data in the recordset is moved to the object's variables, and the connection and recordset is closed.

The retrieve function is the only function that uses a recordset. The other functions create a SQL statement and execute it using the connection object.

Using the Contact Information Object

Once the component is completed it needs to be registered. The Wizard created a <registration> element in the component so the component could be registered. To register the component, right-click on the file within Windows Explorer to display its context menu and select the Register option. A confirmation message box should be displayed that states the registration process was successful.

Figure 15-5 shows a Web page that uses the contact information WSC. This is not the only way to use it. Since it is a COM object, it could be used with any COM-compliant application. We show how to use it with a Web page, but these same techniques can be employed to use the component in other applications.

The Web page's onload event creates the contact information object as follows:

```
var dbLoc = "D:/WSC BOOK/chpt15/Examples/";
var objContact;
function initPage(){
    objContact = new ActiveXObject("contactinfo.wsc");
    objContact.dbLoc = dbLoc;
}
```

The two variables before the initPage function are global variables for the page. The initPage is called when the <body> tag's onload event fires. The initPage function creates the contactinfo.wsc object using the ActiveXObject function. It then sets the objContact object's dbLoc property to the path of the database.

Since the contactinfo WSC is just like any other COM object, its properties and methods are called in the same manner. For example, let's see how the page calls the contactinfo object's retrieve method. To retrieve a contact, the user must enter a last name in the textbox next to the Get Contact By Last Name button and then press the button. The retrContactData function is executed when the button is clicked. The retrContactData function looks like this:

```
function retrContactData(){
    if (frmContact.txtRetLName.value == ""){
        alert("Please enter a last name to retrieve.");
        return;
    }
    objContact.lName = frmContact.txtRetLName.value;
    objContact.retrieve();
    moveObjectDataToForm();
    if (objContact.id == 0)
        alert("Contact " + frmContact.txtRetLName.value + " not found.");
}
```

The retrContactData function makes sure that a last name was entered in the textbox. If a last name was not entered, then an error message is displayed and the function ends. Otherwise, the last name is then placed in the object's lName property, and the object's retrieve method is called. The retrieve method gets the data for the contact from the database and places it into the object's private variables. When the retrieve method finishes, the moveObjectDataToForm function is called. The moveObjectDataToForm function takes the data from the object's properties and places it in the form's fields to be displayed on the screen. A contact's ID value of 0 indicates that the contract was not found, and a message is displayed to that effect. The other properties and methods of the contact WSC are executed in the same manner.

THE DHTML BEHAVIOR INTERFACE

As we already stated, WSCs have three built-in interfaces that give a component a specific kind of functionality. In the previous section we covered the COM interface. In this section we will cover the DHTML behavior interface.

The DHTML Behavior Architecture

The DHTML behavior interface allows a WSC to interact with a browser that supports DHTML behaviors. Currently, only Internet Explorer 5.0 and later support DHTML behaviors. A DHTML behavior extends the functionality of an HTML element on a Web page. The extended functionality is in the form of properties, methods, and events in the DHTML behavior. The behavior can also extend the user interface of the HTML elements.

To create these features, the WSC's DHTML behavior interface has additional properties, methods, functions, and XML elements that are used in creating a WSC DHTML behavior. Table 15-4 lists these items.

DHTML Behavior	Purpose	Type
attach	Binds an event from the containing page to a function in the WSC	XML element
attachNotification	Binds a function in the WSC to a notification message sent from the container	Method
createEventObject	Creates an event object to pass data between the DHTML behavior and its container	Method
element	Defines the HTML element the behavior is attached to	Property
layout	Defines the HTML text that is inserted in the container when the WSC is first instantiated	XML element
fireEvent	Raises an event to the WSC's container	Method

Table 15-4. Properties, Methods, Functions, and XML Elements in WSC's DHTML Behavior Interface

The <attach> XML Element

The <attach> element ties a function in the script code to an event on the container. The syntax of the <attach> element is

```
<attach event="eventName" handler="functionName"
for="elementName"/>
```

The event attribute is the container's event that is tied to the function. The optional handler attribute is the name of the script function that will be executed when the container's event is raised. If the handler is not specified, the name of the function in the script code depends on whether the for attribute is specified. If the for attribute is not specified, the function's name is the same as the event; otherwise the function's name is the for attribute's value and the event attribute's value concatenated together with a _ (underscore) in the middle. The optional for attribute is used to state which of the container's objects the event is for. The valid values of the for attribute are window, document, and element. If the for attribute is not given, then the event that is specified is for the element object.

The following list shows an example of a use of the <attach> element:

```
<implements type="Behavior">
<attach event="onclick" handler="clicked"/>
    <attach for="window" event="onload" handler="initWin"/>
</implements>
<script language="JScript">
<![CDATA[
function clicked(){
    alert("The DHTML behavior was clicked.");
}
function initWin(){
    alert("The window onload event was raised.");
}
```

The above code listing binds two events to the WSC functions. The clicked function is executed when the element that the DHTML behavior is attached to is clicked. The initWin function is executed when the container's onload event is raised. Notice that the <attach> element is placed within the <implements> element. This is because it is a DHTML behavior interface–specific XML element.

The attachNotification Function

The attachNotification function is used by the WSC to execute a function when the WSC receives a notification message from its container object. These messages are sent to the WSC when the element, to which the behavior is attached, has changed or when the browser is finishing parsing the document. The following code listing shows how to use the attachNotification:

```
<script language="JScript">
<![CDATA[
attachNotification (notified);
function notified (sNotification){
    if (sNotification == "contentReady"){
        // element has changed
    }
    else if (sNotification == "documentReady"){
        // the container has finished parsing document
    }
}
]]>
</script>
```

The attachNotification function call is placed in the script to attach the container's notification function and the script's function. It needs to be outside of a function so that the attachment can be executed when the WSC is instantiated. The notified function is called when the container needs to notify the component. The two notifications are checked, and the appropriate code can be placed in each section.

The element Property and the <layout> XML Element

The element property gives the WSC access to the underlying HTML element that has the behavior attached to it. The element property is read-only so it cannot be changed, but the WSC has access to all of the properties and methods of the element so the element can be modified.

The <layout> element is used to set the initial content of the element that the behavior is attached to. This content can be any valid HTML. If the element has content on the container page, <layout> will overwrite that content. The syntax of the <layout> element is

```
<layout>
    HTML code here
</layout>
```

An example of the <layout> element's usage is

```
<implements type="Behavior">
<layout>
    <table border="1" width="100%">
    <tr>
      <td width="50%"> </td>
      <td width="50%"> </td>
    </tr>
    <tr>
      <td width="50%"> </td>
      <td width="50%"> </td>
    </tr>
  </table>
</layout>
</implements>
```

A table is placed in the element when the container is first displayed. The <layout> element is placed inside the <implements> element because it is a DHTML behavior interface–specific XML element.

The fireEvent and createEventObject Methods

The fireEvent raises a custom event from the WSC to its container. Its syntax is

```
fireEvent(sEvent, oEvent)
```

The fireEvent method has two parameters: the event name (sEvent) and an optional event object (oEvent).

The createEventObject method creates an event object, which is used to pass data between the WSC and the container. This event object is really just the event object used in the DHTML object model (DOM). The createEventObject method does not have any parameters. The following code listing shows how to use both the createEventObject and fireEvent methods:

```
<?xml version="1.0"?>
<component>
<implements type="Behavior" id="setBehavior">
    <attach event="onclick" handler="doclick" />
    <layout>Click here!</layout>
</implements>
<public>
    <event name="onClickFinished" />
</public>
<implements type="Behavior">
    <attach event="onclick" handler="doclick");
</implements>
<script language="JScript">
<![CDATA[
function doclick(){
    var sResult;
    objEvent = createEventObject();
    objEvent.result = sResult;
    fireEvent("onClickFinished ",oEvent);
    alert("The Container returned: " + objEvent.result);
}
]]>
</script>
</component>
```

The following Web page could be used to test the above WSC:

```
<html>
<head>
<title>New Page 1</title>
</head>
<script language=JavaScript>
function setResult(){
    window.event.result = "The text got clicked.";
}
</script>
<body>
<div style="behavior:url('c:\temo\sa.wsc')"
    id="wsc" onClickFinished="setResult()">
</div>
</html>
```

The page declares the WSC in the <div> tag. It uses a style and attaches the behavior to the <div> tag. WSCs are instantiate in the same manner as DHTML behaviors. See Chapter 2 for different methods of instantiating a DHTML behavior on a Web page. The url gives the location of where the WSC can be found. The <div> also declares the onClickFinished event and executes the setResult function. The setResult function retrieves the event object and sets the event's result property to a text string. When the function is complete, execution will go back to the WSC after the fireEvent statement. The alert statement will then be executed and display a message.

USING THE DHTML BEHAVIOR INTERFACE

Figure 15-6 shows a picture of scrolling text that is displayed in Teletype fashion. In order to see how the user interface works, you will need to run this example on your machine. Each character of the message is displayed on the screen, one at a time. The font that is being used is the old typewriter style. These two attributes give the component's output the look and feel of an old fashion Teletype machine.

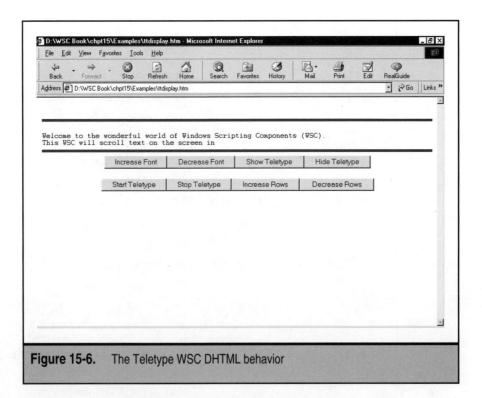

Figure 15-6.   The Teletype WSC DHTML behavior

The Teletype Component

Table 15-5 contains a summary of the properties, methods, and events of the Teletype component.

The <implements> XML element for the component is listed below:

```
<implements type="Behavior" id="Behavior">
    <layout>
    <![CDATA[
        <div id="divTeletype"></div>
    ]]>
    </layout>
    <attach event="onmouseover" handler="MouseOver"/>
    <attach event="onmouseout" handler="MouseOut"/>
</implements>
```

Name	Type	Purpose
Text	Property	Text that will be displayed
Visible	Property	Boolean value that states if the component is to be visible or not
Rows	Property	The number of rows that are displayed for the text to be scrolled in
FontSize	Property	The size of the font
IsRunning	Property	Whether or not the text is being displayed
StartTeletype	Method	Starts the teletype
StopTeletype	Method	Stops the teletype
FireTimer	Method	Used by a timer to display the text
EndOfMessage	Event	An event that is raised to the component's container when the text is finished displaying

Table 15-5. Properties, Methods, and Events of the Teletype Component

The <layout> element creates a <div> HTML tag inside the element that will hold the Teletype component. The reason for this is so that the component has a foundation element, as the component could be placed in any HTML tag. The component also attaches to the containing element's onmouseover and onmouseout events. The purpose of these handlers is to stop the Teletype so a hyperlink can be clicked when the cursor is over the Teletype component and to start the Teletype up once again after the cursor moves off of the component.

When the Text property is set it resets the component to display the text. When the Visible property is turned on, it displays the value in the LastHTML variable. The LastHTML holds the latest text to be displayed because when the Visible property is turned off, the text is still generated but not displayed. The Row property causes at least one row of text to be displayed. This can be overridden by setting the Visible property to false. The StartTeletype method starts the Teletype displaying the text. It creates a timer, which fires every 250 milliseconds. The StopTeletype method stops the text from being displayed by turning off the timer.

The engine for the Teletype component is in the FireTimer method. The following are the StartTeletype and the FireTimer methods:

```javascript
function StartTeletype(){
    if (Timer == 0)
        Timer = window.setInterval(this.id + ".FireTimer()", 250,
"javascript");
    IsRunning = true;
}
function FireTimer(){
var sTemp = "";
var iStart;
var iCount;
var sCurrentLine;
var iEndOfTag;
var sTemp;
    sCurrentLine = TextLines[ArrayLocation];
    LineLocation++;
    if (LineLocation > sCurrentLine.length){
        LineLocation = 1;
        ArrayLocation++;
        if (ArrayLocation > TextLines.length - 1 ){
            ArrayLocation = 0;
            fireEvent("EndOfMessage");
            if (IsRunning == false)
                return;
        }
        sCurrentLine = TextLines[ArrayLocation];
    }
    if (sCurrentLine.substr(LineLocation, 1) == "<"){
        iEndOfTag = sCurrentLine.indexOf(">", LineLocation);
        if (iEndOfTag == -1){
            alert("Missing > in current line:" + sCurrentLine);
            return;
        }
```

```
            sTemp = sCurrentLine.toUpperCase();
            if (sTemp.indexOf("A HREF=", LineLocation) != -1)
                InHref = true;
            else{
                if (sTemp.indexOf("/A", LineLocation) != -1)
                    InHref = false;
            }
            LineLocation = iEndOfTag;
            sTemp = "";
        }
    if (Visible == true){
        iStart = ArrayLocation - Rows + 1;
        if (iStart < 0){
            for (iCount = 1; iCount <= Math.abs(iStart); iCount++)
                sTemp = sTemp + "<FONT face=Courier size=" + FontSize +
"><BR></FONT>";
            iStart = 0;
        }
        for (iCount = iStart; iCount <= ArrayLocation - 1; iCount++)
            sTemp = sTemp + "<FONT face=Courier size=" + FontSize + ">"
+
TextLines[iCount] + "</FONT><BR>";
        if (InHref == true)
            sTemp = sTemp + "<FONT face=Courier New size=" + FontSize +
">"
+ sCurrentLine.substr(0, LineLocation) + "</A></FONT><BR>";
        else
            sTemp = sTemp + "<FONT face=Courier New size=" + FontSize +
">" + sCurrentLine.substr(0, LineLocation) + "</FONT><BR>";
    }
    else
        sTemp = "";
    document.all.divTeletype.innerHTML = sTemp;
    LastHTML = sTemp;
}
```

The FireTimer method is public because it is called by the
DHTML object model's window object's setInterval method in the
StartTeletype method. The this.id refers to the Teletype component.

When the FireTimer method executes, it sets the sCurrentLine, which holds the line of text to be displayed, to the value of the TextLines array's current index, the ArrayLocation variable. The TextLines array contains the entire text. Splitting up the text between <BR> tags creates the elements of the array. The LineLocation value is an index that keeps track of the next character in the text that is to be displayed. If the LineLocation is greater than the text in the current line, then the LineLocation needs to be set back to 1, and the next line of text from the TextLines array needs to be placed in the sCurrentLine variable. If there are more lines in the TextLines array, then the TextLines array's index is reset to 0, and the EndOfMessage event is sent to the container. If the container sets the IsRunning property to false, then the text is stopped from displaying.

The text that is displayed can have hyperlinks in it. The component does special processing for hyperlinks. That is what the second major if statement does in the FireTimer method. If there is a hyperlink in the text, it sets the InHref variable to true and blanks out the sTemp variable. The sTemp variable is used to hold text that is to be displayed.

The third major if statement checks to see if the text should be displayed. Assuming it is to be displayed, the starting line is calculated. The lines of text are always displayed from bottom to top. For example, if there are three rows and one line of text that is displayed, then the first two rows will be blank and the last line will contain the text. Therefore if the starting row is negative, then a blank line must display for the absolute number of rows. Then the rows that have already been displayed in the TextLines array are shown on the page. The current line, from the sCurrentLine variable, is displayed from the beginning of the line up to the current line location, the LineLocation value. Then if the text is in the middle of the hyperlink, the InHref value is set to true and the ending hyperlink </a> tag is appended to the text. The sTemp variable is used to hold all the text that is to be displayed. The sTemp sets the Teletype's innerHTML property to be displayed on the page. It also sets the LastHTML variable so the text can be displayed after it is made visible. This allows the Teletype component to keep generating the display text event though it is not displaying it.

SUMMARY

In this chapter we covered how to use and create Windows Script Components. We learned that there are three default implementations of a WSC: COM objects, DHTML behaviors, and ASP. We covered the architecture of WSC COM objects and a DHTML behavior WSC and saw examples of both of them.

CHAPTER 16

Creating an Active Server Page Scripting Component

In the previous chapter we covered the design of Windows Script Components and introduced you to a special function Windows Script Component to create DHTML behavior components. In this chapter we will show you how to create another special function component that can be used in Active Server Page (ASP) technology. These components are particularly useful for creating reusable objects that have the full functionality of Active Server Pages built into the component environment. In this chapter we will review Active Server Pages and then cover the details of how to create this type of component, including:

▼ The details and syntax for creating an ASP Windows Script Component.

▲ How to call the component from inside your existing ASP pages.

ASP OVERVIEW

First let's briefly review Active Server Page (ASP) technology. The Active Server Page programming environment provides the ability to combine HTML, scripting, and components to create powerful and dynamic Internet applications that run on your server. The general concept of ASP is to include script blocks within an HTML template in order to generate content dynamically. Inside of the script blocks, you can use components that provide additional functionality that is not inherent to the ASP and scripting environments. One of the most commonly used sets of components inside ASP is ActiveX Data Objects (ADO); these objects are used to retrieve data from a database or from another data-store. You can then integrate this data into the output and dynamically build the HTML sent to the client.

Active Server Pages expose a set of five basic objects that are used to retrieve data from the client, send HTML to the client, store data for a particular user or application, and define a server object, which represents the environment that the pages run in. The five objects, listed respectively, are: request, response, session, application, and server. The object model is relatively straightforward (compared to other object models like DHTML), and for most of the programming you will deal primarily with the request object to get data from the client and the response object to send HTML to the client. We will cover the most commonly used functionality of the five objects in this chapter; for a full list of the methods and properties of the objects see Appendix H.

ASP are text files that are saved with the *.asp* extension. Inside of these files you can use any type of Active Scripting Language; however, VBScript and JScript/JavaScript are the two most commonly used scripting languages, with VBScript being the default. It is important to note that the default scripting language can be defined for a particular Web site, so you can choose to use another language besides VBScript. If you decide you want to run a non-default language in your ASPs, you need to add the following line to your ASP before any script:

```
<%@ LANGUAGE=JavaScript %>
```

NOTE: To continue with the theme of the book, we will show all of our examples using JavaScript; however, most of the code we will show is very straightforward and could easily be converted to VBScript.

As you may have noticed from our prior snippet, to designate the code that is to be run on the server, you surround the code with the tags <% ... Code ... %> (we will refer to these as *server script tags*). This tells the server that the code should be run on the server and that none of the code inside of the tags will be directly sent to the client. The <% %> tags are similar to the start and end script tags in an HTML document. It is important to note that you can have as many server script tags in your document as you would like; it is not limited to just one code section.

In addition to the <%...%> server script tags, ASP also supports the more traditional <script > tag by adding an additional attribute, RUNAT=SERVER:

```
<SCRIPT LANGUAGE=JavaScript RUNAT=SERVER>
```

While not recommended for obvious optimization reasons, it is possible to have server-side script written in multiple languages within a single page. To implement such a multiple-language server-side script page, you must use the standard <script> tag with its runat=server and language attributes set for each script block, instead of the shorthand <%...%> tags.

Active Server Pages also provide the built-in ability to use common code that is stored in an external file and then dynamically include the file into your ASP. This provides a simple form of code sharing between pages; however, there are issues with this mechanism, as we will discuss later. It is important to note that these files are included before the ASP processor gets the source, so you can't use script code to determine which files to include. These types of files are called *server side include files* and are generally stored with an .inc extension. Once these files are imported, the functions that are contained in the external file can be called just like a function that exists inside of the ASP's code. In your external code file, you wrap your common code in the server script tags and then make this file available under a virtual directory or though a physical file path (such as c:\includes). To add the code to your ASP, you use the #include directive. This directive has two attributes: one to include a file using virtual mapping (virtual) and another to include a file using physical mapping (file). The following are examples of the syntax that is used to add server side includes to your ASP pages:

▼ Physical path:

```
<!-- #include file="commonSource.inc" -->
```

▼ Virtual path:

```
<!-- #include virtual="includes/commonSource.inc" -->
```

Sending HTML to the Client

The next thing you need to be aware of is how to insert dynamically built HTML into the document. You can insert HTML by two different methods: use the equal (=) operator to insert the results of a single line of code, or use the Response.Write method. Using the equal operator is a fairly straightforward operation. The following is a simple example:

sample1.asp

```
<%@ LANGUAGE=JavaScript %>
<%
var x;
x = 2;
%>
<html>
```

```
<%=x*2 %>
</html>
```

This simple ASP writes the following HTML to the client browser:

```
<html>
4
</html>
```

It is also important to note that we cannot make a server script tag a child of another server script tag. So the following code would *not* work and would result in an error:

sample2.asp

```
<%@ LANGUAGE=JavaScript %>
<%
function sample(){
  var x;
  x = 2;
  <%=x*2%>
}
%>
<html>
<%sample%>
</html>
```

Working with the Response Object

Because we cannot embed server script tags, as shown earlier, there is another method that is made available from the Response object to write HTML to the client. This method is the Write method. The Write method takes one parameter that is the string of text you wish to write to the client. If we take our prior example and change the code to use the Write method, the code would look like

sample3.asp

```
<%@ LANGUAGE=JavaScript %>
<%
function sample(){
  var x;
  x = 2;
```

```
    Response.Write(x*2);
  }
%>
<html>
<%sample()%>
</html>
```

One item that you may wish to set before actually writing out the data to the browser is the content type. The content type specifies how the browser should interpret the data it is being sent. The reason we mention it here is because if you wish to create an ASP that generates XML, instead of HTML, you need to set the ContentType property of the response object to "text/xml" prior to writing any data to the client. The following shows an example of writing XML to the client from an ASP:

sample4.asp

```
<%@ LANGUAGE=JavaScript %>
<%
  Response.ContentType = "text/xml"
  Response.Write("<someXML><xmlNode></xmlNode></someXML>");
%>
```

The final item we want to cover for the Response object is the Redirect method. The Redirect method instructs the browser to connect to a different URL. This method can be useful, for example, if you create your own logon process, and, once the user has been successfully authenticated, you want to point them to the correct starting page. The method has just one parameter, which is the URL that the user should be forwarded to. One important thing to remember about the Redirect method is that you cannot write out any HTML, HTML headers, or cookies to the browser before you redirect the user to the new location. The following is a code snippet that shows the Redirect method:

```
if (isAuthenticated)
  Response.Redirect("startPage.htm");
else
  Response.Redirect("logon.asp");
```

Getting Data from the Client

Depending on your familiarity with HTML, you may know that there are two HTTP methods of sending form data to the server: GET and POST. The GET method appends the name of the form controls and their values to the URL. This combination of the URL and form name/value pairs is referred to as the query string of the ACTION attribute for the form. The query string or GET method has some shortcomings and limitations. For instance, the query string contains the controls values clearly visible in the browser's address box and could easily be intercepted in transit. Also, the amount of data that is sent to the server on the URL is limited to about 1,000 characters (there are minor variations based on the browser type and version). Despite these limitations, the GET method of data transfer can be useful in some simple situations. To retrieve the data on the server side, ASP provides a QueryString collection that is available from the Request object. To retrieve a value based on the name of the form element from the QueryString collection, you would use the following syntax, where txtName is the name of the controls value you want to retrieve:

```
value = Request.QueryString("txtName");
```

If you want to retrieve the complete delimited results that are sent to the server, we would simply call the QueryString method without passing in any parameters.

The following is an example of an HTML form that submits the data to the server using the GET method. When the user clicks the submit button, the form is processed by a simple ASP (shown after the HTML) and writes the values back to the client.

sample5.htm - HTML page

```
<html>
<body>
<form action="sample5.asp" METHOD="GET">
<input name="txtInput1">
<input name="txtInput2">
<input type="submit">
</form>
</body>
</html>
```

sample5.asp Active Server Page

```
<%@ LANGUAGE=JavaScript %>
<%
  var value = Request.QueryString("txtInput1");
  Response.Write("txtInput1=" + value + "<BR>");
  var value = Request.QueryString("txtInput2");
  Response.Write("txtInput2=" + value + "<BR>");
  var value = Request.QueryString();
  Response.Write("The Complete Query String =" + value + "<BR>");
%>
```

Using the Post Method

As mentioned earlier, the other method for sending data to the server from an HTML form is the POST method. The POST method sends the data from the HTML form in the HTTP header instead of in the query string. The POST method does not have a restriction on the amount of data that can be sent to the server. Similar to the GET method, the Request ASP object exposes the Form collection that contains the values from the HTML form, allowing us simple access to the values that were entered into the form's elements. To retrieve a value based on the name of the form element from the Form collection, you would use the following syntax:

```
value = Request.Form("txtName");
```

To implement our prior example using the POST method and the Form collection, we need to change the HTML's form tag to the following (but nothing else changes in the HTML file):

```
<form action="sample6.asp" METHOD="POST">
```

The following is the ASP code we would use to implement our example using the Form collection:

sample6.asp

```
<%@ LANGUAGE=JavaScript %>
<%
  var value = Request.Form("txtInput1");
```

```
Response.Write("txtInput1=" + value + "<BR>");
var value = Request.Form("txtInput2");
Response.Write("txtInput2=" + value + "<BR>");
var value = Request.Form();
Response.Write("The Complete Form String =" + value + "<BR>");
%>
```

Using the Query String for Non-Form Data

One interesting option that using the query string allows is submitting data to the server without the use of HTML forms. This concept can be used to send additional data not in the HTML form from the client or provide an easy way to pass a variable from one ASP to another. The way this is done is to append the data you want to send to the server to the query string from a script. The only thing you need to make sure of is that you append the data using the correct query string format. If you look at how data from a form is sent to the server, you can easily see the format. The following is an example of query string format:

```
txtInput1=val1&txtInput2=val2
```

The format is name=value; & is the delimiter. There is one additional item you need to be aware of: whether your data must be ASCII encoded. What ASCII encoding does is to replace characters that can't be passed on a URL with the ASCII value in hexadecimal format or, in the case of space characters, with a + character. This might sound a little scary, but actually it is pretty easy to handle. First, if your values don't contain spaces and are all alphanumeric characters (A–Z, a–z, 0–9), you don't even have to worry about the encoding. But if your values do contain some of the other characters, you will need to encode these values. To handle this, JavaScript has a method called escape that has one parameter, which is the string to encode; it automatically encodes a character string and returns the encoded string.

Now that you know how to add data to the query string, the next thing you need to be aware of is how to retrieve the data. Because we have formatted our data the same way that a form's data would be sent, we can simply use the QueryString collection to retrieve the values. For example, if we had an HTML page that had two images, and we wanted to return to an ASP the image that was clicked and the location where the user clicked, we could pass the values as part of the query string. The following shows an example HTML page followed by an ASP that shows this functionality. The ASP receives the values and simply returns the values to the client.

sample8.htm

```
<html>
<script language="JavaScript">
function sendToServer(image){
  x = event.offsetX;
  y = event.offsetY;
  escapedImage = escape(image);  //Not really needed, just shown to show
                                 //example of calling escape method
  window.location.href = "sample8.asp?image=" + escapedImage  + "&x=" + x +
"&y=" + y;
}
</script>
<body>
<img src="image1.gif" onClick="sendToServer('image1')">
<img src="image2.gif" onClick="sendToServer('image2')">
</body>
</html>
```

The source for the ASP is as follows:

sample8.asp

```
<%@ LANGUAGE=JavaScript %>
<%
  var value = Request.QueryString("image");
  Response.Write("Image=" + value + "<BR>");
  var value = Request.QueryString("x");
  Response.Write("X=" + value + "<BR>");
  var value = Request.QueryString("y");
  Response.Write("Y=" + value + "<BR>");
  var value = Request.QueryString();
  Response.Write("The Complete Query String =" + value + "<BR>");
%>
```

Storing Values on the Server

There are two different ASP objects that are used to store data in memory on the server side: Application and Session objects. An application comprises all of the files that can be referenced through a single virtual mapping, or aliased directory on a Web server. One Web server can contain multiple applications, and you can also define multiple applications for a site through Microsoft Internet Information Server. An application starts when any client requests an item from that virtual mapping and ends when a Web server is stopped. A session is assigned to each client that requests an item from an application. The session starts when the client requests their first item and ends when the client has had inactivity for, by default, a 20-minute period of time. To track a client's session, ASP uses a cookie to uniquely identify the client. This cookie is passed back and forth from the client and server to uniquely identify the data that is stored for that client.

The Application and Session objects allow you to store values that are associated with the particular application or client, respectively. The data is stored in named value pairs and can be easily stored or retrieved from the Application or Session object by simply using the Object("Name") syntax. If we want to have a Session-level variable called X and we want to store the value of a variable, var, we use the following syntax:

```
Session("X") = var;
```

Similarly if we want to retrieve the value of the Session-level variable X into the variable var, we use the following syntax:

```
var = Session("X");
```

Trapping the Start and End of Sessions and Applications

There may be cases where you would like to initialize variables or load data when a session or application begins or clean up data once they end. To do this, you need to create a special file called global.asa and place that file in the applications root directory. Inside of this file, you can trap the objects' start and end by creating the following specifically named functions (in VBScript they can be subs): Application_OnStart, Application_OnEnd, Session_OnStart, and Session_OnEnd. The ASP processor then automatically calls these functions. The following is an example of a global.asa file that defines a database connection string for the application in an Application variable and stores the time the user started their session in a Session-level variable.

global.asa

```
<Script LANGUAGE="JavaScript" RUNAT="Server">
function Session_OnStart(){
  var currentDT = new Date();
  Session("startTime")= currentDT;
}
function Application_OnStart(){
  Application("connectString")=
"DSN=Sample;UID=admin;PWD=admin;";
}
</Script>
```

The Root Server Object

The Server object represents the root of the ASP object model. The Server object contains several methods that are useful for almost every application. The CreateObject method is the most commonly used Server method. It is used to create ActiveX objects that are not inherent to the ASP environment. One of the things that make the ASP environment so powerful is that it can be easily extended by other server objects. To instantiate a server-based ActiveX object, you call the CreateObject method, passing in the program identifier (progid) that is assigned to each correctly installed ActiveX object. To show you how to use the CreateObject method, we will create one of the most common objects, the database connection object of ActiveX Data Objects (ADO). The following is a code snippet of how to create this object:

```
var database = Server.CreateObject("ADODB.Connection");
```

Now that you have created the object, you can work with it the same way you would work with one of the intrinsic ASP objects.

Another useful method that is available from the Server object is the MapPath method. The MapPath method provides a nice mechanism to determine the physical path on the server to the directory where the ASP is running, keeping the ASP application portable (easily movable to a different server without changing any code). In addition to this, you can pass in paths relative to the ASP to determine their physical path (this could be different because of virtual mapping). The following shows a snippet for determining the physical path to the images directory.

```
var path = Server.MapPath("images");
```

This example might return something like the following:

```
"D:\InetPub\wwwroot\myweb\images"
```

BUILDING ASP WINDOWS SCRIPT COMPONENTS

Depending on how much work you have done with ASP, you may know that one of the issues with developing ASP is that you can end up having the same functionality repeated in multiple ASPs. This is all right if you don't need to change any of these common pieces; however, it presents a problem if you ever need to change this functionality, especially if you need to change it quite often. The way that you can solve this problem is by creating a Windows Script Component that contains all of the ASP application's common functionality. But if you created an ordinary component, you would not have access to all of the built-in ASP objects unless you passed them into each method. Fortunately Windows Script Components implement another interface in the script component runtime (Scrobj.dll) that provides full access to the built-in ASP objects.

You might be thinking, "I don't need to create a component. I will just include the file that contains all of this common logic using server side includes." Well, yes, that is another way of solving the shared code problem; however, there are scalability issues involved with using include files. First of all, include files include all of the code into the ASP no mater if the code is used in your page or not. Because of this, the processor slows down because it needs to parse though your code even though it is not used. Another issue is that every time you use an include file for a different ASP, the common code is not shared across the different pages: each page has its own version of the code loaded into memory. With components, however, these issues are eliminated because the components are shared across pages, and you can control when and if they are instantiated; because of this, we can more closely control what code is used in the page.

The method used to create an ASP script component is the same as you would normally use to create a script component. It is important to note that we will not go over all of the details of the different tags that make up a script component in this chapter. For more information about the basic construct of a Windows Script Component, see Chapter 15.

What we need to add to a normal component is the <implements> element to implement the ASP interface handler. To specify what interface handlers we want to include for the component, we set the type attribute for the implements element. In this case, because we want to implement the Active Server Page interface, we set the type attribute equal to ASP. The implements tag is used to notify the script component runtime engine (scrobj.dll) to load a COM object that acts as a proxy between the WSC and the ASP object model.

By adding the ASP interface handler, we can now access the standard ASP objects—Response, Request, Server, Session, and Application—from inside of our component. The ASP interface handler is a COM object that imports the ASP type library and obtains valid references to all the intrinsic ASP objects. Now we can access and use the ASP objects the same way we would use them in a standard ASP. As we noted earlier, the ASP interface handler is built directly into the script component runtime (Scrobj.dll), so there isn't a requirement for an external interface handler. By adding this support, the object becomes so much like a part of an ASP that if we make a call to the Response object, the output of that call is automatically inserted into the output for the ASP. Once the ASP component is instantiated and run, the component uses the same name space as the ASP that called it. In addition, the script component has access to the same Session and Application variables that the calling ASP does. As you can see, it is a pretty seamless operation for creating reusable ASP objects.

Creating Your First ASP Script Component

To lead you through the process of creating an ASP Windows Script Component (WSC), we are going to create a very simple component that adds a common set of headers and footers for a site. The component has only two methods: createHeader and createFooter that are used to build our header and footer; there are no properties or events.

The easiest way to get started with creating your first component is by using the Windows Script Component Wizard. For more details on the Windows Script Component Wizard, see Chapter 15. Figure 16-1 shows the first step of the Wizard that defines the name of the file, program Id, and file location.

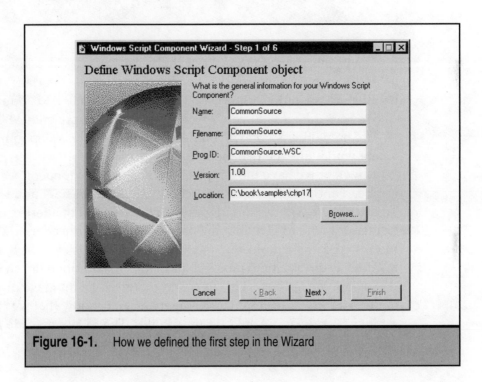

Figure 16-1.   How we defined the first step in the Wizard

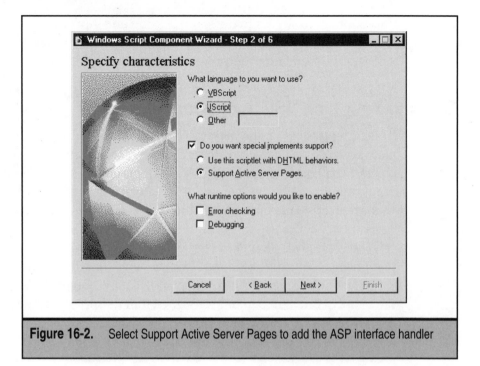

Figure 16-2. Select Support Active Server Pages to add the ASP interface handler

The primary step in the Wizard to be concerned with is the second screen (see Figure 16-2), where we define the interface handlers we want to support. You, of course, want to add "Support Active Server Pages" to your Windows Script Component (WSC).

The only other step that you need for the sample is step four, where you define the two methods (see Figure 16-3).

Now that we have the template built for our component, we can go ahead and add the details to actually build the header and footer. To do this, we will use the Response.Write method to interject our header or footer HTML into the page's output. Our headers and footers are fairly simple, but one thing you may wish to add to the methods is the ability to pass in parameters to conditionally change the look of the outputted headers and footers. One thing we did add to the header was a simple welcome message to show that we can retrieve Session and Application variables. The following code shows our common source Windows Script Component.

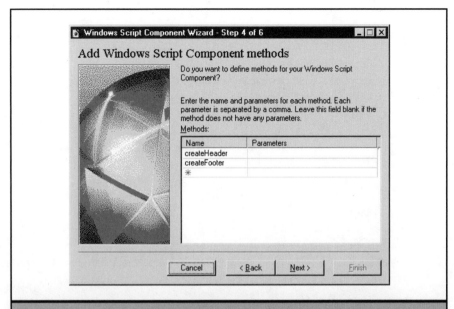

Figure 16-3. We added the createHeader and createFooter methods

CommonSource.wsc

```
<?xml version="1.0"?>
<component>
<registration
  description="CommonSource"
  progid="CommonSource.WSC"
  version="1.00"
  classid="{4c44f8e0-b5ab-11d3-8e91-00207810a286}"
>
</registration>
<public>
  <method name="createHeader">
  </method>
  <method name="createFooter">
  </method>
</public>
<implements type="ASP" id="ASP"/>
<script language="JScript">
<![CDATA[
var description = new CommonSource;
function CommonSource(){
```

```
   this.createHeader = createHeader;
   this.createFooter = createFooter;
}
function createHeader(){
   Response.Write("<table width='100%'><tr><td align='center'><img
src='image1.gif'></td>");
   Response.Write("<td>Welcome " +  Session.Contents("UserName") +
"</td></tr></table>");
   Response.Write("<p align='center'><table><tr><td><a
href='products.htm'>Products</a></td>");
   Response.Write("<td><a href='about.htm'>About</a></td>");
   Response.Write("<td><a href='contact.htm'>Contact</a></td></tr>
</table></p>");
}
function createFooter(){
   Response.Write("<p align='center'><table width='100%'><tr><td><a
href='privacy.htm'>Privacy Statement</a></reserved.</td>");
   Response.Write("<td><a
href='feedback.htm'>Feedback</a></td></tr></table></p>");
}
]]>
</script>
</component>
```

NOTE: There is a problem with using the default property for the
Application and Session objects. If you notice in our example above, we
used the Session.Content("UserName") syntax rather than the normal
Session("UserName"). The reason we did this is that there is a bug in the
current release of WSC related to the default properties that are collections
of a base object. We can easily fix the problem from code by fully
specifying the Content collection, which is the default property. Additionally,
specifying the Content collection prevents the server object from searching
all of its other collections for UserName, optimizing the process.

Calling the Component from Your ASP

Before we can instantiate and make calls to our component, we need
to register the component with the operating system. When you

installed the 5.0 versions of the scripting engines, either by installing IE 5.0 or installing just the script engines themselves, a new context menu item was created to register components from inside Windows Explorer. To register the component, simply open Windows Explorer, select the new WSC, and right-click on the file. You will then be presented with the context menu for this file: choose Register, and Windows will attempt to register the component, returning a message to indicate whether the registration was successful (for more information on the registration process, see Chapter 15).

Now that we have the component registered, we can go ahead and instantiate the component using the Server.CreateObject method from inside our controlling ASP code. The method and syntax for instantiating a WSC is comprised of the same syntax that is used to create any other ActiveX object from an ASP. We can then use this newly created object to access our methods (or properties, if we had properties), just as we would access any other object that we created on the server. The following is a very simple ASP that instantiates and uses our common code component.

sample9.asp

```
<%@ LANGUAGE=JavaScript %>
<HTML>
<BODY>
<%
    var commonSource = Server.CreateObject("CommonSource.WSC");
    Session("UserName") = "Jim";
    commonSource.createHeader();
%>
<p> </p>
<p>Here is where you would put the body of your HTML Document</p>
<p> </p>
<%commonSource.createFooter()%>
</BODY>
</HTML>
```

Figure 16-4 shows the results of our (somewhat unattractive but functional) ASP Windows Script Component.

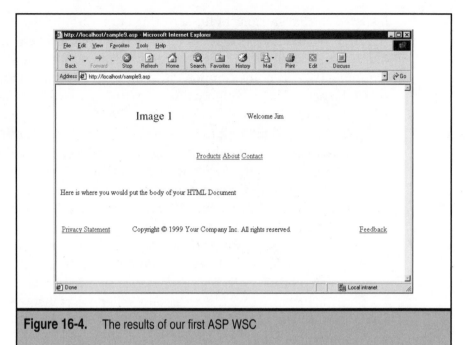

Figure 16-4. The results of our first ASP WSC

Another Sample ASP WSC

To further illustrate the advantages of ASP WSC, we created another
component that could be used to handle displaying a typical HTML
user ID and password login screen. In this example, we emphasized
how you could create a component that could be customized by
the programmer rather than creating components with hard-coded
HTML. To handle this situation, we created properties for the
component that are used by the developer to define what the output
of the component should be. The component will build the table
that contains the login text boxes, captions, and submit button
based on the settings the developer specified. To help illustrate
what the results of the login component look like, see Figure 16-5,
which shows the results of our sample ASP that uses the login
component.

In addition to allowing the user to customize the look of the login,
the login component validates the user against a simple Microsoft
Access 97 database and returns whether the user ID and password
are valid. If the user is validated, the developer can retrieve the name

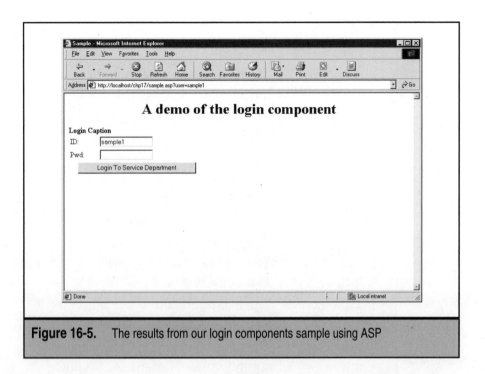

Figure 16-5.   The results from our login components sample using ASP

(retrieved by the component from the database, userName property) of the user who logged in. We use ActiveX Data Objects (ADO) to retrieve the data from the database. The data is accessed using the built-in Admin account for Access and assumes that the database is in a "db" directory under the location of the ASP files. This simple design is not very secure, and you would want to minimally move the database file to a location where it could not be easily downloaded from the server (turn off the anonymous browse and read permissions for the directory) or move out of Access completely if you were to implement this concept. Table 16-1 lists the properties and methods for the component.

The following is the code for the login component:

LoginScript.wsc

```
<?xml version="1.0"?>
<component>
<registration description="LoginScript" progid="LoginScript.WSC"
  version="1.00" classid="{a7884700-b74c-11d3-8e91-00207810a286}" >
</registration>
```

Property/Method	Description
loginWidth	The maximum width that the table containing the login elements should be. Default is 100%.
loginCaption	The caption that appears above the user ID. Default is "Enter Your User-ID and Password."
userCaption	The caption that appears to the left of the user ID text box. Default is "User ID."
maxUserSize	The maximum allowable length for the user ID text element. Default is 10.
password Caption	The caption that appears to the left of the password text box. Default is "Password."
maxPassword Size	The maximum allowable length for the password text element. Default is 10.
submitButton Caption	The caption that should be applied to the submit button. Default is "Login."
userID	Contains the value that was entered by the user after the validateUser method has been called. Prior to calling the buildLogin method, it can also set the value of the user ID to be displayed in the login.
userName	Contains the name of the user (from the database) after a successful login attempt (that is, validateUser returns true).
buildLogin	After setting the customization properties, this method is called to build the customized actual login form.
validateUser	Retrieves the login values from the form and validates the user against the database. Returns true if the user is valid.

Table 16-1. Properties and Methods for the login Component

```
<public>
  <property name="userCaption">
    <get/><put/>
  </property>
  <property name="passwordCaption">
    <get/><put/>
  </property>
  <property name="maxUserSize">
    <get/><put/>
  </property>
  <property name="maxPasswordSize">
    <get/><put/>
  </property>
  <property name="userID">
    <get/><put/>
  </property>
  <property name="userName">
    <get/></property>
  <property name="loginCaption">
    <get/><put/>
  </property>
  <property name="loginWidth">
    <get/><put/>
  </property>
  <property name="submitButtonCaption">
    <get/><put/>
  </property>
  <method name="validateUser" />
  <method name="buildLogin" />
</public>
<implements type="ASP" id="ASP"/>
<script language="JScript">
<![CDATA[
var description = new LoginScript;
function LoginScript(){
  this.get_userCaption = get_userCaption;
  this.put_userCaption = put_userCaption;
  this.get_passwordCaption = get_passwordCaption;
  this.put_passwordCaption = put_passwordCaption;
  this.get_loginCaption = get_loginCaption;
  this.put_loginCaption = put_loginCaption;
  this.get_loginWidth = get_loginWidth;
```

```
    this.put_loginWidth = put_loginWidth;
    this.get_maxUserSize = get_maxUserSize;
    this.put_maxUserSize = put_maxUserSize;
    this.get_maxPasswordSize = get_maxPasswordSize;
    this.put_maxPasswordSize = put_maxPasswordSize;
    this.get_loginCaption = get_loginCaption;
    this.put_loginCaption = put_loginCaption;
    this.get_submitButtonCaption = get_submitButtonCaption;
    this.put_submitButtonCaption = put_submitButtonCaption;
    this.get_userID = get_userID;
    this.put_userID = put_userID;
    this.get_userName = get_userName;
    this.validateUser = validateUser;
    this.buildLogin = buildLogin;
}
var userCaption = "User ID:";
var passwordCaption = "Password:";
var userID = "";
var userName;
var loginCaption = "Enter Your User-ID and Password:";
var maxUserSize = 10;
var maxPasswordSize = 10;
var submitButtonCaption = "Login";
var loginWidth = "100%";
function get_userCaption(){
  return userCaption;
}
function put_userCaption(newValue){
  userCaption = newValue;
}
function get_passwordCaption(){
  return passwordCaption;
}
function put_passwordCaption(newValue){
  passwordCaption = newValue;
}
function get_userID(){
  return userID;
}
function put_userID(newValue){
  userID = newValue;
}
```

```
function get_userName(){
  return userName;
}
function get_loginCaption(){
  return loginCaption;
}
function put_loginCaption(newValue){
  loginCaption = newValue;
}
function get_loginWidth(){
  return loginWidth;
}
function put_loginWidth(newValue){
  loginWidth = newValue;
}
function get_maxUserSize(){
  return maxUserSize;
}
function put_maxUserSize(newValue){
  maxUserSize = newValue;
}
function get_maxPasswordSize(){
  return maxPasswordSize;
}
function put_maxPasswordSize(newValue){
  maxPasswordSize = newValue;
}
function get_submitButtonCaption(){
  return submitButtonCaption;
}
function put_submitButtonCaption(newValue){
  submitButtonCaption = newValue;
}
function validateUser(){
  var conn = Server.CreateObject("ADODB.Connection");
  var path = Server.MapPath("db") + "\\userDB.mdb";
  var password = Request.Form("txtPassword");
  userID = Request.Form("txtUserID");
  conn.Open("Provider=Microsoft.Jet.OLEDB.3.51;Data Source=" + path +
";");
  sql = "select UserName from Users where UserID = '" + userID;
  sql += "' and Password = '" + password + "'";
```

```
      var rs = conn.Execute(sql);
      if (rs.EOF){
        return false;
      }
      else{
        userName = rs(0);
        return true;
      }
    }
  function buildLogin(){
    Response.Write(loginCaption);
    Response.Write("<table border='0' width='" + loginWidth + "'>");
    Response.Write("<tr><td>" + userCaption + "</td>");
    Response.Write("<td><input type='text' name='txtUserID' size='" +
  maxUserSize + "' maxLength='" + maxUserSize + "' value='" + userID +
  "'></td></tr>");
    Response.Write("<tr><td >" + passwordCaption + "</td>");
    Response.Write("<td><input type='password' name='txtPassword'
  size='" + maxPasswordSize + "' maxLength='" + maxPasswordSize +
  "'></td></tr>");
    Response.Write("<tr><td colspan='2' align='center'><input
  type='submit' value='" + submitButtonCaption +"'></td></tr></table>");
  }]]></script></component>
```

To demonstrate the component, we used two ASP pages: one
to present the login (login.asp) and another that validates the user
(validate.asp). The login page simply creates the component, sets
the properties, and then calls the buildLogin function to write the
results to the client. The validation page is also pretty simple in
that it creates the login component and then calls the validateUser
method to validate the user. If the user is successfully validated, the
ASP (validate.asp) simply writes out a message that the login was
successful and a welcome message with the user's name. Otherwise,
if the user is not valid, we redirect the user's browser to the login
page. One other little thing that the validation ASP does is pass
the user ID to the login ASP as part of its query string. This

allows us to display the user ID that was entered on the previous login attempt. The following is the code listings for both of the ASPs:

login.asp

```
<%@ LANGUAGE=JavaScript %>
<HTML>
<HEAD><TITLE>Sample</TITLE></HEAD>
<BODY>
<P align=center><FONT size=6><STRONG>A demo of the login component
</STRONG></FONT></P>
<FORM Method="post" Action="validate.asp">
<%
  var login = Server.CreateObject("LoginScript.wsc");
  login.userCaption = "ID:";
  login.userID = Request.QueryString("user");
  login.loginWidth = "40%";
  login.maxUserSize = "15";
  login.maxPasswordSize = "15";
  login.passwordCaption = "Pwd:";
  login.submitButtonCaption = "Login To Service Department";
  login.loginCaption = "<B>Login Caption</B>";
  login.buildLogin();
%>
</FORM></BODY></HTML>
```

validate.asp

```
<%@ LANGUAGE=JavaScript %>
<%
  var login = Server.CreateObject("LoginScript.wsc");
  if (login.validateUser())
    Response.Write(login.userID + "Successfull Login. <BR>Welcome " +
login.userName);
  else
    Response.Redirect("login.asp?user=" + login.userID);
%>
```

SUMMARY

In this chapter we have introduced you to the concept of Windows Script Components that implement the Active Server Page interface handler. These components can be very useful to create objects that contain reusable ASP code. They are also completely browser-safe because they run on the server, totally independent of the client's browser. Don't forget these valuable tools if you are creating an ASP application that contains repeated output or functionality.

CHAPTER 17

Remote Scripting

One of the Web's great capabilities is that a client program (browser) can request a Web page from a server anywhere in the world. The server sends the Web page to the client; once the client receives it, the page is rendered by the browser for displaying to the user. But there is a down side to this type of sending and receiving—it is not very efficient. Each time the client requests some new information, an entire Web page is sent to it by the server. The reason is that Web pages are used in one of two ways: either it asks the user for information or it gives the user information. For example, if an application needs to look up a person, the server will send two pages to the client (see Figure 17-1). The first page sent is for the user to enter the identifier of the person. The client then sends the data back to the server and requests the information for that person. On the server, the request is processed, and a new page with the person's information is sent back to the client. These types of requests could be handled more efficiently if only the person's data needed to be returned to the client, rather than an entirely new Web page.

Microsoft has introduced a new technology that makes this type of processing more efficient. It is called *remote scripting*. With remote scripting, you can make a request to the server, and the server

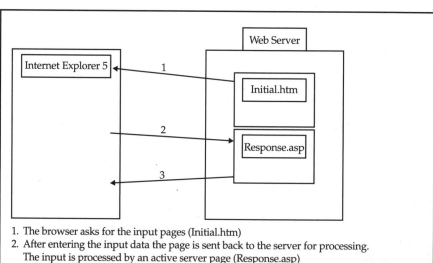

1. The browser asks for the input pages (Initial.htm)
2. After entering the input data the page is sent back to the server for processing.
   The input is processed by an active server page (Response.asp)
3. The Response.asp page sends back a new page with the data

Figure 17-1.   Standard browser/server interaction

returns only the data that the client needs (see Figure 17-2). When the client makes a request to the server, some script code is executed on the server. The server-side script can include database queries, business rules logic, and other server-side tasks. The server-side script that is executed is run inside of an Active Server Page (ASP). In this chapter we will cover the following features of remote scripting:

▼ The advantages and disadvantages of remote scripting.

■ Requirements of the client and how to set up the client to be remote scripting aware.

■ Requirements of the server and how to set up the server for remote scripting.

■ The details of the remote scripting pieces.

■ How ASPs are used with remote scripting.

■ How to call remote scripts synchronously and asynchronously.

■ How to handle remote scripting errors.

▲ How to use remote scripting with other browsers and what is needed to do so.

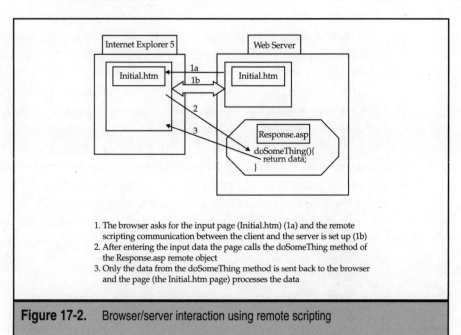

1. The browser asks for the input page (Initial.htm) (1a) and the remote
   scripting communication between the client and the server is set up (1b)
2. After entering the input data the page calls the doSomeThing method of
   the Response.asp remote object
3. Only the data from the doSomeThing method is sent back to the browser
   and the page (the Initial.htm page) processes the data

Figure 17-2.   Browser/server interaction using remote scripting

BENEFITS OF REMOTE SCRIPTING

One problem that remote scripting solves is the statelessness of Web pages. A Web page is stateless by nature. *Stateless* means that the page does not retain internal information from one Web page to another. We presented an example of statelessness with the person information pages (see Figure 17-1). With remote scripting, you can use the same page to request data from a URL and display the requested result. This type of behavior gives a Web page state. To illustrate how a Web page can have state, look at Figure 17-2. The first state of the page is the input data state, and the second state of the page is when the page displays the result page based on the input data.

Remote scripting allows for organizing your application into separate components. For an example, think back to the person's information example used earlier. Suppose that the person's information was updatable on the same page. The page would execute a remote script to return the person's information, based on some inputted data. The user changes the person's information, and the page makes a remote script call, updating the data on the server. The retrieving and updating of the data could be created as separate components on the server; these components could even be COM objects.

Another benefit of using remote scripting is that the calls to the server can be asynchronous. This allows the client-side script to keep executing while the server is executing the remote call. This helps the performance on the client side to be faster because it does not have to wait for the remote script call to return before it can process its code.

Probably the best benefit of using remote scripting is that it is a cross-browser technology. Remote scripting does *not* require Internet Explorer on the client to function. The browser needs to be able to run Java applets and its JavaScript engine must be ECMAScript compliant. Remote scripting works with Internet Explorer 3.x and later and Netscape Navigator 3.x and later, but it works only on Win 32 platforms. Thus, remote scripting will not work for Macintosh and Win 16 platforms.

REMOTE SCRIPTING ARCHITECTURE

Remote scripting uses a proxy Java applet that acts as a communication object between client and server. When remote scripting is run on the client, the server downloads script's files and the applet to the client so the client communicates directly with the server.

Required Files and How to Install Them

Microsoft's scripting Web site has an program for installing remote scripting on a Web server.

> **NOTE:** The remote scripting installation is located at msdn.microsoft.com/scripting, in the remote scripting section. This URL may change at any time, so if it is not valid, then search the Microsoft site for the remote scripting installation download page. Also, the remote scripting installation file is on the companion CD in the Chapter17/RS Install directory. The file is called rs10ben.exe.

The remote scripting installation program will ask you the location of where to install the remote scripting. By default, it will try to install it on the C drive. You need to point it to the inetpub/wwwroot directory. After remote scripting is installed, the wwwroot directory contains all the files needed to do remote scripting: rs.htm, rs.asp, and rsproxy.class. It creates a _ScriptLibrary directory and copies those files there. It will create a doc directory, which contains a set of .htm files, which make up the remote scripting help documentation. The other directory that it creates is a samples directory. There are two files in this directory: simple.htm and simple.asp. Figure 17-3 shows the *simple* sample after the RSExecute Method1 (async) button is pressed.

The Remote Scripting Files

The rs.htm file is a file that an HTML document includes to have access to the remote scripting functionality. This file is placed in the HTML document using a <script> tag and the src attribute. The three main

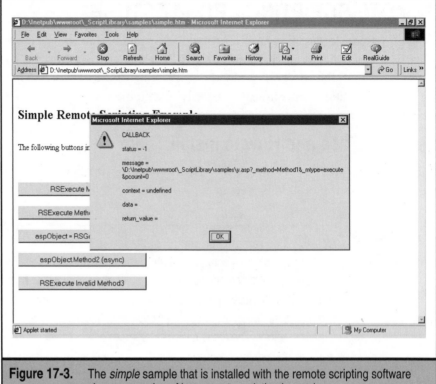

Figure 17-3. The *simple* sample that is installed with the remote scripting software shows examples of how remote scripting is used.

functions, in the rs.htm, that are called by the HTML document are listed in Table 17-1.

The RSEnableRemoteScripting function places a Java applet in the HTML document. The Java applet that is loaded is the rsproxy.class file that is in _ScriptLibrary. This applet coordinates the communication between the browser and the server.

An ASP file is needed on the server that contains the remote scripting logic to be executed by the client. The ASP file must include the rs.asp file. The rs.asp file helps in dispatching the client calls to the ASP page's methods and returning data back to the client. The client calls a method in the ASP file either by using the RSExecute function or by creating an ASP object and calling the ASP object's methods.

Function	Purpose
RSEnableRemoteScripting	Initializes the remote scripting functionality.
RSExecute	Executes a method of the ASP.
RSGetASPObject	Creates an object reference to an ASP. The object then can be used to call the ASP's methods.

Table 17-1.   Client Functions That Make Remote Scripting Available

The Remote Scripting ASP File

As we will see, the remote scripting ASP file can be thought of as a remote object made up of a JavaScript object. The remote object requires a couple of items for it to function as a remote script. The following lines must be added to the ASP file:

```
<!--#INCLUDE FILE="rs.asp"-->
<% RSDispatch %>
```

NOTE: The directory of the rs.asp may need to be changed, depending on its location on the server, relative to the remote scripting ASP page that is including it.

The first line includes the rs.asp file, and the second line executes the RSDispatch function that is found in the rs.asp file.

The remote object also needs to declare its public interface and uses a rather unorthodox way of doing so, with a special named variable called public_description. The following code gives an example of declaring a public interface:

```
<script runat=server language="JavaScript">
public_description = new someASP();
```

```
function someASP(){
    this.getData = methodOne;
    this.updateData = methodTwo;
}
function methodOne(ID){
...
}
function methodTwo(id, name, address){
...
}
...
</script>
```

The ASP's public interface is exposed as someASP by setting the public_description variable to that name. The someASP object is now considered a JavaScript object. The someASP object declares two methods in the someASP function. The someASP function's main purpose is to declare the public interface. It can also be used to initialize variables and/or to do any other initialization for the remote object. It is called when the public_description variable is set with a new instance of the someASP object.

The someASP object's public interface is getData and updateData. The client will call these methods when it needs to execute the remote object. The methodOne and methodTwo functions implement the code for the two public interfaces. If there are any other functions within the remote object, the client does not have access to them.

VBScript Functions

The ASP's public interface can only be written in JavaScript. What if you have an existing ASP that is written in VBScript and you want to use it remotely? You can add the public interface into the page and point the public interfaces to the VBScript functions. The following code listing shows an example of this:

```
<script runat=server language="JavaScript">
function someASP(){
    this.getData = Function('id', 'return methodOneVBS(id)');
    this.updateData = Function('id', 'fullname', 'addr' 'return
```

```
methodTwoVBS(id, fullname, addr)' );
}
public_description = new someASP();
</script>
</script runat=server language="VBScript">
function methodOne(ID)
...
end function
function methodTwo(id, name, address)
...
end function
...
</script>
```

The Function statement is a JavaScript statement that will execute a function. When the getData method is executed, the Function statement will execute the VBScript's methodOne function. There are two <script> tags in the ASP because the ASP interpreter needs to know what language to use when executing the respective lines of code.

The Client-side Files

The client does not require any files to be installed on it to use remote scripting. All the files that it needs are downloaded with the HTML document. To run remote scripting, the HTML document must include the following two lines of code before any other script in the document:

```
<script language="JavaScript" src="rs.htm"></script>
<script language="JavaScript">RSEnableRemoteScripting();</script>
```

NOTE: The directory of the rs.htm may need to be changed depending on its location on the server, relative to the page that is including it.

The first line includes the file rs.htm, which contains the functions to execute a remote scripting object. The second line executes the RSEnableRemoteScripting function to initialize remote scripting for the document. The RSEnableRemoteScripting function takes an optional parameter, which is the path of the rsproxy.class file location on the server. If a path is not passed to the function, it will search for the rsproxy.class file in the _ScriptLibrary directory under the virtual directory of the server or project. After the function executes, the Java proxy applet is now part of the HTML document. The RSEnableRemoteScripting function only needs to be executed once for the life of the page. This execution needs to take place before any references are made to a remote object. The only other processing that is required by the client is to call the server's ASP to execute the remote object's method(s).

CLIENT SCRIPT CODE TO CALL REMOTE OBJECT METHODS

Since the rs.htm file is included in the client's HTML document, it has access to the RSExecute and the RSGetASPObject functions. These two functions are used to execute the remote object's methods. Both of these functions serve the same purpose, to execute a remote method; they just do it using different styles. The RSExecute function is a function-based way of executing the remote object's method, and RSGetASPObject is an object-oriented way of doing the same thing. The RSExecute function implementation is more efficient then the RSGetASPObject implementation because the RSGetASPObject has an extra step, as we will see later.

Calling Remote Objects Using the RSExecute Function

The RSExecute function syntax is

```
RSExecute(url, method [, p1, p2, ...] [, callback [,
errorcallback]
[, context]])
```

The url is the address of the ASP to be called. This page must be in the same domain as the HTML document. The method is the method of the ASP that will be executed; this must be a string value. The p1, p2 values are optional; they are parameters that are required by the ASP method. The parameters can only be basic data types. Structures and objects are not allowed. The parameters are passed as strings from the client to server. The ASP code must convert a parameter's data type if it expects it not to be a string. The optional callback parameter is a function in the HTML document that is called when the ASP method completes. If this parameter is passed, then the call to the method will be *asynchronous*, which causes the HTML document's script code to keep on executing after the RSExecute call is made. If this parameter is not given, then the call is *synchronous*, which causes the code to wait for the remote object's method to complete. The optional errorcallback parameter is also a function in the HTML document. The function is called if a call to the remote object's method cannot completed. The optional context parameter is data passed to the remote object and the remote object will pass it back. The data is used by the callback function to identify which remote method was called.

Using the RSExecute Synchronously

The listing below demonstrates a synchronous remote method call using the RSExecute function:

```
<script language="JavaScript">
function callRemoteMethodSync (dataID){
var co;
    co = RSExecute("someASP.asp", "getData", dataID);
    if (co.status == -1){
        alert("getdata method failed.");
        return;
    }
    alert("Returned data: " + co.return_value);
}
```

The callRemoteMethodSync function is called by the client. It executes the RSExecute function by calling the someASP.asp's getData method. The method takes one parameter, dataID, that is passed to the callRemoteMethodSync function. The optional parameters—callback, errorcallback, and context—are not given because this is a synchronous call. The RSExecute function returns a Call object, which is called co in the code above. The Call object contains return and status information from the call. Table 17-2 shows the Call object's properties and methods.

Properties/ Methods	Type	Purpose
id	Property	Unique ID for a call, generated when the call is first made.
return_value	Property	Data that the method returns, if any.
data	Property	Data returned by the server. This data is enclosed in XML tags.
status	Property	Current state of the method call: −1 means failed; 0 means completed; 1 means pending.
message	Property	Text information about the call. If the call has completed, then it will say "Completed". If the call failed, it can be text from the server or a standard error message.
callback	Property	Name of the callback function.
error_callback	Property	Name of the error callback function.
context	Property	Context value that was passed with this function.
wait	Method	Suspends processing of the client script and waits for an asynchronous remote call to be finished. It does not take any parameters.
cancel	Method	Cancels an asynchronous remote call. It does not take any parameters.

Table 17-2. The Call Object's Properties and Methods

Using the RSExecute Asynchronously

The following code listing shows how to call the previous example asynchronously:

```
<script language="JavaScript">
function callRemoteMethodAsync (dataID){
RSExecute("someASP.asp", "getData", dataID, doneCallBack, errCallBack,
"getdata");
}
function doneCallBack(co){
    if (co.status == -1){
        alert("Call to " + co.context + " method failed.");
        alert("Message: " + co.message);
        return;
    }
    alert("Returned data: " + co.return_value);
}
function errCallBack(co){
var msg;
    msg = "Call to " + co.context + " method failed.";
    msg = msg + "\n\nMessage: " + co.message;
    msg = msg + "\n\nData: " + co.data;
    alert(msg);
}
```

The first thing to notice is that in the callRemoteMethodAsync function, the RSExecute function does not return a Call object, and it does set a callback function, an error callback function, and a context. After the RSExecute function is executed, the client code continues to execute. When the remote object's getData method is finished, it calls the doneCallBack function in the client script. The doneCallBack function receives a Call object when the server calls it. The Call object can be interrogated for its execution status and any data returned to the client. The server calls the errCallBack function if an error occurs when the getData method is called. It is also passed a Call object. The Call object's message property can be used to display the error message. The Call object's data property contains the error message and other information in an XML format that is generated by the server. Figure 17-4 shows an example of an error and what the Call object's data looks like.

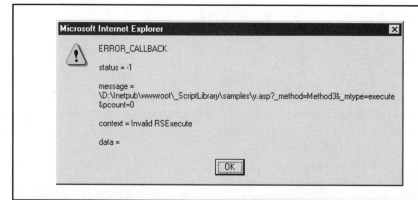

Figure 17-4. The Call object contains information from the server. The data can be interrogated to check the status of the call, the data returned, any error messages, and the raw data sent back from the server.

Using the Context Value

In the preceding example, the context value does not really have much use. Where it comes into play is when you use a general-purpose callback function, either a callback or an error callback. If another remote object call was added to the code, it could use the same callback functions, as follows:

```
RSExecute("someASP.asp", "updateData", dataID, txtName,
txtAddress,
doneCallBack, errCallBack, "updateData");
```

This remote call executes the updateData method in the someASP.asp file using the same callback functions. The doneCallBack function needs to be modified so it can work with both methods, as the following listing shows:

```
function doneCallBack(co){
    if (co.status == -1){
        alert("Call to " + co.context + " method failed.");
        alert("Message: " + co.message);
        return;
    }
    if (co.context == "updateData")
        alert("Update successed.");
```

```
    else{
       if (co.context == "getData")
          alert("Returned data: " + co.return_value);
    }
}
```

The doneCallBack function now differentiates each of the
methods that call it. The errCallBack function could also be changed
to do different error handling for each of the methods.

Using RSGetASPObject to Call Remote Objects

The other way of calling remote objects is to use the RSGetASPObject
function. This function gets a reference to the ASP remote object. The
ASP remote object is then used to call its methods. The following
code demonstrates how the RSGetASPObject is used.

NOTE: The examples that demonstrate using the RSGetASPObject
function are the same examples used to demonstrate the use of the
RSExecute function.

```
<script language="JavaScript">
function callRemoteMethodSync (dataID){
var objASP;
var co;
    objASP = RSGetASPObject("someASP.asp");
    co = objASP.getData(dataID);
    if (co.status == -1){
        alert("getData method failed.");
        return;
    }
    alert("Returned data: " + co.return_value);
}
```

As the name implies, callRemoteMethodSync calls the remote
object synchronously. It first gets a reference to the ASP object by
using the RSGetASPObject function. This function takes a single
parameter, the URL location of the ASP file. Next, the ASP's getData

method is called directly; it is passed its expected parameter data, and the getData method returns a Call object.

The following code shows how to make a call to a remote ASP object asynchronously:

```
<script language="JavaScript">
function callRemoteMethodAsync (dataID) {
    objASP = RSGetASPObject("some.asp");
    objASP.getdata(dataID, doneCallBack, errCallBack, "getdata");
}
function doneCallBack(co) {
    if (co.status == -1) {
        alert("Call to " + co.context + " method failed.");
        alert("Message: " + co.message);
        return;
    }
    alert("Returned data: " + co.return_value);
}
function errCallBack(co) {
var msg;
    msg = "Call to " + co.context + " method failed.";
    msg = msg + "\n\nMessage: " + co.message;
    msg = msg + "\n\nData: " + co.data;
    alert(msg);
}
```

To make an asynchronous call, the callback functions and context are added to the ASP method's call. Notice that when the method is executed, it does not return a Call object. The callbacks and the context are used exactly the same way as they are for the RSExecute function.

CUSTOMER INFORMATION EXAMPLE

The Customer Information page (Figure 17-5) uses remote scripting to display and update customer information. Using the customer ID value and pressing the Get Customer button will retrieve a customer. The four buttons at the bottom allow the user to navigate to a customer. The customer ID must be entered in order for the Prev and Next buttons to work correctly; otherwise these buttons are ignored.

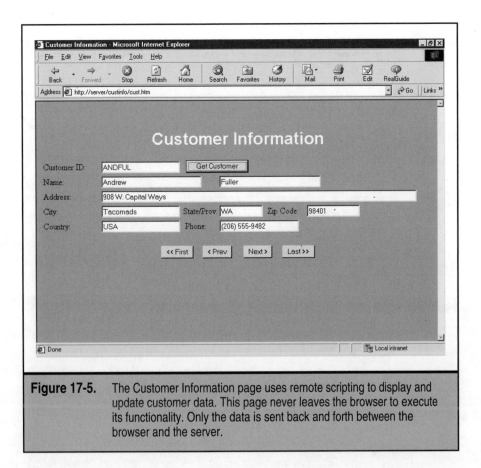

Figure 17-5. The Customer Information page uses remote scripting to display and update customer data. This page never leaves the browser to execute its functionality. Only the data is sent back and forth between the browser and the server.

The First and Last buttons will display the first and last customer, respectively, and they do not need the customer ID to be entered.

A customer's information can be updated by changing the data in the text boxes and pressing one of the four bottom buttons. The Get Customer button does not perform updating.

An Access 97 database, called CustInfo.mdb, is used on the server. This database contains a Customers table. Figure 17-6 shows a snapshot of the customer table and its data. Use the CustomerID column values to retrieve customers by ID. This table is used by custinfo.asp to retrieve and update the customers. The custinfo.asp file is the remote scripting object used by the client (browser).

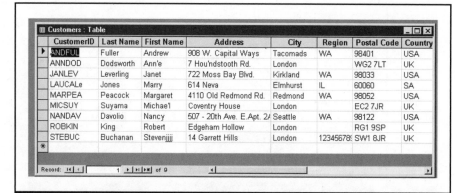

	CustomerID	Last Name	First Name	Address	City	Region	Postal Code	Country
▶	ANDFUL	Fuller	Andrew	908 W. Capital Ways	Tacomads	WA	98401	USA
	ANNDOD	Dodsworth	Ann'e	7 Hou'ndstooth Rd.	London		WG2 7LT	UK
	JANLEV	Leverling	Janet	722 Moss Bay Blvd.	Kirkland	WA	98033	USA
	LAUCALe	Jones	Marry	614 Neva	Elmhurst	IL	60060	SA
	MARPEA	Peacock	Margaret	4110 Old Redmond Rd.	Redmond	WA	98052	USA
	MICSUY	Suyama	Michae'l	Coventry House	London		EC2 7JR	UK
	NANDAV	Davolio	Nancy	507 - 20th Ave. E.Apt. 2/	Seattle	WA	98122	USA
	ROBKIN	King	Robert	Edgeham Hollow	London		RG1 9SP	UK
	STEBUC	Buchanan	Stevenjjjj	14 Garrett Hills	London	123456789	SW1 8JR	UK
*								

Record: ◄◄ ◄ 1 ► ►I ►* of 9

Figure 17-6.   The Customers table contains customer information. This snapshot allows you to see which customers are available to be used with the cust.htm page.

Requirements to Run the Customer Information Page

Since remote scripting deals with the client and the server, some prep work needs to be done to make the Customer Information page work correctly. (This prep work is not anything that you wouldn't normally need to do for any Web site that you run.) You will need to do the following to set up the server:

NOTE: We are using IIS as our Web server. You do not need to use IIS, but you do need to use a Web server that supports Active Server Pages. Also we will not go into details of how to set up the following items in IIS.

1. Create either a Web site or virtual directory in IIS that points to the physical directory from which the Web site will run. The Web pages, ASPs, and the database will be located in the physical directory.

2. Create a virtual directory called ScriptLibrary that will point to the _ScriptLibrary, which contains the remote scripting files.

3. Make sure that ADO (ActiveX Data Object) is installed on the server.

CustInfo.asp Details

The CustInfo.asp page is the remote scripting object that resides on the server. The rs.asp file is included in the custinfo.asp page using the virtual directory, and it also executes the RSDispatch function:

```
<%@ LANGUAGE=VBSCRIPT %>
<!--#INCLUDE VIRTUAL="/ScriptLibrary/RS.ASP"-->
<% RSDispatch %>
```

NOTE: We will not show the entire custinfo.asp file listing in this chapter. Refer to Chapter 1 to find the file location of the example.

The following code listing displays the custinfo.asp public interface:

```
function CustInfo(){
    this.getCustByID = custInfoByID;
    this.getNextCust = nextCust;
    this.getPrevCust = prevCust;
    this.getFirstCust = firstCust;
    this.getLastCust = lastCust;
    this.updateCustData = updateData;
}
public_description = new CustInfo();
```

The public_description variable creates a CustInfo object. The CustInfo object has five public interfaces: getCustByID, getNextCust, getPrevCust, getFirstCust, getLastCust, and updateCustData. Each of the public interfaces is implemented by a function. The first five functions do the same thing. The only exception is that they execute different SQL statements. The code below shows an example of these functions logic using the nextCust function:

```
function nextCust(id){
return loadData('select top 1 * from customers where customerid > "' +
id + '"');
}
```

The nextCust function is passed a customer ID parameter. The customer ID is used to get the next customer in the SQL statement. The nextCust function just calls the loadData function and returns the return value of the loadData function. The loadData function code listing is shown below:

```
function loadData(strSQL){
var dataValue;
var data;
var dbCust;
var rsCustInfo;
    dbCust = new ActiveXObject("ADODB.Connection");
    rsCustInfo = new ActiveXObject("ADODB.Recordset");
    dbCust.Open("provider=Microsoft.Jet.OLEDB.3.5;Data
Source=" + dbLoc +
"customer.mdb;Persist Security Info=False");
    rsCustInfo.Open(strSQL, dbCust, 3, 1);
    if (rsCustInfo.EOF && rsCustInfo.BOF)
        return "";
    for (i = 0; i < rsCustInfo.Fields.Count; i++){
        if (rsCustInfo(i).Value == null)
            dataValue = "";
        else
            dataValue = rsCustInfo(i).Value;
        if (i > 0)
            data = data + "<||>" + dataValue;
        else
            data = dataValue;
    }
    rsCustInfo.Close();
    dbCust.Close();
    return data;
}
```

The loadData function is passed the SQL statement. It creates an ADO Connection object and ADO Recordset object. It opens the database with the connection object. The recordset object is then opened using the connection object and the SQL statement. If the recordset is empty, then a null string is returned to the loadData caller. If a record is found, then its column data is concatenated into a string delimited by the character string <||>. The recordset and the connection object are closed, and the data string is returned to the caller (nextCust), which will return it to its caller, the client.

To update a customer, the customer's data is sent to the server as a string. There, it has to be parsed and an update SQL statement is executed. The updateData function (listed as follows) is used to implement the updateCustData public interface.

```
function updateData(strData){
var strSQL;
var data = new Array();
var rs;
    data = strData.split("<||>");
    strSQL = buildSQL(data);
    rs = new ActiveXObject("ADODB.Recordset");
    dbCust = new ActiveXObject("ADODB.Connection");
    dbCust.Open("provider=Microsoft.Jet.OLEDB.4.0;Data
Source=" +  dbLoc +
"customer.mdb;Persist Security Info=False");
    rs = dbCust.Execute(strSQL);
    dbCust.Close();
    return data[0];
}
```

The updateData function is passed a string of data, which is the customer's data. The string is placed into an array using the JavaScript String object's split method. The array is passed to the buildSQL function, which creates and returns the SQL update statement. It creates an ADO Connection object, opens the database, and executes the SQL update statement. The database is then closed, and the customer's ID is returned to the client.

Calling the Remote Script Object

In this section we describe how a Web page calls the CustInfo ASP using remote scripting. The Web page sets up remote scripting and then calls the methods in the CustInfo ASP to retrieve and update customers.

Setting Up the Web Page to Call a Remote Object

The client calls the remote script on the server. The first thing it needs to do is set up the proxy with the server. This is done with the follow code:

> **NOTE:** We will not show the entire cust.htm file listing in this chapter. Refer to Chapter 1 for the location of the cust.htm file. The cust.htm is used to call the custinfo.asp remote scripting object and is the UI for the customer information page.

```
<SCRIPT LANGUAGE="JavaScript"
src="http://server/ScriptLibrary/RS.HTM"></SCRIPT>
<SCRIPT LANGUAGE="JavaScript">
    RSEnableRemoteScripting("http://server/ScriptLibrary");
</SCRIPT>
```

To include the rs.htm file, its src attribute points to the URL of the location on the virtual Script Library directory on the server. Then the RSEnableRemoteScripting function is passed the path of where the RSProxy.class applet is located on the server. The Web page is now capable of calling any remote scripting object on the server.

Calling the CustInfo Remote Object Synchronously

If the user enters a value in the Customer ID field and presses the Get Customer button, the following code is executed:

```
function displayCustByID(){
var co;
var obj;
    co = RSExecute(aspDoc,"getCustByID", document.frmCust.txtCustID.value);
    if (co.status != 0){
        alert("Error retreiving customer ID " +
```

```
document.frmCust.txtCustID.value + ". Error message: " + co.message);
        return;
    }
    loadDataFlds(co.return_value);
}
```

The displayCustByID function is called by the onclick event of
the Get Customer button. This function calls the RSExecute function.
In this case, the RSExecute function is used to call a remote object
synchronously. The RSExecute function calls the getCustByID method
of the custinfo.asp remote object. The first parameter of the RSExecute
function, aspDOC, is set to this value in the beginning of the <script>
code section. The last parameter that is passed to the RSExecute
function is the customer ID value that is contained in the Customer
ID text box. This parameter is passed on to the getCustById method
of the remote object.

After the RSExecute function had completed executing, it returns
a Call object. The Call object is used to check the status of the called
remote object. If the status is not 0, then an error occurred; a message
is displayed and the displayCustByID function is ended. If the status
returned is 0, then the loadDataFlds function is called, passing it
the Call object's return_value property. The loadDataFlds parses the
data in the return_value variable and places it into the appropriate
<input> tags on the page, using this code:

```
function loadDataFlds(strData){
var data = new Array();
    strDataPassedIn = strData;
    data = strData.split("<||>");
    if (data == ""){
        strOrgCustID = "";
        document.frmCust.txtFirstName.value = "";
        document.frmCust.txtLastName.value = "";
        document.frmCust.txtAddress.value = "";
        document.frmCust.txtCity.value = "";
        document.frmCust.txtState.value = "";
        document.frmCust.txtZip.value = "";
        document.frmCust.txtCountry.value = "";
        document.frmCust.txtPhone.value = "";
        alert("Could not find customer with ID: " +
document.frmCust.txtCustID.value);
```

```
        }
        else{
            strOrgCustID = data[0];
            document.frmCust.txtCustID.value = data[0];
            document.frmCust.txtLastName.value = data[1];
            document.frmCust.txtFirstName.value = data[2];
            document.frmCust.txtAddress.value = data[3];
            document.frmCust.txtCity.value = data[4];
            document.frmCust.txtState.value = data[5];
            document.frmCust.txtZip.value = data[6];
            document.frmCust.txtCountry.value = data[7];
            document.frmCust.txtPhone.value = data[8];
        }
}
```

The loadDataFlds function receives the data string that was created by the remote object. It splits it into an array, called data, using the < | | > value as a delimiter. If the data array is empty, then the input fields are set to blanks; otherwise, they are set to their appropriate data array value.

The Prev and Next buttons use the same type of synchronous calls and logic to process their respective functionality. The only thing that they do differently is to update the customer data if there were any data changes.

Calling a Remote Object as an Object

As we stated earlier, remote scripting can be called either by a function or as an object. In our example, the Get Customer, Prev, and Next buttons use the function format. The First and Last buttons use the object format. Each of these buttons calls the remote object synchronously and executes the same type of logic to display the customer information. The code listing below shows what happens when the First button is pressed:

```
function displayFirstCust(){
var co;
var objCust;
    if (strDataPassedIn != null)
        updateData();
    objCust = RSGetASPObject(aspDoc);
```

```
    co = objCust.getFirstCust();
    if (co.status != 0){
        alert("Error retreiving the first customer. Error message: " +
co.message);
        return;
    }
    loadDataFlds(co.return_value);
    if (co.return_value == "")
        alert("No customers in the database");
}
```

The displayFirstCust function is executed when the First button's onclick event is fired. The function first checks to see if the data on the page has changed by calling the updateData function (we will discuss the updateData function in the next section). It then gets a reference to the custinfo remote object. Then, using the object reference objCust, it calls the getFirstCust method. The getFirstCust method returns a Call object, which is used to test the method's execution status. Assuming the status is okay, it loads the data returned from the server on the page. If the getFirstCust method does not return any data then a message is displayed that indicates that there is no data in the database.

Updating the Customer Data Using a Remote Object Asynchronously

The customer data is updated automatically by the page when the First, Prev, Next, or the Last button is pressed after the data is changed. The following If statement is executed in each of the functions that have update abilities:

```
if (strDataPassedIn != null)
    updateData();
```

This If statement checks whether the variable strDataPassedIn is null, meaning that the data has not been loaded on the page yet so an update is not needed. The strdataPassedIn variable is set in the loadDataFlds function.

If the data has been loaded on the page (strDataPassedIn is not null), then the updateData function is called. The updateData function calls a remote object method asynchronously, as the following code listing shows:

```
function updateData(){
var strDataEntered;
    if (document.frmCust.txtCustID.value == ""){
        alert("The customer ID is required for an update.");
        return false;
    }
    strDataEntered = document.frmCust.txtCustID.value + '<||>' +
document.frmCust.txtLastName.value + '<||>' +
document.frmCust.txtFirstName.value + '<||>' +
document.frmCust.txtAddress.value + '<||>';
    strDataEntered = strDataEntered +
document.frmCust.txtCity.value + '<||>' +
document.frmCust.txtState.value + '<||>' +
document.frmCust.txtZip.value + '<||>' +
document.frmCust.txtCountry.value + '<||>' +
document.frmCust.txtPhone.value;
    if (strDataPassedIn == strDataEntered)
        return;
    if (strOrgCustID == "")
        return;
    RSExecute(aspDoc,"updateCustData", strOrgCustID + '<||>' +
strDataEntered, doCallBack, doErrCallBack, "Update Customer Data -
Customer
ID" + document.frmCust.txtCustID.value);
}
```

The updataData function validates that a customer ID was entered. It then concatenates all of the inputted data into the strDataEntered variable. Next it checks to see if there is a difference between the data that was loaded on the page and the data that is currently on the page. If the two variables are the same, then an update is not needed and the function ends. The strOrgCustID variable is used to save the original customer ID. If this variable is blank, it indicates that the data was not loaded on this page, and therefore, there is also no need to update the customer data.

Finally the RSExecute function is executed to call the custinfo.asp's updateCustData method. It passes the input data prefixed with the original customer ID. The reason for passing the original ID is that the ID may have been changed by the user, so the original ID is used to identify which customer is to be updated. The callback and error callback function addresses are passed to the RSExecute function. The context value then is passed in and is used by the callback function to display a message.

The callback functions are listed below:

```
function doCallBack(co){
    if (co.status != 0)
        alert("Update to customer id " + co.return_value + "
failed. Error msg: " + co.message);
    else
        alert("Customer ID " + co.return_value + " update
successfully.");
}
function doErrCallBack(co){
var msg;
    msg = "Error updating!  Error message: " + co.message;
    msg = msg + "Raw data :" + co.data;
    alert(msg);
}
```

When the asynchronous call is finished executing, it calls the doCallBack function. This function checks the status and displays either an error message or a message that the update succeeded. The doErrCallBack function is called only if there is an error while executing the RSExecute function. It displays the call object's message and data properties.

USING REMOTE SCRIPTING WITH NETSCAPE COMMUNICATOR

As we stated earlier, remote scripting is browser independent. The Customer Information page does run in Netscape's browser (version 4.7) (see Figure 17-7). In order to use the Web page in both browsers, the page needs to use their common functionality. Communicator's

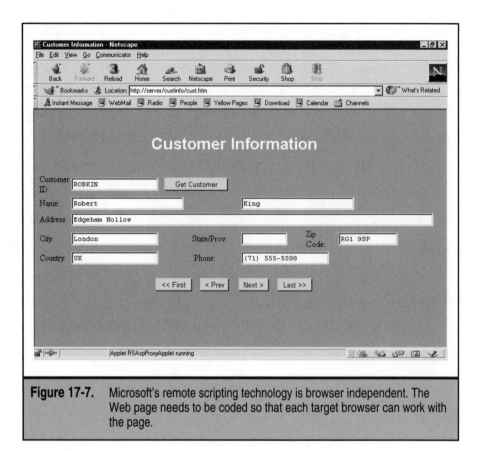

Figure 17-7.   Microsoft's remote scripting technology is browser independent. The Web page needs to be coded so that each target browser can work with the page.

JavaScript coding standards are more stringent than Internet Explorer's, which can cause a problem when using remote scripting. For example, sometimes in Internet Explorer you can get away with not ending a JavaScript statement with a semicolon, whereas Communicator requires one and the page will not work correctly without it. Another example of browser difference is the rendering of a text box. Communicator requires that the text box be contained within a set of <form> tags; Internet Explorer does not have that requirement.

Both browsers' DHTML object models are also different. For example Internet Explorer has cascading style sheets and Communicator has layers. Even the individual objects are different. Internet Explorer has richer objects with more capabilities. For example, Internet Explorer's text box has a readonly property and Communicator's text box does not.

To make remote scripting work in both browsers, we suggest that you start with Communicator since it is more restrictive in its requirements and its DOM has less capabilities. You will need to do some digging for what features will work in both browsers. Also, when you make any changes to the JavaScript code, you'll need to retest the changes with both browsers.

REMOTE SCRIPTING AND SECURITY

Remote scripting has only one security restriction: the Web page and the remote objects that it calls must be located within the same domain. For example, in Figure 17-7, looking at the location fields we can see that the cust.htm page is obtained from a server named server. Inside the cust.htm page, it tries to call the remote object from www.premierbusinesssoft.com/chp17a/, which is on a different server. This causes the error in Figure 17-8 to be displayed.

SUMMARY

In this chapter we covered how to make Web pages more efficient by using remote scripting. Remote scripting is used to send the client only the page elements and data that are needed to change to the client and not a whole new page. Remote scripting uses a proxy

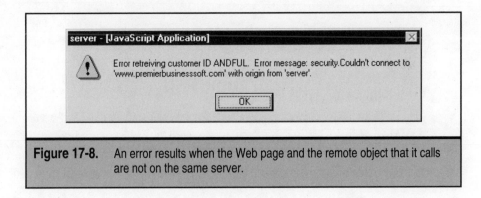

Figure 17-8.   An error results when the Web page and the remote object that it calls are not on the same server.

service (a Java applet) to communicate between the browser and the server. Client Web pages need to include the file rs.htm, which loads the proxy service (rsproxy.class) on the page. Because of this Java applet implementation, remote scripting works on Microsoft Internet Explorer and Netscape Navigator/Communicator 3.0 and later. Once the client is remote script aware, it can then execute a remote script object's methods. The remote object is made up of an Active Server Page that contains a special variable named public_description, which creates a JavaScript object with a public interface. For security reasons, client pages and remote scripting objects must reside within the same domain.

PART VI

Sample Application

CHAPTER 18

Putting It All Together

In the previous chapters, we discussed quite a few of the different scripting technologies. These technologies really show their true power, however, through synergistic use in building a complete application. In this final chapter, we are going to lead you though a sample application that uses most of the technologies covered in this book, resulting in a complete Web application.

NOTE: The complete source code for the Web application can be downloaded from the Downloads section of the Osborne/McGraw-Hill Web site (http://www.osborne.com).

In this chapter, we cover in detail some of the more interesting and important parts of the sample to help you begin to apply the technologies you have learned in this book. We discuss the following topics and technologies:

▼ How to approach the development of the sample application.

■ How to build and reuse DHTML behaviors.

▲ How to use XML as a data store and a data transfer facility.

THE SAMPLE APPLICATION

The sample application is a time keeping application that can be used to automate and streamline the mundane task of creating timesheets. The application is comprised of a client application (an HTML application) that allows a user to fill in the timesheet while being away from the network, as well as an online viewer portion that allows you to view the completed timesheets from any (that is, IE 4 and later and Netscape 4 and later) browser.

The client-based application allows the user to define multiple activities for a given week, the day, the start and end times, the client that the activity was completed for, and a detailed description of the activity. The application gives the user the ability to add, edit, and delete activities for a given week. Once the user has completed the timesheet for the week, they mark the sheet as being completed. At this point, the timesheet can be uploaded to the server and stored in a database.

Once in the database, other users can view either a detailed or summarized version of the timesheet, based on their viewing privileges.

The client application uses HTML components to create a reusable interface and common logic modules. In addition to this, we use XML, XSL, and the XML data source object (XMLDSO) to store, present, and edit the timesheet data. On the server side of the application, we use XML, XSL, XML schemas, Remote Scripting, and Active Server Page Windows Script Components to accept data from the client application and to display the data in the lookup application.

GETTING STARTED WITH THE IMPLEMENTATION

Before we began working on the project, we determined some of the basic requirements for the application. The first of these requirements was that the portion of the application that allows the user to create and maintain timesheets needed to be able to run as a stand alone application that was not always connected to the Internet. This would allow traveling users to be able to fill in their timesheets when they had the time, rather than only when they were connected.

The next major requirement was that we needed the ability to upload and review timesheets. This would allow a manager or a client to review the activities of one of their workers. Additionally, we wanted the ability to review timesheets without being tied to the IE 5 browser so that a manager or client could use almost any browser to access the timesheets. To coincide with this, we also wanted to build security into the server-side processing where we could define rights for a particular user so that they could only see either certain workers' timesheets or certain clients' data.

In addition to these major requirements, we had a couple of other minor design goals that we wanted to implement in the application. The first of these goals was to isolate the entire file saving technique within the client side of the application. This way, if in the future we wanted to convert the client application into a server-based application, we could do so by simply changing where the data was saved. (If we were to do this, we would need additional code on the server to save and retrieve the data.) The final requirement was to reuse some of the concepts and examples we had developed in this book. This not only helped us develop the application more quickly, but it also shows you code reuse techniques you can use.

BUILDING THE CLIENT APPLICATION

We started with the client application and determined what reusable client components (DHTML behaviors) we needed to create. As we began to define the user interface, we decided that we would need a grid to allow the user to enter data into their timesheet. The other user interface behavior we needed to create was a menu component that would serve as the basis for all of the different actions a user could perform with a timesheet (such as creating a new timesheet, closing a timesheet, adding tasks to a timesheet, and so on). The final component we needed to create was a nonuser interface component that would contain all of our common code and file interaction, meeting our design goal of file handling isolation within the client-side of the application.

Building a Grid Component

The types of functionality needed in the grid component are similar to the one we developed back in Chapter 7. There were, however, a few key pieces of functionality that the grid did not support. If you remember, the grid example only allowed you to have text data entry fields. We needed the ability to display drop-down lists, allowing the user to choose the day, start time, end time, and so on. In addition, we needed the ability to display text areas so that the user could enter detailed information for a particular task. And finally, we also wanted to enhance the grid so we could set the column widths and be able to set focus to a particular cell in the grid.

Even though these were fairly large pieces of functionality to create, it was by far easier to use the existing grid as a starting point, enhancing its functionality to meet our requirements. To support the different types of edit items in the grid, we created two new properties to define what type of element to display for the column. The two properties are colTypes (used to set all of the columns' types) and colType (used to set a single column's type). The colTypes property simply takes and returns a comma-delimited string of the column types. To use the colType property, you pass in the column number you wish to set or retrieve the column type for. In our new version of the grid, we support three different types of columns: dropDown (displays a select element), textArea (displays a textarea element), and text (default, displays a text type input element).

The next issue we needed to address was how to define what data should be displayed in the select element for the drop-down column types. We wanted to allow the user of the grid to be able to define both the value to be returned and also the value to display in the drop-down menu. To support this functionality, we decided to create a property, dropDownData, that allows the user to pass in an XML document containing all of the possible values for each of the drop-down columns. The following is the schema for this document and also a sample XML snippet showing the format of the XML document (it is important to note that the columnIndex attribute refers to the column in the grid):

gridDropDownSchema.xml

```
<Schema xmlns="urn:schemas-microsoft-com:xml-data">
<AttributeType name="columnIndex" required="yes" />
<AttributeType name="value" required="yes" />
<ElementType  name="item">
  <attribute type="value" />
</ElementType>
<ElementType  name="column">
  <attribute type="columnIndex" />
  <element type="item" />
</ElementType>
<ElementType  name="dropDownValues">
  <element type="column" />
</ElementType>
</Schema>
```

Here is the sample drop-down definition:

```
<dropDownValues xmlns="x-schema:gridDropDownSchema.xml" >
  <column columnIndex="1">
    <item value="Monday">Monday</item>
```

```
    <item value="Tuesday">Tuesday</item>
    <item value="Wednesday">Wednesday</item>
    <item value="Thursday">Thursday</item>
    <item value="Friday">Friday</item>
    <item value="Saturday">Saturday</item>
    <item value="Sunday">Sunday</item>
  </column>
  <column columnIndex="2">
    <item value="ACME">Acme Corporation</item>
    <item value="XYZ">XYZ Data Manipulation, Inc.</item>
  </column>
  ...

</dropDownValues>
```

Now that we knew what type of control to display and what data to display in the control, we moved on to manipulating the editCell function so that it would display and retrieve the values from our new control types. The implementation of this functionality was fairly straightforward because we could call on our new properties to determine the data type and then display the appropriate control. The trickier task came when we tried to create a borderless select object. We wanted to do this because if we displayed a select object in the table, its border would cause the row to be resized, causing a redraw of the complete table. Unfortunately, the select object does not support the ability to hide the border, as the text input element does. So to hide the border of the select object, we created a clipping region that was used to clip off the border.

The only other issue we needed to deal with in the editCell method was how to hold onto the value of the selected item in the select object. To do this, we created our own user-defined attribute on the table's cell, called currentValue, where we would store the value for the selected item. The following is the new, updated code for the editCell function:

```
function editCell(ele, save){
var eInputItem;
var data = "";
var regExp = / /g;
var objEvent;
var currentValue;
if (save){
```

```
      switch (vcolTypes[vlastEditedItem.cellIndex]){
        case "dropDown":
          var selected =
vlastEditedItem.children(0).options.selectedIndex;
          if (selected >= 0){
            data = vlastEditedItem.children(0).options[selected].text;
            currentValue =
vlastEditedItem.children(0).options[selected].value;
          }
          break;
        case "textArea":
          data = vlastEditedItem.children(0).innerText;
          break;
        default:
          data = vlastEditedItem.children(0).value;
          break;
      }
      objEvent = createEventObject();
      objEvent.data = data;
      objEvent.result = true;
      eeID.fire(objEvent);
      if (objEvent.result){
        ele.removeChild(ele.children(0));
        vlastEditedItem = null;
        ele.innerText = data;
        ele.currentValue = currentValue;
        ele.title = data;
      }
      else{
        eval(element.id + "CellInputItem").focus();
        return false;
      }
    }
    else{
      objEvent = createEventObject();
      objEvent.data = ele.innerText;
      objEvent.column = ele.cellIndex + 1;
      objEvent.row = ele.parentElement.rowIndex + 1;
      objEvent.result = true;
      seID.fire(objEvent);
      if (!objEvent.result)
        return false;
```

```
      switch (vcolTypes[ele.cellIndex]){
        case "dropDown":
          eInputItem = document.createElement("<select id='" + element.id
   + "CellInputItem' ></select>");
          eInputItem.style.height = "100%";
          eInputItem.style.position = "absolute";
          var bottom = ele.clientHeight - 2;
          var right = ele.clientWidth - 1;
          eInputItem.style.clip = "rect(2 " + right + " " + bottom + "
   2)";
          break;
        case "textArea":
          eInputItem = document.createElement("<textarea style='border:0
   none' id='" + element.id + "CellInputItem' ></textArea>");
          eInputItem.innerText = ele.innerText;
          break;
        default:
          eInputItem = document.createElement("<input style='border:0
   none' type='text' id='" + element.id + "CellInputItem' ></input>");
          eInputItem.value = ele.innerText;
          break;
      }
      eInputItem.style.width = "100%";
      ele.innerText = "";
      ele.insertBefore(eInputItem, null);
      if ((vcolTypes[ele.cellIndex]) == "dropDown"){
        var bottom = eInputItem.clientHeight - 2;
        var right = ele.clientWidth - 2;
        eInputItem.style.clip = "rect(2 " + right + " " + bottom + " 2)";
        var currentValue = ele.currentValue;
        //Populates the select object with the data from the XML file
        addItemsToDropDown(ele.cellIndex, currentValue, eInputItem);
      }
      if ((vcolTypes[ele.cellIndex]) == "textArea"){
        eInputItem.style.height = ele.clientHeight;
      }
      eInputItem.focus();
    }
    return true;
  }
```

The final issue we needed to deal with regarding the new data types dealt with the returning and setting of values from the grid. Columns that have the dropDown data type should return the value of the selected item, not the text of the cell. Likewise, if a value is passed into the grid, we want to display the text for that value, not the value itself. These changes were relatively easy to implement (see the grid.htc for full details) because we could retrieve the currentValue for the cell to return the data. Also, when setting the data, we retrieved the text to display from the XML file based on the column and value.

The final pieces of functionality we needed to add were setting the column widths and adding the ability to set the focus to a particular cell. To set the column widths, we created a new property called colWidths. This property takes and returns a comma-delimited string of column widths. Now that we had the widths, we needed to change the buildRow function to incorporate the user-defined values. Finally, we added the setCellFocus method. This method has two parameters: the row and the column to which you wish to set focus. In the setCellFocus method, we check to see if another cell is currently being edited. If it is, we call the editCell function to take it out of edit mode and then call the editCell function again to set the specified cell into edit mode.

Building a Menu Component

The next user interface component we developed was a menu component, providing functionality similar to that of a standard Windows menu. We used the basic mouse capture concept that we began to develop in Chapter 14 as a starting point. We also wanted the menu to be able to support enabling/disabling of menu items and setting of customizable colors for the menu.

The requirements for the timesheet application only require the menu component to support a single level of menu items (no cascading menus). In the menu component, we continued to use mouse capturing to handle the user interaction. The menu is composed of the following HTML elements:

▼ A DIV element that acts as a container element for the menu.

■ One DIV element for each of the highest-level menu items.

■ One DIV to contain the child menu items (built when a parent menu is clicked).

▲ One DIV for each of the child menu items (built when a parent menu is clicked).

Most of the methods and properties are used to define the look of the elements that are used in the component. Table 18-1 describes the public interface (methods, properties, and events) for the menu component.

In addition to defining the look of the menu, we needed an easy mechanism to define the somewhat complex structure and the elements of the menu. Based on this requirement, we decided to use

Method/Property/Event	Description
backgroundColor	The default color for the background of the menu and all of the child elements
childMenuWidth	The width of the container that holds all of the child elements
color	The default color for the text of the menu and all of the child elements
disabledBackgroundColor	The background color of a disabled child menu item
disabledColor	The font color of a disabled child menu item
fontFamily	The font family to use for all of the menu text
fontSize	The font size to use for all of the menu text

Table 18-1.   Public Interface Properties, Methods, and Events of the Menu Component

Method/Property/Event	Description
menuHeight	The height of the menu items, both the parent and child items
menuTop	The absolute position where the top of the menu should be displayed (default: 0)
menuWidth	The width of the complete menu element
parentMenuWidth	The maximum width of the parent menu items
selectBackgroundColor	The background color of a selected child element
selectColor	The font color of a selected child element
separatorColor	The color to set the thin line between the parent menu items and the child container element
xmlFilePath	The path to the XML file that contains the menu layout
disableMenu(menuValue)	Method to disable a specified menu item; pass in the value of the menu item to disable
enableMenu(menuValue)	Method to enable a specified menu item; pass in the value of the menu item to enable
onMenuClick	Event raised whenever a child menu item is clicked; returns the value of the selected item in the menuValue property of the event object

Table 18-1. Public Interface Properties, Methods, and Events of the Menu Component *(continued)*

XML once again to define the layout. The component loads the XML
file defined by the xmlFilePath property and dynamically builds
the menu based on the structure defined in the file. The following
is the schema and the XML document we used to define the menu
for the timesheet application

menuSchema.xml

```
<Schema xmlns="urn:schemas-microsoft-com:xml-data">
<AttributeType name="display" required="yes" />
<AttributeType name="value" required="yes" />
<AttributeType name="status" dt:type="enumeration" dt:values="disabled
enabled" default="enabled" />
<ElementType  name="menuItem">
  <attribute type="display" />
  <attribute type="value" />
  <attribute type="status" />
</ElementType>
<ElementType  name="menuList">
  <element type="menuItem" />
</ElementType>
</Schema>
```

menu.xml:

```
<menuList xmlns="x-schema:menuSchema.xml">
  <menuItem display="File" value="File">
    <menuItem display="New" value="NewSheet" />
    <menuItem display="Open" value="Open" />
    <menuItem display="Save" value="Save" />
    <menuItem display="Close" value="Close" />
    <menuItem display="Set Complete" value="Complete" />
    <menuItem display="Delete" value="Delete" />
    <menuItem display="Send To Server" value="Send" />
    <menuItem display="Clients" value="Clients" />
    <menuItem display="Exit" value="Exit" />
  </menuItem>
  <menuItem display="Tasks" value="Tasks">
    <menuItem display="Add Task" value="AddTask" />
    <menuItem display="Remove Task" value="RemoveTask" />
  </menuItem>
  <menuItem display="Help" value="Help">
    <menuItem display="About" value="About" />
  </menuItem>
</menuList>
```

Because the complete code listing is quite long, we refer you to the online source (menu.htc) for the complete code listing. But what we would like to show you here is the function that does most of the processing: handleClick. This function is called when a click occurs anywhere in the menu or anywhere in the document once the menu has received the mouse capture. handleClick is responsible for hiding and showing the child menu items and also determining when a child menu item is selected. The following is the code listing for the handleClick function.

```
function handleClick(){
  var newElement;
  var source = event.srcElement;
  var menuState;
  //Check to see which menu item was selected
  switch(source.type){
    case "parentMenu":
      //check to see if a menu is already displayed
      if (activeMenu != event.srcElement){
        if (menuContainer != null){
          removeSubMenu();
        }
//create and set the location of the submenu item container
        menuContainer = document.createElement("DIV");
        with (menuContainer.style){
          position = "absolute";
          left = source.style.left;
          top = menuTop + menuHeight;
          borderTop = "1px solid " + menuSeperatorColor;
        }
        this.appendChild(menuContainer);
        var subItems = xmlSource.selectNodes("//menuItem[@value='" +
source.id + "']/menuItem");
      var xmlElement = subItems.nextNode();
        //loop through and build menu items
        while (xmlElement != null){
          menuState = xmlElement.getAttribute("state");
          newElement = document.createElement("<DIV>");
          with (newElement.style){
            width = menuChildWidth;
            overflow = "hidden";
```

```
          if (menuState == "disabled"){
            backgroundColor = menuDisabledBackColor;
            color = menuDisabledColor;
          }
          else {
            backgroundColor = menuBackColor;
            color = menuColor;
          }
          fontSize = menuFontSize;
          fontFamily = menuFontFamily;
          height = menuHeight;
        }
        with (newElement){
          innerHTML = xmlElement.getAttribute("display");
          id = xmlElement.getAttribute("value");
        }
        newElement.type = "subMenu";
        newElement.state = menuState;
        menuContainer.appendChild(newElement);
        xmlElement = subItems.nextNode();
      }
      this.setCapture(true);
      activeMenu = source;
    }
    //second click on the parent menu (remove child menu)
    else {
      activeMenu = null;
      this.removeChild(menuContainer);
      menuContainer = null;
    }
    break;
  //click on sub menu means item was selected
  case "subMenu":
    if (source.state != "disabled"){
      var eventObject = createEventObject();
      eventObject.menuValue = source.id;
      menuClick.fire(eventObject);
      this.releaseCapture();
    }
```

```
        break;
    //click somewhere else in the document
    default:
      this.releaseCapture();
      break;
  }
}
```

Building a Common Source Component

In addition to our components providing user interface services, we wanted to create a nonvisual component that contained logic that could be used in several different locations. In addition to this, we wanted to be able to have our file interaction in one common location (a design goal) so we could easily change the way this functionality works. All of the methods of this module are pretty straightforward helper methods, so we will not go into great detail about the common source behavior. The shared functionality is contained in the commonSource.htc behavior. It is important to note that some of these methods interact with the settings.xml file, which is detailed in the next section. This behavior contains nine helper methods that are listed in Table 18-2.

Defining the Client-side XML Document Formats

In the client application we have three different types of information we need to store: the settings for the application, a list of all of the timesheets, and the actual timesheets themselves. The settings XML document is a very simple file that contains information, similar to an .ini file in Windows. The document stores the following information: the path to the server (used to determine where to send the timesheet data), the path to the local data files (used in the file operations to save and delete files, because you need the complete path), and the last user to create a timesheet (saved so the user does not have to enter their name each time they create a timesheet). Storing the settings information in a file allows us to easily update this information either programmatically or from a simple text editor. It is important to note

Method	Description
addItemToList(list, value, display, selected)	Adds a new option object to an HTML select object
clearList(list)	Removes all of the option items from a list
deleteXMLDocument(file)	Deletes the specified file from the system
getDataPath()	Retrieves the file system path from the settings file of where the data files are stored (settings.xml)
getSelectedListValue(list)	Retrieves the value of the selected option from an HTML select element
getPreviousUser()	Retrieves from the settings file the name of the user for whom the last timesheet was created (settings.xml)
getServerPath()	Retrieves the path from the settings file to the server to which the timesheet data is sent (settings.xml)
savePreviousUser(userName)	Saves to the settings file the name of the user who created the last timesheet (settings.xml)
saveXMLDocument(xmlDoc, saveTo)	Extracts the XML from the XML document and saves it to the specified file

Table 18-2.   The commonSource Behavior's Methods

that we didn't create an XML schema for this document because of its simplicity. The following is the settings.xml we used on our local machine when running the application:

```
<application>
  <previousUser>neyt1</previousUser>
  <dataPath>c:\book\samples\chp18\</dataPath>
<serverPath>http://localhost/chp18/</serverPath>
</application>
```

The timesheet list XML document allows us to maintain a list of all of the timesheets that have been created. This file serves as a type of index, eliminating the need to open all of the timesheet documents and extract the data we need when displaying a list of timesheets.

In addition to simply storing a list of documents, we also wanted to be able to classify timesheets as either being complete (I have entered all of my time for the week) or open (I haven't entered all of the data for the week). By classifying timesheets in this way, users can easily identify the timesheet(s) that are still in progress (needing to be completed). When a user marks a sheet as complete, this also serves as the signal to send the timesheet to the server. Beyond the categorization, we store the file name that corresponds to the timesheet, the name of the timesheet's assigned user, the status of the timesheet (used to determine if the closed timesheet has been sent to the server), and also the date that the user specified as the start date. It is important to note that we store the start date in two different formats: one is the human readable form of mm/dd/yyyy, and the other represents the number of milliseconds between midnight, January 1, 1970, and the specified start date (this is easily obtained using the JavaScript getTime method). You might be thinking, "Why would you store the date in that format?" Well, storing the date in this format allows us to perform easy sorts using XSL and also provides an easy mechanism to load the date into a JavaScript date object. The following is the XML schema for the timesheet list and also a sample timesheet list document.

tsListSchema.xml

```
<Schema xmlns="urn:schemas-microsoft-com:xml-data"
        xmlns:dt="urn:schemas-microsoft-com:datatypes">
<AttributeType name="createdBy" required="yes" />
<AttributeType name="startDate" required="yes" />
<AttributeType name="file" required="yes" />
<AttributeType name="status" dt:type="enumeration" dt:values="sent modified
new" default="new" />
<ElementType  name="timeSheet">
  <attribute type="createdBy" />
  <attribute type="startDate" />
  <attribute type="file" />
  <attribute type="status" />
</ElementType>
<ElementType  name="Completed">
  <element type="timeSheet" />
</ElementType>
<ElementType  name="Open">
  <element type="timeSheet" />
</ElementType>
<ElementType name="timeSheets">
  <element type="Completed" />
  <element type="Open" />
</ElementType>
</Schema>
```

timeSheetList.xml

```
<timeSheets "x-schema:tsListSchema.xml">
<Completed>
  <timeSheet createdBy="neyt1" startDate="1/9/2000" file="947413404310.xml"
startInt="950076000000" status="sent" />
  <timeSheet createdBy="neyt1" startDate="1/16/2000" file="947414891030.xml"
startInt="950680800000" status="modified" />
  <timeSheet createdBy="neyt1" startDate="1/12/2000" file="947715841550.xml"
startInt="950335200000" status="sent" />
</Completed>
<Open>
  <timeSheet createdBy="neyt1" startDate="1/14/2000" file="947913776660.xml"
startInt="950508000000" status="new" />
</Open>
</timeSheets>
```

The final client application XML document type is the timesheet document. These documents store the detailed data for the timesheets and are transported to the server after they have been marked complete. There is one timesheet document for each timesheet created, and it contains one or more task elements. The text of the task elements represents the description of the task, and a task element also contains attributes storing the day the task took place, the start and end times of the task, and the client for whom the task was completed.

There is one important thing to note about the timesheet documents: the schema that is used to validate the document is actually stored on the server, not on the client. The reason for this is to make sure that the format of the data that the server is expecting matches the format of the data that is on the client side. When we load the timesheet document locally, we turn off validating external documents (schemas) so that the application does not try to connect to the server. When we are ready to send the data to the server, we don't disable the validation, verifying the document format with what the server is expecting. If we change the format and the schema of the timesheet document in a future version of the application on the server, and a user has a prior version on their local machine, this will prevent potential problems importing the new data to the server. The following is the server-side validation schema and a sample for the timesheet document:

tsDetailSchema.xml

```
<Schema xmlns="urn:schemas-microsoft-com:xml-data">
<AttributeType name="startDate" required="yes" />
<AttributeType name="day" required="yes" />
<AttributeType name="clientID" required="yes" />
<AttributeType name="startTime" required="yes" />
<AttributeType name="endTime" required="yes" />
<ElementType   name="task">
  <attribute type="day" />
  <attribute type="clientID" />
  <attribute type="startTime" />
  <attribute type="endTime" />
</ElementType>
```

```
<ElementType  name="timeSheet">
  <element type="task" />
  <attribute type="startDate" />
</ElementType>
</Schema>
```

Here is the sample timesheet document:

```
<timeSheet xmlns="x-schema:http://localhost/chp18/tsDetailSchema.xml"
startDate="1/9/2000">
  <task day="Monday" clientID="XYZ" startTime="09:00"
endTime="17:00">Did
investigation into XML and XML Schemas</task>
  <task day="Tuesday" clientID="XYZ" startTime="09:00"
endTime="17:00">Began
working on prototype of XML on an NT Server</task>
  <task day="Wednesday" clientID="XYZ" startTime="09:00"
endTime="18:00">Completed prototype of XML on an NT Server</task>
</timeSheet>
```

Building the Client Application

Now that we have covered all of the infrastructure components of the application, actually building the application becomes pretty easy. The primary functionality of the application is contained in the HTML application file (main.hta). The application file is responsible for trapping all of the menu operations, interacting with the timesheet data, and displaying the data. Figure 18-1 shows the application when it is first loaded.

Creating a Timesheet

We will walk you through the application's functionality, following the path that a user would generally take. The first thing to do in the application is to create a new timesheet, which is done by selecting the New item from the File menu. The application is notified of the selection of the New menu item and displays the Create New Timesheet dialog (newsSheet.htm). Figure 18-2 shows what this dialog looks like.

After selecting the appropriate start date, entering who the timesheet is for, and clicking the Create button, the application goes to work

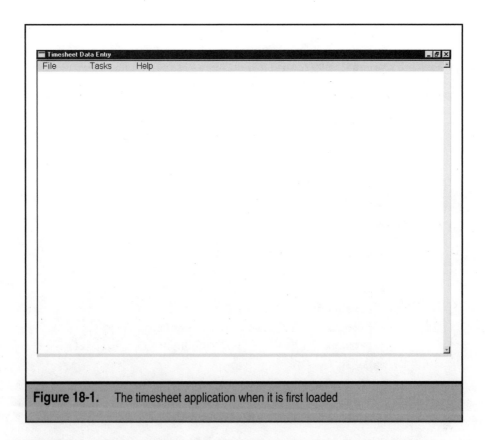

Figure 18-1.   The timesheet application when it is first loaded

adding a new timesheet to the timesheet list and creating a new timesheet document. The new timesheet is stored in the path that is specified in the dataPath element of the settings.xml file. To be certain that our new file is given a unique name, we set the filename equal to the current system date and time as expressed in the JavaScript getTime function. The following code is executed to create the new timesheet:

```
function createTimesheet(){
  var currentDT = new Date();

  //Retrieve the data from the form
  var year = common.getSelectedListValue(cmbYear);
  var month = common.getSelectedListValue(cmbMonth);
  var day = common.getSelectedListValue(cmbStartDay);
  var tsFor = txtFor.value;
```

```
var startDate = month + "/" + day + "/" + year;
var startDateObj = new Date(year, month, day);
var startInt = startDateObj.getTime();

//The new timesheets file name
var fileName = currentDT.getTime() + ".xml";

var dataPath = common.getDataPath();
if (tsFor == ""){
  alert("You must specify who to create the timesheet
for.");
  txtFor.focus();
}
else {
  timeSheetList.async = false;
  timeSheetList.load("timeSheetList.xml");
  //Check to see if the timesheetlist.xml exist if not
create it
  if (timeSheetList.xml == ""){
    timeSheetList.loadXML("<timeSheets xmlns='x-
schema:tsListSchema.xml'><Completed /><Open /></timeSheets>");
  }
  //Add the new timesheet to the open section of the timesheet
list
  var openNode = timeSheetList.selectSingleNode("//Open");
  newElement = timeSheetList.createElement("timeSheet");
  newElement.setAttribute("createdBy", tsFor);
  newElement.setAttribute("startDate", startDate);
  newElement.setAttribute("file", fileName);
  newElement.setAttribute("startInt", startInt);
  openNode.appendChild(newElement);
  //Create and save the template for the new timesheet
  timeSheet.async = false;
  timeSheet.resolveExternals = false;
  timeSheet.loadXML("<timeSheet xmlns='x-schema:" +
```

```
common.getServerPath() +
"tsDetailSchema.xml' startDate='" + startDate + "'/>");
  common.saveXMLDocument(timeSheet, dataPath + fileName);
  common.saveXMLDocument(timeSheetList, dataPath +
"timeSheetList.xml");
  common.savePreviousUser(tsFor);
  window.returnValue = dataPath + fileName;
  window.close();
  }
}
```

The dialog returns the path of the timesheet to the main document, which loads that XML document and initializes the grid. Because there are no tasks in the document (it is brand new), the grid displays only the header. Figure 18-3 shows the results of this action.

Adding Tasks to the Timesheet

Now that the user has a timesheet to work with, they can go ahead and start adding tasks to the timesheet. To add a task, the user simply selects Add Task from the Tasks menu. The main document is notified of the click on the Add Task menu item and adds a new row to the grid. Figure 18-4 shows a new timesheet with several tasks added.

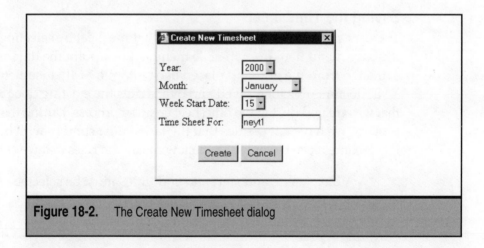

Figure 18-2. The Create New Timesheet dialog

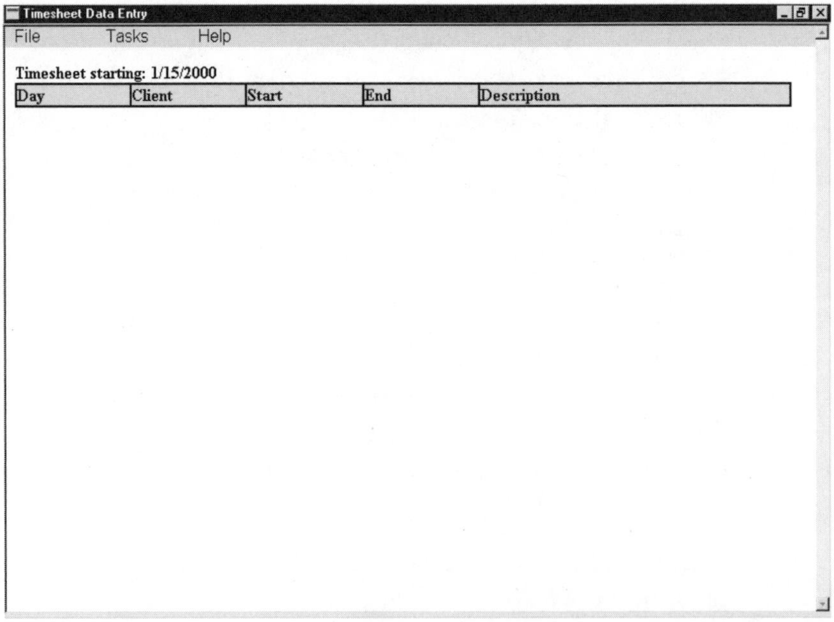

Figure 18-3. The main document after creating a new timesheet

Saving the Timesheet

The user can then save the changes to the timesheet by selecting the Save menu item from the File menu. At this point the data is extracted from the grid and placed back into the XML document. The XML document is then saved and overwrites the existing document that was created during the timesheet creation process. During the save process, we have a few rules that the tasks must comply with before the document can be saved. The following are the rules that we enforce:

▼ A day, client, and start and end times must be selected.

■ You cannot have an end time that is before a start time.

▲ You cannot have two tasks that start at the same time on the same day.

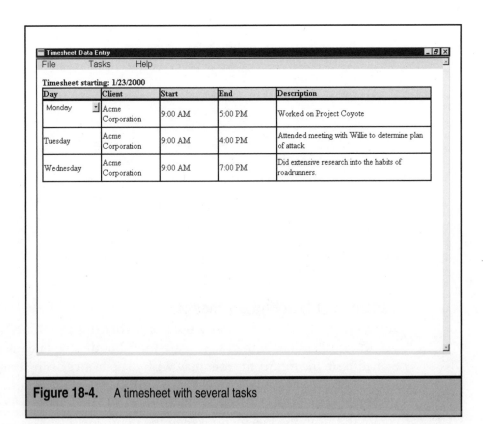

Figure 18-4.   A timesheet with several tasks

These rules are enforced in the validateData function. The code for
the save process is as follows:

```
function saveTimesheet(){
  if (validateData() == false)
    return;
  var resultsArray = workArea.getGridData()
  var rootNode = currentTS.documentElement;
  var clonedRoot = rootNode.cloneNode(false);
  currentTS.documentElement = clonedRoot;
  if (resultsArray != null){
    //loop through the elements from the grid and build the XML document
    for(var count = 0;count<resultsArray.length;count+=5){
      newElement = currentTS.createElement("task");
      newElement.setAttribute("day", resultsArray[count]);
      newElement.setAttribute("clientID", resultsArray[count+1]);
      newElement.setAttribute("startTime", resultsArray[count+2]);
```

```
        newElement.setAttribute("endTime", resultsArray[count+3]);
        newElement.text = resultsArray[count+4];
        currentTS.documentElement.appendChild(newElement);
    }
    common.saveXMLDocument(currentTS, activePath);
    var path = common.getDataPath();
    tsList.async = false;
    tsList.load(path + "timeSheetList.xml");
    var fileName = activePath.slice(path.length);
    var markModified = tsList.selectSingleNode("//timeSheet[@file='" +
fileName + "']");
    markModified.setAttribute("status", "modified");
    common.saveXMLDocument(tsList, path + "timeSheetList.xml");
  }
}
```

Recalling or Deleting a Timesheet

After saving the data, the user would probably close the timesheet or exit the application, both of which are found under the File menu. Sometime in the future, the user may wish to open an existing timesheet to add/modify the tasks, or they may wish to delete the timesheet from their machine. To do this, the user selects the Open or Delete command from the File menu. When the main document is notified of either action, it opens a dialog (selectSheet.htm) that allows the user to select the timesheet they wish to open or delete. To simplify the code required to display the list of timesheets, we use an XSL style sheet (selectSheet.xsl) to specify the display format of the timesheet list. The same document is used for either action, and a parameter is passed into the document to specify which "mode" it is in, complete or open. Figure 18-5 shows the dialog in the open mode.

If the dialog is being used to open a document, both open (documents that have not been set complete) and completed timesheets are displayed. However, if the dialog is being used to delete a document, only documents that are open are displayed. Once the user has selected the timesheet and clicked the Open or Delete button, either the path to the timesheet is returned or the timesheet is deleted and removed from the timesheet list.

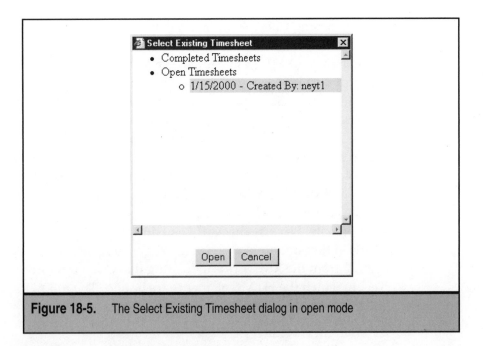

Figure 18-5.   The Select Existing Timesheet dialog in open mode

Marking a Timesheet Complete

After having entered all the data for a particular week, the user will
want to mark the timesheet complete, which serves as a flag to tell
the program the timesheet can be transferred to the server. The way
that the user does this is to open the timesheet they wish to mark
complete and then select Set Complete from the File menu. By selecting
this item, the user is telling the application to move the current
timesheet from the Open section of the timesheet list XML document
to the Completed section of the document, and then saving the
updated timesheet list.

Editing the Client List

One maintenance task that a user may need to do prior to actually
creating a timesheet is add their list of clients. The reason I say *may* is
because the application could be distributed with a preconfigured list
of clients. But in cases where the user needs to modify the client list,
they can easily do so by selecting the Clients option under the File

menu. Choosing Clients displays a dialog that allows the user to add/edit/delete clients. Figure 18-6 shows the Edit Clients dialog.

We used the XML Data source object (XMLDSO) to perform the editing of the client list. We ran into an issue when building this piece of functionality. This issue centered on the fact that what we are editing is actually the dropDown.xml file, and we have an XML schema associated with the document. When we get the XML for the column node we want to edit from the drop-down document (in our case, column two contains the clients), there is an attribute on this node called xmlns. Because of this attribute, a recordset is created to hold the attribute, and another recordset is created that contains the item elements. Because the XMLDSO does not support adding records in this situation, a problem arises. To rectify this, we strip the attribute from the XML prior to loading the XML string into our XML object to which the HTML elements are bound. The following is the code that we used to initialize our XML data source:

```
function initialize(){
  dropDown.async = false;
  dropDown.load("dropDown.xml");
  var root =
dropDown.selectSingleNode("//column[@columnIndex='2']");
  var clonedRoot = root.cloneNode(true);
  clonedRoot.removeAttribute("columnIndex");
  clientList.async = false;
  xmlString = clonedRoot.xml;
  var regExp = new RegExp("xmlns=\".*\"");
  //Strip out the xmlns attribute
  withoutXMLNS = xmlString.replace(regExp, "");
  clientList.loadXML(withoutXMLNS);
  clientList.recordset.MoveFirst();
}
```

After the user has finished editing client list and clicked the Save button, we use the XML node from our XMLDSO and replace the existing XML node in the drop-down document. The following code shows this functionality:

```
function saveClientList(){
  clientList.documentElement.setAttribute("columnIndex", "2");
  var oldElement =
dropDown.selectSingleNode("//column[@columnIndex='2']");
  dropDown.documentElement.replaceChild(clientList.documentElement,
oldElement);
  var dataPath = common.getDataPath();
  common.saveXMLDocument(dropDown, dataPath + "dropDown.xml");
  window.close();
}
```

Sending Data to the Server

The final major piece of functionality in the client application is
sending data to the server. To send the completed timesheets to
the server, the user selects the Send To Server item from the File
menu. The application then retrieves a list of files built from the
timeSheetList.xml file that need to be transferred to the server.
The list contains only those elements in the completed section of
the document that have a status not equal to *sent*, as well as
items that do not have a status (do not have a status attribute).
The application then loops through this list and loads each of
the XML documents, verifying the documents against the current
XML schema that is stored on the server. As stated earlier, this

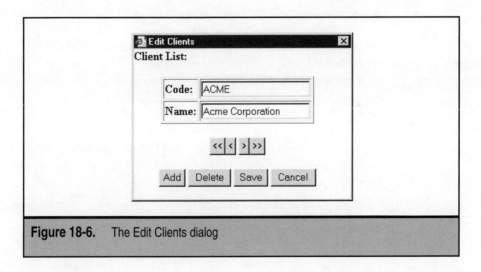

Figure 18-6.   The Edit Clients dialog

validates that the version of the document is compatible with the version of the document the server is expecting.

After verifying the version, the application uses the xmlHTTP object (getClientXML.asp, discussed in more detail a little later) to transfer the XML documents to the server. The server returns "accepted" if the document was successfully saved to the database; otherwise it returns an error. To keep the user informed of the status of the file transfer, we display a dialog that contains that status. The contents of this dialog are built dynamically in code, and in most cases the file transfer happens too quickly to even read the status messages. The following is the code used to transfer the timesheet XML documents to the server.

```
function sendTimesheets(){
  var path = common.getDataPath();
  var serverPath = common.getServerPath();
  var xmlRequestObject = new ActiveXObject("Microsoft.XMLHTTP");
  var sendDocument = new ActiveXObject("Microsoft.XMLDOM");
  var fileName;
  //Display the status window
  var status = window.open("about:blank", null,
"height=200,width=400,status=no,toolbar=no,menubar=no,location=no,resizable=
no,titlebar=no,left=200,top=200");
  status.document.write("Establishing list of items to transfer.<BR>");
  sendDocument.async = false;
  tsList.async = false;
  tsList.load(path + "timeSheetList.xml");
  //Get the list of items to transfer
  var sendList = tsList.selectNodes("//Completed/timeSheet[@status != 'sent'
or not(@status)]");
  var sendSheet = sendList.nextNode();
  var createdBy;
  var result="accepted";
  var count=0;
  //Loop thought list - continue till the end of list or an error
  while (sendSheet != null && result=="accepted"){
    count++;
    status.document.write("Transfering Item" + count + "<BR>");
    fileName = sendSheet.getAttribute("file");
    sendDocument.load(path + fileName);
    //All documents should have XML if there isn't XML then the file
```

```
      // is bad or the version is different
    if (sendDocument.xml == ""){
      sendDocument.resolveExternals = false;
      sendDocument.load(path + fileName);
      if (sendDocument.xml != "")
        alert("The version of the document is incompatible with the
anticipated version of data on the server.");
      else
        alert("An error has occured while loading a timesheet that was to be
transfered. Error Reason: " + sendDocument.parseError.reason);
      sendDocument.resolveExternals = true;
      status.close();
      return;
    }
    createdBy = sendSheet.getAttribute("createdBy");
    //Pass in the information to the server from the list file
    // that is needed on the server
    filePath = serverPath + "getClientXML.asp?file=" + escape(fileName) +
"&createdBy=" + escape(createdBy);
    //Send the document to the server
    xmlRequestObject.open("POST", filePath, false, "", "");
    xmlRequestObject.send(sendDocument);
    sendSheet.setAttribute("status", "sent");
    sendSheet = sendList.nextNode();
    result = xmlRequestObject.responseText;
  }
  if (sendList.length > 0 && result== "accepted"){
    common.saveXMLDocument(tsList, path + "timeSheetList.xml");
  }
  if (sendList.length > 0 && result != "accepted"){
    status.document.write(result);
    alert("An error has occured in the transfering process. Please try
again.");
    status.close();
    return;
  }
  status.close();
  if (sendList.length > 0)
    alert("The data has been successfully transferred to the server.");
  else
    alert("There are no new items to transfer.");
}
```

BUILDING THE SERVER APPLICATION

The application on the server is broken down into two different pieces: the piece that retrieves the timesheets from the client and the much larger piece used to look up timesheets. The retrieval portion of the application simply takes the XML document returned to the server and inserts the data from the document into the database. The lookup portion allows a user to search for a timesheet and view either the details of a timesheet or a summary for the selected timesheet(s).

The Server-side Database

Before we can get into the details of the server application's functionality, we must first talk about the design of the server-side database. The database (timesheet.mdb) is a Microsoft Access 97 database that contains the timesheet information along with user and user-rights information. The tables that are used to store the timesheet data on the server are similar in structure to the timesheet and timesheet list XML documents. The TimesheetList table stores the filename, who created the timesheet, and the start date for the timesheet. In addition to these fields, this table contains an AutoNumber (counter) field (FileID), which is used to relate the timesheet to the details for the timesheet. The details (tasks) for the timesheet are stored in the TimesheetDetail table. Similar to the timesheet files on the client, this table contains the following information for a task: the day of the task, the client ID, the start and end times, the description of the task, and the FileID to relate the task to the TimesheetList table.

The Users table simply contains the user IDs, passwords, and user names for the individuals that are allowed to run the lookup application. This table is simply used by the login component to validate the user. The UserRights and ClientRights tables are used to define which users and clients a user of the lookup application can view. These tables simply contain the user ID and the timesheet creators or clients for which the user can view timesheets. The way the application is designed is that if a user does not have any users or client rights specified, the user can view all of the timesheets. This piece of functionality is important in that it allows you to let a client view the timesheets of all of the people who did work for them, but they cannot see work that was performed for other clients. In addition, you could allow a manager to view only the timesheets of the individuals who work for him or her, not those of all of the other individuals. The viewing rights can also be combined so that a user can only view a particular client's data and can only view certain people who did work for that client. Even though this is a fairly simple structure, it allows you pretty good flexibility in specifying user rights.

Components Used on the Server

Our server-side application uses two different Active Server Page Windows Script Components: a login component and a common functionality component for the server application. The login component (TimesheetLoginScript.wsc) is the same component that we developed in Chapter 16. The only modification we made was to point the component to our new database. The common source component (CommonFunctionality.wsc) allows us to centralize code that would otherwise have to be repeated in several different active server pages. Table 18-3 lists and describes the common methods and properties for this component.

The Data Receiver Portion of the Server Application

The receiver portion of the server application is composed of a single ASP (getClientData.asp). The server page receives data in two forms: from the XML file sent to the server and from the query string passed to the server. The query string's data contains the information that is inserted into the TimesheetList table (the filename, the creator, and the start date). The ASP uses the filename and creator to determine if this timesheet has been sent to the server before. If it hasn't, it creates a new row in the TimesheetList table and then retrieves the FileID for

Method/Property	Description
formatDate(longDateFormat)	Takes the long formatted date (mm/dd/yy hh:mm:ss:ms) that is returned from the database and returns just the mm/dd/yyyy portion of the date.
getDatabaseObject()	Creates an ActiveX Data Object (ADO) database object and automatically connects to the database. Provides a central location that contains the location of the database.
replaceQuotes(dataField, replaceType)	If the replaceType is XML, it replaces quotation marks (") with the XML-friendly &quote. Otherwise it replaces single quotes (') with two single quotes (") to allow us to safely write SQL statements, which contain data with single quotes.
setRightsProperties(userID, addTimeSheetDetail)	Connects to the database and in the tables and where properties with the strings that are used for the client and user rights functionality. The addTimeSheetDetail flag tells the function if the tables property needs to also contain the syntax for the join between the Timesheet and TimesheetDetail tables or if this join is already specified in the calling function's SQL statement.
tables	Contains the tables that need to be added to the SQL statement to limit the data that is shown to the user, based on their user and client rights. Filled in by the setRightsProperties method call.
where	Contains the where clause that needs to be added to the SQL statement to limit the data that is shown to the user based on their user and client rights. Filled in by the setRightsProperties method call.

Table 18-3.   Methods and Properties of the CommonFunctionality Component

the newly inserted timesheet. If the timesheet has been uploaded previously, the server retrieves the FileID for that item and uses the FileID to delete all of the existing detail records in the TimesheetDetail table. At this point, the ASP loops through all of the detail records (tasks) in the XML file and can simply insert the tasks into the TimesheetDetail table. If all of the data manipulation completes successfully, the ASP returns the value accepted; otherwise it relies on the built-in processes of the ASP environment to capture the error in the script and automatically return the error message.

The Lookup Portion of the Server Application

Now that we have all of this timesheet data on the server, we are ready to build an application that allows users to query this data. The lookup application provides a secure mechanism to allow a user to narrow down the data they wish to view. We will cover the lookup application in the same manner that we covered the client application, by leading you through how a user would use the application.

The Login Process

The majority of the login functionality is encapsulated in the login component. All that we need to do is to set the properties of the component in our login ASP (login.asp) and magically we have a login dialog. After the user submits their login information, we use the validate.asp page to instantiate the login component again and validate the user. This page then either redirects the user back to the login (if the login was unsuccessful) or redirects the user to the main application page (if successful). Figure 18-7 shows what our login document looks like. For more details on the login component, see our discussion on the component in Chapter 16.

Defining the Lookup Query

After the user has successfully logged into the application, they are presented with a frames page that contains two frames: one to define the lookup parameters (lookup_timesheet.asp) and another to display the results of the lookup. Initially, the results portion contains

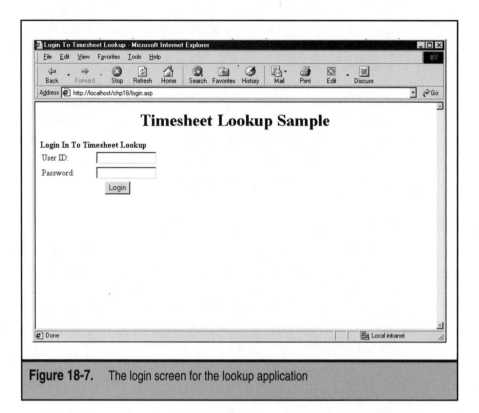

Figure 18-7.   The login screen for the lookup application

an empty HTML document (empty.htm). Figure 18-8 shows the initial view the user is presented with.

When the parameter definition document is sent to the client, the list of names (timesheet creators) is prepopulated with the people for whom the user is authorized to view data. The Client and Date drop-downs are populated only with the all item. When the user clicks on the drop-down, the document uses remote scripting to retrieve the appropriate data from the server (calls remotecalls.asp). It is important to note that when we go to the server to populate both the Client and Date lists, we check to see if a name is selected. If one has been, we pass that name to the server. If a name is selected, the remote scripting ASP then returns only the clients or dates that correspond to that person and that the user is authorized to see. If the user clicks the Date drop-down, the getAvailableDates function is called. Otherwise, if the user clicks the Client drop-down, the

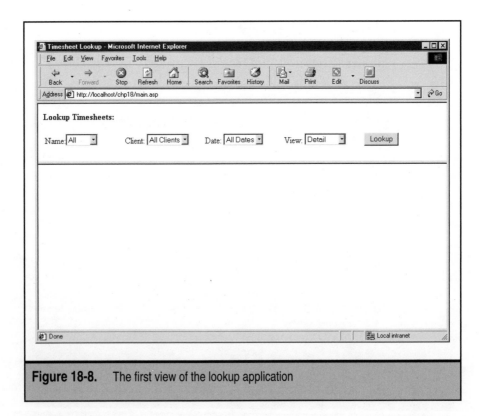

Figure 18-8.   The first view of the lookup application

getAvailableClients function is called. Both of these functions return a delimited string (the delimiter is passed into the function call) containing the available dates or clients, which the lookup document parses and adds to the drop-downs. The following is the ASP code used in the remote scripting operation to return the data to the client:

remoteCalls.asp

```
<%@ LANGUAGE=VBSCRIPT %>
<% RSDispatch %>
<!--#INCLUDE VIRTUAL="/_scriptLibrary/rs.asp"-->
<SCRIPT RUNAT=SERVER Language="JavaScript">
function Description(){
  this.getAvailableDates = getAvailableDates;
  this.getAvailableClients = getAvailableClients;
}
```

```
public_description = new Description();
function getAvailableDates(delimeter, selectedName){
  return commonGetAvailable(delimeter, selectedName, "dates");
}
function getAvailableClients(delimeter, selectedName){
  return commonGetAvailable(delimeter, selectedName,
"clients");
}
function commonGetAvailable(delimeter, selectedName, dataType){
  var nameList = "";
  var common = Server.CreateObject("CommonFunctionality.WSC");

  var conn = common.getDatabaseObject();
  var sql;
  var dataElement;
  var userID = Session("UserID");
  var where = "";
  if (dataType == "dates"){
    sql = "select distinct StartDate from TimesheetList ";
    common.setRightsProperties(userID, true);
  }
  else{
    sql = "select distinct ClientID from  ";
    common.setRightsProperties(userID, true);
  }
  selectedName = unescape(selectedName);
  if (dataType == "dates"){
    if (common.tables != "")
      sql += common.tables;
  }
  else{
    if (common.tables != "")
      sql += "TimesheetList " + common.tables;
    else
      sql += "TimesheetDetail INNER JOIN TimesheetList ON
TimesheetDetail.FileID=TimesheetList.FileID ";
  }
  if (selectedName != "All")
    where = " CreatedBy = '" +
```

```
common.replaceQuotes(selectedName) + "'" ;
  if (common.where != "") {
    if (where != "")
      where += " and ";
    where += common.where;
  }
  if (where != "")
    sql += " where " + where;
  rs = conn.Execute(sql);
  while (rs.EOF == false) {
    dataElement = rs(0);
    if (dataType == "dates")
      dataElement = common.formatDate(dataElement);
    nameList += dataElement + delimeter;
    rs.MoveNext();
  }
  return nameList;
}</SCRIPT>
```

Processing the Query and Returning the Results

After the user has selected the criteria and clicked the Lookup button,
the criteria definition document determines which browser type and
version the user is running. If the user is running IE 5, the results of
the detailsClient.asp are loaded into the results frame of the
document; otherwise the results of the details.asp page are loaded
into the frame. The primary difference between the two results
versions is that the IE 5 version sends an HTML document to the
client that calls back to the server to return an XML document to the
client where an XSL style sheet is used to display the results. The
non–IE 5 version still uses the same XSL style sheet, but all of the
processing is done on the server and only an HTML result document
is sent to the client.

The criteria document passes the values of each of the selected
drop-down options to the server as part of the query string. It is
important to note that we don't want to submit the criteria document
to the server because this would cause us to have to reload this
document. One of the drop-down options the user can choose is the
view of the results, either a detailed view or a summary view. The

detailed view displays all of the tasks including the start, end, and description of tasks grouped by a timesheet creator for a particular week. The summary view shows the amount of time a timesheet creator spent at a particular client for a week. Because these are two fairly different views of the same data, we have two different ASPs (buildTimesheet.asp and buildTimesheetSummary.asp) that read the database and build XML documents based on the criteria. The following are samples of output XML documents generated by each ASP.

Here is the output from buildTimesheet.asp:

```xml
<timeSheetGroup>
<timeSheet startDate="1/9/2000" createdBy="neyt1">
  <task day="Wednesday" clientID="KOM" startTime="09:00 AM"
endTime="06:00 dPM">Completed prototype of XML on an NT Server</task>
  <task day="Tuesday" clientID="KOM" startTime="09:00 AM" endTime="05:00
PM">Began working on prototype of XML on an NT Server</task>
  <task day="Monday" clientID="KOM" startTime="09:00 AM" endTime="05:00
PM">Did investigation into XML and XML Schemas</task>
</timeSheet>
<timeSheet startDate="1/16/2000" createdBy="neyt12">
  <task day="Monday" clientID="KOM" startTime="12:00 AM" endTime="05:00
AM">Fixed crashed hard drive on production server.</task>
</timeSheet>
</timeSheetGroup>
```

Here is the output from buildTimesheetSummary.asp:

```xml
<timeSheetList>
  <timeSheetSummary startDate="1/9/2000" startInt="947397600000"
createdBy="neyt1" clientID="KOM" duration="1500" />
  <timeSheetSummary startDate="1/16/2000" startInt="948002400000"
createdBy="neyt12" clientID="KOM" duration="300" />
</timeSheetList>
```

As stated earlier, in the non–IE 5 version of the results document, the XML document that is generated by the build timesheets ASP is loaded and transformed on the server. The server uses the timesheet.xsl style sheet to transform the document and inserts the results of the transformation into the stream of HTML that is being

sent to the client. The IE 5 version of the results document loads the
XML document to the client and performs the same transformation
also using the timsheet.xsl style sheet. Figure 18-9 shows the output
of a detailed timesheet lookup using IE 5. It is important to note that
the output would look the same in other browsers.

To show you the advantages of using the client-side version of the
transformation, we added functionality to the summary version of
the lookup to be able to sort data, based on the different data elements
returned. All of this processing takes place on the client and is just a
simple retransformation of the data with a different order-by attribute
in our XSL style sheet. One of the difficulties we came across when
developing this functionality was how to dynamically tell the XSL
document how to order the data. What we ended up doing was the

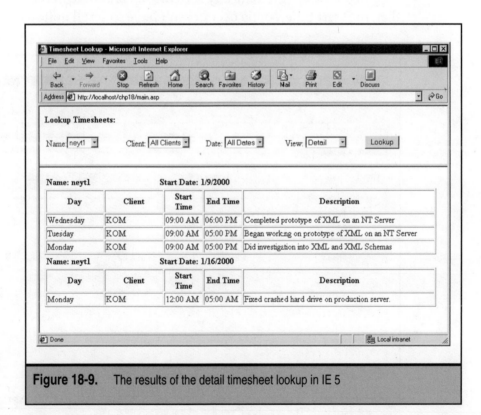

Figure 18-9.   The results of the detail timesheet lookup in IE 5

following: before we run the transformation each time, we modify the order-by attribute in the XSL document using the XML DOM. Figure 18-10 shows our enhanced IE 5 version of the summary lookup.

WHAT'S MISSING FROM THE APPLICATION

While our example application is fairly complete, there are, however, a few items that you might want to add if you were to use the application in a production environment. One blanket statement we can make about the application is that it needs more error checking, both on the client and server side.

On the client side, you would probably want to add some usability features, such as automatically selecting an end time that is greater than the start time, so the user doesn't have to scroll quite as much.

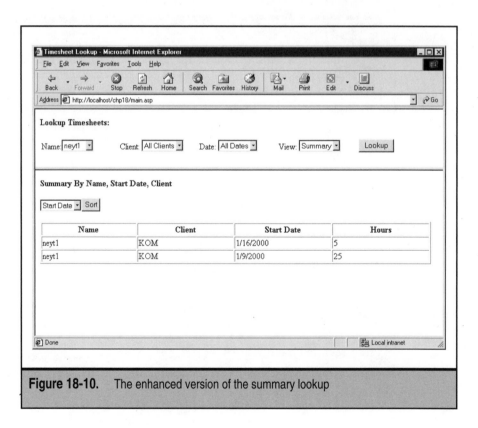

Figure 18-10. The enhanced version of the summary lookup

Additionally, you might want to allow the user to set up default start and end times, storing these values in the settings document. You would also probably need to add more detailed increments into the start and end times, such as 9:00, 9:10, 9:20, and so on, rather than just hourly increments.

In addition to the usability features, you might also want to add the ability for a user to define a period of nonbillable time for a task. For example, let's say we worked from 9:00 AM to 5:00 PM, but we took an hour lunch from 12:00 PM to 1:00 PM. In the current system you could create two tasks: one from 9:00 AM to 12:00 PM and another from 1:00 PM to 5:00 PM. It might be nice to just create one task with a nonbillable time designator.

On the server side, you might want to enhance the lookup to allow sorting on all platforms, not just IE 5. This would, of course, require a complete refresh of the results page, but it might be a nice touch.

The final item you might think about adding—which was out of the scope of our project—is the ability for a person to approve a timesheet online. Once a timesheet was approved, you could then send off a paper invoice, or better yet you could automatically send an XML document that was an electronic version of an invoice. This could significantly improve the whole timesheet process and lead to more efficient and accurate processing.

SUMMARY

Overall, the application is a pretty cool example that shows you how to solve a real-world business problem. As stated, there are a few enhancements we would make before using this application in a production environment; however, it builds a pretty solid foundation. This application touches almost all of the topics that were covered in the book and shows you how complementary these technologies are to one another.

PART VII

Appendixes

APPENDIX A

JavaScript

This appendix covers JavaScript variables and naming, data types, operators, control flow, built-in message boxes, trapping and handling errors, and built-in objects. Let's start off, though, by covering a few JavaScript ground rules.

SOME BASIC JAVASCRIPT RULES

▼ All JavaScript statements should be terminated with a semicolon (;), as shown here:

```
x = 10;
```

■ The equal sign (=) is used to assign a value.

■ JavaScript is case-sensitive.

■ Blocks of JavaScript statements are surrounded by braces ({}). The following function is an example of a block of statements:

```
function x(){
   y=10;
   z=/;
}
```

■ Functions let you wrap several operations into a single name. These operations can also return data. The return statement is used to exit a function and return data (if desired). The following shows a function using a return statement:

```
function x(){
   return 10;
}
```

■ You can place comments in code using either a single-line comment or a block comment. The single-line comment is prefixed with two forward slashes (//). A block or multiple-line comment begins with the forward slash–asterisk combo (/*) and ends with the asterisk–forward slash combo (*/). The following shows both comment types:

```
function x(){
   /*The purpose of this function
     is to return 10
```

```
*/
//Returns ten
return 10;
}
```

ARIABLES AND NAMING

As JavaScript is a loosely typed language, variables in JavaScript technically have no fixed type. Instead, they have a type equivalent to the type of the value they contain. Although not required, it is considered good practice to declare all of your variables prior to using them. To do this, you use the var statement:

```
var x;
```

If you declare a variable, as just shown, the variable exists, but the value of it is undefined. It is important to note that *undefined* is a special value that can be tested for. It is also important to note that you can initialize the variable in the var statement, as shown here:

```
var x = 10;
```

There may be cases where you wish to declare and initialize a variable, but you don't want the variable to contain any particular value. To do this, you can set the variable equal to null (and you can easily test if a variable equals null), as shown here:

```
var x = null;
```

Variable names can be of any length and must start with a letter, an underscore (_), or a dollar sign ($). Subsequent characters can be letters, numbers, underscores, or dollar signs. In addition, variables cannot be named the same as reserved words, which are listed at the very end of this appendix.

ATA TYPES

JavaScript has four main data types: strings, numbers, objects, and Booleans. In addition to the four main data types, a variable or value can be of the type null or undefined. String data types are delineated by single (') or double (") quotes and can be initialized to a zero-length string by setting the variable equal to "" or ". It is important to note that a string is also an object, a topic we will cover later in this appendix. Numbers support both integer and floating-point values. Integers can be expressed in base 10, 8, or 16. Octal integers are prefixed with a leading 0, and they can contain digits 0 through 7. Hexadecimal (hex) integers are specified by a leading 0x and can contain digits 0 through 9 and letters A through F. Booleans contain either the special values true or false. These values *cannot* be used as either 1 or 0.

JAVASCRIPT OPERATORS

Here are JavaScript's assignment operators:

Operator	Description
=	Assignment. Example: x=1.
+=	Addition. Example: x +=y. Result: x = x plus y.
&=	Bitwise And. Example: x &=y. Result: x = x bitwise and y.
|=	Bitwise Or. Example: x |=y. Result: x = x bitwise or y.
^=	Bitwise Xor. Example x ^=y. Result x = x bitwise Xor y
/=	Division. Example: x /=y. Result: x = x divided y.
<<=	Left shift. Example: x <<=y. Result: x = x shift bits to the left y locations.
%=	Modulus. Example: x %=y. Result: x = x modulus y.
*=	Multiplication. Example: x *=y. Result: x = x multiplied by y.
>>=	Right shift. Example: x >>=y. Result: x = x shift bits to the right y locations.
-=	Subtraction. Example: x -=y. Result: x = x minus y.
>>>=	Unsigned right shift. Example: x >>>=y. Result: x = x shift bits to the right y locations and fill 0s in from the left, discarding bits shifted off to the right.

The next list covers JavaScript's computational operators:

Operator	Description
-	Negation.
++	Increment by 1.
--	Decrement by 1.
*	Multiplication.
/	Division.
%	Modulus (that is, return the remainder).
+	Addition.
-	Subtraction.

The next list covers JavaScript's logical operators:

Operator	Description
!	Logical not.
<	Less than.
>	Greater than.
<=	Less than or equal.
>=	Greater than or equal.
==	Equality (two equal signs).
!=	Not equal.
&&	Logical AND.
||	Logical OR.
?:	Conditional. Example: x > y ? return x : return y. Translation: if x is greater than y, then return x, otherwise return y. This provides a mechanism similar to an if…else control flow statement.

Operator	Description
,	Sequential operation. This operator causes two operations to be performed sequentially. Example: for (x=0;x>y; x++, z++).
===	Identity (3 equal signs). This operator is used to perform an equality check without type conversion.
!==	Nonidentity. This operator is used to perform an inequality check without type conversion.

Here are JavaScript's bitwise operators:

Operator	Description
~	Bitwise NOT.
<<	Bitwise left shift.
>>	Bitwise right shift.
>>>	Unsigned right shift. This operator shifts bits to the right and fill 0s in from the left, discarding bits shifted off to the right.
&	Bitwise AND.
^	Bitwise XOR.
|	Bitwise OR.

Finally, here are some other, miscellaneous JavaScript operators:

Operator	Description
delete	Deletes a property from an object, or removes an element from an array.
typeof	Returns a string that specifies the data type of the variable. Possible values: number, string, boolean, object, function, and undefined.
void	Prevents an expression from returning a value.

ONTROL FLOW

Code control flow allows you to check different conditions and execute different code based on the result of a test. There are two types of control flow: conditional statements and looping.

onditional Statements

JavaScript supports two different conditional statements: if...else and the switch case. The if...else statements have the following general form:

```
if (condition)
{   //{Required only if there are multiple statements inside true part
    //code executed if condition is true
}   //}Required only if there are multiple statements inside true part
else
{   //{Required only if there are multiple statements inside false part
    //code executed if condition is false
}   //}Required only if there are multiple statements inside false part
```

The following are some basic rules for an if...else statement:

▼ The else portion is optional.

■ Multiple statements inside of the check must be enclosed in braces.

▲ If statements can be nested.

Switch case statements have the following general form:

```
switch (expression){
  case value:
    //one or more statements
    break;
  case value2:
    //one or more statements
    break;
  default:
```

```
        //one or more statements
}
```

The following are some basic rules for a switch case statement:

▼ Once the expression matches a value in a case statement, the code in the switch will continue running until a break is encountered, even if another case statement is encountered.

■ The default clause is executed if none of the other values match the expression.

▲ You can have zero or more case clauses.

Loops

JavaScript supports four different types of loops, which allow you to execute blocks of code repeatedly. The four loop types are for, for in, while, and do while.

The for loop specifies a counter variable, a test condition, and an action that updates the counter. Just before each time the loop is executed, the condition is tested. After the loop is executed, the counter variable is updated before the next iteration begins. For loops have the following general form:

```
for (counter=0;counter <= x; counter++){
  // one or more statements
}
```

For in loops are a special type of loop that allows you to step through all of the properties in an object. The built-in loop counter steps through all of the indexes in the array of properties. The following is the general form of a for in loop:

```
// obj is an object with several properties
for (property in obj){
  // one or more statements
}
```

While loops are similar to for loops, except they don't use the counter as the test of whether to continue. Instead, the result of an expression is checked to see if it is equal to true. If it is, the code inside the loop is executed; if not, the loop is ended. The following is the general form of a while loop:

```
while (expression > 100){
// one or more statements
}
```

The final loop type, the do while loop, is similar to the while loop except that the do while loop always executes a statement block at least once, repeating execution of the loop until a condition expression at the end of the loop evaluates to false. The following is the general form of a do while loop:

```
do {
  // one or more statements
}
while (expression > 100)
```

There are two statements that are useful in controlling looping execution: break and continue. The break statement provides a mechanism to stop the execution of the loop, and the continue statement automatically jumps to the next iteration of the loop. The following is a very simple example of using the two loop execution control statements:

```
for (counter=0;counter<x;counter++){
  z=myArray[counter];
  if (counter == 0)
    continue;
  if (z=="matching")
    break;
}
```

BUILT-IN MESSAGE BOXES

JavaScript includes three different methods to present information to the user and get user feedback. The simplest of the three is the alert method, which is used to simply display a message to the user with an OK button. The following is a sample of using the alert method (Figure A-1 shows the results):

```
alert("Simple Message");
```

The confirm method allows you to display a message with OK and Cancel buttons. If the user selects the OK button, true is returned by the method;

Figure A-1. The results from using the alert method

otherwise, false is returned. The following is a sample of using the confirm method (Figure A-2 shows the results):

```
confirm("Are you sure you want to delete the item");
```

The prompt method allows you to display a message and a text box to capture user input. The method takes two parameters: the message to display above the text box and the default value to display in the text box. If the user selects the OK button, the value entered into the text box is returned. The following is a sample of using the prompt method (Figure A-3 shows the results):

```
prompt("Enter your favorite day of the week", "Friday");
```

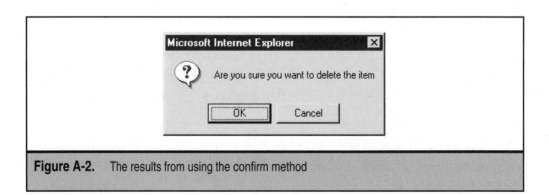

Figure A-2. The results from using the confirm method

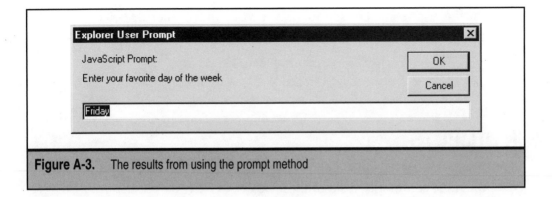

Figure A-3.   The results from using the prompt method

TRAPPING AND HANDLING ERRORS

There may be cases in your JavaScript code when you want to handle unforeseen errors that may occur in a block of code. As you may know, if a JavaScript error is not trapped (in a browser environment), the user will be presented with an error message dialog. What you may wish to do is to trap these errors and display a more intelligent error message to the user. To support error handling, JavaScript has the fairly simple syntax of the try and catch statements. The general format of these statements follows:

```
try {
  //some code that could fail
}
catch (e){
//handle the error
}
```

The catch (e) statement handles any errors that may have occurred in the try block. The variable e in the catch statement will contain an error object that holds information about the error that you can use to display additional detail. The error object contains two properties: description and number (contains the error number).

There may be cases where you wish to raise your own error that could be trapped at a higher level or simply displayed to the user. To raise an error, you use the throw statement, which has one argument that is an expression. You could simply specify the string for the error or the number for the error. However, a more common way to handle this is to create an error object and pass it as the argument. The following shows creating an error object and raising an error:

```
var err = new Error(9999, "This is a sample error);
throw err;
```

BUILT-IN OBJECTS

There are a number of built-in objects in JavaScript. In this section, we will cover the most commonly used of these objects. When we are listing the constructors, we are listing the different methods you can use to create and initialize the object.

Array Object

Here are the array object constructors used in JavaScript:

```
var newArray = new Array();
var newArray = new Array(size);
var newArray = new Array(element0, element1, element2....);
```

In the list below, brackets ([]) denote an optional attribute:

Member	Description
concat(array2)	Returns an array that contains the two arrays combined.
length	Returns the length of the array, which is one greater than the greatest element defined in an array, as arrays are zero-based.
join(separator)	Returns a string object that consist of all the elements in the array concatenated together using the specified separator.
reverse()	Returns an array object with each of the elements of the array reversed (that is, 1,2,3 becomes 3,2,1).

Member	Description
slice(start [, end])	Returns an array object containing a portion of the array. If the end is not specified, it returns from the start position to the end of the array.
sort([sortfunction])	Returns an array object with the elements sorted. If the sort function is not specified, the data is sorted in ASCII character order. If you specify the sort function, the function will receive two values and will return a negative value if the first argument is less than the second argument, zero if the two arguments are equal, or a positive value if the first argument is greater than the second argument.
toString	Returns a string object that consists of all the elements in the array concatenated together using a comma delimiter (,).

Date Object

Here are the date object constructors used in JavaScript:

```
var newDateObj = new Date();
var newDateObj = new Date(dateVal);
var newDateObj = new Date(year, month, date[, hours[, minutes[,
seconds[,ms]]]]);
```

Notes: the dateVal is a number that refers to the number of milliseconds in UTC (Universal Coordinated Time) between the date and January 1, 1970. Brackets ([]) denote an optional attribute.

Member	Description
getDate()	Returns the day of the month for the date, such as 2. Values are between 1 and 31.
getDay()	Returns a number that corresponds to the day of the week for the date. Returns 0 for Sunday through 6 for Saturday.

Member	Description
getFullYear()	Returns the year value for the date in four-digit form.
getHours()	Returns the hours value for the date in 24-hour format. Returns 0 if the hours were not specified for the date.
getMilliseconds()	Returns the milliseconds value for the date. Returns 0 if the milliseconds were not specified for the date.
getMinutes()	Returns the minutes value for the date. Returns 0 if the minutes were not specified for the date.
getMonth()	Returns the month number, with January as 0 through December as 11.
getSeconds()	Returns the seconds value for the date. Returns 0 if the seconds were not specified for the date.
getTime()	Returns an integer that refers to the number of milliseconds between the date and January 1, 1970 UTC. Negative numbers indicate dates before January 1, 1970.
getTimezoneOffset()	Returns the difference in the number of minutes between the time on the computer where the script is running and UTC.
getUTCDate()	Returns the day of the month for the date, such as 2, using UTC format. Values are between 1 and 31.
getUTCDay()	Returns a number that corresponds to the day of the week for the date, using UTC format. Returns 0 for Sunday through 6 for Saturday.

Member	Description
getUTCFullYear()	Returns the year value for the date in four-digit form, using UTC format.
getUTCHours()	Returns the hours value for the date in 24-hour format, using UTC format. Returns 0 if the hours were not specified for the date.
getUTCMilliSeconds()	Returns the milliseconds value for the date, using UTC format. Returns 0 if the milliseconds were not specified for the date.
getUTCMinutes()	Returns the minutes value for the date, using UTC format. Returns 0 if the minutes were not specified for the date.
getUTCMonth()	Returns the month number, using UTC format, with January as 0 through December as 11.
getUTCSeconds()	Returns the seconds value for the date, using UTC format. Returns 0 if the seconds were not specified for the date.
getVarDate()	Returns the VT_DATE value in a Date object. This is only used with ActixeX objects that accept dates in VT_DATE format.

Member	Description
setDate(dateValue)	Sets the numeric date for the object. If the value specified is greater than the number of days in the month or is negative, the date is set to a date equal to the specified value minus the number of days in the stored month. Example: if the current date in the object is May 3, 2000, and setDate(33) is called, the date changes to June 2, 2000. Negative numbers would decrease the current value.
setFullYear(yearValue [,monthValue, dayValue])	Sets the year for the date. You can optionally use this method to set the month and day values.
setHours(hoursValue [,minutesValue, secondsValue, millisecondValue])	Sets the hours for the object. Can also be used to set the remainder of the time values. If the value specified is greater than the number of hours in a day or is negative, the value of date is changed accordingly. Example: if the current date in the object is May 3, 2000 00:00:00:00, and setDate(25) is called, the date changes to May 4, 2000 01:00:00:00. Negative numbers decrease the current value.
setMilliSeconds(millisecondValue)	Sets the number of milliseconds for the date. If the value specified is greater than 999 or is negative, the number of seconds (and minutes, hours, and so forth as necessary) is incremented or decremented by the appropriate amount.

Member	Description
setMinutes(minutesValue [, secondsValue, millisecondValue])	Sets the minutes for the object. Can also be used to set the seconds and milliseconds of the time value. If the value specified is greater than 59, or is negative, the number of hours (and day, month, and so forth as necessary) is incremented or decremented by the appropriate amount.
setMonth(monthValue [, dayValue])	Sets the month for the object (0 for January through 11 for December) and can also be used to set the day value. If the value specified is greater than 11, or is negative, the year of the date is incremented or decremented accordingly.
setSeconds(secondsValue [, millisecondValue])	Sets the seconds for the object. Can also be used to set the milliseconds of the time value. If the value specified is greater than 59, or is negative, the number of minutes (hours, day, months and so forth as necessary) is incremented or decremented by the appropriate amount.
setTime(milliseconds)	Sets the date and time for the object. The specified argument is an integer that refers to the number of milliseconds between the date and January 1, 1970 UTC. Negative numbers indicate dates before January 1, 1970.

Member	Description
setUTCDate(dateValue)	Sets the numeric date of the object, using UTC format. If the value specified is greater than the number of days in the month, or is negative, the date is set to a date equal to the specified value minus the number of days in the stored month. Example: if the current date in the object is May 3, 2000, and setDate(33) is called, the date changes to June 2, 2000. Negative numbers decrease the current value.
setUTCFullYear(yearValue[, monthValue, dayValue)	Sets the year for the date, using UTC format. You can optionally use this method to set the month and day values.
setUTCHours(hoursValue[, minutesValue, secondsValue, millisecondsValue])	Sets the hours for the object, using UTC format. Can also be used to set the remainder of the time values. If the value specified is greater than the number of hours in a day, or is negative, the value of date is changed accordingly. Example: if the current date in the object is May 3, 2000 00:00:00:00 and setDate(25) is called, the date changes to May 4, 2000 01:00:00:00. Negative numbers decrease the current value.
setUTCMilliseconds (millisecondsValue)	Sets the number of milliseconds for the date, using UTC format. If the value specified is greater than 999, or is negative, the number of seconds (and minutes, hours, and so forth as necessary) is incremented or decremented by the appropriate amount.

Member	Description
setUTCMinutes(minutesValue[, secondsValue, millisecondsValue])	Sets the minutes for the object, using UTC format. Can also be used to set the seconds and milliseconds of the time value. If the value specified is greater than 59 or is negative, the number of hours (and day, month, and so forth as necessary) is incremented or decremented by the appropriate amount.
setUTCMonth(monthValue[, dayValue])	Sets the month for the object (0 for January through 11 for December) and can also be used to set the day value, using UTC format. If the value specified is greater than 11 or is negative, the year for the date is incremented or decremented accordingly.
setUTCSeconds(secondsValue[, millisecondValue])	Sets the seconds for the object, using UTC format. Can also be used to set the milliseconds of the time value. If the value specified is greater than 59 or is negative, the number of minutes (hours, day, month, and so forth as necessary) is incremented or decremented by the appropriate amount.
toGMTString()	Returns the date converted to a string, using Greenwich Mean Time (GMT) format. Example: 03 May 2000 00:00:00 GMT.
toLocaleString()	Returns the date converted to a string, using the date and time format specified on the computer running the script.

Member	Description
toUTCString ()	Returns the date converted to a string, using UTC format.
valueOf()	Returns an integer that refers to the number of milliseconds between the date and January 1, 1970 UTC. Negative numbers indicate dates before January 1, 1970.

Global Object

The global object is an intrinsic object that does not need to be instantiated. Its members are automatically made available as global methods and properties and are simply referenced by their name.

Member	Description
escape(charstring)	Encodes the specified string in Unicode format. All punctuation and non-ASCII characters are encoded in %xx (xx is the ASCII character number) or %uxxxx (for characters with a value greater than 255) format.
eval(codestring)	Evaluates the contents of the string and executes the string as JavaScript code. Provides a mechanism that allows for dynamic execution of code.
Infinity	Returns an initial value of Number.POSITIVE_INFINITY.
isFinite(number)	Determines if a number is finite. Returns true if the number is any value other than NaN, negative infinity, or positive infinity.

Member	Description
isNaN(value)	Determines if a value contains the reserved value NaN (not a number). This value is set to a variable where an attempt is made to convert a value to a number that is not a number.
NaN	Returns the special value NaN, indicating that an expression is not a number.
parseFloat(numberinstringform)	Converts a string to a floating-point value. If the value specified couldn't be converted to a number, the value NaN is returned.
parseInt(numberinstringform [, radix])	Converts a string to an integer value. The radix is used to specify the base of the number (acceptable values are between 2 and 36). If the value specified couldn't be converted to a number, then the value NaN is returned.
unescape(characterstring)	Decodes an escaped character string.

Math Object

The math object is an intrinsic object that does not need to be instantiated. Its members are referenced using the following syntax: Math.memberName.

Member	Description
abs(number)	Returns the absolute value of the specified number.
acos(number)	Returns the arccosine of the specified number.
asin(number)	Returns the arcsine of the specified number.

Member	Description
atan(number)	Returns the arctangent of the specified number.
atan2(y, x)	Returns the angle in radians from the X axis to the point (x, y).
ceil(number)	Returns the smallest integer greater than or equal to the specified number.
cos(number)	Returns the cosine of the specified number.
E	Returns Euler's constant, the base of natural logarithms (approximately 2.718).
exp(number)	Returns e (the base of natural logarithms), raised to the specified number.
floor(number)	Returns the greatest integer less than or equal to the specified number.
LN2	Returns the natural logarithm of 2.
LN10	Returns the natural logarithm of 10.
log()	Returns the natural logarithm of the specified number.
LOG2E	Returns the base-2 logarithm of e, Euler's constant.
LOG10E	Returns the base-10 logarithm of e, Euler's constant.
max(number1, number2)	Returns the greater of the two specified numbers.
min(number1, number2)	Returns the lesser of the two specified numbers.
PI	Returns the ratio of the circumference of a circle to its diameter, approximately 3.141592653589793.

Member	Description
pow(base, exponent)	Returns the value of the specified base expression, raised to a specified power.
random()	Returns a random number between 0 and 1. The seed for the number is generated automatically when the JavaScript engine is loaded.
round(number)	Returns the specified number rounded to the nearest integer.
sin(number)	Returns the sine of the specified number.
sqrt(number)	Returns the square root of the specified number.
SQRT1_2	Returns the square root of 0.5.
SQRT2	Returns the square root of 2.
tan(number)	Returns the tangent of the specified number.

Regular Expression Object

A regular expression object stores patterns that are used to search for character combinations in a string. These expressions allow you to go beyond searching for a simple string and let you do more advanced searches, such as wild card and range searches. The pattern in a regular expression is composed of a set of characters and special pattern syntax characters.

Here are the regular expression object constructors:

```
var regularexpression = /pattern/[switch]
var regularexpression = new RegExp("pattern"[, "switch"])
```

The acceptable values for the switch parameter are as follows:

▼ i means ignore case.

■ g means global search for all occurrences of *pattern*.

▲ gi means global search, ignore case.

Before a string is searched, the regular expression must be compiled. If you use the first syntax for the constructor, the compilation happens when the code is loaded. If you use the second construction method, the expression is compiled just before use. Looping using the second method can cause a performance penalty. You can, however, use the second syntax, along with the compile method, which takes two parameters: pattern and the switch. The following shows the syntax for the compile method:

```
var x = new RegExp("t\n");
x.compile("t\n", "g");
```

The pattern syntax is somewhat complex, so we will list here only the most commonly used of the different pattern syntax characters:

Character	Description
\	Specifies that the next character is either a special character or a literal.
^	Matches the beginning of input.
$	Matches the end of input.
*	Matches the preceding character zero or more times.
+	Matches the preceding character one or more times.
?	Matches the preceding character zero or one time.
.	Matches any single character except a new-line character.
a|b	Matches either a or b.
{a}	Matches exactly a times.
{a,}	Matches at least a times.
{a,b}	Matches at least a and at most b times.
[abc]	Matches any one of the enclosed characters.
[^abc]	Matches any character not enclosed.
[a-d]	Matches any character in the specified range.
[^a-d]	Matches any character not in the specified range.
\b	Matches a word boundary, which is the position between a word and a space.
\B	Matches a nonword boundary.

Character	Description
\d	Matches a digit character.
\D	Matches a nondigit character.
\f	Matches a form-feed character.
\n	Matches a new-line character.
\r	Matches a carriage-return character.
\s	Matches any white space, including space, tab, form-feed, and so on.
\S	Matches any nonwhite space character.
\t	Matches a tab character.
\v	Matches a vertical tab character.
\w	Matches any word character, including underscore.
\W	Matches any nonword character.

String Object

There are two methods for constructing a string object: either explicitly (shown below) or implicitly by setting a variable equal to a string literal. Here is the string object constructor:

```
var stringObject = new String("Sample Object");
```

Once instantiated, the following string object methods are available using the syntax stringObj.memberName().

Member	Description
anchor(name)	Returns a string that contains an HTML anchor element (<A>), with the Name attribute set to the specified name, around the string from the object.
big()	Returns a string that contains an HTML big element (<BIG>) around the string from the object.

Member	Description
blink()	Returns a string that contains an HTML blink element (<BLINK>) around the string from the object.
bold()	Returns a string that contains an HTML bold element (<B>) around the string from the object.
charAt(index)	Returns the character that is at the specified location in the string. The index for the string is 0-based.
charCodeAt(index)	Returns the character code (Unicode encoded) that is at the specified location in the string. If the character does not exist, NaN is returned. The index for the string is 0-based.
concat(string2)	Returns a string object that contains the two strings concatenated.
fixed()	Returns a string that contains an HTML <TT> element around the string from the object.
fontcolor(colorValue)	Returns a string that contains an HTML <FONT> element with the COLOR attribute set to specified colorValue around the string from the object.
fontsize(sizeValue)	Returns a string that contains an HTML <FONT> element with the SIZE attribute set to specified sizeValue around the string from the object.
fromCharCode(char1, char2, char3…..)	Returns a string that is made up of the specified Unicode character values. Note: you can pass in an almost infinite set of character code values.
indexOf(substring, startindex)	Returns an integer that indicates the starting position of the first occurrence of the substring in the string, starting with the position specified by startindex. If the string does not exist, it returns –1.

Member	Description
italics()	Returns a string that contains an HTML italic element (<I>) around the string from the object.
lastIndexOf(substring, startindex)	Returns an integer that indicates the starting position of the last occurrence of the substring in the string, starting with the position specified by startindex. If the string does not exist, it returns –1.
length	Returns the number of characters in the string.
link(href)	Returns a string that contains an HTML anchor element (<A>), with the HREF attribute set to the specified href, around the string from the object.
match(regularExpression)	Returns an array that contains the characters of the matching substrings, based on the specified regular expression.
replace(regularExpression , replacementString)	Returns the string with the text replaced based on the regular expression.
search(regularExpression)	Returns the position of the first matching substring, based on the regular expression. Returns –1 if there are no matches.
slice(start [, end])	Returns a portion of the string specified by the start and end positions. If the end is not specified, the remainder of the string from the start location is returned.
small()	Returns a string that contains an HTML small element (<SMALL>) around the string from the object.
split(separator)	Returns an array of strings that are composed of the substrings that are delimited by the specified separator. The separator can also be a regular expression.
strike()	Returns a string that contains an HTML strike element (<STRIKE>) around the string from the object.

Member	Description
sub()	Returns a string that contains an HTML <sub> element around the string from the object.
substr(start [, length])	Returns a substring that starts at the specified location and has a specified length. If the length is not specified, the remainder of the string is returned.
substring(start, end)	Returns a substring specified by the start and end positions. The method uses the lower of the two values as the starting point for the extraction.
sup()	Returns a string that contains an HTML <sup> element around the string from the object.
toLowerCase()	Returns a string that has all of the alphabetic characters converted to lowercase.
toUpperCase()	Returns a string that has all of the alphabetic characters converted to uppercase.

RESERVED WORDS

The following is a list of reserved words in JavaScript:

break	delete	for	super	void
case	do	function	switch	while
catch	else	if	this	with
class	enum	import	throw	
const	export	in	true	
continue	extends	new	try	
debugger	false	null	typeof	
default	finally	return	var	

APPENDIX B

HTML Component Elements, Objects, Methods, and Events

HTC ELEMENTS

ATTACH

The ATTACH element binds an event from the component's container to the component. Usage:

```
<PUBLIC:ATTACH Event = "eventName" For = "document" OnEvent =
"eventHandler" ID ="sID" />
```

Attribute	Description
Event	Specifies the name of a DHTML event or any of the events specific to an HTC. *Required.*
For	Identifies the source of the event. Values are as follows: document refers to the document object for the HTML document; element refers to the element to which the behavior is attached (*default*); window refers to the window object of the browser.
OnEvent	Specifies the name of the function to call when the event is fired or in-line script to process. *Required.*
ID	Specifies the unique identifier for the attach element of the component.

COMPONENT

The COMPONENT element is used in the HTC file to define a component in the file. Usage:

```
<PUBLIC:COMPONENT NAME="name" ID= "ID" URN="URN" > </PUBLIC:COMPONENT>
```

Attribute	Description
Name	Specifies the name by which the behavior is referred to in the containing document.
ID	Specifies the unique identifier for the component element in the component.
URN	Specifies the uniform resource name (URN) that uniquely identifies the component.

EFAULTS (IE 5.5 and Later)

The DEFAULTS element is used to set the default property values of the HTC. This element and each of its attributes are optional. Usage:

```
<PUBLIC:DEFAULTS tabStop="true/false" style="sStyle"
contentEditable="true/false" canHaveHTML="true/false"
viewInheritStyle="true/false" viewMasterTab="true/false"
viewLinkContent="true/false" />
```

Attribute	Description
tabStop	Specifies whether the component may be tabbed to within the parent container page. Default is false.
style	Denotes string used to specify the style of the HTC-defined tag.
contentEditable	Sets user editing of content. By default, the HTC inherits this attribute from its parent, based on whether the parent has the ability to allow user editing of content. Setting this attribute to false disables editing functionality, regardless of the parent's abilities. Setting this value to true enables content editing, still limited by the parent container's abilities.
canHaveHTML	Specifies whether the content of the HTC's tag may contain HTML markup.
viewInheritStyle	Specifies whether ViewLink inherits styles from the main HTML file. Default is true.
viewMasterTab	Specifies whether the master element of the HTC is to be part of the primary document's tab sequence. Default is true.
viewLinkContent	Specifies whether the HTC's markup is used as the ViewLink. Default is false.

EVENT

The EVENT element is used by the HTC to create an event that is fired up to its container. Usage:

```
<PUBLIC:EVENT NAME ="name" ID="eventID" />
```

Attribute	Description
Name	Specifies the name of the event exposed to the containing document. *Required.*
ID	Denotes unique identifier for the event element in the component.

METHOD

The METHOD element is used to declare a public procedure for the component that is called by the container. Usage:

```
<PUBLIC:METHOD Name="name" InternalName="internalName" ID="ID" />
```

Attribute	Description
Name	Specifies the name that the containing document uses to call the method. If an internal name is not specified, this is the name of the function that is called when the method is called. *Required.*
ID	Denotes unique identifier for the event element in the component.
InternalName	Specifies the alternate name of the function to call within the component when the method is called.

PROPERTY

The PROPERTY element is used to declare a public attribute of the component. If the PROPERTY has the get functionality but not the put functionality, the property is read-only from the public interface. Likewise if the PROPERTY has the put functionality without the get, the property is write-only from the public interface. Usage:

```
<PUBLIC:PROPERTY Name="name" ID="ID" InternalName="internameName"
Get="getFunctionaName" Put="putFunctionName" Persist="persist"
Value="defaultValue" />
```

Attribute	Description
Name	Specifies the name of the property exposed to the containing document. *Required.*
ID	Specifies the unique identifier for the property element in the component.
InternalName	Specifies the name by which the property is referred to within the component.
Get	Specifies the function to be called whenever the value of the property is retrieved.
Put	Specifies the function to be called when the value of the property is set.
Persist	Specifies whether to persist the property as part of the page.
Value	Specifies the default value for the property.

TC OBJECTS

efaults (IE 5.5 and Later)

The defaults object is used to programmatically set the default properties on the Element behavior.

Properties	Description
tabStop	Specifies whether the component may be tabbed to within the parent container page. Default is false.
style	Denotes string used to specify the style of the HTC-defined tag.

Properties	Description
contentEditable	Sets user editing of content. By default, the HTC inherits this attribute from its parent, based on whether the parent has the ability to allow user editing of content. Setting this attribute to false disables editing functionality, regardless of the parent's abilities. Setting this value to true enables content editing, still limited by the parent container's abilities.
canHaveHTML	Specifies whether the content of the HTC's tag may contain HTML markup.
viewInheritStyle	Specifies whether ViewLink inherits styles from the main HTML file. Default is true.
viewMasterTab	Specifies whether the master element of the HTC is to be part of the primary document's tab sequence. Default is true.
viewLink	Specifies whether the HTC's markup is used as the ViewLink. Default is false.

document (IE 5.5 and Later)

The document object provides programmatic access to the underlying markup in an Element behavior. The members of the object are the same as the members of the DHTML DOM document object.

element

The element object provides programmatic access to the underlying element that the behavior is bound to.

HTC METHODS

There are two HTC methods:

Method	Description
createEventObject()	Creates a DHTML event object, which is used to pass event information to the containing document when the fire method is called.
eventID.fire([eventObject])	Raises an event to the container. Can only raise events specified in the <event> elements for the component. Allows you to pass an event object to the container that contains details about the event, rather than just raising the event. The eventID contains the ID of the event you wish to raise.

TC EVENTS

The following list covers HTC elements:

Event	Purpose
oncontentready	Fires when the element that the behavior is attached to has been parsed by the browser.
oncontentsave (IE 5.5 and later)	Fires before the contents of an element attached to identity behavior is copied or saved.
ondetach	Fires before the behavior is removed from the element it is attached to.
ondocumentready	Fires when the containing page has been parsed. This event fires after scripts, images, Microsoft ActiveX controls, and other elements on the page have completed being downloaded. This event is fired after the window.onload event fires.

APPENDIX C

The XML Document Object Model

It is important to note that we do not cover all of the different objects in the document object model, only the most commonly used elements. For the complete list of the XML document objects, see http://msdn.microsoft.com/xml/xmlguide/default.asp.

THE XMLDOMNODE OBJECT

This object is implemented by the XMLDOMDocument, XMLDOMElement, and XMLDOMAttribute objects. This means that these objects support the functionality defined in the XMLDOMNode object. In the following list, italic properties are read-only.

Member (Method, Property, Event)	Description
appendChild(newChild)	Adds the newChild to the end of the childNodes collection. Returns newChild if successful.
attributes	Returns an XMLDOMNamedNodeMap (collection) of all of the attributes for the node. For an XMLDOMAttribute object, always returns null.
baseName	Returns the base name (right-hand side of a name space-qualified name). The property returns "base" for the element <prefix:base>.
childNodes	Returns an XMLDOMNamedNodeList (collection) of all of the attributes for the document node.
cloneNode(cloneDescendants)	Creates a new, cloned XML node. If cloneDescendants is true, it will clone child nodes also. If the node is an element, the attributes are also cloned. Returns the new node.

Member (Method, Property, Event)	Description
dataType	Returns the data type for the node. XMLDOMDocument returns String; XMLDOMElement and XMLDOMAttribute return the data type specified in the schema or null.
definition	Returns the specification for the particular node from the schema or DTD.
firstChild	Returns the first child node for this node. Returns null if there aren't any children.
hasChildNodes()	Returns whether the node has children.
insertBefore(newChild, referenceChild)	Inserts the new child prior to the reference child. If the reference child is null, the new child is inserted as the last child of the calling node.
lastChild	Returns the last child of the calling node.
namespaceURI	Returns the universal resource identifier for the name space. The property returns namspaceURI for the name space definition xmlns:x = "namspaceURI".
nextSibling	Returns the next sibling for this node from the parent's list of children. Attributes and document elements always return null because they are not children of nodes.
nodeName	Returns as follows: the Attribute node returns the name of the attribute; Document returns the string constant "#document"; and Element returns the name of the XML tag, including the name space prefix if one is specified.

Member (Method, Property, Event)	Description
nodeType	Returns an enumerated value (an integer) indicating the node type. 1 denotes Element; 2 denotes Attribute; and 9 denotes Document Element.
nodeTypedValue	Contains the node's value, based on its data type defined in the document's schema or DTD. If no data type is specified, it contains a string with the value. For document elements, it contains the text for the element.
nodeTypeString	Returns the node type specified as a string (attribute, element, document).
nodeValue	Contains a string containing the value (attributes) or text (elements) for the node.
ownerDocument	Returns the document object (XMLDOMDocument) that contains the node.
parentNode	Returns the parent node for elements. Document elements and attributes return null because they cannot have parents.
parsed	Returns whether the node and all of its siblings have been parsed and instantiated. Returns true if they have been parsed and instantiated.
prefix	Returns the name space prefix (left-hand side of a name space-qualified name). The property returns "prefix" for the element <prefix:base>. Returns "" if no prefix is specified.

Member (Method, Property, Event)	Description
previousSibling	Returns the previous sibling for the node from the parent's list of children. Attributes and document elements always return null because they are not children of nodes.
removeChild(removeChild)	Removes the node specified by removeChild from the node's childNodes collection. Returns the removed child if successful.
replaceChild(newChild, oldChild)	Replaces the oldChild with the specified newChild in the childNodes collection. Returns the oldChild if successful. If newChild is null, simply removes the oldChild.
selectNodes(pattern)	Uses the specified pattern with the calling node as the current context to return a XMLDOMNodeList (collection) of matching nodes.
selectSingleNode(pattern)	Uses the specified pattern with the calling node as the current context to return the first matching node.
specified	Returns whether a node's value is explicitly specified (true) or is set from a default value (false). Elements always return true.
text	Contains a string that contains the value of the node. This is the concatenated text of all of the node's subnodes.
transformNode(stylesheet)	Returns a string that contains the results of the transformation of the node and its children. The stylesheet parameter can contain either a complete XSL style sheet or a particular XSL style sheet node.

Member (Method, Property, Event)	Description
transformNodeToObject (stylesheet, outputobject)	The output object (an XML object or stream) contains the results of the transformation of the node and its children. The stylesheet parameter can contain either a complete XSL style sheet or a particular XSL style sheet node.
xml	Returns the XML for the node and all of the node's children.

THE XMLDOMDOCUMENT OBJECT

In addition to the members listed here, the XMLDOMDocument object also supports the members in the XMLDOMNode object. In the following list, italic properties are read-only.

Member (Method, Property, Event)	Description
abort()	Cancels an asynchronous download of XML data.
async	Indicates if the asynchronous method of download is permitted. Default is true.
createAttribute(name)	Creates a new XMLDOMAttribute with the specified name. Returns new attribute.
createCDATASection(data)	Creates a new CDATA section that contains the data passed in. Returns new CDATA section.
createComment(data)	Creates a new comment node that contains the data passed in. Returns new comment object

Member (Method, Property, Event)	Description
createDocumentFragment()	Creates a new document fragment object. The new object is not added to the XML tree. Returns the new document fragment.
createElement(tagName)	Creates a new XMLDOMElement with the specified tag name. Returns the new element.
createEntityReference(name)	Creates a new entity reference that is specified by the passed name. Returns the new entity reference.
createNode(Type, name, namespace)	Create a new node of the type specified (for example, NODE_ELEMENT, NODE_ATTRIBUTE). Returns the new node.
createProcessingInstruction(target, data)	Creates a new processing instruction. Example: createProcessingInstruction("xml", "version '1.0'"). Returns the new processing instruction.
createTextNode(data)	Create a new text node, which contains the specified data. Returns the new text node.
doctype	Returns the document type node that specifies the DTD for this XML document.
documentElment	Contains a reference to the element (XMLDOMElement) that is the root of the XML document.

Member (Method, Property, Event)	Description
getElementsByTagName(tagName)	Returns an XMLDOMNodeList (collection), located anywhere in the document that contains the specified tag name. Use an asterisk (*) to return all of the elements in the document.
implementation	Returns the XMLDOMImplementation object for this document. This object is used to query the XML object model to determine its capabilities, such as which version of the XML specification the object supports.
load(url)	Loads the XML document with the source from the specified location (url). Returns true if loading was successful.
loadXML(xmlString)	Loads the XML document with the specified xmlString. Returns true if loading was successful.
nodeFromID(id)	Returns the node that has the specified ID value. For this method to work, you must create an attribute on the element you are looking for that has the data type of ID specified in an XML schema or DTD.
ondataavailable - Event	Fires event during the asynchronous download of an XML document. The event is fired every time a new chunk of data arrives at the XML parser.

Member (Method, Property, Event)	Description
ondataavailable – Write Only	Specifies the function that serves as the event handler for the ondataavailable event.
onreadystatechange – Event	Fires event during the asynchronous download when the readyState changes value.
onreadystatechange – Write Only	Specifies the function that serves as the event handler for the onreadystatechange event.
ontransformnode(xslNode, xmlNode) – Event	Fires event prior to each node in the document being transformed by an XSL style sheet. The xslNode parameter contains the XSL node that will transform the XML node specified in the xmlNode parameter. Returning false from the event handler will stop the transformation process.
ontransformnode – Write Only	Specifies the function that serves as the event handler for the ontransformnode event.
parseError	Returns an XMLDOMParseError object that contains information about the last error that occurred during parsing. The object can be used to debug the error in the XML document.
preserveWhiteSpace	Specifies whether white space (carriage returns, spaces) should be maintained from the original document when using the xml property to retrieve the XML. Default value is false (don't preserve the space).

Member (Method, Property, Event)	Description
readyState	Determines the current state of the XML document during asynchronous loading: loading specifies the load is in progress, but the data has not started parsing yet; loaded says the object is reading and parsing data, but the object model is not yet available; interactive says a portion of the data has been read and parsed and the object model is available on a partial basis, but is read-only; complete denotes that the document has been completely loaded, and if successful, the entire object model is available. *Note: a completed, yet unsuccessful load will also return complete.*
resolveExternals	Specifies if external definitions (such as external name spaces, DTD, XML schemas) should be resolved (downloaded, used).
save(target)	Saves an XML document to the target location. The target can be a file path, ASP Response object, an XMLDOMDocument object.
url	Returns the URL for the last successfully loaded XML document. For documents not loaded via a url, it returns null.
validateOnParse	Specifies if the XML document should be validated during parsing. If set to false, the document is still validated for well formatting. Default is true.

THE XMLDOMELEMENT OBJECT

Besides the members listed here the XMLDOMElement object also supports the members in the XMLDOMNode object. In the following list, italic properties are read-only.

Member (Method, Property, Event)	Description
getAttibute(attributeName)	Returns the value of the specified (attributeName) attribute. Returns "" if the attribute does not have a value or does not exist.
getAttributeNode(attributeName)	Returns the attribute node of the specified (attributeName) attribute. Returns null if the attribute does not have a value or does not exist.
getElementsByTagName(tagName)	Returns an XMLDOMNodeList (collection) of the descendent elements that match the specified tagName. Use an asterisk (*) to return all descendant elements.
normalize()	Combines two or more adjacent text nodes of the element into a single text node. When a new text node (XMLDOMText) is created and added to an element, it is appended to the collection of child nodes; this method combines the multiple text nodes.
removeAttribute(attributeName)	Removes the specified attribute (attributeName) from the element. If the attribute has a default value, this method resets the value of the attribute to the default value.

Member (Method, Property, Event)	Description
removeAttributeNode (attributeObject)	Removes the specified attribute (attributeObject) from the element. If the attribute has a default value, a new attribute is created with the default value and associated with the element. Returns the removed attribute.
setAttribute(attributeName, attributeValue)	Used to set the value of the attribute specified (attributeName) to the value specified (attributeValue). If the attribute does not exist, a new attribute is created and associated with the element.
setAttributeNode(attributeObject)	Adds or sets the value of an attribute. If the attribute already exists, the specified attribute node (attributeObject) replaces the current node and the current node is returned. If the attribute does not exist, the attribute is added and null is returned.
tagName	Returns the name of the element. For the element <sample x="1" />, it returns "sample."

THE XMLDOMATTRIBUTE OBJECT

Besides the members listed here, the XMLDOMAttribute object also supports the members in the XMLDOMNode object. In the following list, italic properties are read-only.

Member (Method, Property, Event)	Description
name	Returns the name of the attribute.
value	Contains the value of the attribute. For attributes with children, it returns a concatenated string with the text of all of the subnodes.

HE XMLDOMNODELIST OBJECT

In the following list, italic properties are read-only.

Member (Method, Property, Event)	Description
item(index)	Returns the node at the specified (0-based) index in the collection. Used for random access.
length	Returns the number items in the node list collection.
nextNode()	Iterates sequentially over the collection of nodes. Initially the iterater's pointer points to before the first node, and the first call to the method returns the first item in the collection. Returns null if there isn't a next node (for example, at the end of collection or an empty collection).
reset()	Resets the iterater's pointer to the starting position of before the beginning of the collection.

HE XMLDOMNAMEDNODEMAP OBJECT

In the following list, italic properties are read-only.

Member (Method, Property, Event)	Description
getNamedItem(name)	Returns the XMLDOMNode object for the specified attribute name. Returns null if the item is not in the collection.
getQualifiedItem(attributeName, namespaceURI)	Returns the XMLDOMNode object for the specified attribute name (attributeName) and name space prefix (namespaceURI). Returns null if the item is not in the collection.
item(index)	Returns the node at the specified index in the collection. Used for random access.
length	Returns the number items in the named node map collection.
nextNode()	Iterates sequentially over the collection of nodes. Initially the iterater's pointer points to before the first node, and the first call to the method returns the first item in the collection. Returns null if there isn't a next node (for example, at the end of collection or an empty collection).
removeNamedItem(attributeName)	Removes the specified attribute (attributeName) from the collection. Returns the removed attribute or returns null if the item is not in the collection.
removeQualifiedItem(attributeName, namespaceURI)	Removes an attribute based on the specified (attributeName) and name space prefix (namespaceURI). Returns the removed attribute or returns null if the item is not in the collection.

Member (Method, Property, Event)	Description
reset()	Resets the iterator's pointer to the starting position which is before the beginning of the collection.
setNamedItem(attributeObject)	Adds or sets an attribute. If the attribute already exists, the specified attribute node (attributeObject) replaces the current node. If the attribute does not exist, the attribute is added to the collection. The newly added attribute is returned.

THE XMLDOMPARSEERROR OBJECT

In the following table, italic properties are read-only.

Member (Method, Property, Event)	Description
errorCode	Returns the error code of the last parsing error.
filepos	Returns the exact position in the file (character number) where the parse error occurred.
line	Returns the line number where the parse error occurred.
linepos	Returns the character position within the line where the parse error occurred.
reason	Returns a detailed description of why the error occurred.
srcText	Returns the complete line of text for the line where the error occurred.
url	Returns the URL of the document that caused the error.

THE XMLHTTPREQUEST OBJECT

In the following list, italic properties are read-only.

Member (Method, Property, Event)	Description
abort()	Cancels the current asynchronous call. Resets the object to the uninitialized state, which requires a call to the open method to reinitialize the object.
getAllResponseHeaders()	Returns a string containing all of the response header name/value pairs separated by a carriage-return line feed. Contents are valid only after the send method has successfully completed.
getResponseHeader(headerName)	Returns the value of the specified response header (headerName). Contents are valid only after the send method has successfully completed.
onreadystatechange – Event	Fires event during the asynchronous request when the readyState changes value.
onreadystatechange – Write Only	Specifies the function that serves as the event handler for the onreadystatechange event.
open(method, url, asynchronous, user, password)	Initializes the HTTP request and tells the object which method, location, and user to connect to. The method contains the HTTP method used to open the connection (GET, POST, PUT). The url must be the absolute path. Asynchronous is true or false; the default is true. If the user and password are not specified and are required, the object displays a login dialog.

Member (Method, Property, Event)	Description
readyState	Determine the current state of the HTTP request during asynchronous loading of a document. Status values are as follows: loading indicates that the load is in progress, but the data has not started parsing yet; loaded indicates that the object is reading and parsing data, but the object model is not yet available; interactive indicates that a portion of the data has been read and parsed, and the object model is available on a partial basis, but it is read only; and complete indicates that the document has been completely loaded, and if successful, the entire complete object model is available. Note: a completed yet unsuccessful load will also return complete.
responseBody	Contains an array of unsigned bytes that represent the contents of the response.
responseStream	Contains an IStream object that represents the contents of the response.
responseText	Returns a string that contains the contents of the returned body from the request. This is the most useful response property for general scripting.

Member (Method, Property, Event)	Description
responseXML	If the response is an XML document, it returns an XML document object (XMLDOMDocument) that contains the parsed but not validated returned body from the request. Note: even if the body is XML, you can retrieve the body using the responseText property.
send(requestBody)	Sends an HTTP request to the specified URL in the open method and receives a response. The request body can be a string, XML document object (XMLDOMDocument), or IStream.
setRequestHeader(headerName, value)	Specifies a header name and value to send to the server during the send method.
status	Returns the value of the HTTP status code after returning from a send method.
statusText	Returns the value of the HTTP response line status after returning from a send method.

APPENDIX D

XSL Elements and Patterns

XSL ELEMENTS

xsl:apply-templates

This element selects the list of nodes specified in the select attribute and tells the XSL processor to search for the appropriate template and apply the template based on the type and context of the nodes. The element can contain xsl:template elements to create locally scoped templates. Usage:

```
<xsl:apply-templates order-by="orderByList" select="pattern" >
```

Attributes	Description
order-by	Specifies a semicolon-delimited list of sort items (-firstItemToSortBy; secondItemToSortBy). The first non–white-space character is used to specify the sort direction: + for ascending (optional/default) and – for descending.
Select	Specifies the context that the template will execute in. If not specified, all of the children of the current node are selected.

xsl:attribute

This element creates an attribute node and automatically attaches it to an output element. The contents of the element are used to set the value of the attribute. Usage:

```
<xsl:attribute name="attributeName">
```

Attributes	Description
Name	The name of the attribute to create.

xsl:choose

This element provides the ability to have multiple condition testing when used with the xsl:otherwise and xsl:when elements. Functions as the block element around the xsl:otherwise and xsl:when elements. Usage:

```
<xsl:choose>
```

Attributes

None

sl:comment

This element is used to generate a comment in the output document. The contents of this element appear between the <!— and —> in the output document. Usage:

```
<xsl:comment>
```

Attributes

None

sl:copy

This element provides a mechanism to copy the current node from the source to the output documents. It does *not* copy the attributes or children of the element. Usage:

```
<xsl:copy>
```

Attributes

None

sl:element

This element creates another element with a particular name in the output document. It is useful for creating output elements that conflict with XSL itself. Usage:

```
<xsl:element name="elementName">
```

Attributes	Description
Name	The name of the element to create.

xsl:eval

This element executes a single line of script to generate a text string. It can be used to call a function in an xsl:script block. Usage:

```
<xsl:eval language="languageName">
```

Attributes	Description
Language	The scripting language to use to execute the code. Default is JavaScript.

xsl:for-each

This element is used to loop through a set of nodes, applying the contents of the tag repeatedly. The element selects the list of nodes specified in the select attribute and iterates through the list. The context for the instructions inside the element is the selected node for that iteration of the loop. Usage:

```
<xsl:for-each order-by="orderByList" select="pattern">
```

Attributes	Description
order-by	Specifies a semicolon-delimited list of sort items (-firstItemToSortBy; secondItemToSortBy). The first non–white-space character is used to specify the sort direction: + for ascending (optional) and – for descending.
Select	Specifies the context that the for loop will execute in. If not specified, all of the children of the current node are selected.

xsl:if

This element is used for a single conditional check of whether to apply a template fragment. Usage:

```
<xsl:if expr="scriptExpression" language="languageName" test="pattern">
```

Attributes	Description
expr	A script expression, the results of which return a Boolean. If the returned value equals true, the contents of the element are outputted.
language	The scripting language to use to execute the code, if code is specified in the expr attribute. Default is JavaScript.
test	Condition to test for in the source data. If the condition returns at least one node, the contents of the element are outputted.

sl:otherwise

This element provides the ability to have multiple-condition testing when used with the xsl:choose and xsl:when elements. The element is used to define the default condition for the multiple-condition test. Usage:

```
<xsl:otherwise >
```

Attributes
None

sl:pi

This element is used to generate a processing instruction in the output document. For example: <xsl:pi name="xml">version="1.0"</xsl:pi> would generate: <? xml version="1.0" ?>. Usage:

```
<xsl:pi name="processingInstructionName">
```

Attributes	Description
name	The name of the processing instruction to create.

xsl:script

This element defines a script section that contains functions or variables, which can be accessed from the XSL elements. Usage:

```
<xsl:script language="languageName">
```

Attributes	Description
language	The scripting language to use to execute the code. Default is JavaScript.

xsl:stylesheet

This element is used as the document element, wrapping one or more xsl:template and/or xsl:script elements. The tag generally is used to define the XSL name space, as shown here: <xsl:stylesheet xmlns:xsl="http://www.w3.org/TR/WD-xsl">. Usage:

```
<xsl:stylesheet default-space="preserve" indent-result="yes"
language="languageName" result-ns="namespace">
```

Attributes	Description
default-space	Defines whether to preserve the white space that appears in the source document. Only the value of default is supported.
indent-result	Defines whether to preserve the white space that appears in the XSL style sheet. Only the value of yes is supported.
language	Specifies the scripting language to use to execute the code. Default is JavaScript.
result-ns	Defines what the output of the XSL processor is. All IE 5 output is XML, so the attribute is not used.

xsl:template

This element is used to define the output for nodes of a particular type and context. Usage:

```
<xsl:template language="languageName" match="nodeContext">
```

Attributes	Description
language	The scripting language to use to execute the code. Default is JavaScript.
match	The context that the template will execute in.

sl:value-of

This element is used to retrieve the value of a node and inserts it into the document as text. If more than one node is returned based on the select attribute, the first node to appear in the document will be used. Usage:

```
<xsl:value-of select="pattern">
```

Attributes	Description
Select	Specifies the value to insert based on the current context. If not specified, the value of the current node is inserted.

sl:when

This element provides the ability to have multiple-condition testing when used with the xsl:choose and xsl:otherwise elements. It's used to specify one of the nondefault (xsl:otherwise) choices. Usage:

```
<xsl:when expr="scriptExpression" language="languageName"
test="pattern">
```

Attributes	Description
expr	A script expression, the result of which returns a Boolean. If the returned value equals true, the contents of the element are outputted.
language	The scripting language to use to execute the code, if code is specified in the expr attribute. Default is JavaScript.
test	Condition to test for in the source data. If the condition returns at least one node, the contents of the element are outputted.

XSL METHODS

The following list describes XSL methods:

▼ **absoluteChildNumber(xmlNode)** returns the number of the node relative to all of its siblings. The first child of an element is assigned a value of 1.

■ **ancestorChildNumber(nodeName, xmlNode)** navigates back up the tree (from the nodeName element) to find a node that matches the nodeName parameter. It returns the child number of that element. If a match is not found it returns a null.

■ **childNumber(xmlNode)** returns the number of the node relative to the siblings with the same name. The first child of an element is assigned a value of 1.

■ **depth(xmlNode)** returns the depth of the node in the document tree. The root node is 0; the first child of the root is 1.

▲ **formatDate(dateValue, formatString, locale)** returns the date value formatted based on the format string and locale. The format string supports the following values:

Format	Result
m	Returns month values as 1–12
mm	Returns month values as 01–12
mmm	Returns month values as Jan–Dec
mmmm	Returns month values as January–December
mmmmm	Returns month values as the first letter of each month
d	Returns the days as 1–31
dd	Returns the days as 01–31
ddd	Returns the days as Sun–Sat
dddd	Returns the days as Sunday–Saturday
yy	Returns the years as 00–99
yyyy	Returns the years as 1900–9999

To use the formatDate function, the date value passed in must come from an XML file that is using a schema that defines the field as a DateTime type.

The local is used to determine the order in which the date values should be returned. If unspecified, month-day-year is assumed.

▼ **formatIndex(integerValue, formatString)** returns the integer formatted, based on the formatString, in the following numbering systems:

Format	Result
1	Standard numbering
01	Numbering with leading zeros
A	Numbering following uppercase character sequence: A–Z, AA–ZZ, and so on
a	Numbering following lowercase character sequence: a–z, aa–zz, and so on
I	Numbering using uppercase roman numerals: I, II, III, and so on
i	Numbering using lowercase roman numerals: i, ii, iii

■ **formatNumber(numericValue, formatString)** returns the number formatted, based on the formatString, in the following numbering systems:

Format	Result
#	Used as a numeric place holder. Returns only significant digits; does not return insignificant zeros.
0	Used as a numeric place holder. Returns zero if there are not that many digits in the number passed in.
?	Adds spaces for insignificant zeros on either side of a number to help in alignment of numbers.
.	Specifies the location of the decimal point in the number.
,	Displays a comma as a thousands separator or scales a number by multiples of one thousand.
%	Displays the number as a percentage.
E- or e-	Displays a number in scientific notation.
E+ or e+	Displays a number in scientific notation and places a plus or minus sign by the exponent.

The following is an example of formatting a number to have a currency-like format with a comma separator and two decimal places:

```
formatNumber(someValue, "#,###.00");
```

■ **formatTime(timeValue, formatString, locale)** returns the time value formatted, based on the format string and locale. The format string supports the following values:

Format	Result
h	Hours in 0–23 format.
hh	Hours in 00–23 format.
m	Minutes in 0–59 format.
mm	Minutes in 00–59 format.
s	Seconds in 0–59 format.
ss	Seconds in 00–59 format.
AM/PM or am/pm	Displays time with AM/PM or am/pm. Hours are displayed based on a 12 hour clock.
A/P or a/p	Displays time with A/P or a/p. Hours are displayed based on a 12 hour clock.
ss.00	Displays the fractions of a second.

To use the formatTime function, the time value passed in must come from an XML file that is using a schema that defines the field as a DateTime type. The local is used to determine the order in which the time values should be returned.

▲ **UniqueID(xmlNode)** returns a unique identifier for a particular node. Can be useful if you need to generate a unique ID for an HTML element or a unique identifier for an XML element.

XSL PATTERNS SYNTAX AND METHODS

Operators and Special Characters

Operator/Special Character	Description
/	The child operator. Indicates that the current context's children should be selected. If the operator is the first in the pattern, it indicates that the children of the root node should be selected.

Operator/Special Character	Description
//	Indicates that the element should be searched for at any level depth based on the current context. If the operator is the first in the pattern, it indicates that the element should be searched for at any level, starting at the root of the document.
.	Used to indicate the current context.
*	Select all the elements in the current context regardless of name (wildcard).
@	Used to signify an attribute.
@*	Selects all of the attributes regardless of their name.
:	The name space separator.
!	Used to apply the specified method to the reference node.
()	Highest level of precedence operator used to explicitly group operations.
[]	Used to specify and apply a filter pattern.
[]	The subscript operator. Used to index into a collection of nodes.

omparison Expressions and Set Operations

Some of the comparison operators have two syntax versions. In these cases, both versions are listed.

Comparison Expression	Description
and, and	Logical AND.
or, or	Logical OR.
not(), not	Opposite or negation.
=, eq	Equality.
ieq	Case-insensitive equality.
!=, ne	Not equal.

Comparison Expression	Description
ine	Case-insensitive inequality.
<, lt	Less than.
ilt	Case-insensitive less than.
<=, le	Less than or equal.
ile	Case-insensitive less than or equal.
>, gt	Greater than.
igt	Case-insensitive greater than.
>=, ge	Greater than or equal.
ige	Case-insensitive greater than or equal.
all	A set operation that tests to see if all of the items in the set meet the condition. If they do, it returns true.
any	A set operation that tests to see if any of the items in the set meet the condition. If any do, it returns true.
|	A set operator that returns the union of the two queries (that is, it returns the combined results of the two queries).

Context-Changing Operators

Operator	Description
ancestor(pattern)	Returns the nearest ancestor matching the specified pattern. The method starts with the parent and checks for a match. If one is not found, it tries the grandparent for a match, and this process continues until a match is found or all of the ancestors have been tested. Returns the matching ancestor or null if a match does not exist.
context(index)	Used to change the context to a node relative to where the query started. Negative numbers indicate positions higher up in the tree from the current context position. An index of 0 is the node that the transformNode was executed against. An index of 1 is the context of the first context-switching XSL element in the style sheet.

Operator	Description
id(expression)	Used to return the element(s) with the specified ID(s). You can return multiple elements by using a pattern inside the method that returns the Ids, or you can use a space-delimited list of IDs. For this method to work, you must create an attribute on the element you are looking for that has the data type of ID specified in an XML schema or DTD.

nformational Methods

Method	Description
date(dateFormat)	The method converts the value to the specified date format that was passed into the method. To use this method, the date value passed in must come from an XML file that is using a schema that defines the field as a DateTime type.
end()	Returns a match for the last element of a collection.
index()	Returns the position of the element within the parent.
nodeName()	Returns the tag name of the element, including the name space.
nodeType()	Returns the type of node. The value is an integer that maps as follows: 1 indicates an element; 2 indicates an attribute; 3 indicates text, representing the text content of an element; 4 indicates a CDATA section; 5 indicates an entity reference; 6 indicates an entity; 7 indicates a processing instruction; 8 indicates a comment; 9 indicates a document object; 10 indicates a document type; 11 indicates a document fragment; and 12 indicates a notation.
number()	Converts the value to a number format.
value()	Returns the typed version of the value based on the schema. If there isn't a schema, it simply returns the text value for the element.

Collection Methods

Method	Description
attribute([name])	Returns a collection of attributes with the matching name for the current context. The name parameter is optional, and if it is not passed in, it returns all of the attributes for the context.
cdata()	Returns a collection of all of the CDATA nodes for the current context.
comment()	Returns a collection of comments in the document based on the current context.
element([name])	Returns a collection of elements with the matching name for the current context. The name parameter is optional, and if it is not passed in, it returns all of the elements for the context.
node	Returns a collection of all the nodes with the exception of attribute nodes and the document node for the current context.
pi([name])	Returns a collection of processing instructions with the matching name for the current context. The name parameter is optional, and if it is not passed in, it returns all of the processing instructions for the context.
text()	Returns a collection of all of the text nodes and CDATA nodes for the current context.
textnode()	Returns a collection of all of the text nodes for the current context.

APPENDIX E

XML Schema Elements and Data Types

XML SCHEMA ELEMENTS

attribute

This element is used to specify a declared attribute type that can appear as part of an element. Usage:

```
<attribute default="value" type="attributeType" required="yes">
```

Attributes	Description
default	Used to specify the default value for the attribute if the value is not specified in the XML document. The default value takes precedence over the default value specified in the AttributeType element.
type	Used to refer to the associated attribute definition (AttributeType). This value must correspond to an AttributeType elements name attribute. ***Required.***
required	Value must be yes or no and is used to specify if the attribute is required in the XML document.

AttributeType

This element is used to create a definition for an attribute that can be referenced in many element type definitions. If the declaration of the element is inside of an ElementType element, that attribute type can only be referenced within the ElementType that contains it. Usage:

```
<AttributeType default="value" dt:type="dataType" dt:values="valueList"
name="attributeName" required="yes">
```

Attributes	Description
default	Used to specify the default value for the attribute if the value is not specified in the XML document. The default value of the attribute element takes precedence over the default value specified in this element.

Attributes	Description
dt:type	Used to specify the data type for this attribute. In IE 5, the supported types for attributes are entity, entities, enumeration, id, idref, idrefs, nmtoken, nmtokens, notation, and string.
dt:values	If the data type (dt:type) for the attribute is set to enumeration, this attribute is used to specify the possible values for the attribute in a space-delimited list.
name	This is used to specify the attribute's name and is also used by the attribute element to reference the AttributeType definition. *Required*.
required	Value must be yes or no and is used to specify if the attribute is required in the XML document.

ataType

This element provides an alternate mechanism to define the data type for an attribute or element (rather than on the AttributeType or ElementType definition). It can be useful if you have an element or attribute that has the same name but different data types. Usage:

```
<dataType dt:type="dataType">
```

Attributes	Description
dt:type	Used to specify the data type.

description

This element is used to contain information about the schema; it's similar to a comment, but you can only have one occurrence in the schema document. Usage:

```
<description >
```

Attributes

None

element

This element is used to specify a declared element type that can appear as part of an element. Usage:

```
<element  type="dataType" minOccurs="0" maxOccurs="1">
```

Attributes	Description
type	Used to refer to the associated element definition (ElementType). This value must correspond to an ElementType element's name attribute. *Required*.
minOccurs	Used to specify the minimum number of times the element can occur inside of its parent element. Supported values are 0 (does not need to occur) and 1 (must occur at least once; default).
maxOccurs	Used to specify the maximum number of times the element can occur inside of its parent element. Supported values are 1 (can only occur once; default) and * (can occur any number of times).

ElementType

This element is used to create a definition for another XML element that can be referenced in many other element type definitions. It is important to note that just setting the model attribute to open does not automatically allow additional content to be permitted. To add other elements not specified in the schema, they must use a name space different than the one used for the schema. Usage:

```
<ElementType content="mixed" dt:type="dataType" model="open"
name="elementReference" order="one" >
```

Attributes	Description
content	Used to specify what types of elements can be contained inside of the element. Valid values are empty (cannot contain content), textOnly (the element can only contain text and no other elements), eltOnly (the element can contain only other elements and no text), and mixed (the element can contain elements and text; default).

Attributes	Description
dt:type	Used to specify the data type for this element. Supported types are listed in the "XML Schema Data Types" section in this appendix.
model	Used to specify whether the element can contain only the elements and attributes defined in the schema or can contain non_specified items. Valid values are open (allow other items) or closed (don't allow other items; default). See note above about the open model.
name	Used to specify the element's name and is also used by the element element to reference the ElementType definition. *Required*.
order	Allows you to specify quantity, and the requisite order of the element's subelements within the document. Valid values are one (allows only one element of the subelements in the document), seq (requires subelements to appear in the order they are specified in the schema; the default value if content attribute is eltOnly), many (allows the subelements to appear or not appear in any order; the default if content attribute is mixed).

roup

This element is useful for specifying groups of elements that you wish to set sequence and occurrences, rather than specifying all of the elements in a particular ElementType definition. Usage:

```
<group minOccurs="1" maxOccurs="1" order="one">
```

Attributes	Description
minOccurs	Used to specify the minimum number of times the group can occur inside of its parent element. Supported values are 0 (does not need to occur) and 1 (must occur at least once; default).

Attributes	Description
maxOccurs	Used to specify the maximum number of times the group can occur inside of its parent element. Supported values are 1 (can only occur once; default) and * (can occur any number of times).
order	Allows you to specify the quantity and order that the groups elements must occur in the document. Valid values are one (allows only one element of the group in the document), seq (requires elements to appear in the order they are specified in the group), and many (allows the elements to appear or not appear in any order).

Schema

This element is the root element of the schema definition, used to identify the start of the schema definition. Usage:

```
<Schema name="schemaName" xmlns="namespace">
```

Attributes	Description
name	The name of the schema.
xmlns	Name space(s) that are to be used in the schema. Most common are xmlns="urn:schemas-microsoft-com:xml-data" (the default schema namespace) and xmlns:dt="urn:schemas-microsoft-com:datatypes" (used to define data types).

XML SCHEMA DATA TYPES

The following is a list of XML data types. In addition to this list, there are also the following ten intrinsic data types: entity, entities, enumeration, id, idref, idrefs, nmtoken, nmtokens, notation, and string.

Data Type	Description
bin.base64	Mime-style Base64-encoded binary blob.
bin.hex	Hexadecimal digits representing octets.
boolean	Contains a 0 (false) or 1 (true) value.
char	Single-character string.
date	Date in a subset ISO 8601 format, without the time information. Example: "2000-01-15."
dateTime	Date in a subset ISO 8601 format with the time information but without the optional time zone. Example: "2000-01-15T12:00:00:00."
dateTime.tz	Date in a subset ISO 8601 format with the time information and with the optional time zone. Example: "2000-01-15T12:00:00:00-08:00."
fixed.14.4	Similar to a number but supports 14 digits to the left of the decimal and only 4 to the right.
time	Time in a subset of the ISO 8601 format, with no date and no time zone. Example "12:30:00."
time.tz	Time in a subset of the ISO 8601 format. Contains time zone but does not contain date. Example "12:30:00-08:00."
i1	An integer represented in a single byte. Can have sign; cannot have fractions or exponents.
i2	An integer represented in one word (2 bytes). Can have sign; cannot have fractions or exponents.
i4	An integer represented in 4 bytes. Can have sign; cannot have fractions or exponents.
r4	A numeric value with no limit on digits. Can have leading sign and optionally an exponent. Values from $3.40282347E+38F$ to $1.17549435E-38F$.
r8	Same as a float. A numeric value with no limit on digits. Can have leading sign and optionally an exponent. Values from $1.7976931348623157E+308$ to $2.2250738585072014E-308$.

Data Type	Description
ui1	An unsigned integer represented in a single byte. Cannot have fractions or exponents.
ui2	An unsigned integer represented in one word (2 bytes). Cannot have fractions or exponents.
ui4	An unsigned integer represented as four bytes. Cannot have fractions or exponents.
uri	Universal resource identifier (URI). Example: urn:schemas-microsoft-com:datatypes.
uuid	Hexadecimal digits representing octets, optional embedded hyphens that are ignored.

APPENDIX F

The HTA Element
and Its Attributes

In the following definition, **bold** text represents the default values for the attribute.

```
<HTA:APPLICATION
    APPLICATIONNAME=value
    BORDER=thick | dialog | none  | thin
    BORDERSTYLE=normal | complex | raised  | static  | sunken
    CAPTION=YES | NO
    ICON=value
    ID=value
    MAXIMIZEBUTTON=YES | NO
    MINIMIZEBUTTON=YES | NO
    SHOWINTASKBAR=YES | NO
    SINGLEINSTANCE=YES | NO
    SYSMENU=YES | NO
    VERSION=value
    WINDOWSTATE=normal | maximize | minimize
>
```

In the following table, an asterisk (*) next to an attribute/property value denotes that it is only a property, with no matching attribute. Italic items are read-only.

Attribute/Property	Description
applicationName	Name of the HTA. If the singleInstance property is set to true, this value is used to test for an instance already running.
border	The HTA's application window border type. This property is only valid when the HTA has a title bar. Note: Setting the border to none removes the HTA's title bar, program icon, and Minimize/Maximize buttons. Possible values: thick indicates a thick window border, plus a size grip and sizing border for resizing the window; dialog indicates a dialog window border; none indicates no window border; and thin indicates a thin window border with a caption.

Attribute/Property	Description
borderStyle	The HTA's content border style. Possible values: normal indicates a normal border; complex indicates a raised and sunken border; raised indicates a raised 3-D border; static indicates a 3-D border typically used for windows that do not accept user input; sunken indicates a sunken 3-D border.
caption	This property states whether the HTA's title bar is displayed.
commandLine *	Retrieves parameters that are passed into the HTA when it is started. This property returns an empty string when the HTA is started via the HTTP protocol.
icon	Path to a 32x32-pixel Microsoft Windows format .ico file.
id	The DHTML DOM identifier of the HTA:Application element.
maximizeButton	States whether the maximize button is displayed. The HTA must have a caption for this button to be displayed.
minimizeButton	States whether the minimize button is displayed. The HTA must have a caption for this button to be displayed.
showInTaskBar	States whether the HTML application (HTA) is displayed in the Microsoft Windows Taskbar. This property, however, has no effect on whether the application is displayed when the user presses Alt+Tab.
singleInstance	States whether multiple instances of the application can run at the same time. The application's applicationName property is used to identify other running instances of the application.
sysMenu	States whether the sysmenu button is displayed. The HTA must also have a caption for this button to be displayed.

Attribute/Property	Description
version	Returns the application version number. The default is an empty string.
windowState	Sets or retrieves the window state of the HTA window (normal, minimize, maximize).

APPENDIX G

Windows Script Component Elements

WINDOWS SCRIPT COMPONENT ELEMENTS

component

This tag is only used to define the debugging options for the component. Usage:

```
<? component error="flag" debug="flag" ?>
```

Attribute	Description
Error	Allows error messages for syntax or runtime errors in the script component file. Set to true to enable.
Debug	Launches the script debugger for a script component. Set to true to enable.

XML

This declaration must be the first tag in a Windows Script Component. Usage:

```
<? XML  version="version" standalone="DTDflag" encoding="encname" ?>
```

Attribute	Description
version	Used to specify the XML level of the file. Should be 1.0.
standalone	Indicates if the XML file includes a reference to an external document type definition (DTD) or schema. Always set to yes (standalone) because WSC don't have external references.
encoding	Used to specify the character set encoding used by the XML document.

comment

This element is used to designate text in a script component file that should be ignored. Usage:

```
<comment > A sample comment </comment>
```

Attributes

None

omponent

This element is used to wrap the entire contents of the WSC definition. Usage:

```
<component id="componentid">
```

Attribute	Description
id	Used if the document contains multiple script components or when you are generating one type library for several script components.

vent

This element is used by the WSC to create an event that is fired up to its container. Usage:

```
<event name="name" dispid="dispid"/>
```

Attribute	Description
name	Used to specify the name of the event exposed to the containing document. *Required*.
dispid	Used to specify the dispatch ID for the event, which is compiled into the component's type library.

nplements

This element is useful because interface handlers can extend the script component runtime. The COM interface handler is added to the component by default. Usage:

```
<implements type="COMHandlerName" id="internalName" default="fAssumed">
```

Attribute	Description
type	Used to specify the interface handler to include with the component. Currently the built-in interface handlers are ASP and Behavior (for DHTML Behaviors). *Required*.
id	Used to provide a mechanism to reference the interface handler in the code.
default	Indicates if the ID is assumed in scripts. By setting to true (default) this adds the members of the interface handler to the default name space and can be called unqualified. Setting to false requires you to use fully qualified calls to the interface handler.

method

This element is used to declare a public procedure of the component that is called by the container. Usage:

```
<method name="methodName" internalName="functionName" dispid="dispID"><
parameter name="parameterID"/></method>
```

Attribute/Elements	Description
name	Used to specify the name of the method exposed to the containing document. *Required*.
internalName	Used to specify the alternate name of the function to call within the component when the method is called. If not specified, the value of the name attribute is used to call the function.
dispid	Used to specify the dispatch ID for the method, which is compiled into the component's type library.
parameter	The parameter tag with its name allows you to specify the parameters that should be passed to the method call. These parameters are compiled into the type library. Note: this is not required.

ject

This element is used to create an object that can be referenced in the component. It is important to note that either the classid or progid must be specified. Usage:

```
<object id="objID" classid="clsid:GUID" progid="progID" / >
```

Attribute	Description
id	Used to provide a mechanism to reference the object in the component.
classid	Used to specify the class ID (GUID) of the object to create. Use "clsid:" followed by the class ID (without curly brackets).
progid	The program ID of the object to create.

ackage

This element is used to enclose multiple script component definitions. Usage:

```
<package >
```

Attributes

None

operty

This element is used to define a public property for the event. It is important to note that the get and put elements are not required, but they provide you with a mechanism to call more complicated code to return and set values. Usage:

```
<property name="propertyName" internalName="propertyVariable" ><get
internalName="getFunctionName" /><put internalName="putFunctionName" />
</property>
```

Attribute/Elements	Description
name	Used to specify the name of the property exposed to the containing document. *Required.*
internalName	Used to specify the alternate name of the variable used to hold onto the properties value. If not specified, the value is stored in the variable specified in the name attribute.
get	The get element and internalName attribute allow you to define a function that should be called to return the value of the property when it is retrieved.
put	The get element and internalName attribute allow you to define a function that should be called to set the value of the property when it is being set.

public

This element is used to enclose the script component's public property, method, and event declarations that are accessible from outside of the component. Usage:

```
<public>
```

Attributes

None

reference

This element is used to reference a type library from an external source, which can be useful because it allows you to use constants defined in the type library in scripts. You must specify either the object or guid attributes to retrieve the type library for. Usage:

```
<reference object="progID" guid="typelibGUID" version="version">
```

Attribute	Description
object	The program ID of the object to derive the type library from.
guid	Used to specify the class ID (GUID) of the object to derive the type library from. Use "clsid:" followed by the class ID (without curly brackets).
version	Used to specify the version of the type library to use.

gistration

This element defines the information used to register the script component as a COM component. Usage:

```
<registration progid="progID" classid="GUID"
description="description"  version="version" remotable=remoteFlag />
```

Attribute	Description
progID	Used to specify the program ID (a text string used to reference your object) of your object.
classid	Used to specify a GUID that is generated using a class ID generation program (such as Uuidgen.exe). If you do not include a class ID, the registration program assigns a class ID to your script component.
description	Used to specify a text description of the script component that is stored in the registry.
version	Used to specify the version number of the component.
remotable	Used to specify whether the script component can be instantiated remotely using DCOM. Boolean value: true (can be instantiated remotely).

source

This element allows you to isolate value in your script component that you want to intermingle with script. Usage:

```
<resource id="resourceID">
```

Attribute	Description
id	Used to specify a unique identifier for the resource within the script component. *Required*.

script

This element is used to specify and wrap the script in your WSC. Usage:

```
<script language="language">
```

Attribute	Description
language	Used to specify the name of the scripting language used in the script component file. Default is JavaScript.

WINDOWS SCRIPT COMPONENT METHODS

Method	Description
createComponent(componentID)	Used to create a component that is in the same WSC.
fireEvent(eventName)	Used to raise an event to the container. Can only raise events specified in the <event> elements for the component.
getResource(resourceID)	Used to retrieve the value of a resource defined in a <resource> element

DHTML BEHAVIOR-SPECIFIC ELEMENTS FOR WSC

attach

This element binds an event from the component's container to the component. Usage:

```
<attach event="eventName" handler="handlerName" for="elementName" />
```

Attribute	Description
event	Used to specify the name of a DHTML event or any of the events specific to a DHTML behavior WSC. *Required*.
handler	Name of the function to call when the event is fired or in-line script to process. *Required*.
for	Used to identify the source of the event. Possible values: document refers to the document object for the HTML document; element refers to the element to which the behavior is attached (default); and window refers to the window object of the browser.

yout

This element is used to define the HTML that should be inserted into the containing document. When the behavior is called, the text in the <layout> element is read into the corresponding element in the containing document. Usage:

```
<layout>
```

Attributes

None

HTML BEHAVIOR-SPECIFIC PROPERTIES
ND METHODS FOR WSC

Italic properties are read-only.

Property/Method	Description
element	Returns the element to which the behavior is being applied.
createEventObject()	Used to create a DHTML event object, which is used to pass event information to the containing document when the fireEvent method is called.

Property/Method	Description
fireEvent(event, eventObject)	Used to raise an event to the container. Can only raise events specified in the <event> elements for the component. Allows you to pass an event object to the container that contains details about the event, rather than just raising the event.

APPENDIX H

Active Server Page Object Model

APPLICATION OBJECT

Member	Description
Contents	Returns a collection that contains a list of the items that have been created and added to the Application object through script commands.
Lock()	Prevents all other users from making changes to the Application object.
OnEnd (Event)	Occurs when the application ends, which generally is when the Web server is restarted.
OnStart (Event)	Occurs when any item (page, file) in the application is first referenced.
Unlock()	Allows users to have access to the Application object properties in order to make changes (typically called to re-enable edits to an application after a Lock() call has been made).

REQUEST OBJECT

Member	Description
BinaryRead(byteCount)	Retrieves the data that was sent to the server from the browser as part of the POST request and returns the number of bytes read. Count should contain the maximum number of bytes to read in; after the call it will return the actual number of bytes read.
ClientCertificate	Returns a collection that contains the values of the client certification fields of the request.
Cookies	Returns a collection that allows you to access the values of the browser cookies sent in by requests.

Member	Description
Form	Returns a collection of the values of the <FORM> elements posted to a request form using the POST method.
QueryString	Returns a collection that contains the values of the variables in the HTTP query string. These variables are the string that follows a question mark in the URL request to the server.
ServerVariables	Returns a collection that contains the HTTP and environment variables. See the "Server Variables" section at the end of this appendix for a full list of the available variables.
TotalBytes	Returns the total number of bytes sent in the body of the request.

RESPONSE OBJECT

Member	Description
AddHeader(name, value)	Adds the specified header name and value combination to the client response. This method must be called before any output is sent to the client.
AppendToLog(output)	Writes the specified string to the Web server's log for this request.
BinaryWrite(binaryData)	Writes the specified nontext to the client response without any character conversion.
Buffer	Returns if the page output being sent to the browser is buffered.
CacheControl	Indicates whether a proxy server can cache the Active Server Page.

Member	Description
Charset	This value is appended to the content-type header contained in the response object.
Clear()	Erases any buffered output.
ContentType	Used to specify the HTTP content type/subtype for the response header.
Cookies	Contains a collection of cookies. Cookies are added in name value pairs, as shown here: Response.Cookies("sample")("cookie") = "thevalueofmycookie"
End()	Tells the Web server to stop processing the script and to return the current results without processing the rest of the file.
Expires	Used to specify the number of minutes before a response from the server cached on the client expires.
ExpiresAbsolute	Used to specify the exact date and time when a response from the server cached on the client expires. The following is an example of this format: Response.ExpiresAbsolute=#January 22, 2000 14:00:00#
Flush()	Sends the contents of the buffer to the client.
IsClientConnected	Returns whether the browser has disconnected from the server since the last Response.Write.
Pics	Used to set the PICS (parental control) rating for the document.
Redirect(URL)	Redirects the client browser to the specified URL.
Status	Returns the value of the HTTP status line returned by the server.
Write(value)	Writes the specified value to the browser or to the buffer if buffering is enabled.

ERVER OBJECT

Member	Description
CreateObject(objectID)	Creates and returns an instance of the specified ActiveX object.
HTMLEncode(encode)	Returns an HTML-encoded version of the specified string characters.
MapPath(path)	Returns the physical path to the specified virtual or relative path.
ScriptTimeout	Specifies the amount of time in seconds that an ASP will run before it times out.
UrlEncode(encode)	Returns a URL-encoded version of the specified string characters.

ESSION OBJECT

Member	Description
Abandon()	Terminates a user's session and removes all of the variables associated with the session once execution of server-side script in the current page is completed.
CodePage	Used to specify which server codepage to use when displaying an ASP. A codepage is a character set used for symbol mapping.
Contents	Returns a collection that contains a list of the items that have been created and added to the Session object.
LCID	Specifies the location identifier that will be used to display the content. Affects the way location-specific data, such as dates and currency, are displayed.

Member	Description
OnEnd (Event)	Event is fired when a user's session has ended.
OnStart (Event)	Event is fired the first time a user accesses any item in the application.
SessionID	Contains a unique identifier for the session.
Timeout	Specifies the amount of time in minutes that an idle session will stay active.

SERVER VARIABLES

Variable	Description
ALL_HTTP	Returns all HTTP headers sent by the client.
ALL_RAW	Retrieves all headers in raw form.
APPL_MD_PATH	Retrieves the metabase path.
APPL_PHYSICAL_PATH	Retrieves the physical path corresponding to the metabase path.
AUTH_PASSWORD	Retrieves the value entered in the client's authentication dialog.
AUTH_TYPE	Retrieves the authentication method that the server uses to validate users.
AUTH_USER	Retrieves the authenticated user name.
CERT_COOKIE	Retrieves a unique ID for client certificate that is returned as a string.
CERT_FLAGS	If the client certificate is present, the first bit (0) is set to 1; if the certifying authority of the client certificate is invalid, the second bit (1) is set to 1.
CERT_ISSUER	Retrieves the issuer field of the client certificate.

Variable	Description
CERT_KEYSIZE	Retrieves the number of bits in Secure Sockets Layer connection key size.
CERT_SECRETKEYSIZE	Retrieves the number of bits in the server certificate private key.
CERT_SERIALNUMBER	Retrieves the serial number field of the client certificate.
CERT_SERVER_ISSUER	Retrieves the issuer field of the server certificate.
CERT_SERVER_SUBJECT	Retrieves the subject field of the server certificate.
CERT_SUBJECT	Retrieves the subject field of the client certificate.
CONTENT_LENGTH	Contains the length of the content header as sent by the client.
CONTENT_TYPE	Retrieves the data type of the content.
GATEWAY_INTERFACE	Retrieves the revision of the CGI specification used by the server.
HTTP_<ABC>	Retrieves the value stored in the header *ABC*.
HTTPS	Returns ON if the request came in through secure channel or OFF if the request is through a nonsecure channel.
HTTPS_KEYSIZE	Retrieves the number of bits in Secure Sockets Layer (SSL) connection key size.
HTTPS_SECRETKEYSIZE	Retrieves the number of bits in server certificate private key.
HTTPS_SERVER_ISSUER	Retrieves the issuer field of the server certificate.
HTTPS_SERVER_SUBJECT	Retrieves the subject field of the server certificate.
INSTANCE_ID	Retrieves the ID for the Internet Information Server (IIS) instance in text format.

Variable	Description
INSTANCE_META_PATH	Retrieves the metabase path for the instance of Internet Information Server (IIS) that responds to the request.
LOCAL_ADDR	Retrieves the server address on which the request came in.
PATH_INFO	Retrieves the extra path information as given by the client.
PATH_TRANSLATED	Retrieves the translated version of PATH_INFO that takes the path and performs any necessary virtual-to-physical mapping.
QUERY_STRING	Retrieves the query information stored in the string following the question mark (?) in the HTTP request.
REMOTE_ADDR	Retrieves the IP address of the remote host making the request.
REMOTE_HOST	Retrieves the name of the host making the request.
REMOTE_USER	Retrieves an unmapped user-name string sent in by the user.
REQUEST_METHOD	Retrieves the method used to make the request.
SCRIPT_NAME	Retrieves a virtual path to the script being executed.
SERVER_NAME	Retrieves the server's host name, Domain Name Server alias, or IP address.
SERVER_PORT	Retrieves the port number to which the request was sent.
SERVER_PORT_SECURE	Retrieves a string that contains a 1 if the request is being handled on the secure port; otherwise it is 0.

Variable	Description
SERVER_PROTOCOL	Retrieves the name and revision of the request information protocol.
SERVER_SOFTWARE	Retrieves the name and version of the server software that answers the request.
URL	Retrieves the base portion of the URL.

Index

B

C

E

F

▼ **I**

M

▼ P

▼ S

T

U